W9-BPE-334

RDR

*"Hillside Architecture is
Landscape Gardening around
a few rooms for use in case of rain."*

— HILLSIDE CLUB YEARBOOK, 1906–1907 —

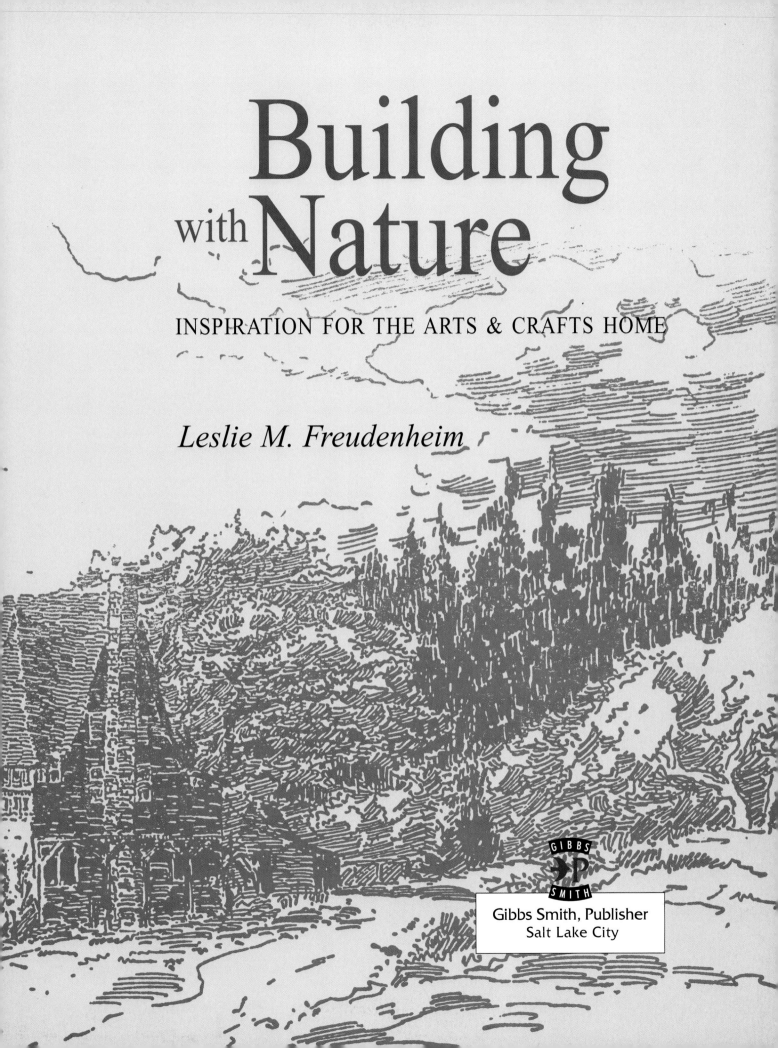

Building
with Nature

INSPIRATION FOR THE ARTS & CRAFTS HOME

Leslie M. Freudenheim

Gibbs Smith, Publisher
Salt Lake City

To Tom,
my husband of forty years,
without whom neither this book nor the earlier one would have happened;
those who know him will understand how lucky I am.

To Elisabeth Sussman,
my dear friend and co-author of
Building with Nature: Roots of the San Francisco Bay Region Tradition,
who graciously encouraged me to expand our first joint effort.

To the Memory of
Ambur Hiken (1915–2002),
whose insightful photography illuminates
the pages of this book.

FIRST EDITION
10 09 08 07 06 05   5 4 3 2 1

Text © 2005 Leslie M. Freudenheim
Photographs by Ambur Hiken © 2005 Leslie Freudenheim and Elisabeth Sussman,
    unless otherwise noted.

Frontispiece/Title Page: The Charles and Louise Keeler house, 1770 Highland Place, Berkeley
(1895), designed by their friend Bernard Maybeck; drawing by Louise Keeler, October 1898.

All rights reserved for all countries, including the right of translation. No part of
this book may be used or reproduced in any manner whatsoever without written
permission from the publishers, except brief portions quoted for purposes of review.

Published by
Gibbs Smith, Publisher
P.O. Box 667
Layton, Utah 84041

1.800.748.5439 orders
www.gibbs-smith.com

Designed by Rudy Ramos
Printed and bound in China

Library of Congress Cataloging-in-Publication Data

Freudenheim, Leslie M., 1941–
    Building with nature : inspiration for the arts & crafts home / Leslie M.
Freudenheim.— 1st ed.
        p. cm.
    Includes bibliographical references and index.
    ISBN 1-58685-463-1
    1. Architecture, Domestic—California—San Francisco Bay Area. 2. Regionalism
in architecture—California—San Francisco Bay Area. 3. Arts and crafts movement
—California—San Francisco Bay Area—History—19th century. 4. Arts and crafts
movement—California—San Francisco Bay Area—History—20th century.
5. Architecture and society—California—San Francisco Bay Area—History—
19th century. 6. Architecture and Society—California—San Francisco Bay Area—
History—20th century. 7. Worcester, Joseph, 1836–1913—Influence. I. Title.
    NA7235.C22S3537 2005
    728'.37'09794—dc22   2004030965

CHULA VISTA PUBLIC LIBRARY

3 3650 01684 9302

Contents

Preface:
A Tribute and an Explanation

IN 1967, WHEN ELISABETH SUSSMAN AND I BEGAN OUR RESEARCH INTO THE SOURCES OF EARLY California architecture, we joined a small group of pioneers whose work was effectively carving out a new field of American architectural history. Esther McCoy's groundbreaking *Five California Architects,* Harold Kirker's significant and classic *California's Architectural Frontier,* David Gebhard's exhibition catalogue *Architecture in California 1868–1968,* Sally Woodbridge's *Buildings of the Bay Area,* and Roger Olmsted and T. H. Watkins' *Here Today*—these became the seminal texts in the field. Their precursor, Elisabeth Kendall Thompson's significant article "The Early Domestic Architecture of the San Francisco Bay Region" (1951), turned out to be prophetic for us, as Thompson alerted us to the possibility that Reverend Joseph Worcester of the Swedenborgian Church in San Francisco may have played a major role in the architectural development of the region from 1876 to 1915.[1]

It has been enormously gratifying to note the outpouring of further research in the field since we published *Building with Nature: Roots of the San Francisco Bay Region Tradition* in 1974, as can be seen in the endnotes and bibliography. Numerous articles and books have impressively augmented our understanding of California's architecture and its role in the Arts & Crafts movement, moving a relatively obscure area of interest into the mainstream of American architectural, intellectual, and social history. One book in particular has been essential: Richard Longstreth's *On the Edge of the World: Four Architects in San Francisco at the Turn of the Century.*

When Gibbs Smith agreed to publish a new edition of our book, we thought we would correct some mistakes and add new photographs. However, when Elisabeth Sussman accepted a job as Curator at the Whitney Museum of American Art, she could not work on this project. I decided to continue my research and generate a new book based on, but different from, the original. When I began, I did not suspect California would turn out to be seminal in the development of the Arts & Crafts movement in the United States.

In this new book I have tried to place this history in the international context it deserves, delving more deeply into the roots of the California Arts & Crafts tradition as we were urged to do thirty years ago by our wise publisher, Gibbs Smith, and pinpointing numerous connections with simultaneous European movements.

So much more information confirming Joseph Worcester's influence has come to light in the past thirty years that I feel it is important to expand upon this theme. Charles Keeler, writing around 1908, credited Worcester with having introduced the "simple home" to the San Francisco Bay Region: *"The work of a small group of young architects originally inspired and guided by a Swedenborgian minister . . . has spread like a leaven in a mass of the commonplace."* [2] And he remarked that Worcester's word *"was law in the select group of connoisseurs of which he was the center."* [3]

Elisabeth Kendall Thompson seconded this view in her important article, cited above. Thompson lists the important architects and influential people in the region and begins by praising Worcester who, *"though he was not a trained architect,"* produced work of *"architectural rightness and dignity,"* and adds that

> *. . . Worcester was designing these simple cottages with a freshness and restraint that, for their period, are all but incredible. . . . According to Bruce Porter . . . it was to Worcester that hopeful young architects, journeying West to seek their fortune, came for advice, and it was to him that they owed their thorough grounding in good taste and simplicity. Hence is possible that to him, in some measure, can be credited some of the underlying philosophy of architectural design in the Bay Region.* [4]

Edward R. Bosley also acknowledged Worcester's impact:

> *The simple, unpainted wood-shingle bungalow he designed for himself in 1877 in the East Bay town of Piedmont is probably the earliest rustic suburban house designed in the West, predating even the East Coast's famous Shingle-style resort houses and bungalows. The house (and its designer) had an important impact on the artists and architects who were in Worcester's informal circle of friends.* [5]

Fig. 0.1: This photo of the East Bay shows the open rolling hills and commanding marine views that drew Worcester to the Piedmont hills in the 1870s, later touted by the real estate companies as they advertised hill property for sale.

Fig. 0.2

Bosley also cites an article in the August 1905 *Craftsman*, which by then was read by architects and designers nationwide, in which Keeler attributes the *"art spirit"* that took hold in San Francisco in the 1890s to Worcester's inspiration.[6]

Sally Woodbridge referred to Worcester as *"an arbiter of taste"* in *Bernard Maybeck: Visionary Architect* (1992)[7] and to Worcester as *"the wizard"*

Fig. 0.2: Joseph Worcester and a group of boys atop Russian Hill, San Francisco, California, after 1890.

Fig. 0.3: J. V. Coleman–M. H. Hecht house, Washington and Octavia, San Francisco (1885). Eastern architect Bruce Price used shingles on this elaborate combination Queen Anne–Shingle Style residence. Whether he designed the original house or renovated what we see here is unclear.

behind the selection of Howard in *John Galen Howard and the University of California: The Design of a Great Public University Campus* (2002).[8]

While acknowledging Worcester's deep interest in handcraft, all types of architecture, John Ruskin, William Morris, and the "simple home" or "humble cottage" as well as his influence in the region, it is not my intention to give Worcester sole responsibility for the pre-1900 growth of the rustic shingled and Mission-Mediterranean Arts & Crafts homes in California, nor to attribute to him alone the increased interest in the ideals championed by the Arts & Crafts movement after 1900. Rather we shall see that Worcester designed and built his first Arts & Crafts–influenced house in 1876–78. When a group of newly arrived young architects became his friends (1889–90), they reacted to what they had seen Worcester accomplish and to what they had seen in the East, in Europe, and in the architectural press. Together they launched the Arts & Crafts "simple home/building with nature" movement in California, thereby helping to move the rest of the country in the same direction.

Fig. 0.3

Introduction:
Setting the Scene

FROM APPROXIMATELY 1876 TO 1910, A GROUP OF CREATIVE AND PIONEERING MEN AND WOMEN IN northern California sought to achieve an architectural expression appropriate to their region. Beginning in the East Bay community of Piedmont, the tradition took tentative root in San Francisco and then spread to Berkeley, where it deepened and matured before extending throughout many parts of California, most notably in Pasadena and Los Angeles. It then combined with growing American interest in the Arts & Crafts movement throughout the United States to help revolutionize middle-class housing.

A desire to get back to nature and to build with natural materials, combined with emerging interest in European architectural developments, California's missions, pueblos, vernacular buildings, and new economic realities, resulted in two major trend-setting California Arts & Crafts interpretations: the California Shingle and the California Mission.

While these architects shared an interest in designing "simple homes," their goals were more than architectural. They believed a well-designed house, like the "humble cottage" that John Ruskin, William Morris, and their followers advocated, could inspire and enhance life. Their aspirations, like those of the European Arts & Crafts movement, were cultural, social, environmental, and economic. It is for this reason they promoted Arts & Crafts values rather than styles. As Richard Guy Wilson explained it:

> The Arts & Crafts Movement, whether in America or Europe, was expressed not in a specific style but as a mood, an attitude, a sensibility. At its core the Arts & Crafts movement advocated a search for a way of life that was true, contemplative, and filled with essences rather than superficialities . . . .[1]
>
> The ultimate concern was not a perfectly designed and handmade bowl, but how that bowl could contribute to a proper life.[2]

Joseph Worcester arrived in San Francisco in 1864 bringing with him a Harvard education, deep personal belief in Swedenborgianism, an acquaintance with transcendentalism, extensive knowledge of architecture, and a firm desire to put into practice the ideals expressed by Ruskin and Morris.

While elsewhere in the United States and England many were discussing affordable housing for the emerging middle class, in 1888 (the same year the Arts & Crafts movement acquired its name) Worcester designed four such houses atop Russian Hill in San Francisco. These intentionally simple homes differed radically from the ornate Victorians that characterized San Francisco at the time. All four were extremely unassuming and featured unpainted shingles on the outside and unvarnished redwood walls inside, and were sited to echo San Francisco's hills. The California Shingle and Mission Style houses (and churches) that followed were justified by

Worcester and his circle, using the same arguments grounded in the Arts & Crafts philosophy: such buildings were rooted in local traditions, did not spoil the landscape, reflected honest work and handcraft, uplifted the soul, and inspired the mind—all goals expressed by Ruskin, Morris, and their many European followers.[3]

As was happening in the United States and throughout Europe, groups advocating handwork and handicraft were fighting the seemingly inexorable march of the machine and the poor living conditions resulting from the Industrial Revolution. Art potteries and home handicrafts sprang up throughout the United States from the 1870s,[4] but the architectural aspects of this revolution developed more slowly.

Among those who came into Worcester's ambit were A. Page Brown, Bernard Ralph Maybeck, Ernest Coxhead, Willis Polk, John Galen Howard, Albert C. Schweinfurth, Julia Morgan, John Hudson Thomas, and Louis Christian Mullgardt.

In Pasadena, Charles Sumner Greene and Henry Mather Greene created Arts & Crafts–inspired bungalows, and Irving Gill, Frederick L. Roehrig, John Kremple, and many other architects found inspiration in the missions. Charles Lummis, the mission's principal savior and advocate, and writer George Wharton James promoted the idea that a new culture would arise from the rough-hewn missions and the "simple" buildings these Native American craftsmen built with local materials and with the landscape in mind.[5] Worcester and many architects shared their sensibilities and felt that the Mission Style also satisfied the goals of the Arts & Crafts movement, bringing art into life.

Sources of inspiration for the California Arts & Crafts home ranged widely: eastern Shingle Style, Spanish Mission Style, Swiss Chalet, Japanese architecture, and the values as well as the architecture of the English Arts & Crafts movement all contributed. Vernacular traditions were equally important: early American salt-box and shed roof houses, American and English barns, late-medieval European villages, and even Yosemite's cabins provided inspiration.[6] And of course, there was the influence of the land itself.

Coxhead came to California from England. The rest of the architects had lived and worked in either the East or Midwest before settling around San Francisco, Pasadena, and Los Angeles, and several had studied and traveled in Europe. All were familiar with architectural developments worldwide; it was a small world even then.[7]

When Worcester decided in 1876 not only to shingle the exterior of his home in the Piedmont Hills but also to use unpainted redwood board for the entire interior, and when he repeated this on Russian Hill in the midst of San Francisco in 1888–90, he stimulated many architects to design affordable yet inspiring houses for newly developing cities and towns.

By 1889 architects in the American West were already familiar with the more elegant Shingle Style houses built in the East by H. H. Richardson; McKim, Mead, and White; and others through their publication of the residences in *American Architect and Building News*.

Moreover, several of the California architects had worked in these eastern architectural firms. Worcester's rustic, suburban, shingled, redwood-interior Piedmont house (1876–78) was almost contemporaneous with Henry Hobson Richardson's W. Watts Sherman house (1874), and yet it was entirely different from it; and his Russian Hill houses along with those designed by his friends after 1890 differed from Shingle Style houses in the East[8]; nor did these California Arts & Crafts houses resemble the combination Queen Anne–Shingle Style houses being built in the

Bay Area, such as one by eastern architect Bruce Price (Fig. 0.3).[9] The results, and the testimony of others, bear witness to this group's success. They set out to change California's architecture—and in the process started what some might term an architectural revolution.

The American West had the topography and climate for indoor-outdoor living; foliage grew year-round, and redwood seemed to be available in unlimited quantities. Architects on both coasts favored the large central living space; but the expansive sitting rooms of Worcester's houses, paneled in wood with an inviting fireplace, provided a focal gathering point, and may be precursors of living rooms as we know them today. They were nothing like the two-story, elegant living halls of the eastern Shingle Style house. Maybeck did use two-story living rooms whenever the budget and client permitted; but they were far simpler than those found in the grand halls of eastern "cottages."

One feature of the California Arts & Crafts house became particularly popular and later spread widely: over-hanging eaves reminiscent of Swiss chalets, mountain architecture, and mission buildings.

Inside California Shingle Style houses, the architects featured unvarnished wood, exposed structure, and beamed ceilings—sometimes flat, sometimes cathedral-like while inside mission-inspired Arts & Crafts houses, architects combined rough-hewn beams with plain white walls and arched openings. California architects eschewed wallpaper (they did not even approve of William Morris–designed paper) and abhorred bright paint as well as elaborately carved furniture and ornate moldings, balusters and paneling. They used simple board and batten to add light and shadow to walls, although Maybeck often used color on his houses and buildings, especially from about 1905.

In 1883 a competition was held to design a mechanic's house or laborer's cottage, which indicates the strong interest in, and demand for, middle-class "simple" and inexpensive housing. *American Architect and Building News* published the entries. Schweinfurth, then living in the East, gave his very modest house a positive shine by naming his entry "Sweete Simplicitie" [*sic*].[10]

Although the demand was there from the early 1880s, Worcester and his circle were among the first American architects, if not the first, actually to deliver Arts & Crafts ideals translated into simple, affordable houses and other structures, designed with nature, art, handcrafts, and the spiritual in mind.[11]

After 1885 eastern architects turned to the Colonial Revival, which, as Scully expressed it, *"became more specifically antiquarian, academic, and unoriginal . . . and academicism struck a deathblow to the shingle style."* In addition, monumentality took over in the East, even in suburban architecture.[12] But in the West this democratic, low-cost, anti-monumental style coincided with the Arts & Crafts movement's call for affordable simple homes and a surge in California's population to produce widespread demand for Arts & Crafts bungalows or simple homes.

However, an architect may show genius, but it takes clients *"whose minds are adventurous, whose liberal acceptance of advanced ideas* [makes possible] . . . [this] *kind of architectural work, particularly in the domestic field . . . ."*[13]

Long before 1876, shingles and redwood boards had been used on California houses; however, most were painted except for the roofs. Theodore A. Eisen, writing in 1883, praised the *"honest shingle roof"* for its lack of sham.[14] As late as 1891 the general attitude had not changed. Alexander F. Oakey wrote that roofs should remain natural and unpainted, but the rest of the house must be painted.[15] According to Scully, even Andrew Jackson Downing, who was enormously

Fig. 0.4: Church of the Holy Innocents, 455 Fair Oaks Boulevard, San Francisco, by Coxhead & Coxhead. Wood double doors dated 1890, studded with nails to resemble strap hinges. Photo ca. 1972.

influential and *"may be credited with starting American domestic architecture along a new path,"* advocated painting wood so that it might blend harmoniously with surrounding landscape rather than rejecting paint because it would hide the material.[16]

Worcester's circle, on the other hand, distinguished between painted and natural finishes, recognizing that materials left in their natural state would provide a subtle means of harmonizing with, rather than standing out from, the existing landscape.

Worcester and his friends advocated Arts & Crafts values as a way of improving life, not just as a way of integrating all aspects of a design into a *gesamtkunstwerk,* or total work of art. They subscribed to Morris's maxim: *"Have nothing in your houses that you do not know to be useful, or believe to be beautiful."*[17] Although Worcester was certainly not interested in the increased business architects would reap if they designed the furniture, light fixtures, hinges, etc., as well as the architecture, his friends undoubtedly understood the financial benefits of this goal as did the entrepreneurial Gustav Stickley, who recognized, David Cathers tells us, that *"a Craftsman house . . . was a big, empty box that his customers would want to fill with Craftsman products."*[18]

In 1890 Willis Polk launched *Architectural News* to provide a forum for some of the group's ideas, and recognition of what these California architects and designers were attempting to achieve continued to expand.

Americans nationwide became supporters of the Arts & Crafts way of life, subscribed to its values, and wanted their houses to reflect them. They were encouraged by *Ladies Home Journal,* which, from 1895, began commissioning architects to design moderately priced houses,[19] and by the architectural press, which began publishing English Arts & Crafts architecture and furniture. Gustav Stickley published plans and perspective views of his first house in May 1903,[20] and his Craftsman House #1, Mission Style bungalow, in January 1904; in addition, he promoted furniture and fittings suited to these homes, which heightened reader interest and helped shape middle-class American taste. All this media attention, combined with personal interactions at expositions, exhibitions, and national/international travel, attracted so many followers to the Arts & Crafts movement that it remained popular until about 1920.

This book reviews the brief span of years in which a new American architecture was developed in California and began to influence the nation. Surprisingly, the ongoing intellectual and aesthetic cross-fertilizations, global and national, make this an international story. I hope this book helps to make this narrative come alive.

Ruskin, Morris, and the First California Arts & Crafts House

1

JOSEPH WORCESTER (1836–1913), REVEREND OF THE SWEDENBORGIAN CHURCH AND THE MAN WHO GAVE the simple Arts & Crafts house in northern California its initial impetus, was an architect by avocation, although he was not credentialed as one. Worcester stands out as a highly influential proponent of unpretentious Arts & Crafts houses built of natural materials to harmonize with nature. Not only did he design and oversee construction of five California Arts & Crafts houses and a church, he inspired, urged, cajoled, and succeeded in convincing many others to follow his design ideas.

While he was best known in California, his friends included such important figures as architects Daniel H. Burnham, Bernard Maybeck, Charles Follen McKim, Willis Polk, Ernest Coxhead, A. Page Brown, and John Galen Howard; artists Bruce Porter, Arthur Mathews, William Keith, Jules Guerin, George Inness, and Mary Curtis Richardson; writers Robert Louis Stevenson, Charles Keeler, Charles F. Lummis, and Jack London; pioneering environmentalists Frederick Law Olmsted and John Muir; philanthropist Phoebe Apperson Hearst; many University of California professors; and at least one San Francisco mayor. All of them play a role in this book.[1]

Worcester, who arrived in San Francisco for the first time in 1864 (perhaps to escape the horrors of the Civil War), left Boston for good in 1867 and came to love California so intensely while traveling through it that he settled in the Piedmont hills east of San Francisco and the bay. Most of Worcester's family members (Fig. 1.2) were prominent Swedenborgians who lived in Boston's Louisburg Square until their move to Waltham, Massachusetts, where Joseph taught school. His studies at Harvard Scientific School were only part of his intellectual training; he also studied drawing and architecture. He was deeply influenced by such writers as Ralph Waldo Emerson, James Russell Lowell, William Wordsworth, and especially John Ruskin and Emanuel Swedenborg. It would be amazing if Worcester did not also know Charles Eliot Norton, who graduated from Harvard before him in 1846 and became a force in cultural and intellectual activity.

Norton knew and admired Ruskin, helped spread his theories and collected his watercolors. It is very possible that Norton influenced Worcester.[2]

Fig. 1.1: Phoebe Hearst (center) with members of the International Jury for the University of California, Berkeley, design competition at Hacienda del Pozo de Verona, Sunol, California, September 1899. Included in this image are Regent J. B. Reinstein (lower left) and prominent architects John Belcher, London (wearing glasses, to Phoebe Hearst's right), replacing R. Norman Shaw who was sick; Walter Cook, New York (sitting in the middle, holding a straw hat); Jean-Louis Pascal, Paris (with long, flowing beard, to Mrs. Hearst's left); and Paul Wallot, Berlin (seated, lower right).

Fig. 1.2: Joseph Worcester's family in a photograph, ca. 1846. Thomas Worcester strongly objected to his son's move to California.

Worcester later found the ideas of his intellectual mentors reflected in the simplicity of California's adobe structures, weathered shingled barns, and miners' shacks, along with the plain wooden houses from his native New England.[3]

Among the other forces in his life were his close friends. Daniel Burnham's family moved to Waltham when Daniel was seventeen. He attended the New Church School kept by the Worcesters and formed a friendship there with Joseph Worcester that lasted throughout his life; Burnham and Worcester were also related by marriage. Even before he became a nationally known architect, Burnham was in San Francisco often, not only to visit Worcester but also to conduct business. In this fascinating tidbit from 1888, Burnham confesses to his wife his professional drive and his excitement at being asked to design a "statue of liberty" for San Francisco:

I am doing my level best to make a client out of [Sutro]. *I am sure he will talk about a building to go on that place; to be his monument and forever command the entrance to the Golden Gate. If we can do that, then no one can ever again pass out or into this country, on the Pacific side, without thinking of us. It will be like Bartholdi's Statue of Liberty, in New York harbor. Dreams are they not? But very happy ones, and with a chance of realization. You see my ambition is insatiable. . . . (The de Young job is contracted for, and that ship fully launched.)*[4]

Worcester's other prominent friends included John Muir, one of the first explorers to walk through the whole of Yosemite Valley, and possibly Frederick Law Olmsted, whose visits to Yosemite Valley coincided with Worcester's. As he matured, Worcester influenced many others, particularly in the fields of architecture and city planning.

Worcester and William Keith (Fig. 1.3), the great California landscape painter, were more than very close friends. Worcester helped sell Keith's paintings, found potential clients for his work, and advised Keith on his technique and style; later, Keith contributed four paintings that were incorporated into the design of the Swedenborgian Church. However, scholars have not resolved the question of when Worcester first met Keith. It may well have been before 1882 when Worcester comforted the painter after the death of Keith's first wife. Perhaps they were friends as early as 1875 when Worcester mentions a "William" to his nephew Alfred Worcester: *"William and I thought how nice it would be for you to come across the Continent and make us a visit."* [5]

We can speculate that the painter and the minister may well have spent time together even earlier. In 1872 and often thereafter, Keith went to Yosemite with Muir, so it is likely that they all knew each other through mutual friendships. [6] In any case, Worcester and Keith developed an intimate relationship, and in his letters from Europe, Keith expressed love verging on worship for Joseph Worcester. He signed his letters to Worcester "with love" or "affectionately" and once, writing from Cologne in 1883, he concluded: *"I think of you so softly & tenderly until I find myself playing the woman, & so I had better stop,"* suggesting a homoerotic attraction, at least on Keith's part. [7]

Considering the lack of modern-day jet travel and information technology, Joseph Worcester's circle of friends was exceedingly well informed, well-traveled, and made up of intellectually curious and knowledgeable individuals who were up to date on what was happening architecturally in Europe as well as on the East Coast. For example, John Wellborn Root's death on January 15, 1891, was received "over the wires" and published in *Architectural News* 3 in January 1891; on June 11, 1871, Worcester wrote his nephew that *"this is no longer a far off land,"* [8] and applauded the receipt of letters sent from the East to San Francisco within one week. (The railroad links that made this possible were completed in May 1869.)

Ernest Coxhead had come to San Francisco from England, where he had been a member of the Royal Institute of British Architects (RIBA), and certainly knew about the developing Arts & Crafts movement and its architectural manifestations in England. He worked first in Los Angeles before moving to the Bay Area where he maintained friendships with Worcester, Polk, Maybeck, Keeler, Howard, and members of the Hillside Club, among others.

Bernard Maybeck read and spoke both French and German, had studied in Paris, and had worked in New York, Florida, Kansas City, Salt Lake City, and San Francisco before settling in Piedmont and then Berkeley. While a student at the École des Beaux-Arts in Paris, he met Thomas Hastings from New York (for whose firm, Carrère and Hastings, Maybeck later worked), Ambrose Russell from Kansas City, Rudolph Dick from Vienna, Enrico Ristori of Florence, and Robert Sandilands from Glasgow. He also met and befriended R. Norman Shaw, who revolutionized English architecture and influenced British Arts & Crafts architects. [9] In California his friends included Keeler, Worcester, Polk, Coxhead, Burnham, Schweinfurth and Howard. His student and friend Julia Morgan established a very successful practice.

John Galen Howard had worked for Boston's premier architect, Henry Hobson Richardson, whom Worcester greatly admired, and yet had been adventuresome enough to travel to Los Angeles in 1887. In 1888 he lived in Paris and by1889 had fallen in love with Italy, as his letters and diary reveal. He returned to work in 1889 for McKim, Mead, and White, first in Boston and then in New York City, but by the end of 1890 he was back in Paris to study at the École des Beaux-Arts. After starting a private practice in New York in 1893, Howard and his partner, Samuel Cauldwell, entered the Phoebe Hearst International Competition to plan the new campus for the University of California, Berkeley, and were among the finalists selected. In late 1901 Howard accepted the university's offer to become supervising architect and moved to Berkeley, becoming part of Worcester's circle. [10]

Fig. 1.3: William Keith, famous California painter and Worcester's closest friend, as photographed by Charles F. Lummis.

Fig. 1.4: Albert Cicero
Schweinfurth, portrait.

Bruce Porter sketched all over Europe in 1889, especially in Italy, visited Burne-Jones' studio in England, and most likely found inspiration for his stained glass in numerous European churches. His friends are known to have included Worcester, Keith, Polk, and Coxhead; he certainly became acquainted with A. Page Brown and Maybeck, his draftsman, when the Swedenborgian Church was under construction.

Willis Polk had worked for Coxhead in Los Angeles before moving to San Francisco to join A. Page Brown's firm in 1889. He crossed the country several times, sketching as he traveled. In 1890 he settled on Russian Hill in San Francisco, maintained his friendships with Maybeck and Coxhead, and developed a close relationship with his neighbor Joseph Worcester, who eventually helped Polk's career by bringing him clients and convincing Daniel Burnham to take Polk into his firm. Richard Longstreth suggests that the two years Polk spent in Burnham's office (beginning in September 1901) revolutionized Polk's architectural designs and significantly increased his ability to attract clients. Once Polk started working with wealthier clients, his taste reverted to the grand.[11] Worcester continued to promote Polk to Burnham and to potential clients once the young architect decided to return to San Francisco.

Charles Keeler was born in Milwaukee in 1871 and came to Berkeley in the late 1880s, attending the University of California, Berkeley, before beginning to work for the California Academy of Sciences in San Francisco in 1891. After befriending Maybeck sometime between 1891 and 1894, Keeler introduced Maybeck to many potential clients and promoted the rustic shingled simple home and the Arts & Crafts spirit through personal contacts, numerous articles, Hillside Club pamphlets, and his book *The Simple Home*. He became part of Worcester's wide circle of friends and wrote a tribute to Worcester's closest friend, William Keith, which appeared in Charles F. Lummis's magazine, *Land of Sunshine,* titled "The American Turner." This article may overstate Keith's importance as a painter; but with this title, Keeler and Lummis connected Keith to Ruskin, who referred to J. M. W. Turner (1775–1851) as "the father of modern art." Keeler also mentions the visionary painter George Inness (1825–1892), a Scotsman, a Swedenborgian, and a mystic, who came to California to paint with Keith a few years before his death.[12]

A. C. Schweinfurth (Fig. 1.4) had worked for Peabody & Stearns in Boston, as well as with A. Page Brown in New York on and off from 1885 to perhaps 1892. He also worked with his architect brother Charles in Cleveland in 1886, and then in Denver from 1889 to 1890. Although Schweinfurth left Denver in 1890, he was not listed in the *San Francisco Directory* until 1893; his whereabouts between 1890 and early 1893 remains to be established. When he finally settled in San Francisco, he remained in the Bay Area and, after working briefly for Brown, developed a successful independent practice with commissions from William Randolph Hearst and his friends. He knew Maybeck, Coxhead, Keeler, Polk, Brown, and probably Worcester. In 1898 he suddenly decided to sail for Europe. Sadly, he died shortly after his return in 1900.

A. Page Brown studied at the École des Beaux-Arts in Paris and worked for McKim, Mead, and White before opening his own architectural office. He had established a successful East Coast practice when, at the behest of the Crocker family, he decided to move west. His success in the San Francisco area was astounding. The list of buildings for which his firm was responsible from 1889 to his tragic death at age thirty-six in 1896 is lengthy. Brown hired many talented draftsmen, among them Maybeck, Schweinfurth, and Polk. Brown, too, had in-depth knowledge of several European cities and their architecture, as can be glimpsed in the one article in which he is known to have given his architectural views: it appears in Chapters 3 and 7 of this book.[13]

To summarize, whether or not they had traveled widely, Worcester and his friends knew what was happening elsewhere almost as it occurred.

Little is known about Worcester's life during several periods. On August 14, 1872, he writes as if he had visited these English cities: *"I hope you will go to Yarmouth Port, and to Bath especially if you are not well."* One wonders whether Worcester might have been to Europe and thus could offer this advice.[14]

During the next four years, June 1871 to 1875, Worcester offers doubts about staying in California *"more than one year."* However, he was already involved in local politics, and on August 1, 1875, he complained to his nephew, much as we do today: *"It seems impossible to elect men to office that cannot be bought up."*[15]

Writing in 1905 to Daniel Burnham (who referred to Worcester as "Uncle Joe"), Joseph Worcester's choice of words is maddeningly unclear; so we cannot tell whether Worcester has actually seen the Florentine buildings he criticizes. Worcester muses:

Dec 31, 1905 from Minadoro, Santa Barbara
I wonder what you will look hardest at in Florence, for . . . it seems to me a great mixture
there of good and bad in what is most admired. I should love to look at it with you.
Ever affectionately, Jos Worcester[16]

If Worcester did not see distant buildings firsthand, he certainly kept abreast of architectural developments from Europe to Egypt, as can be seen in the fourteen scrapbooks he filled with architectural clippings. His library includes numerous architectural publications, among them *Architectural Record* (May 1895), part of the Great American Architects series, with articles on H. H. Richardson as well as Volume 5 of *Monographs of American Architecture* on Richardson's Trinity Church in Boston, and Volume 3 on his Ames Memorial buildings, North Easton, Massachusetts, built near Worcester's former hometowns of Boston and Waltham. He also clipped articles on the firm of McKim, Mead, and White as well as on Albert Winslow Cobb and others, all of whom built in the Shingle Style.[17]

When Worcester wrote home on March 5, 1870, he asked nephew Alfred, who had taken over his old bedroom, *"Is the picture between the door and the bed the one of the East Porch of Chartres that used to hang there?"* suggesting that Worcester's architectural interests went back many years.[18]

Worthy of note is the fact that Worcester's scrapbooks also include clippings and photographs of English cathedrals, church and home furniture, examples of American furnishings, views of Venice, English cottages, French farm buildings, and American buildings such as an Arthur Little shingled house (n.d.) in Brookline, Massachusetts. Worcester cut out words of advice from the editors of the *American Architect,* which he seems to have followed:

Viollet-le-Duc's Dictionnaire Raisonné, article "Maison," contains invaluable information.
Besides these strictly technical works many picturesque books of travel . . . contain hints
which can be used by one who understands what he wants.[19]

Knowing what you want and how to convince others that you are right became Joseph Worcester's mission. What caused Worcester to blossom from a man so tormented by doubts about himself that he left his Swedenborgian pulpit to teach in Piedmont, into a man convinced that his building philosophy could transform entire sections of a city into enclaves built with nature in mind? Could his encounters with the work of Frederick Law Olmsted and John Muir, discussed below, have made a difference?

As Worcester's friend Charles Keeler put it, Joseph Worcester provided *"the original inspiration for civic pride and beautification efforts in San Francisco,"* attributing the latter to *"this man of gentle nature, of devoted love of the beautiful and of exceptionally true, though reserved taste. . . . His word was law in the select group of connoisseurs of which he was the center."*[20]

Alfred Worcester's comment on his Uncle Joe confirms Keeler's observation:

Could I only sketch in barest outline types of the very different classes who felt themselves indebted to him for their greatest blessings, I surely should convince those who never knew him of the extraordinary reach of his personal influence.[21]

As his library reveals, Worcester spent hours studying the world's architecture through books. He also clipped this recommendation:

Read, for a beginning, Viollet-le-Duc's Habitations of Man in All Ages, *transl. Bucknall, pub. by James H. R. Osgood and Co., for $2. Then take up Kerr's* Gentleman's House . . . *continue with Nash's* Mansions of England . . . *[Charles J.] Richardson's* Studies from Old English Mansions . . . *and consult Cicognara's* Venetian Architecture *and Letarouilly's* Edifices of Rome Moderne.[22]

Had Worcester followed even half of this advice he would have become a very sophisticated and knowledgeable architectural historian. The reading advice is not dated; however, the scrapbooks and architectural library are proof that Worcester followed it.

Worcester had begun clipping articles at least by 1876, the year he designed his first house, because his scrapbooks include number three in a serialization of Viollet-le-Duc's *Habitations of Man in All Ages* from the March 11, 1876, edition of *American Architect and Building News*.

Considering the extent of his architectural library and interests, we can guess that Worcester may also have read Charles Locke Eastlake's *Hints on Household Taste,* which Scully informs us *". . . had seven American editions from 1872 to 1883 . . . ,"* and that the *"main importance of his book arose from its popularization of the ethical-aesthetic principles of Ruskin and Morris."*[23]

Aware that his architect friends sought and valued his opinion of their buildings and plans, Worcester drafted his comments accordingly. As his nephew put it, *"When on rare occasions his wrath was aroused, no man . . . could be more withering."*[24]

For example, he did not hesitate to disagree with the newspaper's jury when comparing two new commercial structures in San Francisco. Condemning Albert Pissis' newly constructed Hibernia Bank, he showered praise instead on the Crocker Building, writing its architect and his close friend, A. Page Brown:

September 15, 1892:

Dear Mr. Brown,

The verdict of the Call's jury moves me to say to you that some of us, not on the jury, dissent and feel that we have many reasons for our disagreement as far as the verdict touches the Crocker Building. For some time I have been pestered with questions. How do you like the Hibernia Bank? And I have uniformly replied in effect— . . . correct and utterly lacking in thoughtfulness and refinement—both in its general proportions and in its detail . . . . [whereas] *the Crocker Building has been to me instructive and gratifying beyond all other buildings in the city, and I regard it today as the most beautiful and permanently right building in San Francisco. I have told several to take the Market Street entrance as their cue and let the eye roam from it to the whole.*

Yours gratefully,

Jos. Worcester [25]

Worcester also criticized his friends' buildings when he found them lacking:

March 3, 1902

Dear Dan,

Thanks for Inland Architect—*clippings of the Washington scheme and Club building. . . . I do not recall any design for a similar building that I like as well as Willis's. I did not like or approve his Hayward Building here, but the Club is fine—it is unity and quietness and refinement.* [26]

The letter below suggests that Burnham valued Worcester's opinion. When writing to Burnham in 1905, Worcester laughs at himself, inwardly acknowledging that Burnham is a world-famous architect and that he (Worcester) is not even credentialed. Nevertheless, Worcester considers himself competent and would indeed like to go over Burnham's plans with him. (Note that Worcester and Polk were among those urging Daniel Burnham to submit a grand plan for San Francisco before the 1906 earthquake and fire.) Worcester also thanks Burnham for bringing the renowned architect Charles F. McKim to visit.

December 31, 1905

Dear Dan,

I am very touched by the letter from you . . . and regret being unable to follow and support you in your efforts for our city, I am not able to even get up to twin peaks and study the plans, and latterly not able to fully respond to your many gracious acts towards me, among these coming and bringing with you your friend, Mr. McKim, and the last coming—the morning of your arrival in the city. . . . It makes me laugh to have you suggest my looking over your shoulder at what you are doing; it would be such a pleasure. [27]

Interestingly, Mary Keith indicates that Worcester promoted William Keith to Burnham and McKim much as a dealer might:

July 2, 1930:

Dan H. Burnham . . . leading architect of Chicago, became a warm friend and thru him . . . Charles Follen McKim the leading NY architect, who purchased $15,000 worth of paintings on his first glimpse of Mr. K's studio in San Francisco. [28]

The buildings for which Worcester was responsible ignored local fashion and conventional architectural solutions but expressed his individual vision and personality. He had undoubtedly been mulling over his ideal home for many years. The dream became a reality on August 28, 1876, when he wrote his nephew:

They make me an offer [to tutor the children of his cousins Arthur Bowman and Henry N. Wright] *which will enable me to live comfortably and independently. . . . It will involve building a little house.* [29]

But Worcester did not build along the street of stylish homes where his cousin lived. Rather, he chose an isolated knoll in the Piedmont hills, which afforded magnificent views of the bay and beyond. There he designed his first architectural creation, a shingled bungalow (Figs. 1.5–1.7) reflecting his sympathy for, and understanding of, the humble cottage (simple home) advocated by Ruskin and Morris. According to historian Edward R. Bosley, this was the

. . . First shingle-clad house in the West. Indeed it predated most of the "Shingle Style" resort houses designed by the famous firms of Henry Hobson Richardson; McKim, Mead & White; William Ralph Emerson, and others in Massachusetts, Rhode Island and Maine. [30]

Fig. 1.5: Undated photograph of Joseph Worcester's Piedmont cottage, one of the earliest and most influential houses in California. Jack London's family described it as a "bungalow with a capital B."

Fig. 1.6

Fig. 1.6: The William Keith painting of Joseph Worcester's Piedmont cottage, signed and dated 1883, captures the magnificent vista over San Francisco and the Golden Gate as seen from Worcester's house, including the knoll upon which it sat, among surrounding trees and flowers.

Fig. 1.7: This detail of William Keith's painting of Joseph Worcester's Piedmont cottage, signed and dated 1883, reveals one end of the extensive porch fronting the entire house and its roof overhang. Note the distinctive chimney tops, which recall designs found on nineteenth-century English cottages such as those illustrated by John Ruskin in "On Poetry of Architecture" (1838) on page 47 (illustrated in Craig, *Maybeck at Principia*, 312, Fig. 12.39).

Fig. 1.7

Today, the house at 575 Blair Avenue has been remodeled beyond recognition, but its qualities were captured in a letter by Jack London, an appreciative later tenant who lived in it from 1901 to 1903 before it was altered. (During this time, London penned what is probably his best-known story, *Call of the Wild*, in 1903, as well a story about California poppies in which he mentions ladies trespassing on "his" hill to collect poppies.) London wrote:

> *Am beautifully located in new house. We have a big living room, every inch of it, floor and ceiling, finished in redwood. We could put the floor space of almost four cottages into this one living room alone. The rest of the house is finished in redwood too, and is very, very comfortable. . . . A most famous porch, broad and long and cool, a big clump of magnificent pines, flowers and flowers galore . . . half of ground in bearing orchard and half sprinkled with California poppies . . . our nearest neighbor is a block away (and there isn't a vacant lot within a mile) our view commands all of San Francisco Bay for a sweep of thirty or forty miles, and all the opposing shores.*[31]

Worcester's cottage (Fig. 1.7) was low and one-storied. A hip roof with overhanging eaves covered it and extended far out to shelter the porch that, with built-in benches along its walls, could serve as an outdoor room. Paired windows provided wide views. Vines were trained up trellises attached on the sides of the house. Evenly laid wood shingles, unpainted and unstained, of uniform size rather than of ornamental shape covered both walls and roof and were left unpainted to weather.[32]

The largest amount of space in this modest house was allotted to the living room, which was exceptionally spacious, as was the porch. Two small bedrooms, a kitchen, and a dining room opened off this central space. For comfort on foggy and rainy evenings there was a large fireplace, but in sunny weather the living space was increased twofold by the long sheltering porch. Wide redwood boards covered floor, walls, and ceilings, while heavy beams supporting the ceilings were left exposed. All wood was kept in its natural state.

Worcester's Piedmont house (Figs. 1.5–1.7), although unpretentious, was very influential, and so merits further citing of the Londons' characterization of it. In describing the Piedmont house Worcester and the Londons agree that the living room was quite large, but they disagree about the size of the entire house. Worcester always refers to it as a house, whereas Jack London calls it a bungalow. Worcester refers to it as "little," although construction took an entire year. According to London's wife, Charmian, the house was large and rambling:

> *The squat, weathered thatch of shingle sheltered a large beamed living hall, a small dining room, and three or four bedchambers. . . . Kitchen, laundry and servants' rooms rambled like aimless if charming afterthoughts . . . up-step and down.*[33]

Worcester lived there "quite alone" the first year, but at some time thereafter, he had a Chinese servant, which may imply servants' quarters. Joan London, Jack's oldest daughter, described a large bungalow as . . .

> *. . . rambling, many-leveled and many roomed, with redwood-paneled walls and ceilings, and redwood shingles outside. . . . The living room . . . was huge.*[34]

Worcester's decision not to paint the interior of his home is significant. The Cape Cod houses that he had known in his youth were often sheathed with unpainted shingles, but whitewashed walls and painted wood were standard in eighteenth-century interiors.[35]

The simple and functional New England clapboarded houses of the late seventeenth and eighteenth centuries, with their large fireplaces surrounded by wood paneling and wainscoting that was mostly painted, no doubt provided inspiration; however, many of these also used plaster above the painted wood wainscoting.[36]

Worcester's acquaintance with early New England houses was perhaps revived by the colonial structures featured at the Philadelphia Centennial Exposition of 1876, which created the popular basis for the colonial revival.[37] Additionally, he probably saw the early American Bishop Berkeley house in Middletown, Rhode Island (1729), captioned "Old House at Newport, RI" and published in the *New York Sketch Book of Architecture (NYSBA)* on December 4, 1874. (H. H. Richardson was listed as editor of this journal, but McKim was the real force, according to historian Richard Guy Wilson.) The published photograph emphasizes the rugged rural side of the house with its long sweeping roof rather than the classically symmetrical front. Wilson credits McKim *"as the most important architect searching for an American expression based upon the native vernacular in the 1870s."* Wilson notes that McKim's commentary on these houses called for somebody to write about them as "Architecture." Whereas Worcester seems to have unreservedly admired vernacular buildings, McKim *"commended 'the picturesque surroundings and architectural merit of many of these old* [early American] *buildings' and backhandedly complimented them, observing that they were not 'ugly' or 'at least they are never aggressively so, like so many of their modern neighbors.'"*[38]

Whether Worcester had any knowledge of still another vernacular tradition, the Anglo-Indian bungalow, is not known.[39] Worcester expressed interest in vernacular architecture contemporaneously and perhaps before McKim. (Later in this chapter, see a discussion of Worcester's interest in Yosemite's vernacular architecture, which he encountered in the mid-1860s.) Moreover, Worcester pasted illustrations from the *NYSBA* in his scrapbook, and thus he, along with McKim, emerges between 1874 and 1878 as a very influential proponent of unpretentious vernacular-inspired houses built of natural materials to harmonize with nature. As we shall see, Worcester not only designed his Piedmont home, three houses for Emilie Price Marshall, and his own house on Russian Hill, but he also advised others what to build, which architect to choose, and even what materials to use.

Letters that Joseph Worcester wrote to his family in New England before and after his house was completed confirm that he took great care with the plans and seemed particularly happy that it fit its setting so well. On October 21, 1876, Worcester wrote his nephew:

The house is not yet begun. . . . I have given Theodore much trouble about it, considering that it is to cost so little, but its position is very conspicuous and for my own satisfaction in it I wanted it should be right.[40]

On January 8, 1878, after a fortnight's occupancy, Worcester wrote:

The little house, though rough, is attractive and in harmony with the magnificence of view around it. Friends will be glad to come to it for relief from city life, and it ought to be a good place for some sober thinking on my part.[41]

Fig. 1.8: Hutchings Hotel,
Yosemite Valley, California,
photographed by J. J. Reilly
after 1864.

A year later, Worcester wrote again of how pleased he and his friends were with life in the house:

And now I can say that I never saw more favorable conditions than those that my little house affords. The broad outlook, the modest homely appearance of the house, and the big wooden room with its quiet tone of color; friends say that it is restful. I have been setting out vines about the house this week, climbing roses, passion-vines, begonias, etc. and at a little distance I have set out currant and gooseberry bushes and apple, pear, and cherry trees.[42]

A clue to the house and the architecture that it influenced in northern California lies in Worcester's view of nature, which grew out of his reading and religious training. He saw the natural world as beautiful because it was the work of God; man's creativity, he felt, should harmonize with God's rather than disturb it.

As a Swedenborgian, Worcester believed that specific things in nature—trees, birds, and flowers—were worldly manifestations of aspects of God. His reading of Ruskin, in particular the *Seven Lamps of Architecture,* supported his credo that the most beautiful styles of art and architecture were those that most closely imitated the forms of nature.[43]

Today many have not heard of Joseph Worcester, but Evelyn Craig Pattiani refers to the hill near Scenic and Blair as Worcester Knoll, and Piedmont historian Gail Lombardi notes that early maps indicate Blair Avenue above Highland (formerly Vernal Avenue) was known as Worcester Avenue into the 1920s.

Olmsted, Muir, and Worcester: A Common Inspiration, A Common Meeting Point?

It can be said that in Yosemite, Frederick Law Olmsted, John Muir, and Joseph Worcester found support for their shared belief that it was worth studying nature and landscape in order to increase man's morality, happiness, and sensitivity to all the arts. Furthermore, all three men succeeded in convincing numerous others to share their belief.[44]

Worcester visited Yosemite, as his nephew's memoir reveals:

From the Yosemite he had brought back a wonderful collection of large photographs—"seconds because of some slight imperfection" as he used to explain, and given to him perhaps in return for help he had given to the photographer, or, if bought, then only at a very low price. For during his long stay in the Valley he had been partially earning his way.[45]

According to Yosemite historian Linda Eade, the well-known photographer Carleton Watkins made a second trip to Yosemite in 1865 (his first was in 1861). No artists or photographers are known to have been there in 1864 or 1866. Then in 1867 Eadweard Muybridge made numerous large plates at Yosemite under the HELIOS trademark. So if Joseph Worcester assisted a photographer and brought the photographs back to Boston to show his family, as

Fig. 1.9: Group portrait, ca. 1905—Charles Keeler, John Muir, William Burroughs (seated), William Keith, Francis Brown—probably taken in Keith's studio. Note also the Mission Style chair.

Alfred mentions, he would most likely have been in Yosemite and have worked with Watkins in 1865 or with Muybridge in *early* 1867, since he returned to Boston to be ordained *late* in 1867. However, the details of Worcester's Yosemite trips and exact arrival dates in California need to be further investigated.[46]

Worcester's letters to Alfred document two visits to Mountain House Ranch in the redwood hills twenty-five miles from San Francisco, and indicate that his two trips to California, and perhaps to Yosemite, were four to five years apart.[47]

March 5, 1869

Do you remember when I first met Harry East? Well, here I am again, some thirty five miles south of San Francisco up among the Redwood hills.

Not feeling very well as Spring approached [the mention of Spring approaching suggests he had been in California before Spring] *I wrote down to see if I could be accommodated for a few days here. A cordial invitation came back and within twenty-four hours I was on my way. I have dreamed much of the place since I was here five years ago, and my dreams fall short of the reality.*[48]

This much we can state with certainty: Worcester made two trips to California, one in 1864 and again in 1868, and two trips to the Mountain House Ranch in 1864 and 1869. It is possible, even likely, considering his love of nature that he also visited Yosemite at least twice, but we cannot say so categorically at this time.

Olmsted was in California from 1863 through 1865 and first visited the Mariposa Grove of Big Trees in Yosemite in November 1863; in August 1864 he explored the high country and Yosemite Valley.[49] During his initial visits to Yosemite, Olmsted reports being enraptured and overwhelmed by the grand and subtle elements of its beauty:

The root of all my good work is an early respect for, regard and enjoyment of scenery . . .
and extraordinary opportunities for cultivating susceptibility to the power of scenery. [50]

Like Worcester, Olmsted had read Ruskin and also shared Worcester's interest in Swedenborg. While in England fifteen years before in August 1850, Olmsted had met James J. G. Wilkinson (1812–1899), the English translator of Swedenborg's works, and was quite taken with him:

He showed us manuscripts of [Swedenborg's]. *He is a noble-man—was very genial and*
good with us. I have not [seen] *men that impressed more as a character mingling the good*
with the great. [51]

As Olmsted expert Charles Beveridge explains:

Olmsted used the style of the Beautiful—or as he usually called it, the pastoral to create a
sense of the peacefulness of nature and to soothe and restore the spirit. [52]

Commenting to his wife on the lush foliage he saw when passing through the Isthmus of Panama on his way to California in 1863, he wrote: *"I think it produces a very strong moral impression through an enlarged sense of the bounteousness of nature."* [53]

Worcester arrived in Yosemite with sensitivity to the holiness of nature, direct from Swedenborgian teachings and from Ruskin. For example, rhapsodizing about mountains, Ruskin wrote:

. . . [they] *seem to have been built for the human race, as at once their schools and cathe-*
drals; full of treasures of illuminated manuscripts for the scholar, kindly in simple lessons to
the worker, quiet in pale cloisters for the thinker, glorious in holiness for the worshipper. [54]

As a Swedenborgian, Worcester believed that God is reflected in all of nature.

If Yosemite was not the catalyst that brought Worcester and Olmsted together, it is likely that Worcester heard about the by-then-famous landscape designer who shared his reverence for nature, and Worcester would certainly have been aware of his work in San Francisco, Berkeley, and Oakland between 1863 and 1865. As Beveridge explains: *"It was that quality of nature, and of the Creator behind it, that Olmsted sought to express and present in his designs thereafter . . . ,"* just as Worcester did when designing the Swedenborgian Church and his Piedmont and Russian Hill homes.[55]

John Muir first visited Yosemite Valley in May 1868, four years *after* Worcester's first visit in 1864. If Worcester met Muir at Hutchings' home or hotel (the Hutchings were friends of both Worcester and the Burnham family) as Worcester's nephew-biographer states, we can conclude that Worcester visited Yosemite for the second time in 1868 or 1869; and since Muir built his shelter next door to Hutchings, it would have been odd if they had not met. In any case, they were definitely friends by 1893, when Worcester wrote seeking Muir's assistance in installing native California flowers around the California State Building at the 1893 World's Columbian Exposition in Chicago. (See Chapters 7 and 10.)

Olmsted, Muir, and Yosemite Prove Inspirational

By the time Olmsted was appointed to head the Yosemite Commission in August 1864, he had developed a reputation as the designer of New York's Central Park and had demonstrated his remarkable organizing powers with the Sanitary Commission and the War Department. In San Francisco, Olmsted developed a plan in the 1860s (influential, although never implemented) for present-day Golden Gate Park, and in Oakland he designed Mountain View Cemetery (dedicated May 1865) with curvilinear roads contoured to the land. This cemetery adjoins Piedmont at a location about four blocks from Joseph Worcester's 1876 Piedmont house, and from its heights there is a magnificent view over the entire bay. In addition, on March 7, 1865, Olmsted was officially commissioned by the Trustees of the University of California to develop a plan for a new college campus in what later became the city of Berkeley.

We can imagine Worcester, then a young man of twenty-seven compared with the older Olmsted at forty-two and Muir at thirty, transformed by the raw vitality of his experiences in frontier California, impressed by Yosemite's majesty, and challenged by his meetings with Olmsted and Muir; after all, something convinced him to give up Boston and escape the traditional East Coast milieu, ignoring his family's strong opposition.

Olmsted and Muir's California work had a huge influence on the San Francisco Bay Region as did Worcester's ideas ten to fifteen years later. If not Olmsted and/or Muir, something turned Joseph Worcester from a shy and reserved young man into another man—a more sophisticated,

Fig. 1.10: James Lamon's log cabin, Yosemite Valley (ca. 1859). Photographed by J. J. Reilly ca. 1870; captioned: "The First House in the Yo Semite Valley, Cal."

self-confident individual, convinced of his opinions and confident in his ability to influence others toward what he saw as best.

Muir and Worcester, like Olmsted, shared a reverence for nature and determined to live in houses reflecting that quality. Muir's description of his Yosemite "hangnest" reveals that, though a simple structure, it was designed specifically to bring nature into his home:

I boarded with Mr. Hutchings' family, but occupied a cabin that I built for myself near the Hutchings' winter home. This cabin, I think, was the handsomest building in the Valley, and the most useful and convenient for a mountaineer. From the Yosemite Creek, near where it first gathers its beaten waters at the foot of the fall, I dug a small ditch and brought a stream into the cabin, entering at one end and flowing out the other with just current enough to allow it to sing and warble in low, sweet tones, delightful at night while I lay in bed. The floor was made of rough slabs, nicely joined and embedded in the ground. In the spring, the common pteris ferns pushed up between the joints of the slabs, two of which, growing slender like climbing ferns on account of the subdued light, I trained on threads up the sides and over my window in front of my writing desk in an ornamental arch. Dainty little tree frogs occasionally climbed the ferns and made fine music in the night, and common frogs came in with the stream and helped to sing with the hylas [tree toads] and the warbling, tinkling water. My bed was suspended from the rafters and lined with libocedrus plumes, altogether forming a delightful home in the glorious valley at a cost of only three or four dollars, and I was loathe to leave it.[56]

Whether or not they met in Yosemite, it is clear Worcester shared Olmsted's and Muir's commitment to buildings that were designed to enhance and encompass the natural world. Unfortunately, no description of Yosemite by Worcester seems to have survived; but when he writes Alfred about Mountain House Ranch, he reveals sensitivities to the awesomeness of nature similar to Muir's description of his Yosemite cabin:

March 5, 1869
The [Mountain House Ranch] *stands at the mouth of a mountain gulch, a mile or two in depth and filled with timber (mostly redwood) with a stream tumbling down through it. The air is mild and delightfully clear; the running water, meadow larks, quail, cow-bells, etc. make music, and the views on all sides are beautiful. The doors stand open and great wood-fires blaze or smoulder in the fireplaces and all things conspire to rest and heal a city-worn boy. Horses and dogs stand about in the great yard, free to all. . . . In the night the coyote (a kind of wolf) and the screech-owl bark and hoot and make the dogs answer.*[57]

Seeing Muir's cabin and other Yosemite structures with exposed, untreated wood inside and out, often with the bark left on, may have inspired Worcester when he designed his homes and the Swedenborgian Church, all with exposed untreated wood, allowing his passion for nature to find fulfillment within his buildings.[58]

Furthermore, Worcester's views of Divinity and its revelation in nature were similar to those of his friend Muir, who equated his explorations of Yosemite with acts of religious devotion. In a letter sent from Yosemite in 1870, Muir wrote:

Fig. 1.11: Bernard Maybeck drawing of the Piedmont cottage in which he and his wife, Annie, lived from late 1890 into 1891, located on the property adjoining Joseph Worcester's.

I have not been at church a single time since leaving home. Yet this glorious valley might be called a church, for every lover of the great Creator who comes within the broad over-whelming influences of the place fails not to worship as he never did before. The glory of the Lord is upon all his works; it is written plainly upon all the fields of every clime, and upon every sky, but here in this place of surpassing glory the Lord has written in capitals. [59]

Both Muir and Worcester worked for the Hutchings' hotel in Yosemite. Muir started work there in November 1869 and worked the winter of 1869–70. He had to build his cabin first and then the sawmill. According to Alfred, *"During* [Worcester's] *long stay in the valley he had been doing chores for Hutchings . . . churning and other chores."* [60]

Although the Hutchings' family hotel was built of hand-hewn white cedar planks, he no doubt saw miners' shanties in many modes while traveling to Yosemite: half-board logs chinked with clay and roofed by a tent, or stone-roofed with thatch or shingle. Of particular importance is the fact that shingles were reserved for roofs or outbuildings and were not used to sheath an entire house. This was true of miners' shanties as well as of more permanent homes built in towns in the 1870s and 1880s. A search through photograph albums in the Bancroft Library for brown shingled houses earlier than Worcester's did not uncover pre-1876 or even pre-1885 examples of unpainted shingling used on California residences. However, as noted, there was one, perhaps by Bruce Price, ca. 1885 (Fig. 0.3).

When he built his house in Piedmont, Worcester wanted to capture the hasty directness of natural materials that the miners' cabins revealed, and he may also have been inspired by wood cabins in Yosemite with their barked logs artistically placed in a pleasing pattern such as that used by James C. Lamon for his first cabin (Fig. 1.10) in Yosemite, built in 1859.

Lamon used unusually large logs for his home, but they were so skillfully notched on both the upper and lower sides, and joined so proficiently at the corners, that the result was a very tight, compact little shelter. The logs were graduated in size from the base log up to a small gable which was filled in with horizontal split shakes.[61]

Additional inspiration might have come from Hutchings' addition of a shed-like building encompassing an enormous tree; the giant trunk occupied a large part of a hotel bedroom. Hutchings did this some time before October 1867, so Worcester could have seen this "Big Tree Room" on his second trip to Yosemite, probably 1868 or 1869.

Like Muir and Lamon, Worcester desired to build a house that was itself almost a thing of nature. As Russian Hill historian William Kostura put it: *"He viewed the natural world as a manifestation of God, and felt that buildings should relate well to the environment rather than disrupt it. Nature was beautiful and buildings which resemble nature were the most beautiful of buildings."* [62]

Joseph Worcester must have seen and appreciated the vernacular architecture of the state's early history as well as its rough shelters. In 1876, when designing his Piedmont house, Worcester incorporated elements of Spanish California's adobe architecture: the hip roof with deep overhangs and the long covered porch of the casa de pueblo. He would have seen this style, for example, at the Sanchez Adobe (1842), Pacifica, or at the Alvarado Adobe (1848), San Pablo, both just south of San Francisco.

The bachelor who loved essentials meant his Piedmont home to be a simple, sheltering house such as a common craftsman might design out of the necessities of site and materials rather than an elegant home proclaiming status through "style." His shingles were not used as an Americanization of English hung tiles as they were initially by Shingle Style architects on the East Coast, but rather to make the house more rustic, more natural, more part of nature and the natural environment. The colonial New England house, wood cabins, and adobe house, along with European and perhaps even Asian vernacular architecture, all provided models for such a simple home—an American equivalent of John Ruskin's and William Morris' ideal humble cottage.[63]

Worcester's Piedmont cottage and his letters to Alfred confirm that his knowledge and appreciation of both Morris and Ruskin had begun before 1876, and he would seem to have been among the first, if not the first, to translate this Arts & Crafts ideal into architecture in California.[64]

In the Worcester letters that have been uncovered to date, William Morris is not mentioned; however, the Arts & Crafts spirit is expressed. As Joseph wrote Alfred:

January 17, 1873
I know that music, drawing, or even a trade would be very valuable to you. . . . If you do not much incline to music or drawing why not take hold of carpentering or cabinet making; that is probably the best handiwork to carry along with a profession, and the most generally useful. I think a facility with tools is a fine basis to build character upon.[65]

The Piedmont house delighted its owner and his friends. California artist William Keith, to whom Worcester was religious advisor and critic as well as friend, visited the house frequently in the early 1880s and did several paintings of it (Fig. 1.6).[66] Maybeck (Fig. 1.12), who came to play a large role in the development of the California Arts & Crafts tradition, lived for a time on the property adjoining the Worcester cottage. According to his early client and biographer Charles Keeler, Maybeck was deeply impressed by his first view of it (Figs. 1.6, 1.7):

There came to Mr. Maybeck in his early California days an experience that profoundly affected his whole artistic outlook. He found a cottage in Piedmont on the hills back of Oakland, and next to him the Reverend Joseph Worcester had a little summer retreat. Looking into Mr. Worcester's windows, he saw the interior of the cottage was all of unpainted redwood boards. It was a revelation.[67]

Maybeck's "revelation" and his later work with Worcester on the Swedenborgian Church, along with seeing the exposed redwood in Polk's and Worcester's pre-1894 houses on Russian Hill (discussed in Chapter 2), may have increased Maybeck's desire to expose structure and to use natural materials, fitting his buildings into the land.

Fig. 1.12: Bernard Maybeck as a young man.

Worcester owned his Piedmont property for twenty-four years. He had already built his Russian Hill house by 1890 but still frequented the Piedmont house when Maybeck moved into the cottage on the adjoining property (Fig. 1.10). This was probably before September 1890, as Maybeck needed a home for his new bride, Annie, after they were married October 29, 1890. As Piedmont historian Gail Lombardi discovered, the Block Books show that, until 1902 and perhaps later, Worcester owned his home and surrounding acres.[68] Having few ministerial duties other than Sunday services, and having many friends in nearby Berkeley, Worcester continued to visit his Piedmont house, so it would have been unlikely for him not to befriend and discuss architecture with his newly married architect-neighbor—a friend of his friends Polk and Brown—during Maybeck and Annie's year-long stay nearby.

Russian Hill: An Early
Arts & Crafts Neighborhood

2

WORCESTER MOVED ACROSS THE BAY TO SAN FRANCISCO IN 1887 IN ORDER TO RESUME THE leadership of the Swedenborgian Church he had left ten years before; but he returned frequently to Piedmont, a short ferry ride away, as church services were only on Sundays; moreover, many of his friends (e.g., William Keith, Professor George H. Howison, Professor and Mrs. F. V. Paget, Charles Keeler, and Bernard Maybeck) lived in Berkeley, only about three miles from Piedmont.

In October 1878, he had described to his nephew his *"new undertaking . . . to walk every afternoon a mile and a half and give three hours to a family of bright children. That with my studying and housekeeping and company keeps me very busy."*[1] Worcester seems to have devoted his energies to studying architecture, as he eventually filled fourteen scrapbooks with architectural clippings, some dating back to 1874. Contemporary accounts specify that the "company" he entertained included numerous architects, and letters found to date confirm that his correspondents included philanthropists, artists, politicians, and academics, among many others.

To get to Berkeley he could have taken the Broadway & Piedmont Horse Railroad if he did not own a carriage of his own. When William Keith visited Worcester in Piedmont, he took the horsecars: *". . . I look forward to the time I shall get out of the horsecars at Piedmont & walk up to your hill, & knock at your door."*[2]

Joseph Worcester and Daniel Burnham

No sooner was Worcester relocated at 1407 Jones Street in San Francisco than he decided to design another house, similarly sited atop a hill with a magnificent view. He urged Emilie Price Marshall, one of his parishioners, to build a few houses as an investment on a plot of land the Marshalls owned on Russian Hill. He subsequently designed three houses for David and Emilie Price Marshall (Figs. 2.1, 2.5, 2.10) and a smaller house next door at 1030 Vallejo (Figs. 2.2, 2.10) expressly for himself. Worcester's was different from the others in that it was one story and had an almost 360-degree view over San Francisco and the Golden Gate and may well have been oriented toward the home he still owned in Piedmont.[3]

As we see below, Daniel Burnham wrote to his wife, praising Worcester's development as "an architect." Referring to the Marshall houses and the house Worcester designed for himself,

Fig. 2.1a

Fig. 2.1b

Figs. 2.1a and 2.1b: Emilie Price Marshall house, Vallejo Street, Russian Hill, San Francisco (1888).

Fig. 2.1a: View: entrance façade to one of three Marshall houses designed by Joseph Worcester, possibly assisted by Daniel Burnham from 1888 to 1890. Photo ca. 1972.

Fig. 2.1b: View: end façade of Marshall house seen in Fig. 2.1a. Photo ca. 1972.

Burnham spells out Worcester's architectural role and establishes the fact that all four houses were designed by Worcester, possibly with help from Burnham, before September 17, 1888, when Burnham wrote:

> *He is just blooming out as an architect. There are four little cottages to be put up by a friend of his and the friend wants Uncle Joe to have entire charge, which he intends to do; and I am to help him. . . . I enclose a sketch Uncle Joe just made to show how he intends to treat the fronts.*[4]

Worcester's "Humble Cottage"

Alfred Worcester states that *"the little house was built for* [Worcester] *practically in accordance with his design but not quite."* Only two of the Marshall houses remain today, at 1034 and 1036

Vallejo; however, all three were completed by July 1889 and Worcester's shortly thereafter. When Worcester actually moved into his San Francisco house is unclear as he was still maintaining his Piedmont home and no residence is listed for February–September 1890. All four houses fulfilled Worcester's desire to create a visible rustic city neighborhood on Russian Hill with "simple," affordable houses, "intentionally unassuming," and designed with nature in mind.[5]

The features of the house in Piedmont appear to have pleased Worcester so much that he saw little reason to alter them in his new Russian Hill house (Fig. 2.2), which was also very plain in decoration and simple in outline, form, and mass. Again, the house was a one-story hip-roofed structure with natural shingles covering walls and roof. It was oriented to the views, not to the street, and the side that faced the Golden Gate had *"large plate glass windows for the glorious outlook."*[6]

As in the Piedmont cottage, the central wooden living room dominated the space (Figs. 2.3, 2.4); only a small bedroom and kitchen opened off it. Nothing detracted from its rustic natural qualities. The floor was wood as were the ceilings and walls. Branches, reeds, and pinecones ornamented the fireplace wall. Again, landscapes by Keith, reminders of the California countryside, hung over the books, and the changing moods of sky and water could be glimpsed from the large windows. Here, Alfred says,

> . . . *he lived superbly, entertaining largely and giving beautiful presents. His clothes, exquisitely tailored of finest materials, never seemed to need replacing, much less cleansing. The dust and dirt of this world seemed to avoid him. Housekeeping with him was a fine art. He knew just how to cook his oatmeal and make his tea, where to buy the best bread, the best butter and cream. This with perhaps some marmalade or Pecan nuts was all that he ever served.*[7]

Fig. 2.2: Joseph Worcester house, 1030 Vallejo, Russian Hill, San Francisco (1888–90; destroyed), reproduced from a woodblock carved by Brother Cornelius, William Keith's biographer, n.d. Worcester designed and sited the one-story rustic shingled house, possibly assisted by his cousin and friend, Chicago architect Daniel Burnham.

Worcester's house and the gracious though simple life he led there delighted the friends who visited him on Russian Hill. Charles Keeler, a regular visitor, expressed his admiration in a description of his first view of the San Francisco cottage:

Opening the gate in the board fence, we found ourselves in a little garden adjoining the residence of the portrait painter Mary Curtis Richardson. This was one of the Marshall houses. Mr. Worcester's home, covered with unpainted shingles, was the one story cottage of a bachelor. Redwood panels, an ample buff colored terra-cotta fireplace with a great heap of ashes and a glowing fire, some charming portraits by Mrs. Richardson and some Keith landscapes, shelves of books and a big bunch of pine cones on the mantle. . . . But the whole room was subordinated to the big windows fronting on a panorama of the Golden Gate, with the roofs of houses in the foreground. [8]

Worcester's friends came to enjoy more than the beauty and serenity of his home. Although he was not a professional architect, many of his visitors were, and they often sought his advice. Even the architects who were planning the University of California buildings in Berkeley asked for suggestions from Worcester, as we shall see in Chapter 8. Edmund Sears describes the situation well:

Fig. 2.3: Worcester house, Russian Hill, view: fireplace end of living room, designed by Joseph Worcester, possibly with the help of Daniel Burnham, seen as it was when Worcester lived there. Worcester brought nature into his home using unpainted redwood for the walls and ceiling as well as for paneling above the mantel over the terra-cotta brick fireplace surround. Note the Oriental and bearskin rugs on the floor, as well as wooden bookcases, Keith paintings, and the foliage and pinecones collected from nearby wooded hills.

And to many besides those who sought his spiritual counsel he had much to give. If a promising young architect came to the city he was sure to know him, to go to him and consult him and get wise suggestions. [9]

Russian Hill: Its Influence

A cohesive yet lively townscape was formed by Worcester's cottage (Figs. 2.3, 2.10) and the three Marshall houses (Figs. 2.5, 2.10), all covered with natural wood shingles. Although Eastern architect Bruce Price had designed two partially shingled mansions in the Bay Area—the 1885 Coleman-Hecht residence, San Francisco (Fig. 0.3), and the 1886 house for George Howard, San Mateo, never executed—they were elaborate combinations of the Shingle and Queen Anne styles with picturesque massing, multiple gables, and differing wall textures; they were not at all "simple" Arts & Crafts houses for the new middle class, such as Worcester and friends were advocating. William Kostura has noted:

The three houses were staggered in their relationship to the property on Vallejo St. The westernmost house, #1036 was placed closest to the street, the next house, #1034, was set

Fig. 2.4: Worcester house, Russian Hill, view: the bay window end of the living room described in Charles Lummis' notes as a real "arts & crafts" design. It was designed by Joseph Worcester, possibly with the help of Daniel Burnham, and is seen as it was when Worcester lived there. Note the built-in bench and bearskin rug, globe lights and Indian textile on the rocker. Redwood board and battens add light, shadow, and depth to the walls as do beams to the ceiling. Photographed by Charles Lummis in 1898 although not published in *Land of Sunshine* until August 1902.

back on the lot a slightly greater distance, and the easternmost house #1032 was set back farther still. This progression of setbacks forced the viewer to regard the three houses as individual structures in a dynamic, unified arrangement. . . . [Worcester's] residence did not impede 1032 Vallejo's eastward views of the bay, and it incidentally allowed Worcester to have a large back yard [and garden]. [10]

The Worcester house in Piedmont and the houses on Russian Hill signaled the beginning of a new era: the development of simple, affordable, artistically designed homes built with nature and handicraft in mind.

It seems likely that Worcester and this lively townscape inspired Willis Polk to attempt something similar on his side of Vallejo Street. A 1918 article describes how he came to live on Russian Hill. The story sounds very much in character:

The Polk home was a house built by Horatio P. Livermore. . . . Willis Polk and Emil Carsen, the artist, discovered the place one night while they were rambling the hill in quest of inspiration. The house was deserted and had practically no window panes left unbroken . . . but it looked very beautiful in the moonlight and Willis decided there and then to live in it if he could. [11]

The following morning Polk sought out Livermore who told him, *"I don't want to bother about fixing up the place but if you care to take it as it is and look after it you may have it rent free."* Polk took the offer and fixed up the house still standing at 40 Florence Street (Fig. 2.6). [12]

It is likely that Worcester met Polk when the latter worked for his friend A. Page Brown, or through their mutual friend Maybeck. In any case, they met before December 1890 when Polk, not yet twenty-three, began renovating the Livermore house for himself on Russian Hill. That same month he wrote an editorial for *Architectural News,* a magazine he had just started, that could in some respects be considered the Arts & Crafts clarion call for well-designed, modest houses for the middle class:

Fig. 2.5: Marshall houses, designed by Joseph Worcester, possibly assisted by Daniel Burnham; view: Russian Hill after 1890 and before 1892, showing how the three Marshall houses cap the summit of Russian Hill and yet echo nature's nearby peaks.

The fact that dwelling houses should express, without affectation, the simplest object of its being, that of furnishing a comfortable shelter to the home-life, avoiding anything tending to display, and without imitating the pretentious houses of men of wealth of which few are models of anything but poor taste, is the real basis for the proper conception of an ideal home of moderate cost.[13]

McKim, Mead, and White chose redwood for the interiors of many of their Shingle Style houses in the 1880s but those sprawling country houses are distinctly different from the modest interiors at which Worcester and his friends were aiming in the very early 1890s. Vincent Scully suggests that in some of these Shingle Style houses *". . . the client is meant to feel himself a baron."* For example, Scully refers to the Victor Newcomb house (1880–81) in Elberon, New Jersey, as *"this beautiful villa"* where *"the main areas of the plan are magnificent."* His description of the Robert Goelet house (1882–83) in Newport, Rhode Island, shows just how far these houses were from what Worcester was trying to achieve: *". . . the Goelet hall . . . is a baronial evocation. . . . The main hall is forty-four feet long, thirty feet wide and twenty four feet high and the fireplace is large enough for a man to walk into."*[14]

Mocking the so-called "cottages" that he and his fellow Shingle Style architects were building, Bruce Price wrote in 1886:

It is the fashion to call these country houses cottages but the cottage exists only in name. The cliffs of Newport, the rocks of Mt. Desert . . . have cottages that would be mansions in England, villas in Italy or Chateaux in France. The "cottage" is an amiable deception . . . our countrymen . . . seek the beauties and comforts that wealth can furnish.[15]

In northern California, on the other hand, architects did more than advocate the simple rustic cottage; from the end of the 1880s on, they actually built them in cities as well as in

Fig. 2.6: Horatio P. Livermore house, 40 Florence Street, Russian Hill, San Francisco, remodeled by Willis Polk, shown in 1904. Redwood board walls and a terra-cotta brick fireplace recall Joseph Worcester's home across the street; however, the large fluted column prefigures the much more elaborately decorated elegant houses that Polk designed later.

Fig. 2.7: Polk-Williams duplex, 1013–1019
Vallejo (1892–93), by Willis Polk. It features
a brown shingled exterior with white trim. The
large Gothic window and upwardly curved eaves
resemble late-medieval French houses such as
those still visible today in Provins, east of Paris,
and in Brittany (Fig. 2.8). Polk probably decided
to use unpainted shingles to keep in step with the
rest of the neighborhood, which was designed by
Worcester, although the interior of the duplex is
more elegant than Worcester's "simple" home.

Fig. 2.8: Rue de Paris, Vitre, Brittany, France; view: window treatment. Similar houses can still be seen just east of Paris in the historic town of Provins.

suburbs. Although by 1884 the Shingle Style had become *"a natural way of construction, limited only by the fact that its method extended mainly to one or two family homes, summer clubhouses, or summer hotels. . . . It was a country and suburban architecture,"* according to Scully. Moreover these California Arts & Crafts shingled homes were designed as affordable primary residences, not as secondary residences in the countryside or at the shore.[16]

Polk remodeled the Livermore house (Fig. 2.6) with redwood paneling left in its natural state, and installed a buff-colored terra-cotta fireplace similar to Worcester's. Polk and Worcester, though opposites in many ways, became fast friends, and Polk, along with Ernest Coxhead, disseminated the Arts & Crafts "simple home" philosophy—at least for a few years. Ernest Peixotto described his friend's remodeling of the Livermore residence as follows:

> *The room designed by Mr. Polk is finished throughout in large panels of redwood, dovetailed where the paneling is too large to be made of one board. The ceiling is supported by heavy beams, ornamented with delicate mouldings. His beautifully designed mantels and picturesque staircases are notable features of his interiors. His redwood is always left either in natural finish or simply waxed, so as to show the exquisite color and texture of the wood.*[17]

As Kostura expresses it: *"Except for a fluted Doric column, also made of redwood, which gave the room a classical touch, the design resembled nothing so much as Joseph Worcester's living room just across the street."*[18]

When Mrs. Livermore discovered that Polk had made her Russian Hill house quite livable, the architect, who had no lease, had to leave. In 1891, when Polk's practice was suffering, Worcester's parishioners gave Polk a commission: he added a half-timbered façade—a late-medieval tradition that influenced the Arts & Crafts—to the William Boericke residence at 1812 Washington Street in San Francisco.[19]

Fig. 2.9: Polk-Williams duplex. Around the living hall's four walls runs a balcony lit by tiny windows that open onto breathtaking views of the entire bay region. On the ground floor, wood piers somewhat screen this room from another.

Thereafter he built a two-family house (Figs. 2.7. 2.9) opposite Worcester's house. As Kostura points out: *"It was actually built as a common-wall duplex, the other half belonging to Dora Norton Williams . . . best known today for her close friendship with* [Scottish novelist] *Robert Louis and Fanny Stevenson."* The Williams half was completed by October 1892, but work was still being done on the other half into early 1893.

The Polk-Williams duplex (Fig. 2.9), as it is now known to historians, still stands, and one can see how its unpainted shingle exterior would have complemented Worcester's house and the Marshall houses. However, its "Gothic" window resembles the treatment given late-medieval French houses—such as those still visible today in Provins, east of Paris, and in Brittany (Fig. 2.8), and recalls the timber-framed Gothic window that Coxhead used on his All Saints Church (1888–89) in Pasadena—rather than Worcester's bungalow; and its interior is far more elegant than Worcester's home. Nevertheless, it continued the "rustic city house" tradition Worcester had initiated.[20] Although Polk featured three buff-colored fireplaces similar to his neighbor's, he added a balcony with carved wood balusters and fancy moldings and, at some point, elegant square piers separating two rooms (Fig. 2.9). The cathedral ceiling in the studio loft of the Williams unit is lit by the large Gothic window inside the flared gable, visible in the illustration.

According to Kostura, *"The duplex was a remarkable synthesis of east coast shingle style, medieval Brittanic [and Provins-like] urbanism, Joseph Worcester's love of natural materials, hilltop Bohemianism, and Willis Polk's creative genius."*[21]

Worcester took an active role in ensuring that Russian Hill would be developed as he saw fit, and Polk had conceived street improvements as early as 1894, as we see in this letter from Polk to a potential client:

October 26, 1894
Dear Mr. Scott:
Mr. Worcester tells me that, without exception, Mrs. Harvey's lot commands the finest view in the city and that it cannot be cut off. I was with him on the lot this morning, and I quite agree with him. Mrs. Harvey asks for her lot $15,000 or but a little more than $100 per front foot. These prices are exceedingly low. With the goat path up Vallejo street properly converted into a series of terraces, and these lots properly improved, there could be no prettier place in San Francisco. . . .[22]

An interesting sidelight reveals the multiple connections among the so-called Bohemian groups on Russian Hill and in Berkeley and how these connections led to architectural commissions. According to Kostura (and as we can see from Worcester's letter on page 32), Robert Louis Stevenson was much admired by the Russian Hill group. It is even possible, although we lack proof to say so categorically, that Worcester came to know Stevenson before the author left for the South Seas in 1888. In any case he and Polk met Fanny Stevenson after her husband's death when she returned to San Francisco and lived with Dora Williams in her Russian Hill house in the latter half of 1895.[23]

Since Bruce Porter and Willis Polk ended up designing a San Francisco memorial to Robert Louis Stevenson before January 1895, it is likely that they had met Fanny Stevenson prior to her

Fig. 2.10: Marshall houses and Worcester house, Russian Hill, San Francisco; photographed after 1890 and before 1892. Worcester conceived the three Marshall houses in late 1888, possibly with the help of Daniel Burnham. Note that he carefully placed the Marshall houses in a dynamic spatial arrangement. His own house (far right) was completed by the end of 1889.

move back to San Francisco. Furthermore, she must have remained friendly with Polk because later in 1900, when Mrs. Stevenson built a duplex home for herself and her son (from her first marriage) on the north slope of Russian Hill at the northwest corner of Lombard and Hyde, Polk and his firm—Percy and Polk—designed the house. However, she did not live there very long. According to Keeler, she chose instead to move to Berkeley, where she joined the group building brown shingle homes designed so as not to destroy the beautiful hills.[24] Also, according to Worcester's letter to George H. Howison, it would appear that Worcester not only knew Mrs. Stevenson but had been introduced, probably by Mrs. Stevenson, to Graham Balfour (another British connection), whom she had selected to write her husband's biography:

> *Jan. 1st 1900, 1030 Vallejo, San Francisco*
> *Dear Prof Howison,*
> *. . . I wonder if you have met Graham Balfour in Oxford. He has some position as school examiner and now he has undertaken the Life of Robert Louis Stevenson, at Mrs. Stevenson's request. I met him when he was in San Francisco, and took a great liking to him as a very genuine character.[25]*

These multiple friendships and interconnections also helped spread the "simple home" or "humble cottage" philosophy as appropriate for use inside the city so that when Maybeck built a house for himself in Berkeley in 1892, he shingled the exterior and left the wood unpainted and exposed on the inside. Three years later he built a brown shingle house for Keeler on Highland Place in Berkeley. Emulating what Worcester had accomplished on Russian Hill, Maybeck wanted the Keeler house neighborhood to serve as an example of what could be accomplished when residents work together.

The Swedenborgian Church and the First Mission Style Chair   3

Ruskin and an Early Arts & Crafts Church in America

IN THE EARLY 1890S JOSEPH WORCESTER TURNED HIS ATTENTION FROM BUILDING homes to building the Church of the New Jerusalem for his Swedenborgian congregation at 2107 Lyon Street, San Francisco (Fig. 3.1). At first view, the church might astonish by its modesty. This is not a grand cathedral, nor is it a bright white wooden church with a soaring spire such as Worcester would have known from his New England upbringing. The door of the church is accessible only after passing through a quiet garden (Fig. 3.12). Nor does the church really feel as though it is in the city; it is barely visible from the pavement (Fig. 3.3), its sanctuary being framed by a tranquil, wall-enclosed garden. Moreover, the church is quite small. Therefore, it takes a moment to realize that this is a legendary church, listed on the National Register of Historic Places, an icon of the American Arts & Crafts movement.

Once inside we are astonished. The Swedenborgian Church is renowned for its nave supported by madrone trees with their bark left on (Fig. 3.2). However, its quality and its effect upon us is spiritual (rather than physical), and nearly everyone who enters falls under its spell (Fig. 3.4).

Fig. 3.1: Drawing of "Swedenborgian Chapel and Residence. NW Corner Washington and Lyon Sts. San Francisco, Calif. A. Page Brown, Architect, 1894."

Fig. 3.2: Swedenborgian
Church, view: detail of two
madrone trees used as vertical
posts and as arched supports
for the roof of the church,
completed in 1895. William
Keith donated the paintings
that appear between the posts.
Reverend Joseph Worcester
inspired and directed the
architect, A. Page Brown,
and his draftsman, Bernard
Maybeck, to produce this
Arts & Crafts icon.

Fig. 3.3: Swedenborgian
Church, view: the street
entrance does not lead to the
church, but to a loggia from
which the visitor proceeds
into a garden. Only after passing through nature's beauty
does one enter the church.

Fig. 3.2

Fig. 3.3

As Keeler expressed it:

The spirit of the [Swedenborgian] *church, with all its quiet restfulness, its homelike charm, its naïve grace, has sunk deep in the lives of a small but earnest group of men and women. . . . The message of the builder has reached his mark, and here and there through city and town, homes have been reared in the same simple fashion—plain, straightforward, genuine homes, covered with unpainted shingles, or built of rough brick, with much natural redwood inside, in broad unvarnished panels. . . . To find this spirit, which would have been a delight to William Morris, so strongly rooted as to assume almost the aspect of a cult, is, I take it, one of the most remarkable features of a civilization so new as that of modern San Francisco . . . and homes have been reared in the same simple fashion.*[1]

Clearly the Swedenborgian Church and its creators had a major impact on beautification efforts in San Francisco.

Ruskin Influences the Swedenborgian Church

The Worcester letters uncovered to date express the Arts & Crafts spirit. In *The Building Must Teach Its Lessons,* Alan Thomsen, an expert in the field of historical Arts & Crafts literature and a member of the San Francisco Swedenborgian Church, explains how Ruskin's aesthetic ideals find spiritual expression in the church. Worcester's letter of March 1, 1892, to Alfred, remarked:

I hope our plan will not be too aesthetic, but my artist friends are much bent on making it so. They want to build a little church, but a pretty church I do not think I could stand; I prefer the little congregation in the bare hall.[2]

Fig. 3.4: Swedenborgian Church, as Joseph Worcester used it; view: note Bruce Porter's round window in the gable featuring a dove on a fountain, the off-center chandelier and podium, and the branches rather than formal flowers.

Fig. 3.5: Joseph Worcester never allowed himself to be photographed, but this sketch rings true because it was drawn by an artist who attended *"Sunday at the church that teaches Honesty by its Construction,"* and who specified in his caption: *"Sketched by an 'Examiner' artist of the interior and the exterior of the second New Church, and of the minister, the Rev. Joseph Worcester."*

Thomsen points out that it was not a matter of forcing an aesthetic to "fit" Swedenborgian thought, but of recognizing the convergence between the two. Worcester consciously wanted to convey his Swedenborgian theology through the design of the building, as is revealed in an article entitled "A House that Teaches" in which Worcester is quoted:

> *I could have done nothing without the architect but he was very patient with my suggestions. Sometimes he said that an idea of mine was not good architecture. I answered him that I cared nothing for the canons of architecture—the building must teach its lessons.* [3]

In attempting to assign the Lyon Street church its rightful place in the history of the American Arts & Crafts movement, Thomsen explains, it is useful to step back in time to consider the empathy and enthusiasm Swedenborgians felt for the reforming ideals of Ruskin and their application a generation later by William Morris (1834–1896). The *Swedenborgian* (July 1859) reviewed Mrs. L. C. Tuthill's *The True and the Beautiful in Nature, Art and Religion: Selected from the Writings of John Ruskin:*

> *Ruskin . . . has attacked the false traditions of the past with a force and power that have seldom been exhibited by any reformer; and in his manly efforts to restore the true standard of taste in Art, he has shown an appreciation of the first principles of things which entitles him to a prominent place among the thinkers of the age.* [4]

In 1859, the year of the review, Worcester was just twenty-three years old and still eight years away from continuing the family tradition of entering the ordained ministry—a tradition he nearly broke by the temptation to pursue a career in architecture. Yet, given his immersion in the Swedenborgian milieu, he recommended that his nephew read Ruskin. Later, William Keith, writing from Europe on May 18, 1884, acknowledged receiving from Worcester an enclosure of art criticisms by Ruskin.[5] Thomsen concludes:

> *Can we be surprised that his church, devoid of architectural shams, would adhere to Ruskinian arts and crafts principles? Clearly the aesthetic and design of the church are products of a lifetime of considered thought. The architect-pastor and spiritual philosopher first shared Ruskin with those he loved, and then through his extraordinary church he shared him with the world.* [6]

The British Aesthetes vs. Morris and Ruskin

Worcester's denigration of the term "aesthetic" when writing his nephew about the church reveals his sophistication and subtle understanding of the difference between the British aesthetes Oscar Wilde and James McNeil Whistler, considered decadent by many, and William Morris and John Ruskin.[7]

Writing on March 1, 1892, Worcester goes on to clarify to his nephew that he wants to avoid merely a *"pretty church"* [8] because it might imply taking pleasure in beautiful things as did Wilde and Whistler, as if art were an end in itself with no wider moral implications.

Instead, Worcester adhered to Ruskin's beliefs—strongly connecting art and morality—as did other prominent Americans, including Polk, Maybeck, Keith, and Keeler, as well as Frederick Law Olmsted and John Muir. For example, it is easy to imagine Worcester as the author of the passages cited below from John Muir and William Morris (while writings of Maybeck and Keeler make the same points). Muir wrote: *"Everybody needs beauty as well as bread, places to play in and pray in, where nature may heal and give strength to body and soul alike."* [9]

Worcester seemed to pattern his life after Morris and Ruskin. The former *"betook himself to the task of remaking Society as he had in his earlier days to woodcutting; the reasons being always the same—namely, that somebody must."* Morris also believed an individual could make a crucial difference: *"Everything having a spark of vitality in it is subject to change, and that the direction it takes may be affected, if not determined, by individual effort."* [10]

A Collaborative Effort

The architect commissioned by Worcester for the Swedenborgian Church was A. Page Brown. Worcester worked closely with Brown, as the *Scientific American* (August 1899) points out: *"It is but fair to state that in the preparation of these plans the architect* [A. Page Brown] *was greatly indebted to the Rev. Joseph Worcester."* This thought is again echoed in a feature story on the Swedenborgian Church in *House Beautiful* (February 1901), which mentions Brown as architect and then adds that the church embodies Worcester's thought. [11]

Since Brown assigned Maybeck to serve as draftsman for the project, Maybeck may well have influenced its conception as well as having been influenced by it, although Brown was the architect of record, not Maybeck. (For Schweinfurth's possible role, see below.)

Worcester's group of artist friends helped decorate the interior of the church. Keith created four pastoral paintings that were set window-like into the walls. Worcester, Brown, and Maybeck designed the chairs. The collaboration of architects and artists in a total decorative scheme, with paintings, windows, and furniture all designed expressly for a particular building, was similar to the approach advocated by William Morris and his followers.

An earlier collaborative approach to church design, inspired by Morris, had been undertaken from 1872 to 1876 by H. H. Richardson (1838–1886) at Trinity Church in Boston, Massachusetts, involving John LaFarge, Augustus St. Gaudens, and the English artist Edward Burne-Jones, one of Morris' circle. Although the resulting elaborate Trinity Church seems to have nothing else in common with the quiet, small, unobtrusive Swedenborgian Church, Worcester collected numerous articles on Trinity Church and pasted them in his scrapbooks, so he was certainly aware of these collaborative efforts (in 1882 Richardson visited Morris in England). [12] Worcester asked his friend and designer Bruce Porter to create at least one and possibly two of the stained-glass windows. The round window features a dove resting on a fountain, the other St. Christopher bearing the Christ Child. As early as March 1893 one of the Porter windows was finished and Worcester shipped it to Burnham (it is unclear why):

March 13, 1893
Dear Dan,
Bruce Porter has made a beautiful little window and will send it in a few days.
Yours affectionately,
Jos Worcester. [13]

A few days later, he wrote the following:

March 20, 1893
Dear Dan:
Bruce Porter's little window is boxed and will be started in a day or two. I hope you will,
for awhile, have it near enough to you to feel its great beauty. I hope it will not add to your
great load.
Affectionately,
Jos Worcester [14]

April 5, [no year but presumably 1893]
Dear Mr. Burnham:
Allow me to introduce to you my dear friend Mr. Bruce Porter, the designer of the beauti-
ful window we sent to your care.
Affectionately,
Jos Worcester [15]

If the window referred to was the round window, then that would suggest he envisioned a gabled street façade before March 1893. Worcester's letter of March 1, 1892, mentions his determination to avoid a *"pretty"* church (cited above); these facts suggest that discussions about the Swedenborgian Church design began in 1892. [16]

Indeed, we can see from this letter to Mr. Warren that the building was already "contemplated," and fundraising was underway.

February 21, 1893
Dear Mr. Warren:
We thank you very much for your kind offering toward our contemplated building, the
greater outlay will go into the land, as is suitable, and the building will be no more than
a decent [unclear word] improvement to the lot. This is in an old part of the town, but not
deteriorating and not changing in its uses. . . .
Very affectionately yours,
Jos Worcester [17]

On March 13, 1893, land at Taylor and Jackson Streets was surveyed *"for Rev. Joseph Worcester."* But one year and four months later, the church rejected this lot and chose a lot on Lyon Street, surveyed on August 28, 1894. [18]

Apparently it took a year to raise the funds (perhaps due to a financial depression in 1893). Worcester confirmed the intention to build and stated that the church would be small:

January 9, 1894
Dear Mr. Hinkley:
Our little body is just about ready to build a very small church with a capacity only for
about 120. I have not a certain understanding of the wisdom of it. But I have tried to help

them to see it in all its meanings, and I can not question their right to provide themselves
a permanent house of worship.
Sincerely affectionately
Joseph Worcester [19]

Interestingly, Maybeck, who eventually became Brown's draftsman for the Swedenborgian Church project, worked with Brown for some of 1891, most of 1892, as well as during 1893 and 1894,[20] the years when discussions pertaining to the design of the church must have been going on. We can see from these letters that Burnham too was probably kept abreast of its design and progress. That Porter designed a second window seems clear from a letter Worcester wrote to John Galen Howard in 1900: *"Bruce Porter made the windows of the little church."* [21]

Italian Inspiration for the Swedenborgian Church

The round window centered on the gable is an essential feature of the Swedenborgian Church, with sources from Italy and France to California. However, it was Italy that inspired Worcester and his friends. It is striking that Ruskin, in the preface to *The Seven Lamps of Architecture,* focused chiefly upon the *Italian* Romanesque and Gothic, and in nine out of the fourteen plates, he illustrated examples from Italian churches rather than French, English, or German. Furthermore, Worcester's library contained a whole volume of images and plates primarily from Italian churches. In fact, it may have been Bruce Porter who found the actual Italian church after which the façade and tower were perhaps modeled.

Reverend Othmar Tobisch, Worcester's most important successor as minister of the church, seems to have been the first to link Bruce Porter not only with the windows of the Swedenborgian Church, one of which drew its inspiration from sixth-century Ravenna mosaics, but also with its exterior design. *"Mr. Bruce Porter a distinguished San Francisco artist had furnished sketches from an Italian village church, near Verona in the Po Valley, for the exterior of the Church."* [22]

Worcester confirmed the Verona source to an interviewer just after the church opened: *"The device of the exterior is similar to a little church near Verona."* Around 1900 Worcester reiterated the Italian connection to Miss Vesta Bradbury, who commented, *"Our belltower looks exactly like those on little country churches in Italy."* Worcester replied: *"And well it may, for it was built brick by brick from a photograph of one of them."* [23]

Bruce Porter was in Europe in 1889. Although correspondence from Porter to Worcester has not been found (most of Worcester's letters were burned at his insistence), there is a letter from Porter to his brother, C. B. Porter, describing buildings he had seen in England and mentioning that he had visited the Burne-Jones studio and was *"sketching."* Furthermore, this letter is filled with tiny sketches.[24]

An "Italian Church" (Fig. 3.7), sketched by Gustavus Trost, was exhibited in the fourteenth Annual Exhibition of the Chicago Architectural Club in 1901, and several of its elements confirm that the Swedenborgian Church design did indeed have some Italian roots: the gable has a round window in the peak, there are arches below, and the belfry is gabled with a double arch beneath the gable.[25]

The wrought-iron screens filling the arches and doorway of the entrance loggia to the

Swedenborgian Church are decorated with scallops, each of which is filled with a cross (Fig. 3.8). These also seem to be a direct quote from an Italian source: they repeat the design found on the sixth century crypt bronze window grill from Ravenna's renowned Sant' Apollinare in Classe church (Fig. 3.9).[26] Furthermore the dove on a pedestaled basin in Porter's round window is an image seen repeatedly in sixth-century Ravenna mosaics.

A Combination of Church and Home

No matter how many friends contributed ideas, there is no doubt of Worcester's personal involvement in both planning and constructing the building. *"The whole thing is Worcester's personal expression of himself, each shrub and flower put there with distinct choice and meaning,"* wrote Dr. Richard C. Cabot, a visitor from the East. *"In laying the brickwork Worcester wanted the mortar so pointed that each brick should cast a distinct shadow."* Cabot went on to quote Worcester's explanation to the bricklayers, who couldn't understand what he wanted: *"I had to take my trowel and follow the workmen around and as they laid each row I pointed the mortar."* The church succeeded in recapturing the warmth and modesty of Worcester's houses. Contemporaries were quick to recognize in it

> . . . *a new note . . . a combination of church and home, an intimate, subdued, aesthetic something that with all its simplicity set it apart from anything that had been built before in the West. . . .*[27]

Or anywhere else, for that matter. Two details seem to have no precedent in church architecture: the fireplace inside the church sanctuary (Fig. 3.15) and the trees with their bark left on as roof supports (Figs. 3.2, 3.4). Other unusual features include individual rush-bottomed chairs rather than pews (Fig. 3.4), paintings of landscapes that do not appear to have any direct Christian reference (Fig. 3.2), and foliage brought in from the hills rather than formal flowers (Fig. 3.4). (It is interesting that Frank Lloyd Wright designed his "Weed Vase" ca. 1893, indicating he shared an interest in untamed nature.)[28]

Mission Inspiration for the Swedenborgian Church

In addition to the Italian sources, the mission buildings of Spanish California inform the rough wall, pierced by brick-edged arches on the street façade, as well as the garden flanking its nave. This was not accidental; interest in the missions was certainly strong in San Francisco by the time Worcester was beginning to formulate ideas about his church. The 1899 *Scientific American* corroborates this idea: *"The design is an adaptation of the 'Mission' style . . . and is one of the larger and more complete in miniature."*[29]

Fig. 3.7

Fig. 3.6 (facing): Saint John the Evangelist, San Francisco (1890–91), by Ernest Coxhead. Worcester was certainly familiar with this church, which featured a prominent gable punctured by a large round window over three arches, designed by his friend. He clearly was aiming at a totally different effect at the Swedenborgian Church.

Fig. 3.7: This small Italian church (or one like it), sketched by Gustavus Trost, provided inspiration for the Swedenborgian Church.

Fig. 3.8: Swedenborgian Church, view: note the carefully pointed brick, the rugged masonry wall, and the wrought-iron screens in this loggia arch— a repeating cross inside a scallop shape.

Fig. 3.9: The crypt of Sant' Apollinare, Classe, Ravenna, Italy; view: detail of one of its sixth-century bronze window screens decorated with superimposed Latin crosses. Art and Archaeology National Museum, Ravenna, Italy.

Fig. 3.8   **Fig. 3.9**

Mabel Clare Craft repeats the same thought in her 1901 article "A Sermon in Church Building": *"In general lines, the church follows the mission architecture of California. . . ."* Like Worcester, many of his friends were attracted to the missions' simplicity and their appropriateness to the California landscape.[30]

As early as 1883 and probably at Worcester's suggestion, William Keith and his new bride, Mary, traveled up the coast from San Diego to visit and to paint the missions.[31]

Since he wanted to create a historical record, Keith painted the old ruins in realistic detail. He explained his purpose in a letter: *"I have secured all the best Missions, and with the sketches and memoranda, they will form a collection of unique and historic value."*[32]

Meanwhile a major "Mission Style" complex was being planned south of San Francisco in Palo Alto. Worcester could hardly have ignored the widely publicized development of Stanford University, constructed between 1887 and 1891 in the Mission Style (Fig. 3.10). The first published references to using the Mission Style at Stanford were made in the *San Francisco Call* and then more explicitly in the *San Francisco Examiner,* April 28, 1887, when Leland Stanford himself took credit for proposing an adaptation of Spanish-style architecture.

> *When I suggested to Mr. Olmsted an adaptation of the adobe building of California, with some higher form of architecture, he was greatly pleased with the idea . . . creating for the first time an architecture distinctively Californian in character.*[33]

In a June 1889 letter to the Stanford site engineer, Olmsted asked about "the mission survey." It is not known if, at the request of the Stanfords and before designing the campus, Charles Allerton Coolidge of the architectural firm Shepley, Rutan and Coolidge, actually did make a thorough study of the extant mission buildings. However, as early as 1886, Olmsted and General Francis A. Walker (who agreed to serve as consultant but refused the Stanfords' offer that he become Stanford's first president) urged one-story buildings connected by an arcade. (Note that Olmsted cared about the architecture as well as the landscaping.)

Mr. Olmsted and myself are fully agreed that, with proper architectural treatment, buildings of this character, made of massive stone, connected by an arcade, may be made singularly effective and picturesque, upon the plain of Menlo.[34]

A single story and an arcade links Stanford to the California missions as well as to Mediterranean and Romanesque architecture from which the missions derive. If by any chance Worcester missed this publicity, which is doubtful, he would also have heard about Stanford's Mission Style from another close friend, David Starr Jordan, the first president of Stanford University.[35]

Fig. 3.10: Lithograph: Stanford University and Memorial Chapel (originally designed ca. 1887). Worcester certainly knew this chapel and probably knew Leland Stanford himself.

In 1887, before Willis Polk became Worcester's friend and neighbor on Russian Hill, he had sketched "An Imaginary Mission Church of the Southern California Type," published in *Architecture and Building* on April 12, 1890. The same year, Polk ran a series of articles entitled "Old California Missions" in his magazine *Architectural News*. Furthermore, Worcester himself had spent time exploring the mission ruins. On a trip to Mission San Miguel, he came upon an old cross that he gave to friends in Santa Barbara, who later sent it to San Francisco to be installed in the garden of the Swedenborgian Church.[36] Another building closer to home that Worcester certainly knew well was San Francisco's Mission Dolores.

A. Page Brown on Architecture, City Planning, and the Mission Style

Worcester's architect, A. Page Brown, not only used the missions as inspiration for his California State Building at the 1893 World's Columbian Exposition in Chicago, but also advocated the Mission Style for San Francisco. (For a discussion of the reasons behind choosing the Mission Style for the California State Building, and for Daniel Burnham's and Worcester's involvement, see Chapter 10.) Since Brown died at a young age in 1896, almost nothing expressing his architectural interests and sophistication exists. The detailed expression of his thoughts set out below does not appear to have been published in full elsewhere since 1894. Therefore it is worth citing this rare article titled "Architecture in California," published in the *San Francisco Chronicle* on December 30, 1894, after the success of the Mission Style California State Building and while the Swedenborgian Church was being constructed. Brown not only advocates buildings in the Mission Style for San Francisco, he also predicts the disaster that fire and earthquake will bring to the city if it does not stop building with wood, and expresses environmental concerns that are advanced for their day.

I have been asked to write something about the possibilities of the future architecture of San Francisco. The present aspect of the city, viewed from such an eminence as the tower of the Chronicle building, shows that a new and more monumental class of buildings is beginning to make an impression on a city of possibly the most uninteresting collection of wooden structures ever erected. A sweeping fire, accompanied by earthquake, would accomplish great good if we could have it without loss of life.

Phoenix-like there would, perhaps, arise a city which would eclipse any American seaport. Even a dozen competing railroads could not do as much universal good. The Chicago fire was a blessing in disguise, for the type of buildings erected before that great fire was similar in many ways to the type we have here so many examples of along our main thoroughfares—buildings which were erected for immediate use and revenue. The haste is pardonable in many instances, but the time has come when these early structures must give way to more substantial and attractive buildings and fortunately, I do not think that some of our modern buildings are any more expensive.

San Francisco has many examples of good architecture, erected when both brick and stone were imported from China. Now, however, we have both abundance of native building material and the best of skilled labor. There is no reason therefore why this city should not have a style of architecture both appropriate and interesting. There is no doubt in my mind that the architectural abominations of San Francisco are the cause of much of our lack of progress in other directions.

San Francisco has limitless possibilities as approached from the waterfront. What a splendid opportunity is offered for a boulevard and for quays flanked by public buildings. The Custom-house buildings for the reception of emigrants pilot-house, ferry houses and many other much-needed structures should grace our waterfront where they would be not only more convenient, but ornamental.

When the waterfront shall have been rebuilt, and the gateway at the foot of Market Street completed, San Francisco will, I trust, make a more presentable appearance. On the Eastern seaboards the seaport towns have been made most attractive by walks, drives and interesting architectural features. A space for trees and shaded drives is left [also one of Olmsted's major tenets]. *What could be more interesting than the Battery at Charleston? The commercial interests as well as the domestic are taken care of. Instead of locating gas works and other nuisances along the bay front between the Presidio and the ferries, why not improve the value of the property overlooking the water? There is ample room for manufacturing, and shipping interests in the Bay of San Francisco without occupying what should be the best residence portion of the city.* [Unfortunately, it took San Francisco many years to recognize Brown's foresightedness.]

As to the development of an architectural style which shall become almost universal, in a city like this the variety of requirements makes it necessary that the exterior treatment should, in any way, suggest exterior [probably he means interior] *requirements. But we should have a unity and harmony of general outline with a scheme of color which would take away the gloom and chill produced by the present condition of things.*

Note that Brown does not advocate brown shingled or wood houses or buildings to blend with the landscape as Worcester did, but rather white buildings to take away the chill of San Francisco fogs. However, like Worcester, Brown condemns existing Victorian buildings in a tone similar to what Charles Keeler uses four years later and advocates buildings that are *"simple without being painfully stupid."*[37]

The domestic architecture of the city has given almost no evidence as yet of refinement of outline or detail. The imitations of chateaux and copies of fragments of palaces, carried out in thin wooden, box-like structures, with bay windows and small corner towers and turrets should never be repeated. The most difficult thing in designing buildings, as in music or painting, is to be simple without being painfully stupid. Taste in architecture is varied and personal, but must not be confounded with narrow prejudice. To bring about a better state of things in the architecture of San Francisco and the State we must free ourselves from narrow-minded views and not condemn every new piece of work because it surprises us. If the architect has the right kind of stuff in him his effort and object must be considered before the result is condemned.

Santa Barbara has a climate which suggests a revival of the old mission type of architecture, and certainly no style has been offered since that brought by the Mission fathers which has given as universal satisfaction, and a revival of it may be looked for which will bring about good results.

The use of adobe for walls will probably never be revived except for illustration of the early type of building. The employment of red tile for roofing will come into general use before long as it is better adapted for the purpose than almost any other material, and lends itself to the generally desired artistic effect.

It is clear from what follows that Brown did not abandon the Mission Style after using it for the California State Building at the 1893 Chicago Exposition as some scholars have stated. Quite the contrary. He argues that the lighter color of Mission Style buildings complements San Francisco and that the style works well for *"low buildings"* if *"carried out properly."*

The attempted revival of the old mission style of architecture as applied to low buildings in this State seems to be a successful one if carefully studied and carried out properly.

The lighter shades of color (even of almost white) if generally employed for external treatment, in a city like San Francisco, would be most successful. [One wonders what he thought of the brown shingled neighborhood Joseph Worcester fostered on Russian Hill.]

When Alfred Parsons, the well-known English artist, was here a few years ago, he told me that his scheme for color for San Francisco would be white and I have often heard the same remark from other artists. The few examples we already have seem to lend strength to this opinion. The clouds of yellow dust we have in summer [probably from unpaved roads] *show less on a wall of similar color and in our fogs it certainly is better than the lead-colored buildings now so much in vogue, and gives warmth and satisfaction to our feelings.*

Brown concludes by advocating architectural competitions:

The selection of plans for artistic and monumental work in large cities and for the improvement of our streets and parks should be obtained in competition, and thereby the best original conceptions obtained, and no great project should be executed without ulterior studies made with a view to improving the original idea. A. Page Brown[38]

Japanese Inspiration

Another architectural tradition revealed in the Swedenborgian Church was that of Japan. Just as the church was being built, interest in Japanese architecture (which had been growing since Commodore Matthew Perry opened Japan to Western trade in March 1854) was rekindled in San Francisco by Japan's gift of buildings and gardens to the California Midwinter International Exposition held in 1894, also known as the 1894 San Francisco Midwinter Fair. However, four years *before* the installation of the San Francisco Japanese tea garden, Worcester and Maybeck and many of their visitors would have been familiar with the Japanese use of wood from the teahouse (Fig. 3.11) erected in Blair Park, about five blocks from their cottages. Piedmont historian Gail Lombardi uncovered this *Oakland Daily Evening Tribune* article describing it as

> *. . . an exact replica of an ancient teahouse in Japan. It was constructed in Yokohama, then broken down and shipped to Blair Park. Rebuilt on site in the Japanese style (1890) its fitted joints were tightly secured with ropes. Nails were used only to hold the roof tiles. It was open on three sides with a circular Japanese window.*[39]

The knots and irregularities were not planed out of the wood or bamboo poles and the structure itself was entirely exposed. In addition, an adjacent Japanese garden was planted with a thousand Japanese lily bulbs, roses, and purple and white wisteria—all of which may have provided additional inspiration.

Even if Worcester did not see the Japanese Tea House in Blair Park, he would surely have noticed articles on Japanese architecture even before the church was designed. For example, *California Architect and Building News* for June 1892 printed a floor plan and elevations of a Japanese building, and in 1894 the *Architect and Builder* commented on Japanese buildings; it is likely that Worcester or someone in his circle owned Edward S. Morse's very influential *Japanese Homes and Their Surroundings,* which was published in 1886.[40]

Fig. 3.11: An exact replica of an ancient teahouse in Japan, erected in Blair Park, Piedmont, California, in 1890, just a few blocks from the Maybeck and Worcester cottages.

Also, in his December 1893 scrapbook, the architect of record for the church, A. Page Brown, reveals his own interest in things Japanese. He cut out and pasted in it an illustrated article entitled "Japanese Life and Customs," picturing a geisha playing on stage; to the right is a tree, with its bark left on it, supporting the doorframe.[41]

In Japan, as at the Swedenborgian Church, sacred shrines are enclosed by high walls or fences and are entered by passing through a gate and then through a garden. The church garden's careful composition of blossoming plum and crabapple trees suggests the artful landscaping of Japanese gardens. To Worcester the church's garden was primarily a captured piece of nature, and since he believed in the holiness of nature, to him the garden was an outdoor church. In the specific Swedenborgian sense, each plant and tree placed in the garden (Fig. 3.12) was a spiritual symbol; the cedar of Lebanon, for instance, represented *"wisdom of the ages, intellectual honesty. Hoary thoughts of wise men. Solomon's proverbs."* Reverend Othmar Tobisch entitled his pamphlet on the Swedenborgian Church *The Garden Church of San Francisco.* In it Tobisch refers to the incorporation of *"tones of the Orient"* and mentions a bronze bell from a Tokyo temple, a vase with poems (ca. 1820) by Sanetomo of Japan, and the garden.[42]

A Unique Arts & Crafts Interior

Once inside the church, the sense of intimacy was (and still is) immediately astonishing. Dr. Richard Cabot wrote to a friend that it was *"a little place, no bigger than the two parlors of your Waltham house thrown together."*[43]

The interior suggested a living room. The nave, lacking side aisles, terminated at the east in an altar placed off-center and at the west in a large brick fireplace flanked by built-in benches (Figs. 3.13, 3.16). This fireplace was also off-center, its tall chimney meeting the roof just to one side of the ridge (Fig. 3.14).

The chandelier at the east end was not hung from the center line but rather slightly to the right of the altar.[44] The asymmetry of the focal points suggests the imperfections in vernacular

Fig. 3.12: Swedenborgian Church, view: newly planted garden. Note the Italian-inspired bell tower, shadows created by the pointing of the brickwork, and the arched entry connecting the garden with the covered loggia facing Lyon Street.

Fig. 3.13: Bernard Maybeck's undated sketch for an unknown building of an asymmetrical fireplace flanked by a bench with an S-curved end, possibly related to, or inspired by, the Swedenborgian Church.

Fig. 3.14: Swedenborgian Church, view: the interior features wood benches with S-curved ends flanking an off-center brick fireplace, reflecting Worcester's preference for asymmetry.

Fig. 3.13

Fig. 3.14

Fig. 3.15

Fig. 3.16

architecture, where a building's forms reflect the hand of the individual craftsman rather than the finish of an architectural plan.

The Church of the New Jerusalem, like his Piedmont and Russian Hill homes, demonstrated Worcester's preference for simple forms and natural materials. The interior decoration of the church was decidedly domestic rather than ecclesiastical. There was a fireplace and there were no fixed pews; instead, each parishioner drew up a chair. As a visitor to the church described the scene:

> *I could still believe that we had ventured into some simple, restful home. The brick fire-place, where logs were smoldering although it was a summer's day, the comfortable rush bottomed chairs grouped around it, the decorations, the little parlor organ, glimpses of books in a reading corner contributed to this effect. Soon the congregation began to come in. We'll not call them a congregation because they seemed more like arriving guests.* [45]

Wooden wainscoting and ceilings in the church echoed Worcester's houses and were left as natural as possible. The madrone tree trunks that supported the ceiling were left gnarled with their bark on, and arch gently upward and inward just as they had in the forest where Worcester found them. The story of the madrone logs appeared in a February 1901 *House Beautiful* article (one of the magazines most influential in promoting the Arts & Crafts to Americans) by Mabel Clare Craft. *"But best of all is the story of the trees,"* she wrote.

> *Reverend Joseph Worcester was in the Santa Cruz Mountains, and he selected the lusty young madrones for the pillars of the temple. He told the young mountaineer on whose wood-lot they grew the purpose for which they were destined. The mountaineer was a*

Fig. 3.15: The Outdoor Art Club, Mill Valley (1904). Bernard Maybeck places his fireplace off-center as in the Swedenborgian Church; the crossbeams and exposed roof provide the room's principal decoration.

Fig. 3.16: Swedenborgian Church, view: detail of the S-curve end of one of the benches flanking the fireplace.

practical young fellow to whom the tree meant nothing more than its market price. But as he cut the trees he grew thoughtful. . . . One day he said to the clergyman: No hands but mine have touched those trees, and I can't bear to think of them being handled as freight. If you will let me carry them to the city in my wagon, it shall not cost you any more than by train. So the mountaineer harnessed his horse to his heavy wagon, took the trees. . . . At last the jingling team drew up in front of the unfinished church, and the trees were put into place—still by the same hands that cut them. And this was the spirit which built the Church of the New Jerusalem, and which still maintains it in all its charming simplicity.[46]

On September 20, 1894, Joseph Worcester recorded in his diary: *"Mr. & Mrs. Martin came with trees from the mountains, arriving in evening."* By January 11, 1895, the roof of the Swedenborgian Church had been constructed and a bill for $680 had been sent.[47]

As Kostura expressed it, *"[Worcester] viewed the natural world as a manifestation of God, and felt that buildings should relate well to the environment rather than disrupt it. Nature was beautiful and buildings which resemble nature were the most beautiful of buildings."*[48]

Fig. 3.17: A few years after this "recently built" San Francisco church was published in the *California Architect and Building News* (March 1882; no precise date or address was given), Bernard Maybeck began work for its architects. Note the nave's exposed construction with the chamfering left visible, as well as its gently arched vault.

Wright and Sanders (for whom Maybeck once worked) might also have provided inspiration. In their 1882 San Francisco church (published without name or locations), the roof, crossbeams, and timbers that spring from their columns to form a gently arched vault are the highlights of the interior space. As in a Norwegian stave church, some chamfering is visible (Fig. 3.17). Logically, Worcester would have looked carefully at every new church in the area to satisfy his architectural curiosity, with dreams of his own church in mind.[49]

Shared Sensitivities

Judging from their work, both Maybeck and Schweinfurth produced original exciting buildings that deserve our attention. From Keeler's statements, detailed above and below, we know that Worcester's house and church influenced Maybeck; numerous descriptions of Maybeck as well as his own comments reveal a spiritual and idealistic kinship between the two men. Although we have less information documenting Schweinfurth's friendship with this group, he clearly knew Polk, Maybeck, and Brown from work at Brown's firm, knew Keith sufficiently to recommend him to William Randolph Hearst as we shall see, and must have met Worcester and Coxhead upon arriving in San Francisco.

Sadly, there is no record from Schweinfurth himself, from Keeler, or from anyone who witnessed the construction of the church as to whether Schweinfurth worked on the church, admired it, influenced Worcester, or was influenced by Worcester. (See discussion of Schweinfurth's possible role below.)

As noted, Worcester's friend Charles Keeler, who was Maybeck's first client and earliest biographer, described a profound experience from 1891 that affected Maybeck's whole outlook. *"Looking into Mr. Worcester's windows, he saw the interior of the cottage was all of unpainted redwood boards. It was a revelation."*[50]

Worcester continued to visit his Piedmont home through 1902. (There are records from 1892 to 1902 showing he paid taxes on his house and surrounding acreage.) Keeler calls it Worcester's "summer retreat." Moreover, when Keeler explains Maybeck's work, it becomes clear that Maybeck shared Worcester's admiration for Ruskin:

> *Mr. Maybeck proposed to restore the handcrafts to their proper place in life and art. Two boards might be glued together, edge to edge, to give the effect of one wide board. But if dove tail joints were let in to hold them, these dove-tailings made the fastening more secure and at the same time added a note of ornamental design. Wooden pegs and wedges driven in slots to hold boards tightly in place, are also ornamental features to be emphasized. No doubt Mr. Maybeck had learned much from William Morris, but he was by no means a slavish imitator of anyone. He was interested in the simple life which is naturally expressive and consequently beautiful. He believed in handmade things and that all ornament should be designed to fit the place and the need. He did not mind how crude it was, provided it was sincere and expressed something personal. Everything that concealed the construction should be done away with. There should be no shams, no false fronts. At last the mystery of why Mr. Maybeck wore sash instead of a vest was revealed. To be sure, a vest has a front to match the suit, but its back, hidden under the coat, is of cambric, merely to hold that sham exposed part in place. Mr. Maybeck was seeking honest expression in all life.*[51]

Keeler confirms Maybeck's esteem for Worcester. Although Keeler knew Schweinfurth from his work on the Moody house (see Chapter 7), he testifies it was Maybeck who *designed* the Swedenborgian Church *as Joseph Worcester wanted it.*

> *He became acquainted with Mr. Worcester and in time designed for him the famous Swedenborgian Church in San Francisco. It had a fireplace. The big overhead madrono [sic] timbers were braced with "ship's knees." There was a new note in this church, a combination of church and home, an intimate, subdued, aesthetic something that with all its simplicity set it apart from anything that had been built before in the west. It was the result of Mr. Worcester's influence on Mr. Maybeck.*[52]

In one of the few surviving descriptions of his own buildings, Maybeck is revealed as a lover of nature who designs and builds with the sensitivities of a painter. Referring to Wyntoon (1902–3), the medieval-castle-like country estate he designed for Phoebe Apperson Hearst (Fig. 3.18), Maybeck wrote:

> *The dark height of the room [some of the ceilings were covered with slabs of tree bark], the unobstructed archways, the deep blues, reds and yellows of the cathedral window, to which time had given maturity, the tapestries, the little flicker of fire, and the roaring of the*

Fig. 3.18: Wyntoon (1902–3),
Phoebe A. Hearst's country
estate (destroyed), McCloud
River, Siskiyou County, by
Bernard Maybeck.

*river outside; and you, satiated, tired and inspired by the day's trip among hazel,
dogwood, great aged pines, rocks, cascades, great trunks of trees fallen years ago,—
a disheveled harmony,—here you can reach all that is within you.*[53]

Schweinfurth recognized Maybeck's ability and artistic sensitivities. Although he might have
disliked his Bohemian appearance, Schweinfurth respected Maybeck as an architect. The letter
below is often misquoted or cited only in part so that it appears Schweinfurth thought Maybeck a
freak. In reality Schweinfurth praised Maybeck; writing to the *Wave* on November 28, 1896, about
the University of California's international competition, he said:

*We agree Bernard Maybeck is a freak but he has great regard for architecture as an art
and undoubtedly the ability to direct a competition as Mr. R [Regent J. B. Reinstein]
assumes that he is to direct.*[54]

Kenneth Cardwell, arguably Maybeck's most sensitive biographer, relates an experience that
permanently focused Maybeck's attention on the emotional impact of architecture and reveals his
sensitivity to medieval church architecture and to music:

One day he was passing through the transept of Saint Germain des Près in Paris and stopped to hear "lovely singing." The music brought over him "the most awesome feeling as though the architecture and the music had blended." From this time on whenever he visited works of architecture, he consciously tried to relate feeling to form [an idea akin to Joseph Worcester's concept that "a building must teach its lessons"].[55]

Maybeck shared this sensitivity with Worcester, who wrote his nephew: *"It is a rare treat for me to hear any music, and I know it must be partly because it affects me so much."*[56]

Although we lack documents that might tell us if Schweinfurth felt passionately about music as Maybeck and Worcester did, Schweinfurth expressed sensitivity to art, praised William Keith, and suggested Hearst hire Keith because he *"paints such things as no one else can."*[57] Like Maybeck and Worcester, Schweinfurth admired art and the irregularities of handicraft. Describing the *"aboriginal labor"* that the *"poor Padres"* were forced to employ in the early days, Schweinfurth writes:

The work that they produced has a charm and a sentiment that completely obscures all mechanical defects, and in looking at their work one does not stop to think that the door jambs are not exactly plumb . . . ; in fact, these very defects seem to add to the charm of their work.[58]

Schweinfurth also provides a poetic description of the *"Manana Manana"* mood he and William Randolph Hearst wished to create at the Hacienda del Pozo de Verona. Unfortunately it is not clear whether this reflects the architect's or the client's ideas; in any case, it captures the poetry of the site. In a letter to Edward H. Clark, dated December 20, 189? (no year given; probably 1895), which is really intended for Phoebe Apperson Hearst, Schweinfurth writes,

When we started out to build the house up there it was the intention to produce a restful, quiet country home entirely in keeping with the climate, the surroundings, and totally different in every way from the ordinary country house. It was, as I supposed at the time, to be a place where a man tired out with the cares and responsibilities of an active metropolitan life could find an absolute change; where the surroundings would be entirely different from those which we find on every side . . . and where everything would express to a greater or less extent that he was in the land of poco tiempo, and where the feeling of Manana, Manana could be cultivated, and where the effect of so complete and perfect a change in every respect would tend to the renewal of life. . . . The nearest neighbors of the Hacienda are aborigines, the Mexican Indian settlement directly opposite the house, on the other side of the Creek would seem to indicate that the house as planned and built should have the accessories and decorations of the distinctly Spanish-Californian character. This was Mr. Hearst's original idea. . . .[59]

Who Designed the Swedenborgian Church?

The Swedenborgian Church in San Francisco, which was always considered Joseph Worcester's inspiration, with Brown as architect and Maybeck as draftsman, has grown more and more popular over the years as visitors discover the charm of its tranquil atmosphere and quiet garden.

However, since 1978 some scholars attributed the design to Schweinfurth, who also worked as a draftsman for Brown but who left the firm before February 26, 1894; this was before the lots at Lyon and Washington were surveyed (August 27 and 28, 1894) and purchased, and before construction on the church began. In her excellent thesis on Schweinfurth, Carol Louise Calavan writes: *"In what capacity the architect functioned as a member of the Brown firm is debatable."*[60]

Schweinfurth in San Francisco

Schweinfurth made several attempts at establishing an independent practice in the East and Midwest before arriving in California to work once again with Brown. However, his arrival date in San Francisco is unknown.

Between 1891 and 1892 he could have been anywhere. The record remains unclear.[61] For this story, it is noteworthy that he is not listed in the *San Francisco Directory* until 1893, which means he could have arrived anytime after the May 1892 directory went to press and before the 1893 directory was published in May. Longstreth tells us that Brown maintained offices in New York as well as in San Francisco and that *"presentation drawings dated as late as 1892 refer to both offices . . ."*[62] Other than Brown's Lemon Curer Warehouse, which Longstreth states Schweinfurth designed for Brown's firm in 1891, there seems to be no work by Schweinfurth for Brown in 1891 or 1892. Moreover, the Lemon Curer drawing is not signed, and the arched recessed windows surrounded by splayed brick also appear in Brown's Crocker Old People's Home, delineated by Polk, as do the short, bulbous columns (Fig. 5.2). This debated attribution is important; without it we lack proof that Schweinfurth actually did work for Brown as planned in 1891.[63] What we do know is that he remained with the firm less than two years, departing in early 1894 probably to work for the wealthy and powerful William Randolph Hearst.[64]

During 1891–92, when Schweinfurth does not seem to have worked for Brown anywhere, Maybeck worked with Brown in San Francisco. Indeed, Longstreth acknowledges that in 1892 Maybeck worked for Brown *"for the better part of that year."* In 1893 both Schweinfurth and Maybeck appear to have worked for Brown on the San Francisco Midwinter Exposition (construction was well underway in November 1893.) Maybeck worked for Brown in 1894 as well whereas Schweinfurth left Brown in February 1894.[65] As noted, Maybeck had friendly contacts with Worcester from the time he lived in Piedmont in a cottage near Worcester's (November? 1890 into 1891). Maybeck commuted to work in San Francisco on the ferry, along with Keith and Keeler, both close friends of Worcester's. Unfortunately we lack any evidence as to Schweinfurth's friendship with Worcester, though it is likely they knew each other through Brown, Maybeck, Polk, Coxhead, Keith, or Keeler.

Maybeck, Schweinfurth, and Brown's Office

According to published records listing the courses and hours Maybeck taught, he did not begin as a part-time instructor at University of California, Berkeley, until 1895, leaving him time to work for Brown and sometimes for others.[66]

Longstreth acknowledges that Maybeck *"is known to have had a hand in Brown's design for the Church of the New Jerusalem [Swedenborgian Church]."*[67] A. Page Brown employed many draftsmen. However, the evidence does not appear to support the contention that Schweinfurth did most, or all, of the firm's designing or that *"the Swedenborgian Church was one of the last designs Schweinfurth produced in Brown's office."*[68]

Schweinfurth departed Brown's office at Suite 238 in the Crocker Building and moved to his own office down the hall at 229 in early 1894, as the *San Francisco Chronicle* announced on February 26, 1894: *"Schweinfurth is now in business for himself,"*[69] Longstreth demonstrates that Schweinfurth was successful:

> *In [April] 1894 Hearst commissioned Brown to remodel his Sausalito residence. The project was abandoned, but a few months later [still 1894] Hearst retained Schweinfurth alone to design a building for the Children's Hospital . . . funded by the San Francisco Examiner. Soon thereafter [still 1894] Hearst gave his new architect a much more important assignment: the creation of a large country house.*[70]

As noted, Schweinfurth seems to have arrived in San Francisco in late 1892 or before May 1893; also, Schweinfurth left Brown's firm at least five months before the lot on Lyon Street was surveyed on August 28, 1894, and before construction had begun, whereas Maybeck still worked for Brown during the church's construction and the year before (1893). It is difficult to ascertain whether *"Schweinfurth must have maintained some sort of an association with Brown under which the Church of the New Jerusalem and other work was designed,"*[71] especially since Schweinfurth worked independently and successfully, and not for Brown, from *early* 1894 into 1895, while the Swedenborgian Church was under construction (see Chapters 7 and 10). There seems to be no documentary evidence for the statement that Schweinfurth stayed with Brown and held "control" for the next four years.[72]

The Poetry of Architecture

Worcester cared deeply about architecture, and it is easy to imagine that the "little church" occupied much of his thoughts. Yet the self-effacing Worcester gives the credit to his friend Brown. However, the special meaning and expressiveness of the weathered tree trunks and the drama they lent the sanctuary was a motif that was definitely not suggested by the architect. Brown, who was accustomed to more conventional architectural solutions, opposed the use of the trees and did not consider them architectural. Worcester never mentions any other designer but he did tell a story to his nephew, criticizing Brown:

> *Mr. Brown, the architect of the little church, had rather discouraged any use of logs as rafters nor was he ever willing to admit their use was architectural. Of the church as finished he said, "This is not architecture." But when Richardson (?) his fellow worker and now head man of McKim, Mead and White, after Brown's death . . . looked over the little church and asked Uncle Joseph what Brown said when it was finished and was told, he said "Yes, he knew it was not architecture but more: it is the poetry of architecture."*[73]

This comment shows widespread awareness among architects of Ruskin's writings entitled "The Poetry of Architecture," first published in *Architectural Magazine* and reprinted in 1892.[74]

Who Played What Role?

It is significant that Maybeck is mentioned as the draftsman of the church by five people (even though he was an unknown architect at the time), three of whom knew and admired Worcester and witnessed the church's construction—Charles Keeler, Mrs. A. Page Brown, Bernard Maybeck himself, Reverend Othmar Tobisch and his wife, Margit—whereas, no one who lived through the design and construction of the Swedenborgian Church mentions Schweinfurth either as draftsman or designer. Maybeck's involvement as draftsman is accepted; the question really is whether Maybeck, Schweinfurth, or both had any input in the actual design of the church itself.

Perhaps Schweinfurth did serve as Brown's chief designer at some point; but did he hold that position when Worcester, Porter, and friends were looking at sketches from Italy and elsewhere, and were discussing, planning, and designing the church? And even if he did, what did he contribute to the design? Given the Italian and Mission roots for the exterior façade, bell tower, and loggia's metal screens, the probable Japanese and Mission inspiration for the garden and its carefully selected plants, and the extent of Worcester's input, what essential features were left for a designer to contribute? The architect or draftsman may have suggested bold wrought-iron straps to hold the arching trees to the vertical tree posts, but the decision to leave the bark on the trees was clearly Worcester's (Fig. 3.2). Worcester went to the forest and selected the trees himself, which indicates the extent of his involvement, and his comment on the "natural beauty of the bark" confirms that the decision to leave the bark on the trees was Worcester's.[75]

We also know from Worcester that Brown (who came from a more classical, formal tradition practiced by McKim, Mead, and White) opposed the use of trees, considered them nonarchitectural, and did not like Worcester's preference for asymmetry.[76]

Furthermore, are there any indications that if Schweinfurth had designed the Swedenborgian Church, he would have placed the fireplace off-center without Worcester's instruction to do so? We have seen that Worcester loved asymmetry, and he criticized Brown for his rejection of it. In Schweinfurth's designs, there are no asymmetries or off-center fireplaces as in Maybeck's work; examples include a clubhouse in the redwoods (Fig. 3.25), the Hopps house, the Outdoor Art Club (Fig. 3.15), and the E. C. Young house.[77]

Schweinfurth designed both the Hacienda del Pozo de Verona and the First Unitarian Church *"with a rigorous order through the use of axial symmetry . . . ."*[78] At the hacienda especially, the huge site permitted, and Pueblo architecture would have suggested, an asymmetrical structure; yet Schweinfurth opted for a symmetrical composition (Figs. 10.12, 10.13).

Nevertheless, Schweinfurth's First Unitarian Church (1897–98) and Bradford house (1896) (see Chapter 7) offer a rustic simplicity that could reflect Worcester's influence and that, in any case, Worcester would surely have admired. So the question of Schweinfurth's possible involvement in this icon of the Arts & Crafts movement requires further analysis.

Further primary source documentation demonstrates Maybeck's sympathy and understanding of what Worcester wanted. Mrs. John Baeck, the granddaughter of Judge Rearden, a very close friend of Worcester's and a long-time parishioner, repeated what Worcester told her grandfather, namely that he was delighted to have the services of the *"talented draftsman Maybeck . . . who felt so keen an interest in the work"* at the Swedenborgian Church.[79] Except for the one very questionable interview described below, no mention is made of Schweinfurth at all, either as designer or draftsman, by anyone connected with the Swedenborgian Church at that time.[80]

Porter and Schweinfurth

Two scholars contend that Brown had assigned Schweinfurth to design the Swedenborgian Church, based on an interview with Elisabeth Kendall Thompson when she was 84 (she died at age 87). Thompson is said to have learned this information from Bruce Porter in 1948, *"shortly before* [Porter's] *death."* If so, one cannot help wondering why Thompson did not include this important fact in her excellent pioneering article in which she is perhaps the first person to highlight Joseph Worcester's role and influence and in which she discusses Schweinfurth at some length.[81]

Thompson published the article in 1951, shortly after she interviewed Porter. In that article, "The Early Domestic Architecture of the San Francisco Bay Region," Thompson discusses three major Schweinfurth projects and includes the Unitarian Church in Berkeley *"because of its domestic character."* Therefore, if Porter had actually told her that Schweinfurth was the "key figure" on the equally if not more "domestic" Swedenborgian Church, would she not have mentioned it in her article? But she does not. In fact when Thompson lists the important architects and influential people in the region, she begins by praising Worcester, who, *"though he was not a trained architect,"* produced work of *"architectural rightness and dignity,"* and adds that *"it is possible that to him, in some measure, can be credited some of the underlying philosophy of architectural design in the Bay Region."*[82]

Thompson quotes Porter at least four times and yet not in relation to Schweinfurth's having been "assigned" to the Swedenborgian Church. Why not? In the article, Thompson praises Worcester, Maybeck, Morgan, Mullgardt, and Greene & Greene, but she is slightly less praiseworthy of Schweinfurth. Comparing Greene & Greene and Schweinfurth: *"Of the two firms, the work of Greene and Greene was by far the more remarkable and influential, though it consists of a single example"* (the Thorsen house in Berkeley, discussed in Chapter 9). Thompson then continues, *"Of A. C. Schweinfurth's work there are three notable examples"*: the Moody house, Hearst's Hacienda del Pozo de Verona, and the First Unitarian Church. Why, one wonders, did she not mention the Swedenborgian Church as Schweinfurth's if Porter had told her that Schweinfurth was responsible for it?[83]

Reverend Othmar Tobisch came to the church in 1929 and was an extremely reliable source, as he had direct links to principals in the project: Tobisch knew Maybeck and he was a close friend of Porter, who lived around the corner from the church and designed at least one of the stained-glass windows. When he was researching his 1945 pamphlet on its history, Tobisch surely would have asked Porter who designed the church. Furthermore, Tobisch also knew the artist Mary Curtis Richardson, an active insider at the time of the building of the church. In addition to being a parishioner, she was also Worcester's neighbor and friend. If Schweinfurth had been involved in a significant way, surely Tobisch would have heard about it from Richardson or Maybeck, if not from Porter, and would have included this information in the later editions of his pamphlet. But he did not.[84]

A Previously Unpublished Drawing of the Swedenborgian Church

A drawing of the Swedenborgian Church has hung in the church library for as long as anyone can remember.[85] According to those working at the church and to the historians at the Swedenborgian House of Studies, the drawing's authenticity has never been questioned. It has always been referred to as Maybeck's work, although there is also a possibility it could be by Worcester (see Fig. 3.19).

Considering the dispute, if Schweinfurth had been the chief designer of the church, why did no one refer to the drawing as Schweinfurth's? Could Maybeck have executed the drawing to Schweinfurth's and Worcester's design? Since Worcester encouraged the Arts & Crafts cooperative spirit, this is not impossible, but it does not appear to be supported by the evidence.

Several facts point to Bernard Maybeck's authorship of the drawing. First, as stated above, Tobisch, who knew Porter, Richardson, and Maybeck, ascribes the "drawing of the compound" to Maybeck:

> *The architectural drawings were made in the office of A. Page Brown, designer of San Francisco's world famous Ferry Building. Mr. B. Maybeck, later also to become a well-known architect, was the draughtsman. His drawing of the compound can still be seen in the Library.*[86]

In addition, Tobisch researched the church carefully before he published his booklet, as he wanted his published statements to be correct. So fastidious was he that while checking his facts in 1939, he sent the following information to Keith's biographer, Brother Cornelius of St. Mary's College of California, who had asked about William Keith's role in the church design.

> *I have written a little pamphlet about the church in which I say: "Under the influence of William Keith & indirectly thru the latter by John Muir, the Rev. Joseph Worcester conceived the idea of creating a house of worship which would mold the forms of nature into a testimony for the Eternal's glory. Mrs. Hobson [who was active in the congregation during*

Fig. 3.19: Swedenborgian Church, view: this drawing of the church may date from March 1893 or before, and was probably executed by Bernard Maybeck for the lot at Taylor and Jackson, later rejected for a lot at Lyon and Washington.

the building of the church], *to whom I sent the proof takes exception & says: 'The first para-graph of your leaflet gives a false impression concerning the creation of the Lyon street church. Mr. Worcester was the creating moving spirit & all others interested including Mr. Keith fell in, because of sympathy with his noble artistic design.' "*[87]

No matter who executed the drawing, its date merits examination. It may well have been done in late 1892 or early 1893 as it shows only the church, not the parish house. Only one lot was surveyed on March 13, 1893, so the congregation planned to build only one building—the church. The decision to buy two lots for the church and a parish house was made over a year later on May 1, 1894. A possible early date for this drawing is also suggested by the fact that fundraising was underway in February 1893, and Worcester might have wanted a drawing to show potential donors. In addition, the drawing shows the nave with four windows on the garden side, not the three actually built; and a loggia with four arches is seen rather than the three that were constructed. Since the round window was ready to ship on March 13, 1893, it had probably been designed in late 1892 and made in early 1893. So this drawing could even date back to late 1892 or whenever Worcester and others decided to center a round window in the gable.[88]

A Photograph Provides Clues

The photograph of a man standing at the Swedenborgian Church construction site, wearing a hat and holding a roll of drawings (Fig. 3.20), shows the madrone trees in place; therefore, the photograph must have been taken sometime after their delivery on September 20, 1894. This man is

probably not Schweinfurth as he had left the Brown's firm in February 1894.[89] Also, comparing his face with the portraits of Brown (Fig. 3.21) and Schweinfurth (Fig. 1.4), shows a closer resemblance to Brown than to Schweinfurth. Brown shapes his moustache downward, as does the man with the hat, whereas Schweinfurth trains his moustache more horizontally and curls it up at each end. Furthermore, Brown and the man in the hat share a high forehead but Schweinfurth's face is rounder, his hairline lower on his forehead.[90]

Conclusion: An Arts & Crafts Cooperative Effort Led by Worcester

Although Brown was the architect for the church, as noted, there is extensive evidence from Worcester himself that he and Brown did not always agree. For example, he did not approve of Brown's *"penchant for symmetry."* Worcester answered Brown *"that I cared nothing for the canons of architecture; the building must teach its lessons."* In addition Brown discouraged any use of trees as rafters.

Keeler says firmly that Worcester influenced Maybeck and that Maybeck designed the church *"as Joseph Worcester wanted it."* We do not know whether, or to what extent if any, Maybeck or Schweinfurth influenced the design. However, it is perfectly possible that many of Worcester's friends made suggestions, just as we have seen Keith and Porter did.

All the available evidence clearly makes the design of the Swedenborgian Church a group effort, with Joseph Worcester very much in control.[91] Neither A. Page Brown, the architect of record (who died January 21,1896, about a year after the Swedenborgian Church opened to great acclaim and publicity), nor A. C. Schweinfurth, one of Brown's many draftsmen (who died September 27, 1900), took credit during their lifetimes for having been the designer of the church; it is not listed in either obituary nor in Maybeck's. Perhaps Worcester convinced his circle to believe, like Swedenborg, that *". . . the art of architecture comes from heaven."*[92]

The information presented above corroborates Edward R. Bosley's statement that *"the church's creation paints a picture of true Arts and Crafts collaboration, inspired by a minister."*[93] Documentary evidence confirms Brown as the architect of record, Maybeck as the draftsman, Porter as designer of at least one window and most likely two, and Keith as donor of his own paintings. Coxhead, Schweinfurth, Maybeck, Polk, and painter Mary Curtis Richardson may well have contributed ideas to the project; if so, they all responded to the wishes of the architecturally sophisticated and knowledgeable Joseph Worcester, who oversaw every detail. Richard Guy Wilson suggests that *"the specifics are not so important as the general effect of calmness and meditation."*[94] Yet the question of attribution has haunted the story of the San Francisco Swedenborgian Church for a century. Considering how influential this church is in the history of architecture and the development of the Arts & Crafts movement in the United States, resolving the attribution question is equally important.

Fig. 3.21

Fig. 3.20 (facing): Swedenborgian Church, San Francisco, under construction (after September 20, 1894). The man standing in the foreground is probably A. Page Brown, but definitely not A. C. Schweinfurth.

Fig. 3.21: A. Page Brown, 1893. Published in *The Messenger,* April 1, 1893. From the Brown Scrapbooks, California Historical Society, San Francisco.

The Origin of Mission Style & Craftsman Furniture

In November 1894, A. J. Forbes began making the first Mission Style chairs for the San Francisco Swedenborgian Church (Fig. 3.23). (Thus the chairs were designed in 1894 or even before.) The maple chairs, handmade without nails, were notable enough to be mentioned by many visitors:

> They had seats woven of tule rushes from the deltas of the Sacramento and San Joaquin rivers, and in front of each was a "Japanese" woven grass mat. . . . The chairs, beautifully modeled, are suggestive of the primitive old mission furnishings.[95]

These blocky chairs with their rush seats and squashed foot eventually served as prototypes for the Mission furniture made by Joseph P. McHugh in New York, which subsequently stimulated competitive lines from Gustav Stickley and others.

Sometime between 1896 and 1897, McHugh, owner and operator of a very successful New York furniture store called the Popular Shop, and his newly hired designer, W. J. H. Dudley, received one or more examples of the Swedenborgian Church chair and drew up detailed specifications to begin copying it. In 1898 McHugh added a matching settee (Fig. 3.22). pronounced them both "Mission Style," began their manufacture, and advertised them widely.[96]

According to his recent biographer David Cathers, Gustav Stickley, who had been manufacturing *"unremarkable revival-style chairs"* since the early 1880s, became increasingly anxious to produce *"more meaningful work."*[97] But, it seems to me that when he saw McHugh's Mission furniture, he recognized a new design trend and a marketing opportunity.

Stickley and other American manufacturers could also have seen fairly simple furniture illustrated in *International Studio,* which began its American edition in 1897, a year before McHugh launched his very successful Mission furniture line. Cathers writes that Americans could have perused *"over one hundred pages in five issues."* These were published from late 1899 to 1900 and featured the London Arts & Crafts Exhibition Society's sixth exhibition.

Like McHugh, Stickley recognized that an increasing number of Americans wanted to rid themselves of Victorian excess and to adopt the new taste for simplicity. Stickley furniture resembled McHugh's Mission line and also similar pieces that had been produced in England, especially furniture designed by M. H. Baillie Scott, illustrated in *International Studio* from ca. 1900. However, as Cathers explains, Stickley may owe something to Baillie Scott but *"no one would mistake it for anything but a Stickley creation."* Stickley steered clear of the term *Mission,* naming his furniture *"the structural style of cabinet making"* (generally referred to as "Craftsman") instead.[98]

Wendy Kaplan and David Cathers note that by 1905, Stickley had to compromise to reach his democratic goals. To achieve affordability and profitability, he shifted toward *"plainness and standardization"* so that by 1904 he had turned to machine manufacture. Whether A. J. Forbes made a similar shift or continued to make each chair by hand, and if so for how long, remains to be explored.[99]

California Women Help Launch Mission Style Furniture

The revolution in taste away from Victorian clutter toward the Arts & Crafts *gesamtkunstwerk* stimulated the growth of interior design firms. The simple home was intended to be a total work

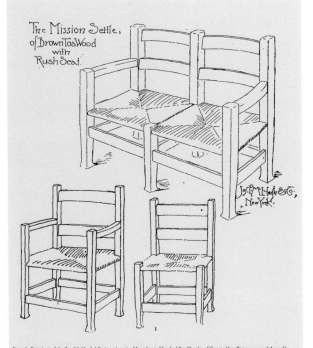

Figure 6. Drawings of the first McHugh Mission pieces in *More than a Hundred Pen Sketches of Certain Very Picturesque and Agreeable Furniture Designed and Adapted by Joseph P. McHugh & Co. and Sold at the Sign of the "Popular Shop"* (1898). Courtesy Warshaw Collection of Business Americana, Archives Center, National Museum of American History, Smithsonian Institution, Washington, D.C.

Fig. 3.22

Fig. 3.22: Drawing of the first McHugh Mission pieces in *"More than a Hundred Pen Sketches of Certain Very Picturesque and Agreeable Furniture Designed and Adapted by Joseph P. McHugh & Co. and Sold at the Sign of the 'Popular Shop' (1898)."* Note that McHugh copies the Mackmurdo squashed foot from the Swedenborgian Church chair.

Fig. 3.23: The first Mission Style chair, originally designed for, and used at, the Swedenborgian Church, San Francisco (1894–95).

Fig. 3.23

of art, filled with handmade objects that would reflect the owner's interest in reading, culture, and family life. Interior design firms soon multiplied to satisfy the desire for simpler everything, from curtains to furniture to the architecture that would house it.

It is likely that one design firm in particular was instrumental in launching Mission Style furniture. Shortly after the first chair was made, Bruce Porter and two San Francisco women, Eudora Martin and Mary Ingalsbe (listed as partners in a decorating business with Bruce Porter in 1892, 1893, and 1894), along with Mary Curtis Richardson, saw the handcrafted maple chair with rush seat that A. J. Forbes & Son had made for the church. Between 1894 and 1897 someone sent McHugh an image of the chair or perhaps the chair itself. This could have been either Richardson or Martin, a colleague of McHugh's, who studied in New York with Candace Wheeler, *"the first professional woman interior designer in America."* Or the chair could have been sent by Bruce Porter, a close friend of Worcester's, who was in business with Martin and Ingalsbe, had contacts in the East, and had contributed to the design of the church. [100]

In 1900 the *San Francisco Chronicle* acknowledged that this mostly female firm, established *"well along in the eighties,"* pointed a new way for working women:

> *What these women have accomplished others may do. The hard pioneer work has been endured and the way made possible. The vanguard has done the things which provide employment for many women, but they have also demonstrated that there is a good market for original ideas and a welcome for brave women.* [101]

A. J. Forbes Makes Several Mission Style Chairs from 1894 to 1902

On November 1, 1894, A. J. Forbes offered to make the chairs and their rush seats for the Swedenborgian Church: *"I haven't made a rush seat for thirty-five years but I think I can remember how to make these and I will teach others."* Forbes made this charming proposal:

> *To Mr. P. Brown & Co. Architects,*
> *We will make the eighty chairs for the following prices.*
> *In Pine, less the mats: $4.00 each*
> *In Maple, " " " " 4.50 each*
> *We will furnish you with the proper flag, make a soaking bot for the boys and learn them to make a cottage mat, i.e. not fancy, at the following terms.*
> *I will pick it (the flag) out and learn the boys to put in a good cottage mat for Nothing.*
> *Soaking bot Nothing*
> *If we get the job, we can commence immediately.*
> *Respectfully submitted,*
> *A. J. Forbes & Son* [102]

After seeing an image of himself as he worked, sketched by Richardson, Forbes wrote to Worcester, saying that *". . . he was worried that people might think he was influenced to do this work by religious feeling. He wanted it understood that all religious feeling had been driven out of him by the churches!"* [103]

In California, Forbes Manufacturing Company continued to sell the chairs designed for the church. This might explain why examples of the chair can be seen in Schweinfurth's Moody house (1896), in Pattiani's Los Gatos country house (he purchased it in July 1898), in Maybeck's Rieger house (1899), and at the fabulous country estate Wyntoon (1903) that Maybeck designed for Phoebe Apperson Hearst. Keeler suggests that someone donated the cost of the chairs to the Swedenborgian Church, possibly Phoebe Apperson Hearst, a friend of Worcester's. Mrs. John Baeck, granddaughter of Judge Rearden, a close friend of Worcester's, confirmed the donation, as we see in the letter cited herein: *"by some unforeseen generosity the church was provided with beautiful rush-woven chairs."*[104]

Meanwhile, half a dozen or more chairs may have been shipped from the Martin-Ingalsbe firm to McHugh in New York City *"in the spring of 1896 or possibly 1897."* After quickly selling those, McHugh and Dudley began making a scaled-down version of the chair. Meanwhile, as noted, A. J. Forbes had continued to make the Swedenborgian chair for Martin and Ingalsbe, who were able to supply northern California architects and homeowners as well as McHugh.[105]

Who Gave Mission Style Furniture Its Name?

Who coined the term "Mission Style"? Did the Californians who discussed the chair design with Worcester and who purchased those chairs refer to them as "Mission," "Mission style," or "Mission inspired" before New Yorker Joseph McHugh did? Consider the evidence. Even before the church or chairs were constructed, the Swedenborgian *New-Church Pacific* states in July 1894 that

> *. . . the Society . . . is to have a new house of worship . . . decidedly unique as far as America is concerned, being low and modest, in the Italian style, its tiled roof and arched doors suggesting the California mission class of architecture. . . .*[106]

Furthermore, it stands to reason that Brown's and Worcester's shared interest in the California missions, visible elsewhere in the church, sparked their determination to have old-fashioned, hand-tooled, simple, sturdy chairs with rush seats.[107] Worcester pasted numerous articles on church furnishings in his scrapbooks, and individual chairs are still used in most Romanesque and Gothic churches in Europe. Keith, Keeler, Porter, and John Galen Howard had all sketched the missions before 1894. Worcester, Keeler, and Keith knew Charles F. Lummis personally, and they were familiar with his efforts to save the mission structures.[108] In addition, Brown's California State Building for the 1893 Chicago Fair, designed between January and February 11, 1892, inspired architects to design numerous buildings in the Mission Style.[109] Thus, the term was in use for architecture before Worcester and his friends began using it to refer to "their" chair.

Another factor popularizing and broadening interest in everything "Mission" was Helen Hunt Jackson's novel *Ramona,* which first appeared in 1884. Sometime thereafter, Bruce Porter sketched two adobe structures: *Ramona's home* and *Ramona's marriage place.*[110] The book's enormous success and subsequent editions aroused further awareness of California's Indian and mission past. Finally, the *San Francisco Call* refers to the chairs on February 10, 1896, as *"of the style in vogue generations ago."* It does not seem unreasonable to conclude that the chairs were largely mission-inspired and referred to as Mission Style.

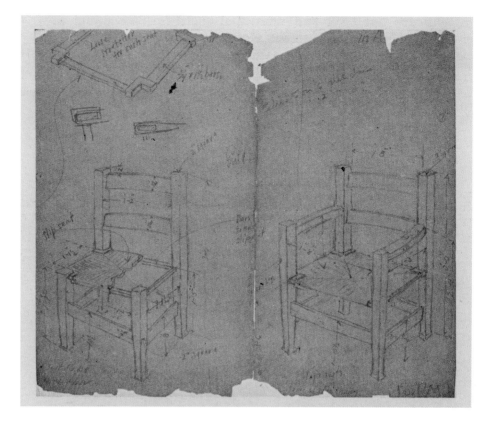

Fig. 3.24: Mission Style chair construction details from original sketches by Walter J. H. Dudley for New York manufacturer Joseph McHugh, after 1896 when Dudley was hired.

Design of the Mission Style Chair and the Mackmurdo Foot

The *San Francisco Examiner* of September 30, 1895, states that *"heavy square-framed chairs were designed,"* without saying by whom except to add that *"the Scotchman* [A. J. Forbes] *was at work upon them when he learned that 'the minister could find . . . no one who knows how to make the rush seats upon which* [Worcester] *had fixed his mind.'"* Forbes offered to make the rush seats and the "cottage" mats to be placed in front of each one.[111]

Who determined the design and the blocky outlines of the chair, and why did the design include the tapered leg that flares at the bottom to form a squashed or flared trumpet foot? The otherwise straight-lined chair uses the Mackmurdo foot, named after the English Arts & Crafts designer Arthur Heygate Mackmurdo, who first used this leg on a desk circa 1885. Could Mackmurdo have particularly appealed to Worcester, Brown and Maybeck because he traveled to Italy with Ruskin, established the Century Guild in 1882, and wrote on the spiritual in art?[112]

Mackmurdo mastered several crafts himself and developed a reforming passion that might also have inspired Worcester and Maybeck. Furthermore, like Worcester, Mackmurdo envisioned the Arts & Crafts movement as more than advocacy of the beautiful; Mackmurdo wanted the movement to engage and enhance man's spiritual nature.[113]

Brown and Maybeck studied, lived, and traveled in Europe before 1894 and may have seen first-hand the move toward simpler, vernacular-inspired furniture. For example, they could have known Morris's rush-bottomed "Sussex" chair, developed before 1870. Maybeck especially would have seen Morris and Mackmurdo furniture (the latter was shown in several European cities) while working for Pottier and Stymus furniture makers in Paris. These English designs, however, were somewhat more refined and less blocky than the chair they designed for the Swedenborgian Church.[114] McHugh copied the Mackmurdo foot from the Swedenborgian Church chair.

First Mission Style Chair: A True Cooperative Effort

No written evidence has yet been found to suggest that Maybeck designed the first Mission Style chair, but he may well have drawn up the specifications. As noted, on November 1, 1894, Forbes presented the contract for the chairs to Brown; clearly the design had been prepared and was ready to be executed before that date.

Up until 1899 the California press referred to the chairs as "Mission," or "old fashioned," and told the story of the rush seats. From 1899 on, most articles restate the *Scientific American*'s August 1899 contention that Brown designed the chair as Worcester wanted:

> *. . . the seats are chairs of maple frame and rush, designed by the architect but in preparation of these plans the architect was greatly indebted to the Reverend Joseph Worcester. I have never seen seats which so perfectly fitted their environment as these. Perhaps the congruity arises from the fact that they too were designed by the architect A. Page Brown.* [115]

However, Brown had no experience designing or making furniture, nor did Schweinfurth, who, in any case, had left Brown's firm by February 26, 1894. (In other words, Schweinfurth had left the firm nine months before the chairs were made.) On the other hand, Maybeck, who served as draftsman for the Swedenborgian Church, had extensive experience in designing and making furniture. Maybeck worked twice for Pottier and Stymus, a firm specializing in custom furniture design: once in New York with his father, a specialist in custom furniture and cabinetry, and again in Pottier's Paris studio in 1881 at age nineteen. Even during his time at the École des Beaux-Arts, it is possible that he continued working for Pottier as money was short. Moreover, once Maybeck arrived in the Bay Area in late 1889 or early 1890, he took a job with still another

Fig. 3.25: Bernard Maybeck designed this clubhouse in the redwoods and its furniture. The bench, with S-curved ends, is reminiscent of the one in the Swedenborgian Church, as is the off-center, asymmetrically placed fireplace. Photograph ca. 1903.

custom furniture and interior design firm, Charles M. Plum Company, and soon became its principal designer.[116]

Dudley's drawings for McHugh based on the Swedenborgian example (Fig. 3.24) demonstrate how complex the construction was of an apparently simple chair.

We do not know whether Maybeck, Worcester, or Brown suggested softening the chair's otherwise blocky appearance with the distinctive Mackmurdo foot. It would have been odd if Maybeck, working for firms specializing in furniture design, had been ignorant of a revolutionary new design. However, if Maybeck had missed seeing the Mackmurdo foot, any one of Worcester's widely read and well-traveled friends could have suggested using this distinctive element.[117]

In addition, one cannot help wondering whether the benches flanking the fireplace, with their S-curved ends, came from the same furniture designer's hand—Maybeck's? As noted, Maybeck drew a very similar bench flanking a deliberately asymmetrical fireplace in an undated Maybeck sketch (Fig. 3.13), and he designed another remarkably similar bench for a clubhouse in the redwoods (Fig. 3.25) ca. 1903.

As with the design of the Swedenborgian Church, the chair would appear to have been a collaborative effort. When Maybeck was still alive, Keeler stated in his 1906 article entitled "San Francisco, the Home of Mission Type of Furniture" that Brown had originated the Mission Style.[118] Therefore, it stands to reason that Maybeck agreed with him and gave Brown the credit for the conception, if not the specifications, of the chair. This attribution makes sense; Brown had been associated with the Mission Style since 1892.

In conclusion, the evidence to date suggests that Maybeck did the detailed specifications for the chair after listening to the wishes of, or seeing a sketch by, Worcester and Brown. However, in keeping with the spirit of cooperation sought by Worcester, it is also possible that Porter, Polk, Schweinfurth, or Coxhead could have been involved.

Widespread Influence of Worcester's Church and Homes

Worcester's homes and the Swedenborgian Church had a lasting effect. Those touched by them included contributors to the artistic and cultural life of California: Maybeck, Muir, Porter, Keith, Coxhead, Polk, Lummis, Burnham, and Phoebe Apperson Hearst, as well as congregants Felicien Victor Paget and Mrs. Warren Gregory, who built houses (Figs. 5.3, 5.4, 8.6–8.10) reflecting the taste for natural materials, simple construction, and harmony with nature. As Keeler expressed it:

> *During the years when civic pride was dormant in San Francisco an art spirit that is yet destined to wield an important influence in the future city of the Golden Gate was taking possession of a small but increasing number of people. If one were to look for its original inspiration, they would not go far astray in attributing it in large measure to a certain quiet and retiring minister,—a man of gentle nature, of devoted love of the beautiful, and of exceptionally true, though reserved taste. From the inspiration of his modest little home, and the picturesque church built under his direction, and more especially from direct contact with the man himself, a group of architects, decorators, painters, and lovers of the beautiful have acquired a new point of view. They have gained the ideal of a quiet, spiritual, reserved type of beauty which has found expression in homes, stores, and indeed in many important forms of art work.*[119]

The First American Arts & Crafts Society, San Francisco, 1894

4

APPROXIMATELY ONE MONTH BEFORE THE MISSION STYLE CHAIRS WERE BEING MADE for the Swedenborgian Church and while that building was under construction, the earliest American Arts & Crafts society was formed—not in the East, not in Chicago, but in northern California. In 1894, six years after the English Arts and Crafts Exhibition Society gave its name to the movement, Worcester's friends established the Guild of Arts and Crafts of San Francisco.

The *Wave* heralded the "permanent" organization of the Guild of Arts and Crafts in San Francisco on September 22, 1894:

> *The Arts and Crafts will be permanently organized this week. William Keith . . . Arthur F. Mathews, Albert Pissis . . . Bruce Porter, Willis Polk and many others are already actively interested. The membership will be limited to 50, and not to 40 as had been erroneously reported by my contemporaries."* [1]

The Boston Society of the Arts and Crafts did not hold its first meeting until three years later, on June 28, 1897, although it held an exhibition in April of that year; Chicago's Arts & Crafts group first met October 22, 1897.

A piece of stationery in Willis Polk's collection at EDA, headed "The Guild of Arts and Crafts of San Francisco," lists guild officers as Bernard Moses, president; Bruce Porter, secretary; and its directors, including A. Page Brown, Douglas Tilden, and Sigmund Beel. The *Wave* mentions two additional architect members, also Worcester's friends: Ernest Coxhead and Clinton Day. Ruskin, Morris and the British movement may have inspired its lofty goals. Moreover, the San Francisco guild specifically stressed "an improvement" in architecture as had the St. George's Art Society formed by assistants working in R. Norman Shaw's office in 1883 and the Art Workers Guild. [2]

The Guild of Arts and Crafts of San Francisco's purposes are typed out on the same piece of stationery mentioned above:

> *Whereas the Guild of Arts and Crafts, having in view the maintenance of an artistic standard in the future architecture of this City, and as the Guild believes that it will be*

possible, through a Board of Public Works to foster and encourage an artistic feeling in the development of our City; therefore be it

> *RESOLVED: That the Honorable Board of Freeholders be, and hereby is, respectfully urged to give due and proper consideration to the Department of Public Works in relation to its discretionary powers in connection with the selection and approval of all designs and plans for public buildings and works, and to regulate the construction of private works.*

> *RESOLVED: That a law creating a Board of Public Works in and for the city and county of San Francisco be included in the Charter that they are now framing.*

> *Signed: The Board of Directors of the Guild of Arts and Crafts.*

The guild intended to control the design of private homes as well as public buildings. A handwritten version, presumably earlier, intends to give the guild real power: *". . . the Board of Public Works shall have 5 members: including the San Francisco Art Association, SF Chapter of AIA, Builders Exchange and Guild of Arts and Crafts."*

The author claims the same authority seen in *"Eastern cities and foreign countries"* and intends that *"the Board shall review not only public building plans but any private building exceeding in cost 1000 dollars."*[3]

On November 24, 1894, the *Wave* applauded the guild's intentions:

> *The Arts and Crafts organization may elevate the standard and contribute toward educating the popular mind to a discriminating sense which will distinguish merit and true art in the various arts & crafts. I am told that the organization proposes to be something beside a passive body of contemplative geniuses indulging in mild, monotonous monthly meetings with no excuse for existence outside of self admiration. It intends, I believe, to encourage an improvement in our architectural vagaries and if this alone be accomplished then Arts and Crafts will not have lived in vain.*[4]

The *San Francisco Chronicle* chimed in: *"The voice of the Guild should be that of the highest authority among us and must carry weight even to the minds of the Philistines."*[5]

Overland Monthly reviewed the San Francisco Guild's exhibition and commented that its name and fundamental idea derive from Ruskin, Morris, and the British Arts & Crafts movement:

> *The [San Francisco] society took its name . . . and fundamental idea from the annual exhibition instituted largely through the efforts of William Morris . . . and Walter Crane. The whole movement is due to the indirect influence of the teachings of Ruskin. . . . The scheme . . . at . . . the Guild of Arts and Crafts in London was the revival of the old handicraft in workmanship . . . not only among working men, but throughout the mass of the population. Nothing gives a man so much respect, both in his own eyes and in those of other men, as the power to make . . . as it tends to remove the barrier between the artist and the artisan. . . . Something may be done for California in this direction.*[6]

Californians had many additional connections with England. In his December 1894 article, Brown stated that well-known British painter Alfred Parsons visited San Francisco *"a few years ago."* Parsons was a member of the Art Workers Guild (1884) that, with the English Century Guild (1882) and the Guild of Handicraft formed by C. R. Ashbee in 1888, used the medieval-referenced term *guild* in their names. One can guess that the founders of the Guild of Arts and Crafts of San Francisco knew their English sister organizations and, of course, the medieval reference, and chose the name accordingly. Moreover, like the Art Workers Guild in London, the San Francisco guild began by inviting only certain people to join. When reviewing the guild's second exhibition, the *San Francisco Examiner* remarked upon the many scenes painted in France and England, confirming the group's first-hand experience in Europe.[7]

Before Boston or Chicago started their Arts & Crafts societies, the Guild of Arts and Crafts of San Francisco spawned a Ruskin Club in Berkeley (1895). Charles Keeler, who greatly admired Worcester and Maybeck, and who certainly knew members of the San Francisco Guild of Arts and Crafts, established the Ruskin Club *"that called people's attention to the need for beautiful and simple surroundings, the necessity of art in life,"* and in 1898 he and the Hillside Club began a Handicraft Guild. That same year a group of writers and artists in Piedmont formed another Ruskin Club.[8]

Although the San Francisco guild died sometime after April 24, 1897, as a result of squabbling among its members, having presented only two exhibitions,[9] it had been publicized to a readership beyond California—in *Overland Monthly* and undoubtedly in other journals as well as by personal contacts—and may have helped to stimulate similar organizations elsewhere in the United States.

Soon other Californians who undoubtedly knew what was happening in San Francisco and the rest of the world from publications, personal contacts, and perhaps from visits to the California State Building at the 1893 Chicago Fair and to the 1894 San Francisco Midwinter Exposition became more sympathetic to the ideas and style of the Arts & Crafts movement. These included Charles Sumner Greene and Henry Mather Greene of Pasadena, Frederick Eaton and Elisabeth Burton in Santa Barbara, and George Wharton James in Los Angeles. From his post at the *Los Angeles Times* beginning in 1885, as president of the Landmarks Club in 1895, and as editor of *Land of Sunshine* (renamed *Out West* in 1901), Charles F. Lummis, friend of Keeler, Keith, and Worcester, was able to promote interest in Native American handicrafts and mission structures found in the West and Southwest.

Keeler also operated his own publishing house, The Sign of the Live Oak, and his wife, Louise, illustrated their books with her own Morris-inspired designs reminiscent of productions from Morris' Kelmscott Press (Fig. 6.7: bookplate designed by Louise Keeler). For example, Louise Keeler's bookplate resembles Morris' frontispiece for his 1892 edition of *News from Nowhere,* which featured the *"old house by the Thames to which the people of this story went"* surrounded by a foliate border with boxed text below the image[10]; she too featured their living room–library with a flowery border and boxed text. Some of Keeler's poetry was similar to that written by William Blake, who had, at one point, been very attracted to Swedenborgianism. Keeler practiced what he preached and aimed to show the necessity of art in the home, homemaking, and decoration. To that end he and Louise initiated a home-based handicraft guild and also produced furniture for sale.[11] These two organizations were among the *"hundreds of organizations"* devoted to handicraft and home industries that, according to Wendy Kaplan, sprang up in the United States from 1890 to 1910.[12]

Fig. 4.1: Charles and Louise Keeler house, 1770 Highland Place, Berkeley (1895). This is the interior after Maybeck added the industrial sash window-wall mirroring the shape of the room. As Keeler described it: *"At the lowest point of the elevation was the living room library . . . designed like a little chapel, open into the peak. It was only one story, jutting out from the two story part of the house back of it."* The term "cathedral ceiling" derives from designs such as this, which in turn were inspired by medieval cathedrals.

"A Cottage All of Our Own":
Polk and Coxhead

5

An Architect and Client Exchange Words, 1891

FUTURE RESEARCH MAY DEMONSTRATE THAT SIMPLE ARTS & CRAFTS HOMES WERE promoted elsewhere in America before Worcester's homes and church became influential. But current research suggests the move to generally adopt and build this type of housing blossomed from 1889 in northern California where architects took Ruskin's and Morris' advice and designed *"a cottage all of our own, with its little garden, its pleasant view."* [1]

In addition to Ruskin, Morris and Worcester's influence, there were many other factors: awareness that Europe was becoming interested in middle-class, affordable, "simple" homes; the abundance of cheap redwood; a climate that made the humble cottage and garden possible; clients willing to try something new; familiarity with the East Coast's Shingle Style; and a desire to preserve the spectacular landscape. These combined to help popularize the California Arts & Crafts home.

Plenty of small houses had been built in the Bay Area in the 1880s, often decorated with fancy-cut painted shingles and with bric-a-brac. At the end of the 1890s when the trend toward *un*painted or brown shingle homes became fashionable, some owners reshingled with unpainted shingles. However, before that there was a transitional period when architects began to get rid of the excesses of the Queen Anne style with its gingerbread, machine-made decoration, towers, turrets, painted and wallpapered walls. During this period Queen Anne elements such as oriel, eyebrow, and round bay windows still appeared on unpainted shingled homes.

When Worcester suggested to philosophy professor George H. Howison, his close friend, that he employ A. Page Brown as architect for his house at 2731 Bancroft, Berkeley (Fig. 5.1), Brown replied: *"Why don't you* [Worcester] *do it."*

This unusual and, apparently, previously unpublished exchange demonstrates that even for a "simple" Arts & Crafts home there were a myriad of details to be determined. In this instance which style might be suitable is not discussed and seems to have depended upon which architect was hired.

Brown's confidence in Worcester's architectural skills reveals Worcester's intense active involvement not only with the selection of the architect but also with the design, construction, cost, and choice of materials for Howison's brown shingle house, and perhaps for others. It also

Fig. 5.1: George H. Howison house, 2731 Bancroft (1890–91). This early brown shingled house in a flat area of Berkeley was designed with the help of Joseph Worcester, Willis Polk, and possibly A. Page Brown. The architect-builder of record, George W. Pattiani, also may have contributed to the design.

Fig. 5.2: Crocker Old People's Home, San Francisco (1889–90), by A. Page Brown, done in the latest Shingle Style. Willis Polk drew the published drawing (published in *Architecture & Building,* July 27, 1889) while working for Brown.

Fig. 5.1

Fig. 5.2

demonstrates his close friendship with Brown and his willingness to promote him, his familiarity with other architects' work, and his knowledge and understanding of the mechanics of the architectural profession. Furthermore, by signing one of the letters "*Not architect but your friendly advisor,*" Worcester expresses self-confidence in his ability to advise others on their architectural projects[2]:

Monday morning, 1030 Vallejo

Dear Mr. Howison,

Your pleasure in Mr. Brown's work made me feel like approaching him again about your house. I saw him this afternoon and told him of our pilgrimage and great interest in his work at the Old People's Home [Fig. 5.2]. He was much gratified and said he should be very glad to assist you and to a certain extent he might be able to do so. He said that this week he should finish the drawings for the Crocker building and should be comparatively free, and that he had got his old draughtsman Schweinfurth from the East, and should have therefore more efficient help than he had had.[3]

He could not undertake the superintendence of the house, but he might make the more important drawing. He said also, "But why don't you do it and let me help you?"

I told him that I had had no training, that the most I could do for my friends [note the plural] was to avoid bad things, that I could not do good things and should not allow myself to stand in the way of those who could. I tell you this partly to set myself right— and partly to give you an alternative (always a pleasant thing to do) in case you should be deterred by thought of the expense or of Mr. Brown's penchant for symmetry or any other reason. Mr. Brown's charges are high, ten percent of the cost, tho' this includes super-intendence, and they would be less for the drawings simply. Where it can be afforded I am sure that the impress upon the building of his thought would add more than that to the value of it.

With the certainty that I feel after our Saturday's experience, that you would rather not go to [architect Clinton Day] I think I will not ask him for the loan of his photographs.

Affectionately yours,

Jos Worcester

Friday PM, 1030 Vallejo

Dear Mr. Howison

I had but a moment with Mr. Malone after you went, but I asked how he made the sheathing so costly. He figured it up again and said—"It would be 31.5 cents plus 10% for labor." I said, then .35 would cover the cost per square yard? He replied—"It might possibly be something more than that for the first grade of either pine or redwood, but .40 would more than cover it."

I did not have time to ask him, but I think for the smaller panels .25 per square foot is all that it need cost; well seasoned half-inch stuff would be heavy enough for this.

Not architect but your friendly advisor,

Jos Worcester

Worcester may not have felt he could call himself an architect but he certainly provided expertise to his friends. At some point Brown was out of the picture and Worcester may have recommended his architect friend Willis Polk to Howison. In any case, Polk seems to have made only one drawing (at least that is all that remains), a plan of one wall with a large fireplace, wood paneling, windows and window seats, and small bookcases for the Howison living hall or living room. But in the end Howison chose the architect/builder Alfred Washington Pattiani, who was adept at designing in the latest styles (and perhaps executed them for less money than other architects did) and who quickly adopted the unpainted shingle house for several clients.

In a recent lecture, historian Paul Roberts pointed out that J. Cather Newsom's pattern books *Artistic Homes of California 1892–93* include two shingled houses from 1891, both of which are not in the Queen Anne style, use unpainted shingles, and are by Pattiani. While building the house for Howison, Pattiani could have seen Shingle Style houses on his several trips east or Worcester, Polk, and Coxhead's versions of the simple shingle house. In any case, Pattiani designed and built three similar houses in 1891–92, one for M. G. King in Berkeley at 2313 Durant Street and two next to each other on Grand Street in Alameda.

The exchange between Howison and Pattiani is fascinating. Pattiani's bills are filled with pleas to be paid, arguments over which material to use, requests for final design decisions regarding a myriad of details, and disputes over the costs involved. It is likely this exchange begins in late 1890 or early 1891 and continues through 1891, as the contract notice with architect A. W. Pattiani dates from May 7, 1891 (filed 5/9/91 for $4,763). However, as late as November 1891, Howison had still not accepted the house.

Examples are numerous. For instance, on July 18, 1891, Pattiani wrote,

> *Your house, #232—situated on North line Bancroft way near Audubon Street has the roof shingles, wall & gable shingles on and chimney built. We are therefore entitled to the first payment of $1300 as per terms of contract dated May 7, 1891.*[4]

Howison marked the bill *"Paid, 7/22/1891."* And when Pattiani demanded further payment on November 19, 1891, Howison annotated the bill: *". . . did not know any due but paid it Sat. Nov. 21 (1891) with provis that house was not completed nor accepted."*[5]

Willis Polk: Simplicity, Dignity and Refinement

At the time that Worcester was intimately involved with Howison's house in Berkeley, he was simultaneously influencing developments on Russian Hill. Whatever the depth of influence exerted by Worcester on Polk, the latter was certainly a man with a cosmopolitan outlook with knowledge of architectural developments in the East as well as in England, the Continent, and elsewhere.[6] Polk's first houses in San Francisco reflected his awareness of the eastern Shingle Style and of homes designed by A. Page Brown as well as his admiration for the designs of his friend Ernest Coxhead and the much simpler homes advocated by his friend and neighbor Joseph Worcester. He certainly did not learn about shingled homes in California. Before meeting Worcester and coming under his influence, his designs reflected the more elaborate, sometimes Queen Anne–inspired Shingle Style in vogue in the East and Midwest. For example, the pre-1890 buildings Polk worked on as a member of his father's firm, W. W. Polk and Sons, are shingled but are certainly not simple homes. In 1888 he shingled the First Presbyterian Church in Liberty, Missouri, but gave it a stone base. And although Polk used shingle sheathing and a tower after the manner of H. H. Richardson for his 1887 Lockwood house in Kansas City, it sported a grand melange of styles and materials, hardly a simple Arts & Crafts home.[7]

Polk had traveled widely before settling in San Francisco in 1889. In the last months of 1887 Polk had moved to Los Angeles, where he worked with Coxhead and met Howard. At least two published designs from 1888 were labeled "Ernest Coxhead, architect, Willis Polk, del. [delineator] and were published in *American Architect and Building News*."[8]

By November 1888 Polk had gone to New York, during which trip he became acquainted with McKim, Mead, and White and was hired by Brown, who had established his own practice in 1884. Proof of Polk's widespread travels can be seen in *Specimens of Wrought Iron Work*, which he sketched prior to 1889. These sketches included "Arch for Carriage Gateway" and a lamp from "old People's Home, San Francisco, A. Page Brown, Architect"; window grille, "city of Mexico 1887"; window grille, "at Kansas City"; glass lantern, "in New Orleans"; keyhole, "St. Saveur, Bruges"; lamppost, "Bleeker St., N.Y."; plus various other sketches that were neither placed nor labeled. *American Architect and Building News* published them.[9]

Dissatisfied with the established architectural journal *California Architect*, Polk began his own magazine a year after he arrived in San Francisco; he was only twenty-three at the time. Although only three issues of *Architectural News* appeared, it provides a valuable record of contemporaneous architectural thinking. Writing as editor of his journal, Polk stated its purpose (which sounds significantly Worcester-influenced), proposing to follow Ruskin's advice to *"cultivate the field of architectural art, and to pay little or no attention to architecture as a science."*[10] *Architectural News* sought to encourage the design of moderately priced simple houses that would integrate interior and exterior architectural design with the realities of the lives of their inhabitants. Polk praised the laborer and emphasized careful design of his housing in all three issues between 1890 and 1891. In the same magazine, he also lauded John Calvin Stevens and Albert Winslow Cobb's 1889 book *Examples of American Domestic Architecture* for its socialist position and its adherence to William Morris' ideals, terming it

> *. . . a guide for houses for working men . . . with a touch almost socialistic, and a feeling akin to the works of William Morris,* [Stevens and Cobb] *outline the "tendency to magnificence" in American architecture and its effect upon American domestic life. It would be unreasonable to expect all architects to . . . become respectable socialists; but surely the very best men in the profession have already assumed this position, that is of designing houses of moderate cost in a simplicity of treatment that expresses a "more general domestic virtue and happiness." . . . it is to be hoped that the seed thus planted will . . . inspire an healthy and permanent appreciation of the value of simplicity.*[11]

Polk stated that one of the purposes of his magazine was to stress *"the value of simplicity"* in home building:

> *. . . a dwelling-house should express, without affectation, the simplest object of its being, that of furnishing a comfortable shelter to the home-life, avoiding everything tending to display, and without imitating the pretentious houses of men of wealth, of which but few*

are models of anything but poor taste, is the real basis for the proper conception of an ideal home of moderate cost. [12]

And he continued stressing the significant role architects could play:

Could these houses be designed by men having an adequate appreciation of the value of simplicity, and who would reserve their ingenuity, curb their ambition, and act entirely in a rational manner, the result would surely play no small part in directing the popular taste, thereby creating a demand which would eventually have its effect in establishing a healthy art feeling and develop an architecture worthy of our great country. [13]

Architectural News also included news from Kansas City, Boston, New York, and Chicago, as well as sketches of buildings in England, France, Germany, and Greece.[14] Clearly, Worcester's circle knew about developments on the East Coast as well as internationally.

Like many Europeans and the rest of this group, Polk believed the Arts & Crafts movement was not a style but an attitude and set of values that encompassed all the arts. Besides stressing *"the value of simplicity"* in home building, Polk wrote in the *Wave,* echoing Charles Follen McKim, who championed beauty as architecture's ultimate goal. However, like Worcester, Polk condemned art for art's sake. Longstreth quotes from and explains Polk's attitudes expressed in the *Wave* ca. 1892:

Unlike English aestheticism which celebrated art for art's sake, the creation of beauty was viewed [by Polk] *as performing an important spiritual role in society debased by material-ism. "Simplicity," Polk emphasized, must be "the prime ruler of all artistic work." . . . "Simplicity, dignity and refinement" were fundamental values for Polk and his generation.* [15]

In 1891, at the time he was working on the Horatio Livermore house, Polk published a draw-ing in *Architectural News* for a wooden house *"nearing completion"* for Francis Avery in Sausalito.[16] This house, featuring two polygonal towers with an open loggia between, was remi-niscent of Shingle Style houses designed by Richardson and by McKim, Mead, and White on the East Coast. The resulting spatial complexity had no counterpart in the simple wooden houses of Worcester, yet the use of unadorned natural materials inside and out suggests local influence. As Polk described the building, it sounded like a house by Worcester:

The interior will be finished throughout in redwood, simply waxed. The exterior is covered entirely with split white cedar shingles put on without stain or oil, which are expected to weather to a silvery gray. [17]

In 1891 Polk designed an entirely half-timbered house for Worcester's friend Professor Felicien Victor Paget at 2727 Dwight Way, Berkeley; it was shingled before 1898 (Fig. 5.5), and, except for the diamond patterning and some fancy-cut shingles, the details of the shingled façade recall Worcester's design for the Marshall houses. One cannot help wondering if Worcester was involved in this design, because he treasured a tiny photograph of the Paget's interior stairwell and hall, and kept it until his death (Fig. 5.3).[18]

Fig. 5.3

Fig. 5.4

Fig. 5.5

Fig. 5.3: Felicien Victor Paget house, 2727 Dwight Way, Berkeley (1891), by Willis Polk. The stair and entrance hall is done in redwood. Joseph Worcester may have helped design this house, as he kept this photo until his death, and the board-and-batten design reflects Worcester's use of redwood in his Russian Hill living room.

Fig. 5.4: George H. Boke house, 23 Panoramic, Berkeley (1901–2), by Bernard Maybeck; view: stair hall.

Fig. 5.5: Paget house, view: except for its decorative diamond and scalloped shingles, the main façade (shingled sometime before 1898) is reminiscent of Worcester's Marshall houses on Russian Hill. Professor Paget was a member of Joseph Worcester's Swedenborgian Church.

After these relatively simple early projects, and after the 1893 Rey house (discussed in Chapter 10), Polk's houses grew more complex. The elegant touches he grew fond of, and which his wealthier clients sought, could be better executed in brick or stucco than in wood, and he designed only a few more houses that showed the lingering influence of eastern Shingle Style and the simple Arts & Crafts home.

Despite his writings advocating simplicity, even his other early projects were not so simple. In his magazine, *Architectural News*, he illustrated his own designs. He combined shingles with towers, turrets, and finials borrowed from Loire Valley chateaux. He also used classical columns, Georgian and Palladian window detailing, and elaborately paneled interiors. Examples of his more elegant work in San Francisco for wealthier clients include the W. B. Bourn house (1896) and the Charles S. Wheeler house (project only, designed 1898), among many others. On the other hand, his California Mission Style house for Frank McCullagh (1901) evokes the simplicity of the missions with bare white walls and tiled roofs.[19]

An Englishman and the Arts & Crafts Spirit

Ernest Coxhead was born in 1863 in Eastbourne, Sussex, to the family of an Anglican minister. After leaving England for Los Angeles in late 1886, he moved to the San Francisco Bay Region in late 1889 or early 1890, where he established a practice with his brother, Almeric; carried on the friendships he had established in Los Angeles with Polk and Howard; and became a close friend of Worcester, Maybeck, and Keeler. He probably also knew Schweinfurth through the Volney Moody family, the Hillside Club, and via Polk. (However, Schweinfurth and Polk may have been enemies as they publicly attacked each other in the *Wave*.[20]) Coxhead developed a client base in Berkeley as well as in San Francisco, and practiced in the area until his death on March 27, 1933.[21]

Two letters demonstrate Worcester's friendship with Coxhead and an appreciation of his architectural skills. When Worcester was lobbying John Galen Howard to take the position at University of California, Berkeley, he wrote Howard: *"There is a little group of us, Polk, Coxhead, Porter, Faville and Bliss . . . who are still saying we wish you could come, study the site with us."*[22]

They maintained their friendship and Worcester kept Burnham informed, as we see from this letter to Burnham, written from Bolinas, June 25, 1902, in which Worcester urges him to help his friend Coxhead:

> *My particular object in writing is to speak of the competition which we understand is about to be arranged for the new Customs house here. We are told that ten architects will be invited to enter, five of them will be of San Francisco. I do not know how the men will be selected but it can not mean more to any one than it does to Ernest Coxhead and if a word of endorsement could be given by you without forcing the matter I should be very glad. I suppose the supervising architect at Washington must have the arrangement. Shall we see you soon?*
> *Ever affectionately,*
> *Jos Worcester*[23]

It is possible that Coxhead played a key role in bringing the English Arts & Crafts aesthetic to California and may even have introduced Worcester to architectural manifestations with which he was not familiar, but it is just as likely that Worcester knew British architecture long before meeting Coxhead. In any case, an interaction between the two men certainly took place. We can imagine their lively conversations during which Worcester would share his reverence for Ruskin and Swedenborg along with his desire to build with nature, while Coxhead might describe English houses by Ernest George and Harold Peto, half-timbering by Norman Shaw, and domestically scaled houses by C. F. A. Voysey and Mackay Hugh Baillie Scott, who *made the cottage a work of architecture. . . ."*[24]

It is easy to imagine Worcester and Coxhead in sympathy with British architects including Baillie Scott and Voysey in their quest to meld the Arts & Crafts aesthetic with cottages (simple homes) to give the "average man" (i.e., the middle class) more independence and healthful living.

As James Kornwolf expressed it:

Both Voysey and [Baillie] *Scott disparaged Shaw's villas. For* [Baillie] *Scott the "so-called Queen Anne bijou residence" represented a bourgeois mannerism that offered at most a "doll's house like prettiness." Instead both architects turned to . . . Carlyle, Ruskin and Morris where they were advised to look . . . at a cottage all of our own, with its little garden, its pleasant view, its surrounding fields, its neighboring stream, its healthy air, and clean kitchen, parlours, and bedrooms.*[25]

Furthermore, English architects eagerly sought information on the latest American trends in domestic architecture, just as American architects looked to England for inspiration. Cross fertilization took place internationally via periodicals, exhibitions, travel, and personal contacts, as recently demonstrated by Wendy Kaplan, Karen Livingstone, and Linda Parry, among others. For example, Voysey attended the 1893 World's Columbian Exhibition in Chicago where his two-dimensional designs were on display. However, he had published a design for his own house in *Architect* in 1888 and received a commission to do a variation on it; thereafter, he published numerous designs, including "A Country Residence," "An Artist's Cottage," a "Verandah House" in *British Architect* and even published in *American Architect and Building News* as early as 1890. Thus Voysey established his reputation and by the time of his 1893 visit had made his designs accessible to architects worldwide.[26]

Kornwolf's description of the 1880s advocacy in England by factions of the intelligentsia and working classes for better conditions and improved housing parallels pressures from the middle class in the United States. Some English reformers were active participants in the socialism of the time, including Morris, Mackmurdo, Ashbee, and Lethaby. Others remained aloof, as did Voysey, Baillie Scott, and Lutyens. No evidence has thus far surfaced demonstrating that Worcester, Coxhead, Maybeck, Brown, Schweinfurth, and others were socialists. However, Worcester, Polk, and Keeler did attack California's materialism and lack of culture and sympathized with the working man, at least in the early 1890s.[27] As we have seen on page 77, for a brief moment in his youth Polk (and perhaps some of his circle?) advocated that architects should be *"respectable socialists."* Indeed, before Polk obtained wealthy clients, he criticized the *". . . universal and insane eagerness for wealth and social standing . . ."* in the first issue of

Fig. 5.6: "Study for
Memorial Church
of the Holy Innocents
S.F." (1890), by
Ernest Coxhead.

Architectural News; and he devoted his opening remarks to "The Poor Man's House of Today: An Improvement Suggested," in which he continued:

> *. . . the mere and misleading appearance of wealth and superiority to labor has been substituted for all that is beautiful in honest labor and domestic life. . . . We have to remember that we are all laborers. . . . To really feel this is to restore labor to its place of honor.* [28]

Just as the work of British Arts & Crafts architects marked a shift in emphasis *"from the English manor to the cottage with its middleclass connotations,"* so the work of this California group signaled a move away from elaborate Italianate or Queen Anne houses to the "simple" Arts & Crafts home for the middle class and university community. According to Kornwolf, Baillie Scott had not studied and read Ruskin and Morris until the early 1880s, at least ten years after Worcester. Baillie Scott began his practice about 1890 and *"reached his early maturity"* in 1898. Voysey's characteristic style (totally different from Worcester's) did not manifest itself until the late 1880s, about the same time Worcester designed the Marshall houses on Russian Hill. Kornwolf sees Voysey's houses, like Baillie Scott's, as small houses, cottages really, that were not meant to be anything more; he points out that Voysey's generation was inspired by both American domestic architecture and the Arts & Crafts movement, and that both coalesced in 1889 or 1890. [29]

Philip Webb's Red House for William Morris (1859–60), which is most often considered the ultimate source for the "small" house made into a work of architecture, did not spawn imitators or a real movement until twenty years later, when its influence was expressed in California in 1876 by Worcester simultaneously with the adoption of Morris' goals by Henry Hobson Richardson and others in the eastern United States. [30]

While Coxhead was still in London, he would likely have seen a trend toward simplicity and the Shingle Style highlighted in an exhibition of recent American architecture at the Royal Institute of British Architects (RIBA). Moreover, the *British Architect* presented examples of the Shingle Style and praised them for their simplicity. Kornwolf and Scully both point out reasons for this British interest in American architecture: namely, that the Shingle Style *"owed its initial and continuing inspiration to English precedents, especially to Shaw and the Queen Anne revival,"* and furthermore,

> . . . [the] *Shingle Style was more original than derivative: it was a fresh vernacular archi-tecture, in many ways more compatible with Morris' literary references to architecture of the Arts and Crafts objectives than was English domestic architecture. . . . It is also obvi-ous that American social structure, unlike that of the English, had gravitated toward a middle-class norm, which helps to explain the early development of moderately sized but well-designed houses.*[31]

Thus, California joined architects worldwide as they began focusing on the simple, affordable house.

As noted, Coxhead moved to San Francisco while Worcester's rustic shingled houses on Russian Hill were being built. He chose to cover his first San Francisco church (the Church of the Holy Innocents, 455 Fair Oaks, San Francisco, 1890) with unpainted shingles (Fig. 5.6).[32]

Gothic-style parish churches had been built in the area, but these had been clapboarded or finished with board and batten, and the wood was painted.[33]

At St. John's Episcopal in Monterey (1890–91), Coxhead's shingles covered so much of the building that it has been nicknamed "Saint Roofus" (Fig. 5.7).

Perhaps Coxhead considered shingles appropriate for the whole surface of the Church of the Holy Innocents and St. John's Episcopal because they were humble, not monumental structures. The inspiration for a shingled church may have come from any one of several sources; for exam-ple, William Ralph Emerson's Church of St. Sylvia on Mount Desert Island in Maine, which was published in the *American Architect* in 1881. The shingled exterior of Holy Innocents was rustic and unpretentious, creating an image of charming simplicity, quite different from the shingled but chateauesque "House at San Mateo for Mr. James Davies" that Coxhead had published in *Architectural News* in 1891 (Fig. 5.8).[34]

By the time Coxhead introduced a shingled version of the vernacular English cottage to San Francisco with two houses on Green Street, he had simplified his style radically; perhaps Worcester influenced him too, or perhaps he had absorbed the growing English interest in ver-nacular simple buildings from architects such as Voysey. His earliest shingled house seems to have been the one for James C. McGauley at 2423 Green Street (Fig. 5.9). This was designed and built in 1891–92, just after Worcester completed the Russian Hill houses and while Polk was working on the Vallejo Street duplex. The McGauley house was a brick and half-timber structure with tall, paired, leaded-glass windows. A shingled roof, thick and rolled at the edge to imitate thatch, projected forward on the street façade.

At his own house (2421 Green Street, next door to the house for his friend McGauley), Coxhead built a narrow town house deep into the lot[35] (Fig. 5.9). Rather than the typical town house of the period, generally a painted wood structure embellished with fancy carved decoration,

Fig. 5.7

Fig. 5.7: St. John's Episcopal Church, Monterey (1890–1891), by Coxhead & Coxhead. It features a large round window puncturing the shingled gable over an arched doorway. The shingles roll over the side entry, soften the gable and dormer edges, and flow almost to the ground—a fairytale vision of an English country church nicknamed "Saint Roofus" for its broad, sheltering roof.

Fig. 5.8: James Davies proposed house, San Mateo (1891), by Coxhead & Coxhead. One wonders whether Coxhead designed this early brown shingle in the chateauesque style before Worcester's influence took hold or if he designed it to suit his client's demands.

Fig. 5.8

Fig. 5.9

Fig. 5.10

Fig. 5.9: Ernest Coxhead house, 2419–2421 Green Street, San Francisco (1893), by Coxhead and Coxhead, who used a scalloped wall to link the masonry base of his own house (left) with the earlier James C. McGauley house (right), 2423 Green Street (1891). Although these are city houses, Coxhead uses brown shingles on large parts of both. The steeply peaked gables, half-timbering, and linking walls recall English examples.

Fig. 5.10: Streatham Common houses, London, by British architects Ernest George and Harold Peto, who used a single dip wall punctured by an entrance arch to link the houses. Coxhead used two arched entrances, each puncturing a wall abutting his own house on Green Street in San Francisco (Fig. 5.9), and linked his house with the one next door with a dipped wall. (See also Fig. 5.14.)

Fig. 5.11

Fig. 5.12

Fig. 5.11: Beta Theta Pi, 2607 Hearst Avenue, Berkeley (1893), by Coxhead & Coxhead. By dividing the building into sections, using steeply pitched gables intersecting at right angles, and combining brown shingle with stucco and half-timber, Coxhead suggests a miniature streetscape rather than a single building.

Fig. 5.12: W. E. Loy house, 2431 Ellsworth, Berkeley (1893), by Ernest Coxhead. This "severely plain" house is a good example of the rustic "simple home."

Coxhead's version was novel in its stark simplicity. Its top section, covered with smooth unpainted shingles, contrasted with the whiteness of its very lowest section. Another unusual aspect was the asymmetrical composition formed on the smooth-shingled surface by the windows. Inspiration for the window arrangement might have come from Voysey's plan for the Forster house near London, which appeared in the *British Architect* in 1891.[36]

Coxhead had been recommended to the RIBA by George Wallis and Fred Chancellor and could also have been influenced by "visitors," among them G. E. Street, Alfred Waterhouse, and Richard Norman Shaw.[37]

However, Coxhead's interest in half-timbering probably did not derive from the late-nineteenth-century English manor house, such as the much-discussed half-timbering used by Shaw at Leyes Wood, Sussex (1868), but rather from the revival of small, half-timbered country cottages appearing in English architectural magazines by the late 1880s.[38]

Moreover, he would have seen vernacular cottages while growing up in England, such as the large sketch of a "Thatched Cottage, Kenley, England," published in Polk's magazine, *Architectural News* (January 1891), to which he was a contributor. Coxhead may also have been directly influenced by Voysey as Kornwolf suggests: *"Forming an even more obvious bridge between England and America is the work of Ernest Coxhead . . . whose design for* [2421 Green Street; 1893–94] *is an equally spirited response to Voysey."*[39]

The way Coxhead handles the walls connecting McGauley's house and his own, and the dip in the wall Coxhead uses at the James Brown–Reginald Knight Smith house (Fig. 5.14) resembles the way two other British architects, Ernest George and Harold Peto, link with a dipped wall the Hambly houses at Streatham Common (Fig. 5.10). Coxhead joins the two freestanding houses with more than one dip, resulting in a scalloped masonry wall edged with bricks (Fig. 5.9). The roof shingles of the McGauley house link it visually with the shingles used for the walls, roof, and dormers on his house. So well are they joined that one cannot help wondering if the two houses were conceived at the same time. Further research might answer this question and might also reveal whether Coxhead could have worked with George and Peto's firm, as did several of the later exponents of the Arts & Crafts movement, including Lutyens. In any case, George and Peto's work was certainly known by both Coxhead and Polk; indeed, the latter published a drawing after an Ernest George watercolor in the November 1890 *Architectural News*.[40]

Moreover, while he lived in England, Coxhead would have had plenty of time to see these 1877 houses at Streatham Common before their publication in an 1896 *Architectural Record* article entitled "The Smaller Houses of the English Suburbs and Provinces."[41]

If his early San Francisco cottages were inspired by English designs, they nonetheless paralleled the rustic houses built by Worcester and Polk on Russian Hill. Longstreth described Coxhead's paired houses: *". . . the overriding simplicity of detail lends cohesiveness to the whole. . . ."* and the *". . . studied casualness owes a major debt to the English arts-and-crafts work."* [42]

At the Beta Theta Pi fraternity house (1893–94), Coxhead treated two sections of the building with brown shingles for a rustic look (Fig. 5.11). The rest probably derives from Coxhead's familiarity with English and other medieval streetscapes and perhaps from Baillie Scott's houses at Douglas on the Isle of Man. Both Coxhead and Baillie Scott sometimes edged white plaster walls with wood beams, leaving the breadth of wall unornamented while delineating its perimeter. Other walls, in contrast, were entirely decorated with half-timbering, which was used on the interior as well as on the exterior.[43]

The house Coxhead discussed as early as 1890 but did not build until 1893 for William E. Loy in Berkeley was also a shingled house in the English cottage, Arts & Crafts "simple home" tradition without ornament. This house (Fig. 5.12), which no longer exists, is best described in the owner's own words:

> *It is perfectly plain—severely plain in fact—nothing has been wasted in ornament. The sides and roof are both shingled with sawed cedar shingles, and these will be left unpainted and allowed to weather. There is no ornamental cornice or fancy front, and no real bay window. There is in front an alcove window, which from the outside looks somewhat like a plain square bay window. . . . The living room and hall will be paneled in natural wood (no paint or varnish) to the height of the doors. . . . The entrance is at the north side, consequently we have sunshine in all the rooms, but not in the hall. We thought a hall only a means of entering a house, and that it was far better to have the sunshine in the rooms where one lives.* [44]

Fig. 5.13: Anna Head School, 2538 Channing Way, Berkeley (completed August 22, 1892), by Soule Edgar Fisher, who designed this beautiful shingled structure with multiple façades, each of a different design. Anna Head was a friend of Joseph Worcester.

Fig. 5.14: James Brown–
Reginald Knight Smith
house, San Francisco (1895),
by Coxhead & Coxhead, who
used English touches in the
gently curved wall, arched
gate entrance, leaded-glass
windows, and towering
chimneys of the house.
Perhaps Worcester encour-
aged his friend Irving M.
Scott to commission Coxhead
to design this house, celebrat-
ing his daughter's marriage
to Dr. R. K. Smith.

The Loy house was diminutive in scale; the roof, with its exaggerated low-dipping slope and upward curve at each end of the ridge, combined forms expressive of Japanese and European roofs, and served the practical purpose of keeping rainwater off the walls. The interior of the house was finished with oversized redwood panels covering three-quarters of the wall's height. The evidence suggests that Worcester referred William Loy to Coxhead. Like Worcester's houses, the emphasis was on simplicity, rusticity, and the living room. The two-story living hall found in many English and East Coast Shingle Style houses disappeared with Worcester. Some may consider Maybeck's two-story living rooms its reincarnation, but they served a very different purpose. The living room, with its fireplace, not a grand entrance hall, became the home's center or focal point. (After the mid-twentieth century, the center shifted to the kitchen.)

At about the time Polk and Coxhead were building "simple" Arts & Crafts brown shingle houses, Anna Head began her first building for what was to become the largest and one of the earliest planned complexes of (fourteen) shingled buildings in the Bay area—the Anna Head School (Fig. 5.13). Not surprisingly, she was a friend of Worcester's. The oldest building—a sophisticated interpretation of the eastern Shingle Style, was designed by Soule Edgar Fisher, Anna Head's cousin, and completed in 1892.[45] The building at 2538 Channing Way, Berkeley, still stands but has been turned into offices by the University of California, Berkeley.

As with Polk, Coxhead's interest in the simple home dominated his practice only in the very early years of his career. Thereafter he was hired to build several large, expensive San Francisco mansions filled with ornamental details and most often built of brick; naturally he designed to satisfy his clients' demands and budget (Fig. 5.14).

The early Polk and Coxhead houses and churches advanced the cause of simplicity in construction and use of natural materials. However, it remained for Maybeck, Keeler, and the Hillside Club to galvanize a large group of supporters who would henceforth demand natural shingle "simple" homes that were integrated with, and complemented the rugged beauty of, the natural landscape.

Hillside Architecture: Maybeck and Keeler

6

"IN THOSE DAYS I USED TO WEAR AN OLD FASHIONED BLACK BROADCLOTH CAPE . . . AND I carried a gold headed cane," Charles Keeler said of himself at the time he met Bernard Ralph Maybeck (Fig. 1.12). His vivid recollection of meeting the man who was to become his good friend and the architect of his house (Fig. 6.1) is one of the best profiles of the lively and likeable Maybeck:

> *Back in 1891, or thereabouts, I was working at the California Academy of Sciences in San Francisco, and I generally returned to Berkeley on the five o'clock commuters ferry. My attention had been attracted by a man of unusual appearance. . . . He was of a solid build with a round face and chin. . . . His complexion was ruddy, like an outdoor man's, although he evidently worked in an office. His eyes were dark and his expression benign. He seemed to me like a European rather than an American. . . . Instead of a vest he wore a sash, and his suit seemed like a homespun of a dark brown color.*[1]

Fig. 6.1: Charles and Louise Keeler house (1895), 1770 Highland Place, Berkeley, designed by their friend Bernard Maybeck; drawing by Louise Keeler, October 1898.

Fig. 6.2: Muriel Ransome, bridesmaid, at Minnie Ray Wilson Olney's wedding, April 26, 1904, in the living room of the Charles Wilkinson house, then owned by James and Katherine Bunnell. Mrs. Bunnell's sister Louise married Charles Keeler. Muriel is standing before the Maybeck fireplace, part of his 1902 remodel of the living room and front porch. Above the mantel can be seen brass-studded leather panels; the walls of the room were finished with redwood board-and-batten paneling and topped by a heavy sculptural cornice.

The handsome polished man with the gold-headed cane became friends with the simple man in the dark homespun. Charles Keeler's family lived in the Charles Wilkinson house, the large Victorian on Dwight Way (Fig. 6.2).

Keeler became a prolific author; he wrote as a zoologist and ornithologist and for Charles Lummis' *Land of Sunshine,* the California Promotion committee, the *Craftsman* magazine, the Hillside Club, and left several unpublished manuscripts. Although Maybeck became the architect of solid principles and great influence, the articulate Keeler recorded his ideas. In "Friends Bearing Torches," an unpublished collection of reminiscences about notable Californians at the turn of the century, he gives an invaluable picture of Maybeck's early career and his architectural philosophy. And in 1904 he dedicated *The Simple Home* to *"my friend and counselor, Bernard Ralph Maybeck,"* advocating the Arts & Crafts philosophy as a way of life.

If Maybeck was the less articulate and more down-to-earth of the two, he was by no means the less creative. Born in New York City in 1862, the son of a German woodcarver, he served a boyhood apprenticeship with a furniture maker before studying at the École des Beaux-Arts in the atelier of Jules André.

Maybeck's practical experience and family background had nourished his respect for craftsmanship. From his Beaux-Arts master's exposed stick-like constructions in the Jardin des Plantes and Viollet-le-Duc's theories, he absorbed a rational approach to architecture emphasizing structural expression. These teachers, along with Olmsted's designs for Berkeley, Stanford, Oakland, and the Chicago Fair, and his friend R. Norman Shaw's work at Bedford Park, helped stimulate Maybeck's interest in landscape and the relationship between buildings and their environment.[2]

In 1886, when Maybeck returned to New York, the newly established firm of Carrère and Hastings hired him to work on the huge Tiffany-decorated Ponce de Leon Hotel in St. Augustine, Florida.[3]

In 1889 Maybeck moved west, stopping first in Kansas City where he met his future bride, Annie White, and then, after returning to claim her, settled in Piedmont, renting a cottage (Fig. 1.11) near Worcester's home (late 1890–91), which proved *"a revelation."* In 1892 he and Annie built (or renovated?) a house at Grove and Berryman Streets in Berkeley and possibly built and sold cottages managed by Annie, his wife and business partner. Simultaneously he worked for several firms, including A. Page Brown,[4] but he longed for a private practice and glimpsed the possibility of fulfilling this goal when he met Charles Keeler, who was to become his first client.

The two men were instantly sympathetic to each other. In conversations during their daily ferry crossings to San Francisco, they found that they shared many of the same ideas. Both knew Joseph Worcester and his Piedmont and Russian Hill houses and both admired not only the simple Arts & Crafts home but also handcrafted furnishings. Enthusiastically sharing his theory of art with Keeler, Maybeck told him he proposed to *". . . restore the handcrafts to their proper place in life and art. He believed in handmade things and that all ornament should be designed to fit the place and the need. He did not mind how crude it was, provided it was sincere and expressed something personal."*[5]

As noted, Keeler formed a Ruskin Club in 1895 and a Handicraft Guild in 1898.[6] He designed the family's wooden beds and may have helped Maybeck determine the design of the broad, hammered iron hinges on the door to his home.

Instead of using mass-produced hinges and doorplates found on most Victorian homes, Maybeck designed strap hinges for the Keeler house (Fig. 6.5). Like the hinges used by Henry Hobson Richardson for Trinity Church in Boston (1872–76) and like those on the door to the Swedenborgian Church (Fig. 6.5a), these decorative hinges were meant to recall medieval hand-hammered hinges. English architects such as Baillie Scott also turned to *"broad iron hinges with a decorative-structural role of tying together the planks"*; one was published in the *Studio* (April 1895), the most widely read British art journal in America.[7]

Keeler may have been stimulated to build a rustic shingled home by watching one go up. While living with his stepfather in the Wilkinson house, Keeler watched the construction of a brown shingle house for Worcester's friend Professor Felicien Victor Paget, directly across the street on Dwight Way in 1891 (Figs. 5.3, 5.4). Keeler later worked with Maybeck on the Gifford McGrew house at 2601 Derby Street, Berkeley (1898–1900) (Fig. 6.3), in which both exterior and interior reflect English design, and the long, low sloping roof is intended to resemble an English country inn.[8]

Keeler kept abreast of the Arts & Crafts movement. He wrote of the Roycrofters of New York State and similar Arts & Crafts societies in California: *"There has been a great impetus to the growth of arts and crafts work in various cities in California, and several arts and crafts societies have recently been formed to foster this work."*[9] As late as 1928 Keeler advocated converting the East Bay Water Company properties in Berkeley to an art colony.[10]

Interestingly, in 1871 Worcester had dreamt of starting *"a new settlement somewhere on the right basis, shutting out objectionable people and things and having a free field for trying experiments . . . there has seemed a chance out here* [in California] *to do something of the kind.*[11]

Fig. 6.3: Gifford McGrew house, 2601 Derby Street, Berkeley (designed ca. 1898; built ca. 1900); house designed by Bernard Maybeck, possibly executed by Charles Keeler, with advice from McGrew's friend Joseph Worcester. In the living room, redwood board and battens make a rich pattern on the walls, and are complemented by inglenook seating with an S-curve end to the bench and a brick fireplace in the English Arts & Crafts tradition. Note the lamps indicating Arts & Crafts architects adopted electricity shortly after it became available.

Fig. 6.4: Charles and Louise Keeler house, 1770 Highland Place, Berkeley (1895), by Bernard Maybeck, who designed the house with a shingled exterior to *"fit into the landscape as if it were a part of it."* One of the *"stupid white painted boxes"* Keeler detested is visible just above his home to the left. The white Wilson-Arbogast house was later shingled, as were most of the white-painted houses in the vicinity. The photograph was taken before 1908.

When Maybeck built his first house—a home for his family in Berkeley in 1892—Keeler was quick to see in it the craftsmanship he admired in the ideals of the Arts & Crafts movement.

[Maybeck's house] was something like a Swiss chalet. The timbers showed on the inside and the walls were of knotted yellow pine planks. There was no "finish" to the interior, for the carpenter work finished it. There was a sheet iron, hand built stove, open in front and with brass andirons. Most of the furniture was designed and made by Mr. Maybeck himself. It was a distinctively handmade home! [12]

Worcester, Polk, and Coxhead had designed houses with wooden interiors, but the paneling on their walls had covered the structural frame of the house, and Coxhead had used wooden wainscots with plaster above. Maybeck, however, designed the Keeler house (Figs. 6.1, 6.4), leaving the structure exposed throughout the interior—an unusual feature for the region and the period. Several buildings with exposed structure could have contributed to this design. In 1890 Maybeck worked for Wright and Sanders and may have seen their 1882 San Francisco church nave with all supports visible (3.17).[13] He undoubtedly recalled rural churches he had admired in Europe; and, as Longstreth pointed out, probably saw the Norwegian stave church with its rugged structural interior illustrated in Gottfried Semper's *Der Stil,* a text he much admired and had planned to translate for *Architectural News.* [14]

To Keeler's delight, Maybeck enjoyed the association with his receptive friend and proposed to build him a house. Keeler wrote,

One day he told me that he had heard I owned a lot up in the hills north of the University grounds. How he had found this out I have no idea, but it was true that I had bought a lot

there with a beautiful old live-oak tree upon it. It was near the rim of a charming little canyon, and commanded a superb view of San Francisco Bay. Mr. Maybeck told me that when I was ready to build a home there, he would like to design it. He told me that he would make no charge for his services as he was interested in me and wanted to see me in a home that suited my personality. [15]

In 1894 Maybeck began work on Keeler's house, a brown shingle with multiple peaked roofs intended to blend with the hillside. Anthony Bruce, executive director of the Berkeley Architectural Heritage Association (BAHA), explains the situation at the time the Keeler house was being built in 1895:

Before 1889 there were only a few scattered houses in the hills. However, things changed dramatically that year with the opening of Daley's Scenic Park, a subdivision incorporating Highland Place and the streets immediately around it. This was Berkeley's first formal development in the hills, with lots for sale to home builders. [16]

The evidence suggests that Maybeck and Keeler and those who adopted their ideas and eventually formed the Hillside Club were upset that many of the houses built on these lots after the tract opened were painted. They recognized that a whole new way of conceiving a home for a *hillside* lot was imperative. What had worked in the flatlands of the *village* was going to turn the all-important hills into an eyesore.

In addition, by 1895 Maybeck had surely seen the successful neighborhood of rustic unpainted shingled houses on Russian Hill by his friends Worcester and Polk; he had also seen the Howison house by Pattiani and Worcester on Bancroft (1891) (Fig. 5.1) and could not have missed Soule Edgar Fisher's brown shingled school for Anna Head (1892) (Fig. 5.13). Moreover he would have known Coxhead's two rustic city houses on Green Street in San Francisco (1892–93) (Fig. 5.9); would have seen Coxhead's Loy house in Berkeley (1893) (Fig. 5.12); and would have noted Beta Theta Pi (1893–94) (Fig. 5.11), which combines vernacular medieval forms, half-timbering, and unpainted

Fig. 6.5a

Fig. 6.5a: Swedenborgian Church, Lyon and Washington Streets, San Francisco (1894–95); view: its door has a medieval-type strap hinge.

Fig. 6.5b: Charles Keeler house, 1775 Highland Place, Berkeley (1895); view: this medieval-type strap hinge was designed by Bernard Maybeck.

Fig. 6.5b

Fig. 6.6: Keeler house, view: living room–library, shown as it was when the Keelers lived there after 1895 but before the later renovation.

shingles.[17] So when Maybeck found that his first client was willing and anxious to convince others to build brown shingle houses similar to the one he planned for Keeler, he jumped at the opportunity; together they set out to fight the construction of more Victorians—such as the white-painted Maher House (1890) and the Wilson-Arbogast House (1895), visible from Keeler's windows (Fig. 6.4)—before the hills were further defaced.[18]

However, Maybeck's house for Keeler was by no means the first brown shingle house in this hilly section. For example, in 1891 Maxwell Bugbee designed a brown shingle house for H. Murphy at 2537 Hilgard Avenue, contracted November 1891; John White, Maybeck's brother-in-law, designed a brown shingle house for Winthrop W. Sargeant at 1633 Arch Street near Virginia in 1894.[19]

Berkeley historian Daniella Thompson adds a third unpainted shingle house (originally meant to be a barn) that preceded the Keeler house. The *Berkeley Daily Advocate*, August 1, 1894, described the temporary house on Ridge Road for Frank M. Wilson, the owner-developer of Daley's Scenic Park, as

> . . . *in the Swiss cottage style . . . completed at a cost of over $2000 by Fred Esty, the contractor. It is the barn of the elegant residence soon to be erected, but is really very attractive in its appointments and as handsomely furnished as many more pretentious homes. All the rooms are plastered and on the first floor are beautifully finished in natural woods, oiled. The large carriage rooms serve as parlors, the other half of the building as living rooms.*[20]

Thus the situation was complicated; as early as 1891 and perhaps before, unpainted brown shingle houses were being built simultaneously with Victorian painted houses.

The fact that in the flat sections of Berkeley, as well as in this hilly tract, unpainted, brown shingle houses were being built before the Keeler house was constructed suggests that the desire for unpainted shingle houses had as much to do with their practicality (no paint needed) and low cost (abundance of redwood) as with the fact that they blended into the trees and did not mar the landscape. About 1889 Stevens and Cobb in the East promoted the affordable home, and Polk editorialized for simplicity in *Architectural News* in January 1890 (see Chapter 5). Worcester's circle knew about European interest in vernacular architecture, affordable housing, and architects' desire to design the house as a total work of art (*gesamtkunstwerk,* in German) via individual contacts, travel, exhibitions, and publications. It is likely the need to house new immigrants to California, knowledge of what was happening in Europe, and economic realities all combined to help launch the new simple, affordable home. Although Maybeck emphasized the handmade, medieval-referenced aspects of the Arts & Crafts simple home, he was not alone in bringing to the hills of Berkeley the tradition that Worcester, Polk, and Coxhead had started.

Maybeck's first effort for a client, the Keeler house, expressed his principles and educated the residents of north Berkeley. Maybeck believed *"a house should fit into the landscape as if it were a part of it."* In addition, Keeler quotes Maybeck's dictum that a building should expose the material of which it is constructed, as had the buildings of his French teacher, Jules André. For Maybeck it followed that *"the design was in large measure determined by the materials of which the structure was to be built. If wood was to be used then it should look like a wooden house."*[21]

Keeler's house at 1770 Highland Place, Berkeley, still stands today although its original shingled exterior was changed to stucco after the 1923 Berkeley fire. Again Keeler informs us:

The ground plan of the house was in the form of a cross; the elevation rose with the ascending hill. At the lowest point of the elevation was the living room library . . . designed like a little chapel, open into the peak. It was only one story, jutting out from the two story part of the house back of it.[22]

Keeler emphasized that *"all the timbers were exposed on the inside and upon them on the outside were nailed redwood planks which made the inside finish."*[23] The wooden walls of the room had no decorative detail; instead, interest was derived from the exposed structure, not unlike the architect's own house:

. . . [Maybeck's] principle was that whatever was of structural importance should be emphasized as a feature of ornament. He called attention to the fact that, in the old Gothic cathedrals the rafters which upheld the pointed arches, the succession of pillars which gave strength to the walls, the flying buttresses that helped to hold them firm were all necessary to the solidity and stability of the building. The repetition of exposed columns and rafters were like the beats in music or the metrical emphasis that gives accents to poetry. That is why Ruskin speaks of architecture as frozen music. . . . But a room with smooth plastered walls creates no sense of rhythm, and its machine-stamped wall paper is applied to relieve the barrenness of its box-like effect.[24]

Fig. 6.7: Louise and Charles Keelers' bookplate, hand-drawn by Louise Keeler before 1907 in the Arts & Crafts style, was influenced by William Morris' typeface and floral designs. The bookplate features many details visible in the ca. 1895 photograph of the actual living room library (Fig. 6.6), which was designed by Bernard Maybeck. Note the many books, Japanese lanterns, exotic freestanding screen, cathedral ceiling, french doors, multiple curtained windows, and exposed structure of the kind Ruskin referred to as "frozen music." See also Fig. 11.1.

Fig. 6.8: Keeler house, view: an industrial sash window and large concrete fireplace, which replaced the original brick one built in 1895. Maybeck stuccoed the exterior after the 1923 Berkeley fire. Note the continued emphasis on exposed structure as decorative.

Writing in 1895, the British architect Baillie Scott expressed concerns similar to Maybeck's: *". . . there should indeed be no arbitrary division between construction and decoration . . . everywhere construction is decorative and decoration constructive. . . ."*[25]

In addition to its English and medieval sources, hints of Japanese architecture appear in the asymmetrical massing, the pavilion-like living area, and the upward curve to the gable ends of the three small peaked shingle roofs. Presumably the living room's wood dividing screens with gold-painted lattice grillework edging the top were added when the window wall and existing french doors were enlarged (Fig. 6.6); however, even earlier, as we see in the Keelers' bookplate featuring their living room library (Fig. 6.7), the Keelers used a freestanding screen. At the 1894 California Midwinter Exposition, San Franciscans got a firsthand look at Far Eastern architecture if they had not already seen the Japanese Teahouse erected in 1890 in Piedmont's Blair Park. Keeler himself sketched the Japanese village from the San Francisco International Exposition of 1894 for his 1901–2 book, *San Francisco and Thereabout.*[26]

Since Maybeck may have worked on Keeler's house while assisting with Worcester's church, it is not surprising that one echoes the other. The nave-like peaked space of what Keeler refers to as their *"living room library,"* with its stick-like straight and diagonal lines, vertical wooden posts, and exposed rafters, recalls the rhythm found in medieval churches and in the Swedenborgian Church sanctuary. Throughout his career, Maybeck emphasized the beauty of wooden beamed ceilings, walls, and vertical supports, as in the Aikin house (Figs. 8.4, 8.5), Faculty Club (Figs. 10.7, 10.8), Outdoor Art Club, Mill Valley (Fig. 3.15), Boke house (Fig. 5.5), Town and Gown Club (Fig. 7.16), Keeler studio (Figs. 6.9–6.13), and many more.[27]

When the house was finished, Maybeck and Keeler were not content with their own success. They wanted others who bought land near Keeler's house to adopt similar styles; to recognize that *"the shape of the hills is the result of nature's forces working on natural material for ages"*; to plan houses that would not detract from the beauty of the hills; to design floor plans so that the long

Fig. 6.9: Keeler studio (1902, or possibly 1905), 1736 Highland Place. This view of the main entrance façade, ca. 1972, shows how the sharply peaked gable, precisely bisected by the chimney, flares outward over the entrance porch in a Japanesque manner.

dimension was horizontal, *"parallel not perpendicular to the slope"*; to build with natural materials that repeated the colors of rocks and trees; and to plan trellises and plant vines so that the house *"hides among the browns and greens of the hill and is finished for all time."* Aware that he and Maybeck had *"taken nothing away from the hill"* but had *"grouped* [the Keeler house] *with what is there,"* Keeler, with Maybeck's encouragement, began establishing a building program for Berkeley that would foster Maybeck's principles and eventually result in the development of site-sensitive architecture as a fundamental part of the California Arts & Crafts tradition.[28]

Keeler and Maybeck wanted others to join them to create a cohesive townscape and neighborhood that would nestle into the hilly landscape. Like A. Page Brown, Keeler especially wanted to avoid the construction of more *"stupid white painted boxes all around him,"* such as the one that stood within eyesight of his front door (Fig. 6.4).[29]

The Keeler house must have attracted much attention because the house and its owner lured other clients to Maybeck. Except for the first Lawson house of "Spanish style" built on Warring Street in 1895 (Chapter 10), Maybeck's earliest group of houses were within sight of each other, and all were in the picturesque brown shingle style with exposed post-and-beam structure developed for Keeler: the Laura G. Hall house (1896; Fig. 6.14), the Williston Davis house (1896),[30] and the William P. Rieger house (1899). All were brown shingled with redwood interiors and were designed to fit the land and relate one house to another in a cluster. In addition, the Hall house had an open plan and the Hall and Davis houses sported picturesquely peaked roofs.[31] Describing a house he built in Palo Alto for Emma Kellogg in 1896, Maybeck characterized it as *"Californian in style."*[32]

These Maybeck houses and the Keeler studio (1902 or possibly 1905)[33] (Figs. 6.9–6.13), like

Fig. 6.10

Fig. 6.10: Keeler studio, view: detail of the second-floor bedroom with redwood walls, brackets, and ceiling supports.

Fig. 6.11: Keeler studio, view: redwood door designed by Maybeck to expose its simple construction.

Fig. 6.11

Fig. 6.13

Fig. 6.12

Fig. 6.12: Keeler studio, view:
living room looking toward the
front door, brick fireplace,
repeating sash windows separated by wood posts, redwood
floor, ceiling, and walls.

Fig. 6.13: Keeler studio, view:
living room looking toward the
stairs, with exposed ceiling
beams and simple post stair
rail. The large windows may
be replacements.

Fig. 6.14: Laura G. Hall house, 1945 Highland Place (1896), by Bernard Maybeck. Shown as built, it was shingled to match the other Highland Place houses. This is one of the earliest open-plan houses; Maybeck intended all first-floor rooms to interconnect and flow into one large space. (Demolished)

the houses by Worcester, Polk, Schweinfurth, and Coxhead, demonstrated how homes could enhance rather than destroy the landscape and how a fairly inexpensive home could have style and character.

Maybeck and Keeler championed homes designed to preserve and enhance their natural surroundings. Olmsted's 1865 plans for Berkeley, Mountain View Cemetery in Oakland, Riverside village, outside Chicago, and work at Stanford ca. 1887 (see Chapter 10) must have proved inspirational. Furthermore both men undoubtedly knew Shaw's integration of housing with landscape at Bedford Park on the western edge of London (1877–ca. 1880), W. H. Lever's planned community Port Sunlight in Cheshire (from 1888) and recognized the birth of the City Beautiful Movement that grew out of the 1893 Chicago Fair for which Olmsted designed the elaborate grounds.[34]

In 1898, to help promulgate their own ideas and those of Maybeck and Keeler, the women of the neighborhood formed a group dedicated to galvanizing others to their viewpoint. They awakened community pride and increased demand for the "simple homes" Worcester, Polk, and Coxhead's early work exemplified. The *San Francisco Call* reported on their success:

> *The Hillside Club sprang into existence October 5, 1898. . . . Its object was primarily to protect the hills of Berkeley from unsightly grading and the building of unsuitable and disfiguring houses; to do all in our power to beautify these hills and above all to create and encourage a decided public opinion on these subjects.*[35]

Early Environmentalists, Yosemite, and a Garden Suburb

7

Muir, Olmsted, and Yosemite

SHOULD WE REFER TO THOSE ADVOCATING "BUILDING WITH NATURE" AS EARLY ENVIRONMENTAL-ISTS? In 1865, following his extensive work on Central Park and the Sanitary Commission, Frederick Law Olmsted resided in California for a two-year period. As chairman of the Yosemite Park Commission established by Congress, Olmsted insisted a road was needed to bring timber into Yosemite Park to remove *"the necessity or the temptation to cut down* [Yosemite's] *groves and to prepare its surface for tillage. . . . Until a road is made it must be very difficult to prevent this."* [1]

Olmsted urged Yosemite be managed for *"the preservation and maintenance as exactly as is possible of the natural scenery."* To that end, he conceived the divided road separating the *"comings and goings"* subsequently adopted by many city planners. Clearly he valued trees as essential to beautiful forests, not just as potential lumber. However, the other members of the commission made sure Olmsted's report never reached the state legislature. Not until 1952 was this most important document advocating total preservation of the forests finally discovered and published for the first time. Yosemite historian Alfred Runte wrote: *"Of all the might-have-beens in national park history, the suppression of Olmsted's report was among the most significant."* It was obvious that Olmsted treasured the existing forests and meadows of Yosemite and, therefore, should be considered an early environmentalist. [2]

John Muir, too, immediately recognized the glories of Yosemite on his first trip in 1868. In "Wild Wool" (1875), he urged mankind to recognize wilderness forests as more than timber, stressing that forests help breathe a life-giving force into city folk and deserve preservation:

> *Thousands of tired, nerve-shaken, over-civilized people are beginning to find out that going to the mountains is going home; that wildness is a necessity; and that mountain parks and reservations are useful not only as fountains of timber and irrigating rivers, but as fountains of life.* [3]

In the first *Sierra Club Bulletin* (1896), Muir urged his readers to experience forest splendor for themselves:

Few are altogether deaf to the preaching of pine trees. Their sermons on the mountains go to our hearts; and if people in general could be got into the woods, even for once, to hear the trees speak for themselves, all difficulties in the way of forest preservation would vanish. [4]

Of course Muir and Olmsted were not architects, and if Olmsted cut trees to create a desired effect in his pastoral landscape, he replaced them with others. How, we may wonder, did architects, builders, and their clients "building with nature" approach the environment?

Veneration and Exploitation of Redwoods

The 1882 *California Architect and Building News* acknowledged growing concern for the forests and ran two small articles and a very brief editorial on their destruction: "Logging in California" pinpoints the damage: *"Redwood sawed in 1881 was 140,000,000 feet; of this 95,000,000 came to the port of San Francisco."* The second article, "Uses of the Steel Square," justifies using wood as a low cost commodity: *"San Francisco can . . . justly lay claim to being . . . the largest wooden built city in the world . . . not due to the absence of quarries for granite and other materials, but the expense of getting them to San Francisco and labor to place more durable material in buildings."* Finally, outrage is expressed in "The Redwoods"; the editor complains of *". . . wanton destruction of redwood forests . . . [and decries] clearing lands for the sake of convenience."* [5]

Other California publications probably expressed similar awareness so that by the early 1890s, when the simple Arts & Crafts house took hold in northern California, its proponents simultaneously espoused the *"veneration and exploitation of redwood"*; the two went hand in hand. Aesthetics, spiritual aspiration, and the profit motive collided in pursuit of the American Dream, creating a tragic paradox that continues to cast a shadow over the American landscape.

Today, environmentalists commonly place a premium on the preservation of native flora. The situation then was equally complex. For example, Worcester, with a group of San Francisco women, sought Muir's help to convince powerful men to allow *"a field of flowers,"* specifically *"California flora,"* around the California Building at the 1893 World's Columbian Exposition in Chicago. [6] Worcester expressed his astonishment that anyone could oppose such a move:

Feb. 18, 1893

Dear Mr. Muir,

I understand that Miss Butler has written to you. I have a little fear that she does not make it clear how important to us all her undertaking is, and how much she needs help.

She has charge of the exhibit of the California flora and she has done much and excellent work not only in drawing the flowers in their habitat, but in getting the plants and seeds with the purpose of making a field of flowers around the California building. She can not carry out the well-devised plan for this without help and she has found it very difficult to interest the men in it, so she has appealed to some of the ladies of the Century Club . . . (but) they much and justly fear that Miss Butler's repressed manner will chill rather than warm her auditors.

Do it in your own way, with the drawings, the seeds, anything in your hand, and
[writing unclear: either consume from twenty to thirty minutes or convince from twenty
to thirty ministers].

Excuse, and believe me,
Yours sincerely, Jos. Worcester [7]

On the other hand, although Worcester thought God resided in nature, his impulse to bring nature into the Swedenborgian Church overrode his conservationist attitudes and he was caught in a terrible, if perhaps unconscious, contradiction: To bring nature's holiness into his church he requested that madrone trees (dear to their owners) be cut from an old-growth forest in the Santa Cruz Mountains and brought to San Francisco to enhance the nave of his church.

When the old couple of the Santa Cruz Mountains were approached about giving the beautiful madrones of their place, they declared that they could never part with them—that their grandfather had planted them.—However, when they learned that they would form part of a church, they decided to cut them down and brought them to San Francisco. [8]

A. Page Brown's Environmental Awareness

The architect of the California Building at the 1893 Chicago Fair, about which Worcester expressed concern (see also Chapter 10), was of course the same architect he chose for his Swedenborgian Church—A. Page Brown. Since Brown published almost nothing in his short life, it is worth quoting at length his personal statement revealing sensitivity to the built and natural environment published in the *San Francisco Chronicle,* December 30, 1894. Brown not only stressed the importance of light, air, city parks, green spaces, and curvilinear streets, he also disapproved of wood buildings and suggested that the forests would not last forever. (Although when properly managed they seem to.)

Writing about street planning, Brown opposed the grid and advocated contoured roads such as Olmsted planned in 1865 for Berkeley's residential district and had executed in 1869 for Riverside Village outside Chicago—ideas that Maybeck and Keeler advocated at about the same time Brown published his article:

It is most unfortunate that when the streets were originally laid out so little attention was paid to artistic and architectural effects. A great opportunity was lost in not making a striking and beautiful feature of winding roads and terraced gardens which would give a setting to dwellings and other buildings on our hills that could not otherwise have been obtained. It is not too late to remedy this in some ways, however, as nearly all the buildings are of material [wood] *which cannot last many years.*

His environmental perspective, advanced for his time, encouraged readers to value city parks: *"Even small parks are a relief to the long lines of uninteresting buildings. . . ."* Olmsted had expressed something similar in his 1866 report to the Trustees of the College of California.

Brown perspicaciously feared the inevitable march of taller and taller buildings *"solely for revenue."* If San Francisco had heeded his advice and imposed a height limit on tall buildings, as did Washington, D.C., and Vienna, Austria, the city would have retained the feeling of its unique topography and much more of its magnificent setting. Brown continued:

> *The broken skylines of occasional lofty buildings is a necessary misfortune which we can-not avoid, but which we may in many ways soften and ameliorate. For all buildings erected solely for revenue, rational limitations should be imposed. Sanitary reasons alone* [and today we might add security reasons] *should bring about legal limitations as to the height of buildings here as elsewhere. The rigidity of the building laws of Vienna gave that city the beautiful Ring Strasse, and most of the European cities have become architecturally beautiful by the enactment of similar laws regulating the character and appropriateness of permanent structures. The lofty office building has revolutionized the architecture of our great American cities, and the problems of lighting, of ventilation and of traffic through the streets have been complicated.*

Brown also opposed commercial billboards, which gave owners a profit at the expense of beautiful scenery and handsome buildings: *"The erection of large sign boards throughout the city . . . should be made a criminal offense. The effect of the best buildings is often ruined by the prox-imity to these abominations."* [9]

He disapproved of wood for domestic buildings, nor was he concerned with "simple," "hum-ble," Arts & Crafts homes for the new, upcoming middle-class, having mostly wealthy clients.

The Garden Suburb, Village Improvement Society, and Hillside Club

The Hillside Club, formalized in 1898, has been widely researched, but its roots are rarely discussed. This was not Berkeley's first neighborhood improvement group; the "Athens of the West" established a Village Improvement Society on November 19, 1880.

The Improvement Society laid out roads, planted trees and flowers, mended fences, and urged owners to keep their houses freshly painted. In 1881 Albert Sutliffe describes professors' houses as "modern" and "Californian," and includes Swiss Chalet (probably referring to painted Victorian houses with exposed, decoratively carved roof brackets) among the styles being used—all of which leaves us wondering what specifically he meant.

He acknowledges that although the town organization dates from 1878 (the university first occupied its buildings in 1873), people were attracted to the area and *"built substantial houses. . . . The architecture of Berkeley . . . is not limited in regard to style. Touches of the renaissance are mingled with traces of the time of Queen Anne, outlines of the Swiss chalet, and ideas that are strictly modern and Californian."* [10]

Sutliffe then goes on to mention numerous improvements:

> *Streets have been named . . . and thoroughfares have been set with ornamental trees. . . . The air of refinement and good keeping about nearly every place in the village, whether it*

is the home of wealth or of moderate means, evinces a local pride that animates the entire population. . . . Although planting season for 1880–81 was well advanced when the association was organized . . . it has already set nearly one thousand trees, and stands ready to furnish at simple cost as many more as their fellow-citizens may desire to use for public or private decoration. [11]

Sutliffe lists twelve people who own *"substantial elegant houses,"* and concludes with this architecturally ambiguous statement: *"The professors of the university live in different neighborhoods. They are all well housed, and in much the same style as regards cottage architecture and floral environment."* Sadly, he does not define *"cottage architecture"* or *"floral environment."* [12]

Frederick Law Olmsted Inspires a Garden Suburb

As mentioned, Olmsted's earlier plan for the Berkeley Property tract, to be sited on the eastern slope adjacent to the university campus property, was laid out for the Trustees of the College of California in 1865. The plan as adopted from Olmsted's 1865 map provided for gracious streets designed to follow along the natural contours of the hillside. Surprisingly, his 1866 report *Berkeley Neighborhood: Report upon the Projected Improvement of the Estate of the College of California at Berkeley, Near Oakland* was published in both New York and San Francisco and thus attracted a large audience. [13] Olmsted elucidated principles for his first residential plan, which became his design trademarks. He did not restrict himself to landscaping: a subdivision should be integrated with a park or public spaces (in the case of Berkeley, the university campus); lots should be ample to encourage large homes behind *"garden set backs"*; and a central divided *"parkway with overbowering trees"* should create a natural setting for the *"comings and goings."* To meet the last requirement, he laid out the 100-foot width of Piedmont Way as it exists today, a divided road with trees in the median as well as on the sides (recently designated a California State Historical Landmark, Site #986).

Olmsted's ideas were still alive in 1881, when Sutliffe wrote about the 1880 Village Improvement Society's planting of a thousand trees, and added: *"[Olmsted] preferred such division and ornamentation as would preserve the natural features and flowing outlines of the place, a plan that has since been somewhat varied."* [14]

The Hillside Club, formally established in 1898 but conceived by Maybeck and Keeler in 1895, derived many of its ideas and goals from Olmsted, who had written in his 1866 report:

It is desirable that scholars at least during the period of life in which character is most easily moulded, should be surrounded by manifestations of refined domestic life, these being unquestionably the ripest and best fruits of civilization. The first requirement of a plan for the improvement of the locality is that it should present sufficient inducements to the formation of a neighborhood of refined and elegant homes in the immediate vicinity of the principal College Buildings. [15]

To quote from Lesley Emmington's introduction to the Berkeley Architectural Heritage Association's 1995 brochure:

. . . [Olmsted's] task, therefore, was to create not only a campus . . . but also . . . a residential community directly adjacent . . . that would be suitably pleasant, enjoyable, healthful, and tranquil to serve the needs of faculty, staff and students. Shelter was a given, but sunlight and fresh air were also important and were "indispensable to the preservation of health and cheerfulness". . . . Private living spaces should be set into good neighborhoods with common roads and walks, gentle, safe and pleasant to use, protected from mid-day sun with "an overarching bower of foliage." Olmsted's plan advocated curvilinear streets that followed the natural contours of the land, connected to the campus by "shaded roads" and "tree-lined lanes."[16]

Perhaps Worcester helped keep Olmsted's ideas alive. In any case, many in his circle shared his belief that architecture should reflect and enhance the natural environment, beliefs that must have been fortified by his experience with old barns, cabins at Yosemite, and buildings such as Henry Hobson Richardson's Ames Gate Lodge (1881), where medieval ideals from Ruskin and Morris fuse with Japanese temple forms. Richardson perhaps acquired from his collaboration with Olmsted, begun in the 1860s, his interest in bouldered walls, Japanese gardens, and rustic buildings. The lodge especially, with its massive boulder walls, connects with nature. In it Richardson incorporated inglenook seats on each side of the fireplace, sculpture by Augustus Saint Gaudens, and Persian blue glass tile by Tiffany over the mantel, all inside an asymmetrical, dynamic composition.[17]

Fig. 7.1: Berkeley hills before the construction of houses, ca. 1900.

As noted, Maybeck and Keeler undoubtedly knew Olmsted's Village of Riverside outside Chicago, planned by 1869, and English garden suburbs such as Shaw's design of Bedford Park, William Lever's Port Sunlight (1888), Burnham (and Worcester's?) interest in The City Beautiful

(ca. 1892), and probably the term *garden city* introduced by Ebenezer Howard in his 1898 book.

The conservation of such spectacularly beautiful natural settings as the California hills was a common concern of Americans in the late-nineteenth and early-twentieth centuries (Fig. 7.1). Hillside Club members were particularly farsighted in seeing the necessity to complement the environment and to create a road system and architecture that would suit it.[18]

Charles Keeler was more than a missionary; he was a well-educated and informed naturalist, artist, writer, and poet. He loved his house, the Berkeley hills, and the aesthetic and architectural principles that had united them. He visualized other houses like his own in the undeveloped cul-de-sac of Highland Place. Maybeck, too, wanted to see its qualities preserved, and he encouraged Keeler to persuade neighborhood newcomers to build homes of materials in harmony with his house rather than painted Victorians. Soon Keeler reported, *"It was not long before we found families to agree to buy the lots surrounding us and have Mr. Maybeck design their homes."* Together the friends aimed for a cohesive neighborhood architectural style, a goal that reflected their farsighted interest in environmental planning.[19]

Albert Cicero Schweinfurth: Rustic Buildings and the Hillside Club

The reputation Daley's Scenic Park had for picturesque and artistic houses was enhanced by the Volney D. Moody house built at 1725 (now 1755) Le Roy Avenue from November 1896 into 1897 (Fig. 7.2). It was designed by the talented, volatile, and elusive architect Albert C. Schweinfurth (1864–1900), who had trained with the well-known Boston firm Peabody and Stearns, worked as a draftsman in A. Page Brown's New York office, and then worked independently in New York and Denver, where he insulted his patrons and left in a huff. Schweinfurth eventually rejoined Brown in San Francisco, about late 1892 or early 1893.[20]

As noted in Chapter 3, by February 1894 Schweinfurth had left Brown to set up his own independent practice, having obtained a very major client early that year—William Randolph Hearst (see Chapter 10). Thereafter, Hearst seems to have been responsible for all of Schweinfurth's other commissions with the possible exceptions of the James Ward house and the First Unitarian Church.[21]

Upon arriving in San Francisco, Schweinfurth's work changed radically. Designs for the Mission-Moorish Style California Building for the 1893 Exposition in Chicago were probably completed before his arrival (Brown was announced the winner on February 12, 1892). The 1893 California Building was such a success that buildings for the San Francisco Midwinter Exposition in Mission, Moorish, Egyptian, and Mediterranean styles were underway by November 1893.[22] As we see from drawings he exhibited in the First Annual Exhibition of the San Francisco Chapter of the AIA held in early 1894, Schweinfurth was not immune to these influences.[23]

Schweinfurth's drawings included *Winter Residence at Santa Barbara* (1894) *". . . of a most interesting design . . . in line with a style of architecture thoroughly characteristic of California and something of which we should see more,"* and a design for a proposed hotel near Montalvo (1894) in the "pueblo style."[24] These two proposed project drawings represented a major shift in Schweinfurth's style. One cannot help asking what caused this change, especially since anyone examining Schweinfurth's Denver work would have to agree with Carol Louise Calavan, who remarks: *". . . the Denver residence was unimaginative in its interpretation and bore none of the visual impact so noticeable in the architect's later California work."* [25]

Several things impelled Schweinfurth to seek inspiration in the California missions and Southwest pueblos: moving to California; seeing (and possibly assisting with?) the 1892 competition drawings for the California Building in Chicago (drawings for which were required to be in the Mission-Moorish style; see Chapter 10) and assisting with drawings for the San Francisco Midwinter Exposition in the various styles just mentioned. Most important was his meeting William Randolph Hearst, who wanted something very Californian and unique for his Hacienda del Pozo de Verona. In addition, interacting with Worcester, Polk, Maybeck, and Coxhead, and seeing their California Shingle rustic buildings, could have provided the impetus that attracted Schweinfurth to the increasingly popular Arts & Crafts rustic shingled style, which he then beautifully adapted for the Bradford house in San Francisco and for the First Unitarian Church (Fig. 7.7) in Berkeley.

Inexplicably, right in the middle of his greatest financial success, having designed exciting buildings that received acclaim, and after completing the Moody house, Schweinfurth left for Europe in 1898, while the First Unitarian Church was still under construction. He died in 1900, almost immediately upon his return to the United States. [26]

Fig. 7.2: Historic view of Volney D. Moody house, "Weltevreden," 1725 (now 1755) Le Roy Avenue, Berkeley (1896–97), by A. C. Schweinfurth. The principal entrance was from the garden, over the bridge spanning the creek, to the elevated verandah.

Dutch and Arts & Crafts Influences in Schweinfurth's Work

Keeler describes how Volney D. Moody and his son-in-law E. S. Gray came to visit the Keeler home, *"and we persuaded them to join our group. They had already picked another architect, Mr. Schweinfurth, to design a "Dutch" house for them."* [27]

In November 1896, the *Berkeley Daily Advocate* reported that contracts were signed for a house *"in the Flemish style, of brick . . . and the entrance will be in the rear . . . over a bridge spanning a creek."*[28]

Their desire for a "Dutch" house would seem to explain the stepped gable ends of this house and its name "Weltevreden' (Fig. 7.2), the Dutch equivalent of the German *wohlzufrieden,* meaning "well satisfied." Instead of the neighborhood's predominant brown shingle, Schweinfurth used a charred "clinker" brick, which *"was the redwood shingle's textural counterpart in masonry."*[29]

Sensitive to the environment, Schweinfurth faced an open loggia, raised above the ground to the first-floor level toward a stream on the property, and added a bridge. (Raised first-floor veran-dahs, or *stoeps,* also appear in South African Cape Dutch architecture [Fig. 7.3].) The choice of brick for the exterior and the paneled and beamed interior is said to have reflected the architect's touch; however, his client, a former banker, clearly had the resources necessary to pay for a brick house and gold leaf.[30]

> *In the living room an application of Florence leaf will be made, producing an effect of iri-descent gold between the beams, . . . In the dining room the ceiling beams are left rough, without planing, and are painted a dull, dead blue without gloss, while the plaster panels between are in a reddish tone of gold.*[31]

Further research reveals possible English and South African sources for the so-called "Dutch" characteristics at Weltevreden. Dutch gables can be seen on brick houses at Collingham Gardens SW, London (1885), by Ernest George and Harold Peto; at Redroofs, Streatham Common (1888); and at the Edwin Long house, Hampstead (1888), by R. Norman Shaw.[32]

Although the Moody house gable steps down at right angles in the classic Amsterdam man-ner, many English and South African Cape Dutch gables step down with curves. In addition to the

Fig. 7.3: Schweinfurth may have been influenced by South African Cape Dutch architecture such as this house known as Tokai near Capetown, architect unknown. It features a *stoep,* or verandah, raised above ground level with stout non-tapered columns. Both details appear at Schweinfurth's Moody house.

raised *stoep,* two other Cape Dutch features might have provided inspiration: both the Moody house and Cape Dutch houses feature entrance halls that bisect the entire house, front to back, to allow cross drafts. In many Cape Dutch houses, the living room, dining room, and hall often feature mammoth horizontal beams, as does the Moody house: *"The interior features* [of the Moody house] . . . *will be its open and exposed construction."*[33] However, in South Africa the beams are not painted as at the Moody house. In South Africa, Indonesia, and other former Dutch colonies, houses and towns still retain the name "Weltevreden," so it is difficult to know from which country Moody, Gray, and Schweinfurth took inspiration.[34]

A contemporary account of the Moody house implied more than *"mere slavish adherence to drawings made in an office."* Schweinfurth *"selected the bricks for the brick layer with his own hands and indeed often laid them himself to prove that the work could be done as he intended,"* as did Worcester at the Swedenborgian Church (1894) as well as Charles Sumner Greene and Henry Mather Greene at the Thorsen house (1908–10).[35]

After settling in California, Schweinfurth introduced stout, non-tapered columns into his work. He may have seen Brown's 1894 design for George Roe's Mission-Mediterranean-inspired house, where thick untapered columns flank the entrance; or perhaps he helped create that design. In any case, he used them effectively on the Moody house verandah (1896–97) (Fig. 7.2), on the sketch for a hotel near Montalvo (1894), as well as at the Hacienda del Pozo de Verona (late 1894–96) (Figs. 7.5, 10.12, 10.13). Perhaps inspired by the Swedenborgian Church, where trees with their bark left on support the roof (1893–95), Schweinfurth used actual tree trunks, bark and all, as porch columns for the James Bradford house in San Francisco (1896) and for the First Unitarian Church in Berkeley (1897–98) (Fig. 7.7).

The First Unitarian Church maintained the rustic shingled look. The church membership included several architecturally sophisticated individuals: Maybeck and his client-friends J. S. Bunnell, Clifford McGrew, and Charles Keeler; along with Allen Freeman, Coxhead's client; the Volney Moodys, Oscar Maurers, and other members of the Hillside Club, including the Warren

Fig. 7.4: Stepped gables that may have inspired A. C. Schweinfurth, E. S. Gray, and Volney D. Moody can be seen in the Dutch Colonies, including South Africa (as at Groot Schuur, Capetown, South Africa, architect unknown, shown here) as well as in Holland, and were also visible in nineteenth-century English architecture.

Fig. 7.4

Fig. 7.5

Fig. 7.5: Hacienda del Pozo de Verona, Sunol, California, by A. C. Schweinfurth. Begun in 1894, the hacienda was built for William Randolph Hearst. The thick, untapered columns and tile roofs suggest a Mediterranean source while the projecting downspouts, small windows, and white boxy shapes recall Native American pueblos of the Southwest.

Fig. 7.6: Schweinfurth designed the hacienda with low ceilings to emphasize the rooms' horizontality.

Fig. 7.6

Fig. 7.7: A. C. Schweinfurth designed this stunning "big gable" façade for the First Unitarian Church, Berkeley (1897–98). He placed one redwood tree trunk column at each end of the gable, creating a balanced symmetrical, yet rustic façade.

Gregorys, who were close friends of Worcester's and became clients and friends of John Galen Howard.[36] It is likely that several of these people knew and admired the Swedenborgian Church, and some may have influenced the First Unitarian Church's design.[37]

E. S. Gray, a prominent member of the congregation, who Longstreth tells us hired Schweinfurth to design his father-in-law's house—the Volney Moody house (Fig. 7.2)—asked Schweinfurth to prepare plans for the First Unitarian Church *"before an architect had been officially chosen."* Maybeck could have contributed ideas in 1897, but in 1898 he was in Europe, supervising the University of California, Berkeley's international competition; however, Worcester and other friends remained in the area and could possibly have had input. Gray superintended construction of the building while Schweinfurth was in Europe.[38]

The First Unitarian church is a masterpiece of the Arts & Crafts Movement in California . . .
a rare nonresidential use of the rustic, handcrafted, open-beamed redwood "back to nature"
style. . . . In the center of the symmetrical west façade is a large circular window twelve feet in
diameter and glazed with amber glass set in an industrial metal sash frame.[39]

Schweinfurth created a simple yet elegant façade using only rustic materials: sawtooth-cut shingles edge the top of the circular window and then step outward toward the two entrance porches. One sturdy redwood tree trunk column with its bark left on supports each end of the descending gable, creating two matching, deeply recessed porches in a balanced symmetrical composition (Fig. 7.7). In his excellent article entitled "The Big Gable," Richard Guy Wilson mentions many architects designing big gables from the 1880s on.[40]

Schweinfurth's shallow-gabled, triangular façade is similar to "big gables" such as Frank Mead's "Nest" and to John Calvin Stevens' "House by the Sea" (Fig. 7.8), which were well known at that time and which Schweinfurth would have seen illustrated in the *American Architect,* for which he had worked in 1880.[41] Closer to home, inspiration might have come from Coxhead's churches with shingled, gabled façades bisected by a large round window (Monterey, Fig. 5.7;

San Francisco, Fig. 3.6), but they did lack the crisp, sharp edges of Schweinfurth's gable. In Monterey Coxhead decorated the section over the door with sawtooth-cut shingles, a small detail but interestingly one that Schweinfurth also used at the First Unitarian Church.

Both Maybeck and Schweinfurth remind us that wood used in buildings comes from living trees, and they sometimes featured the tree bark itself. As noted, Schweinfurth left the bark on his tree-trunk columns at the Bradford house (1896) and at the First Unitarian Church (1898) (Fig. 7.7). Maybeck exposed tree bark for the ceiling of at least one room in Wyntoon, the medieval-inspired country lodge he designed for Phoebe A. Hearst (1902–3), and created a tree house for the 1904 Bohemian club, of which he was a member from 1899 to his death. There, historian Sally Woodbridge tells us that *"bundled tree trunks rise through the deck floor from the building's base where diagonal braces are concealed behind the redwood-bark slabs."*[42] In his own 1892 house, *"the timbers showed on the inside and the walls were of knotted yellow pine planks. There was no 'finish' to the interior . . ."*[43]

Maybeck also left the chamfering visible on the wood beams in the Wallen Maybeck house living room (Figs. 7.9, 7.10), and painted the chamfering gray on the J. H. Senger house porch (1907–8; Bayview Place, Berkeley) to set it off from the blue trim.[44]

All these buildings followed the Swedenborgian Church, which may have provided inspiration; however, the idea might also derive from Japanese buildings, which often use unbarked trees as posts; or from vernacular mountain cabins, or from the Adirondack camps with their twig balconies and split-log siding, several of which had been built by the 1890s. In addition, art historian John Arthur points out that Maybeck, while working at the Ponce de Leon Hotel (1886–88), would

Fig. 7.8: Architect John Calvin Stevens' "House by the Sea" was among the many "big gables" being designed from the mid-1880s that inspired Schweinfurth's design for the First Unitarian Church. (Published in *American Architect and Building News* 18, September 12, 1885.)

Fig. 7.9

Fig. 7.9: Wallen Maybeck
house, 2751 Buena Vista
(1932–33), by Bernard
Maybeck. Note the flat boards
framing the balconies, an inexpensive solution to balusters.

Fig. 7.10: Wallen Maybeck
house, view: living room. Note
the emphasis on the rugged
chamfered beams, gently arched
as were the trees in the
Swedenborgian Church.

Fig. 7.10

certainly have seen the artists studios just behind the hotel where "palm columns" with their bark left on support the porch. Arthur adds, *"the rail is set into the trunks rather than nailed to them, which is a detail commonly seen in Japanese temples and shrines and vernacular architecture in almost every country, including the interiors and exteriors of Scandinavian churches."*[45]

In summary, Schweinfurth preferred stout, non-tapered columns with the defined and more regular round shape of a tree's trunk rather than the jig-jag irregularity of a tree's limb seen at the Swedenborgian Church, and used such massive columns repeatedly, smooth or shaggy bark, from his first work in California.[46]

At the First Unitarian Church, Schweinfurth followed the domestic precedent set by the Swedenborgian Church and included a fireplace. However, he used plastered walls without any wainscoting, and colored them deep red *"to give a rich and subdued effect."*[47]

Rough-hewn ships knees transfer weight from the ceiling's massive horizontal beams *"stained dark brown"* to the vertical posts between each arched, multipaned, industrial sash window.[48]

Even in the First Unitarian Church (Figs. 7.11–7.13) where he might have wanted to suggest aspiration, and where vertical beams support the peaked gable, the overall effect is horizontal, as it was in the Hacienda del Pozo de Verona (Figs. 7.5, 7.6; see also chapter 10). Apparently Schweinfurth did not approve of *"architectural soaring"* or even arching, preferring rooms that had a *"pervasive horizontality."*[49] We see this aversion expressed in Schweinfurth's letter to Hearst:

> *In considering the* [hacienda] *designs I submit I ask you to bear in mind the extremely low ceilings which prohibit any architectural "soaring" and this consideration has governed me in the choice of breadth of effect. . . .*[50]

His ceilings are more massive than light, more flat than arched, similar to heavy-beamed ceilings found in mission churches such as Asistencia of Pala, a branch chapel of the Mission of San Luis Rey.[51] Schweinfurth's masterpiece (since the hacienda's destruction) synthesizes Hillside Club goals with his own creativity; the result startles and delights to this day.[52]

Women Activists and the Garden Suburb

Site planning, a respect for craftsmanship, and artistic taste continued to be explicit goals in developing Daley's Scenic Park, which included several streets around Highland Place. The success of this neighborhood and a deepening interest in the ideals of William Morris and the Arts & Crafts movement encouraged the energetic Keeler to forge ahead with community plans. Continuing the Arts & Crafts interests of his friends Worcester, Maybeck, Coxhead, and Lummis, he founded the Handicraft Guild in Berkeley in 1898, the same year the Berkeley Hillside Club was organized.

California's vernacular architecture was not the only craftsman-produced architecture to play a large part in determining characteristics of the "simple" home. As we have seen, vernacular buildings from many countries, including English, Scandinavian, German, and Swiss, provided inspiration. For example, in 1890–91 *Architectural News* published a large illustration of a rustic, humble cottage in Kenley, England, with a thatched roof and what appear to be shingled sides, drawn by Henry L. Merritt of San Francisco.[53]

Fig. 7.11

Fig. 7.12

Fig. 7.13

In *The Simple Home*, Keeler encouraged emulation of European vernacular: *"For general types of architecture, the Swiss Chalet, old English, old Nuremberg, old Italian, and old Spanish homes may be studied for suggestion and inspiration."* However, Keeler emphasized that style is not important as long as the home is *"adapted to the climate, the landscape, and the life in which it is to serve its part."*[54]

Women activists formalized the Hillside Club to make sure the ideas expounded by Keeler and Maybeck reached a wider audience. To bring pressure to bear upon city government, the men who had originated the ideas were asked to join. These included Maybeck, Almeric Coxhead (Ernest's brother and partner), Keeler, residents of Keeler's neighborhood, and upon his arrival, John Galen Howard.[55] The members' goal, as stated by Keeler, was *"to carry out through a formal club what we had been attempting to do informally in persuading a neighborhood to adopt the Maybeck principles in architecture."*[56]

Similarly, in late 1893 a group of women under the leadership of Miss Tessa L. Kelso of the Los Angeles Public Library started to raise funds to repair the California missions; when they decided they needed help, they approached the energetic Charles F. Lummis (Fig. 7.14), and by 1894 he was actively planning the Landmarks Club, which was dedicated to restoring and preserving California's crumbling missions.[57]

One of the women active in organizing the Hillside Club was Margaret Robinson, daughter of Mrs. Mary Robinson Moody of the Moody house. In June 1899 Robinson's article in the widely read *House Beautiful* publicized designs for, and theories behind, the northern California simple home designed with nature in mind, and demonstrated the major role women played in the Garden Suburb affordable housing movement.[58] Of course Berkeley was not a totally planned garden suburb; but the Hillside Club was influenced by the movement and adapted many of its ideas. Berkeley can be called a garden suburb in the sense that a group of like-minded citizens cooperated to ensure a new kind of town; their goals were cultural, social, political, as well as architectural. They advocated buildings that would fit into the landscape as well as roads that would maintain the hilly contours of the land.

The Hillside Problem

The suburban home all about this glorious bay of ours has for its resting-place, with but few exceptions, the foothill. Our cities have barely room for their busy centers on the level strips that frame the bay, before the land begins its higher sweep from rise to rise, until the nature-lover, the home-lover, the peace-lover, seeks the hillside against which, or upon which, to rest his hearthstone.

Fig. 7.11 (facing): First Unitarian Church, Bancroft Way, Berkeley (1897–98); view: for the sanctuary of the church, Schweinfurth chose arched rather than rectangular windows, and used industrial sash.

Fig. 7.12 (facing): First Unitarian Church, view: interior of the sanctuary, looking toward the round window.

Fig. 7.13 (facing): Schweinfurth had the rugged ceiling beams and ships knees in the church sanctuary stained dark brown.

Fig. 7.14 (left): Charles F. Lummis in 1889, titled *The Southwesterner,* photographer unknown.

But O, such hearthstones! Such blots on the fair sides of green slopes as menace the eye! And why? Because home builders have not yet awakened to the truth that hillside-building is an art in itself; that however pretty or "freshly painted" the town house may be, it becomes an enormity when transplanted and placed as a part of the contour of the hilly landscape.

Any lover of the beautiful knows what a source of irritation and misery this thoughtlessness proves to be.

One looks toward God's everlasting hills for rest and peace; but where can rest and peace be found, so long as our portion of these, God's hills, is scarred with such unhealthy growths, such freaks of houses?

Let us admit, then, here and now, that the suburban hillside home is a problem, and set ourselves bravely and heartily to solve it. There is one general principle given us from which to start; the principle read in the harmony and symmetry of Nature about us. She offers herself with all her grace and color as background. If we but come in touch with the spirit she suggests, the harmony of outline, the soft tints and shades,—if we but love and understand her and her teachings, we cannot go far astray. . . .

Should the knoll be the first site chosen for consideration from our new point of view, a moments's thought will discover that, as the hill itself spreads and broadens at its base, so the ground-construction of our edifice should be distributed squarely and well over the surface of the level, its base distinguished by a breadth more generous than is given to the upper portion.

Pronounced height should be avoided; but the outline of the roof must be so composed as to continue the contour line of the hill.

The side-hill site may admit of more than one solution; but in most instances the broad side of the house should greet the eye, with well-grounded spread of base. Half way up, or even nearer the top it may have ventures, but once finding its niche, it should establish itself broadly and with firm foothold. Even in case the town road passes on either side, do not let your structure turn to look, and thereby imperil its position. As long as the hill sweeps upward and beyond, Nature's broad background should be trusted, and the house should rest closely and expansively against it.

But here there has been no climbing. This home is less venturesome and would rest at the foot of the hill. Then be sure it does rest, close against the rise behind it; the sweep of garden invitingly in front, the broad, pleasant face of the home one's first welcome up the garden path. . . .

Much more might be said about this natural adjustment to the locality chosen—about such interesting and important details as color and materials. But it is enough to utter here an earnest plea for better building, for a return to the spirit of nature about us, which should be our inspiration and our delight.

Civic Action Mandates Rusticity and Domesticity

Between 1898 and 1900 three public buildings reflecting the influence of the Hillside Club were built in Berkeley: a schoolhouse, a church, and a civic clubhouse. Common to the design of each was the unusual use of domestic features such as fireplaces and rustic materials, a precedent already set by the Swedenborgian Church. One of these Berkeley buildings influenced by citizen action was the Hillside School in the vicinity of Highland Place.[59] Mrs. Frank Morton Todd, a charter member of the Hillside Club and wife of the editor of San Francisco's daily *Argonaut*, gave a vigorous and amusing account of citizen participation in the design of the Hillside School, *"built after Hillside Club plans"*:

The Trustees of the Town of Berkeley decided the growing district north of the campus needed a primary school. So they bought a lot on the southwest corner of Le Roy and Virginia. The school was to be a conventional two story building. Now there was a group of women who had a study club in this district and they didn't want that kind of a school house. So they got busy. They appointed a committee to go to the Trustees and ask to be allowed to plan a school suited to little children and the hillside. They promised it would not cost the city anything extra. They had already a sketch by an architect of such a building and knew it could be managed. The Trustees agreed but made them promise they would pay anything over and above the original plan. So a very charming one-story school house was built, the Hillside School; (once built, the Club also held its meetings there).[60]

In his 1901 article entitled "Art in America," Keeler reported that the school was *"notable for its homelike interior, its large open fireplaces, and its quaint relief from the humdrum lines of public buildings."*[61] Covered with shingles and finished on the interior with unpainted redwood, the school complemented the Highland Place homes.

The First Unitarian Church by Schweinfurth and the Hillside School were nonresidential buildings reflecting Hillside Club ideals. The Town and Gown Club of 1899 (Figs. 7.15, 7.16) completed the trilogy of *public* buildings exemplifying the growth of a community-based aesthetic ideal.

Fig. 7.15: Town and Gown Club, 2401 Dwight Way, Berkeley (1899), by Bernard Maybeck, who used outrigger brackets on the shingled exterior of the club as well as on the Rieger house (1899).

Fig. 7.16: The Town and
Gown Club features two rows
of wooden posts and novel
lighting. The posts are slightly
askew intentionally, making
the room memorable. This
was perhaps part of the
"game" of architecture that
was also played by Lutyens
and Baillie Scott.

Maybeck designed the Town and Gown Club soon after his return from an extensive trip to Europe, where he had been exposed to a wide variety of materials and designs; he used native wood inside and out. A contemporary newspaper account remarked on the *" '. . . severe simplicity' of the perfectly plain, flat-roofed wooden building, whose shingle covered exterior was enlivened only by pronounced L-shaped outrigger roof bracketing."* The same year he used outrigger bracketing on William Rieger's house.[62]

The sole decorative elements inside were the richness of the wood, the rhythm and pitch of the post-and-beam supports, and the glow of light above them from lightbulbs hidden behind pieces of amber-colored glass.

The Town and Gown Club may be regarded as part of an attempt to join the campus and the city in an architectural and environmental scheme. As the University of California embarked on an extensive plan for the development of its campus, the Hillside group turned its attention to plans for the environment and architecture of the north Berkeley hills. Having motivated some residents to choose site-sensitive architecture, they now wanted to ensure its success by involving the total community.

Streets That Can't be Unwound, Trees That Must be Accommodated

The Hillside Club made its views on neighborhood planning known through yearly suggestion pamphlets and membership activities. By 1902 its influential members included leading spokesmen for the area's artistic and architectural community.[63]

As early as 1898, in an article entitled "What the Club Advocates," the Hillside Club's Advisory Board recommended *"that hillside streets be made convenient and beautiful by winding at an easy grade,"* resembling *"narrow country roads or lanes, except in case of important thoroughfares."*[64] Underlying this plan was the Club's conviction that local topography must be conserved. Specific proposals presented in their 1906–7 pamphlet show both an indebtedness to Olmsted and some original solutions:

Roads should follow contour lines. . . . The steep parts can be handled in various ways, terraced in two levels as on Hearst Avenue, divided into narrow ways for driving with footpaths above and below and connecting steps for pedestrians. [65]

Today many streets of north Berkeley are terraced in two levels, following contour lines and preserving natural landmarks, all thanks to the Hillside Club's concerned activism typified by another of Mrs. Todd's lively anecdotes:

When Cedar Street was cut through just like a city street (straight) there was great consternation! Down to the Town Hall to protest to the Trustees. It seemed the Trustees were annoyed and said, "No, they wouldn't plan the new streets as winding roads following the contours of the hills." The women [of the Hillside Club] *were stopped for a short time. They decided to call on the men for help—invited them to a meeting at night. That's the reason we have those lovely winding roads. They are winding all right and they can't be unwound.* [66]

In its first year (1898), the Hillside Club also advocated that *"the trees be planted the length of streets suitable to the locality and of uniform variety."* [67] When some streets were planned without regard to trees, members unleashed strong rhetoric to defend all natural landmarks—in this case, trees:

Fig. 7.17: Rose Walk, a public pedestrian walkway connecting Euclid and Le Roy, was designed by Bernard Maybeck and completed in 1913 with donations from the neighbors. Classically styled, it consists of stairways, terraces, balustrades, benches, walls, and planters built of pink and grey concrete. Henry Gutterson designed the houses bordering the walk (1923–26).

Fig. 7.18: This historic photograph shows Le Roy Street bisected by the California oak that Annie Maybeck saved from destruction.

The few native trees that have survived centuries of fire and flood lived because they had chosen the best places. They should be jealously preserved. Bend the road, divide the lots, place the houses to accommodate them![68]

In much the same tone William Morris had pleaded for the preservation of trees in nineteenth-century England:

What do you do with the trees on a site that is going to be built over? Do you try to save them? Do you understand what treasures they are in a town or suburb?[69]

An anecdote reveals the Hillside Club's activism. One day Annie Maybeck came upon workmen preparing to fell an oak tree in the middle of Le Roy Avenue. She persuaded them to wait until she and one or two other women hitched up a horse and drove to city hall to plead with the authorities to save the tree. They were successful and the tree was saved (Fig. 7.18). In the 1980s, after the tree had died, the city planted a young oak to replace it.[70]

Hillside Architecture Is Landscape Gardening

Like Raymond Unwin and Barry Parker in England, Hillside Club members did not think it necessary or desirable to line up houses facing the street.[71] Rather, such factors as sunlight, view, and topography should be decisive in determining each house's placement.[72]

Charles Keeler, in the Hillside Club's 1901 pamphlet, suggested a slight variation from the routine frontal alignment of houses to the street. He wrote:

Fig. 7.19 **Fig. 7.20**

Fig. 7.19: Tufts house, 2733
Buena Vista, Berkeley (1931),
by Bernard Maybeck. This
sharply peaked gable, which
protrudes forward and embraces
a floor to ceiling window
divided into small panes, recalls
Maybeck's 1905 pastel drawing
for the Hillside Club entrance.
(Drawing in EDA: Maybeck
Collection, illustrated in *The Arts
and Crafts Life in California:
Living the Good Life.*)

Fig. 7.20: Tufts house, view:
the exposed ceiling structure
and interior half-timbering
that provide decorative detail.

*If a block had six lots fronting a street, the houses on the other two corners might be placed
forward and the other four backward on the lot, making a hollow square in front, to be
treated in effect like one garden.*[73]

Rectangular lots were difficult and considered undesirable. Maybeck used these assumptions
to divide the large tract of land his wife, Annie, bought in the Berkeley hills along what is now
Buena Vista Way. The land parcels, portioned out along the contour-regulated road, were
pie-shaped and pentagonal, at different angles to each other and to the street. The random effect
can still be seen along Buena Vista above La Loma Avenue.

Club pamphlets quoted Maybeck's Beaux-Arts master, Jules André, *"the great Landscape
Architect,"* in support of their views: *"never take away what is there, . . . but group it in with what
you add to it."* And they added, *"Hillside Architecture is Landscape Gardening around a few
rooms for use in case of rain."*[74]

The Hillside Club also printed a statement by Bruce Price, the New York architect responsible for the combination Shingle Style–Queen Anne house built in San Francisco in 1885,[75] stressing color as the first consideration when designing a house to complement the land:

*The California hills are brown, therefore, the house should be brown. Redwood is the nat-
ural wood of the country, therefore, it is natural to use it. A house should not stand out in
a landscape, but should fit in with it. This is the first principle that should govern the
design of every house.*[76]

More specific suggestions for fitting the house organically to its hillside site were offered in
subsequent pamphlets:

Fig. 7.21: Fairbanks house, 149 Tamalpais, Berkeley (built between 1906 and 1909), architect unknown; altered in 1921 for Chester Rowell by John Hudson Thomas. This house was built for Professor Harold and Bertha Fairbanks, members of Hillside Club. Rough textured boulders and oversized shingles enhance the rustic appeal of this façade.

Fig. 7.22: Fairbanks house, view: the irregularities of the projecting beam end, rugged stucco wall, and tree all complement each other.

Fig. 7.22

124 BUILDING WITH NATURE

Once the lot is bought, use what is there. Avoid cutting into the hill; avoid filling up the hollow. The man who wants a flat lot does not belong on the hillside. Build around the hill on contour lines, or step the house up against the hill, one story above and back of the other. The correctly planned hillside house is parallel not perpendicular to the slope. It avoids the wind by hugging the hill, is firm and enduring because braced against it.[77]

The Hillside Club issued recommendations for building houses and published these simultaneously with environmental plans from 1898 on. The following points are of particular interest: first, that *"only natural materials . . . such as shingles, shakes, rough stone or klinker brick"* be used; second, that *"no oil paint be used inside or out"* because *"no colors are so soft, varied and harmonious as those of wood colored by the weather"*; third, that trimmings are unnecessary but if used should be treated with *"dull brown paint"*; fourth, that a wood house should *"follow straight lines"* that are appropriate to the material; fifth, *"that over-hanging eaves add to the beauty of a house with their long shadows and help to protect it"*; sixth, that *"inside furnishings should be simple"* and built in, and should be included in the architect's plans; seventh, that *"hinged windows, swinging out, are cheaper, more picturesque and afford uninterrupted view,"* curtained with *"denam [sic], burlap, Oriental cotton crepes or crash toweling."* For further suggestions, the club recommended a conference with its Board of Directors.[78]

Keeler and the Arts & Crafts Simple Home

The culminating statement of the Hillside Club's aesthetic principle was Charles Keeler's book *The Simple Home.* Although the book was not published until 1904, Keeler had been expressing similar thoughts in Hillside Club brochures from 1898 on, and probably from his first meetings with Maybeck ca. 1891. Like the Hillside Club literature, this book did not dictate a particular outward form for the simple hillside home, but it did reflect Keeler's increasing knowledge of theories expressed by William Morris and John Ruskin as well as an understanding of the earlier English Gothicist A. W. N. Pugin (1812—1852) and of the French rationalist Viollet-le-Duc's ideals. As historian Robert M. Craig pointed out, *"Keeler expressed Viollet-inspired ideals when he wrote: 'Anything that tends to emphasize the constructive quality of the work enhances its value,' and later Keeler virtually quoted . . . Pugin in saying 'ornament should grow out of the construction.'"*[79]

As Keeler's and the Hillside Club library reveal, it is likely Keeler learned these ideas by reading and studying as well as by hearing them from Maybeck, Worcester, and his other architecturally oriented friends.

The Simple Home certainly advocated qualities and characteristics that had been constant in the genre since its earliest appearance in California in 1876. Indeed, passages from *The Simple Home* could apply to a description of Worcester's first house in Piedmont.

Keeler preferred interior and exterior walls, floors, and ceilings of wood. It should be used honestly, and when combined with another material such as plaster, the construction should be visible, not disguised as something else. Ornament should grow out of construction and should be inspired by animals and plants when possible rather than by slavish copying of European architecture. Keeler preferred the warm tones of redwood as a neutral background for furniture but also recommended undyed satin-finished burlap and Japanese grass cloth for wall coverings, and paintings chosen to harmonize with their setting. Furthermore, he wrote, the simple home should have masses of books because their ornamental value is heightened by the idea of culture that they embody. (As noted Keeler's house had a combination living room–library.)

As self-appointed spokesman for the simple home, Keeler developed a rationale similar to that being espoused in England by Arts & Crafts proponents, combining historical styles and some detail (preferably handmade) with a cultural concept of the simple home. He titled his book *The Simple Home* although he bowed to the growing popularity of pre-industrial European styles, and admitted that almost any "old" style could be adapted to simple California living as long as certain fundamentals were followed that tied the house to nature. The house was to be an artistic whole, which the Germans referred to as a *gesamtkunstwerk.* It was to uplift and inspire. Like Worcester, Maybeck, and the other followers of Morris and Ruskin, Keeler felt that modern materialism demanded unfair sacrifices: men became slaves to business to live ostentatiously. These adherents of this type of home advocated a simpler standard of living that allowed the entire family more time for art and culture, more time for family life. Like several English architects, including Voysey and Baillie Scott, they felt that people were ready for *"this idea of the simple home"* and that it was far more than a style; the Arts & Crafts house would inspire men of all classes to *"beauty and character."*[80]

Fig. 7.23: R. H. Mathewson house, 2704 Buena Vista, Berkeley (1916), by Bernard Maybeck.

John Galen Howard and "His Wizard" Continue Two Arts & Crafts Traditions

8

HAVING SEEN HIS FRIENDS FOLLOW HIS RUSSIAN HILL EXAMPLE ON HIGHLAND PLACE, Worcester set out to influence the University of California's architecture. The formal Beaux-Arts axial plan for the campus, chosen in international competition in 1899, differed greatly from the new Arts & Crafts tradition until Worcester went into action.

In the 1974 edition of *Building with Nature,* Elisabeth Sussman and I suggested that Worcester was intensely involved with the selection of John Galen Howard as architect for the university. Since that time, the role of Worcester and his friends has been generally accepted and further documented. Why Worcester lobbied for Boston architect John Galen Howard rather than for French architect and competition winner Émile Bénard, imbued with École des Beaux-Arts training, is a fascinating story.[1]

To attract Howard, Worcester wrote to him, apparently for the second or third time, reiterating his prior request that Howard come *"study the site."* Significantly, he includes himself (without any embarrassment) among the architects he wants Howard to study the site with: *"There is a little group of us, Polk, Coxhead, Porter, Faville and Bliss, who are still saying we wish you could come, study the site with us."*[2]

Worcester also met Émile Bénard, knew the latter's schedule, kept abreast of changes in the scheme, and apparently filled his "crowded" social schedule with opportunities to lobby against Bénard and for Howard. As he wrote his friend Professor Howison:

> *You will want to know how it stands with Bénard and the University Scheme. R.* [Reinstein, the regent who first opposed and then supported Maybeck's call for an international competition] *is at the Paget's getting the data for a modification of his scheme—to be worked up on his return to Paris.*[3]

Worcester's pleas on behalf of Howard worked, and when Howard moved to Berkeley in 1901, he wrote his wife that he saw Worcester, who

> *. . . has espoused my interests with ardor. Bruce Porter said, when I told him about the circumstances of my coming here, that he loved fairy stories . . . and believed this was all due*

to that wizard on the hill, that is to say, Mr. Worcester. I told you about his tiny perch crest-
ing Russian hill, did I not? I lunched there Monday. . . .[4]

Keeler's also mentions Worcester's role:

What finally determined the Regents in the selection of John Galen Howard to the post
of Professor of Architecture and Architect of the University Buildings was not made pub-
lic. His plans were among those winning prizes, but he was not second in line. Mr.
Howard was from New York with much prestige as an architect. Nevertheless to many of
us, who had fallen under the spell of Maybeck and a number of others of the young
architects of California—the Coxheads, Willis Polk, Schweinfurth, Julia Morgan,
Matthews and others—Howard's work seemed cold and formal, even though his person-
ality was gracious and charming.[5]

It was not long however, before even Mr. Howard, in the designing of homes at
least, fell under the spell of Maybeck's genius. The charm of open timber interiors, with
redwood surfaces, once discovered was too enticing to be resisted. When Mr. Howard
built a home for himself on a hill in North Berkeley, it had many qualities suggestive of
a Maybeckian influence.[6]

In her excellent book on the university's architecture, Sally Woodbridge describes Worcester
as the "wizard" responsible for bringing Howard to the University as dissatisfaction with the
notion that a "foreign" architect could design a "California" campus increased. Worcester may
also have been behind this change in attitude. Two years after Polk endorsed an international competition, he reversed course and declared that *"architecture suitable to California must lose its*
significance when poured through the academic sieve of the Beaux-Arts."[7]

While studying his opportunities at the university, Howard reported socializing with many of
Worcester's influential friends: the Maybecks, Bruce Porter, Coxhead, Bliss of Faville and Bliss,
Keeler, and Polk, and he added: *"The Reverend seemed to be present at every social occasion."*[8]

Merging European and Californian Arts & Crafts Traditions

How did Worcester's circle know Howard? From 1885 to 1886 Howard worked for Henry Hobson
Richardson, whose work Worcester documented in his scrapbooks. Both came from Boston, had
read Ruskin, admired Richardson, and had the courage to go west. In August 1887 Howard met
Polk and Coxhead in Los Angeles and together they sketched landscape, vegetation, abandoned
adobe houses, and missions. Howard maintained those friendships, and when Polk started
Architectural News in 1890, Howard wrote several articles for it about California's adobe buildings. Howard wrote his mother:

March 1888
They attract little enough attention and interest but to me they offer one of the greatest
charms of the place. There is a naturalness about them, a frank acknowledgement of their

limitations and an easy accomplishment of all possible effect within those limitations, a modest dignity in striking contrast to the "loudness" of the smart, pretentious, vulgar loudness of the mansions being built now. [9]

And about the San Fernando Mission:

March 15, 1888
Imagine a long, low rambling pile of a building of sturdy walls and naïve distribution of voids and solids, once whitened but now stained and enriched with warm yellows and browns and greens and falling into an almost unkempt decay—and all crowned with the soft, deep red of the hillocked tile lichened and weather beatened. . . . Behold the Mission! [10]

In the *American Architect* for May 5, 1888, Howard published an "Artist's Country House," with long low roofs sloping almost to the ground, drawn in 1887 while sketching the roofs of adobe buildings. His scheme seems to have been the first artist's house published, even before others by British architects.

Howard certainly knew McKim's interest in vernacular architecture (see Chapter 1), having worked for that firm in both Boston and New York. Moreover, he had lived in France and Italy from November 1888 to February, 1889 and later spent three years in Paris as a student at the École des Beaux-Arts (1890–93); thus he had seen firsthand the growing European interest in rustic vernacular buildings, peasant clothing, textiles, and other manifestations of handicrafts promoted by the Arts & Crafts movement; and subscribed to the *Architectural Review for the Artist & Craftsman.* [11]

About the same time or just after Howard's design was published, Voysey and other British architects began transforming the functional roof into art:

Voysey's method of making such forms artful was to emphasize, even exaggerate, them by eliminating ornament, by simplifying the forms themselves, and by stressing the natural textures of materials. The roof was given particular emphasis in the house as the most basic element in a building: functionally, it symbolized shelter; formally, it symbolized security. Steep dominant roofs became a primary characteristic of the Voysey, Baillie Scott and Arts and Crafts house. [12]

Thus, when it came time to dismiss Bénard and find a replacement, Polk and Coxhead knew that Howard, one of the winners, was the logical choice because he appreciated California's architectural past, its missions and old adobe structures, and that he was au courant with the European Arts & Crafts movement.

Worcester not only engineered Howard's selection, he also commented on his plans. Seeing Howard's proposal for the Hearst Memorial Mining Building (Fig. 8.1), submitted in late 1901, Worcester, the architectural critic, fired back, pinpointing what he thought should be changed:

In thinking of your front, I could wish that the three arched openings could be simplified to the very line, and the face of the one made quiet as possible; and then that all the vertical lines both front and side could spring from a platform so broad and simple that the building would seem to rest upon it. You must learn to take my suggestions in your own province well, as Mr. Keith takes them in his, as showing a friendly interest but not as embarrassing or interfering. [13]

Howard gave the university buildings "California" character with red tile roofs and, when freed from university constraints, designed in the rustic mode his friends advocated. Woodbridge describes the architecture department's building: "The Ark," clad in redwood shingles, was constructed in 1905–6; Howard was known as "Father Noah"; Phoebe A. Hearst donated many architecture books for the library; and President Wheeler wanted the department to influence California architecture. In 1904 Howard produced another brown shingle complex, Cloyne Court (Fig. 8.2), the first faculty apartment building, and before designing the Senior Men's Hall (1906) of 2,940 redwood logs, Howard, like his mentor, studied log cabins in the California mountains. [14]

Cloyne Court was a project of the University Land and Improvement Company, a development group, [15] and Howard was permitted (or encouraged?) to use brown shingles. Three redwood façades face a once lovely, once beautifully planted, sheltered courtyard. As Howard was well aware, Cloyne Court would have blended right in with the nearby partially shingled Beta Theta Pi fraternity house on Hearst Avenue (Fig. 5.11) that Coxhead had designed in 1893, as well as with the shingled houses Maybeck and others had designed for Highland Place, Ridge Road (Fig. 8.3), and elsewhere in Daley's Scenic Park.

These three shingled buildings reveal Howard's commitment to California's version of the Arts & Crafts as do the houses he designed. Shortly after 1902, Howard selected a lot near Highland Place and created a home, combining the rustic and Mission styles in an Arts & Crafts manner (Fig. 8.3). Its tiled roof and squared central tower were inspired by California's missions, and the redwood interiors by the Worcester group–Hillside Club tradition. The front door was an *"immense solid plank of redwood"* and

Fig. 8.1: "Formal presentation of Hearst Memorial Mining Building drawn in 1901–2," by John Galen Howard.

. . . the back of the house was clad in long redwood shingles laid in overlapping rows in which the bottom row extended about two inches below the row above, producing a deep shadow line . . . retaining walls of round river boulders contributed to a rustic look. . . . The living room was a grandly proportioned space with an exposed heavy timber ceiling that peaked above a mezzanine.[16]

Figs. 8.2: Cloyne Court, 2600 Ridge Road, Berkeley (1904), by John Galen Howard; view: garden courtyard.

Keeler enthusiastically praised this house:

Even Mr. Howard, in the designing of homes at least, fell under the spell of Maybeck's genius. The charm of open timber interiors, with redwood surfaces, once discovered was too enticing to be resisted. When Mr. Howard built a home for himself on a hill in North Berkeley, it had many qualities suggestive of a Maybeckian influence.[17]

Living rooms with balconies had been used in the Bay Area previously by Polk for the duplex house on Russian Hill (Fig. 2.9), by Walter J. Mathews in a house for Borax pioneer Francis Marion Smith, a house for which Maybeck designed the furniture, and perhaps by others.[18] Interestingly, Maybeck repeatedly used the balconied living room with an exposed timber ceiling throughout his practice; in fact, it might be considered one of his trademarks (e.g., houses for S. H. Erlanger, E. C. Young, and Charles Aikin [Figs. 8.4, 8.5]).

Rustic wooden cabins from the California countryside as well as knowledge of Worcester's two houses lie behind Howard's design of the Warren Gregory house (1903; expanded in 1906–7), which continued this eastern architect's conversion to the western "simple home" Arts & Crafts tradition.

The Gregorys, members of the Hillside Club and the Swedenborgian Church, were among Berkeley's most affluent citizens; yet in 1902 they commissioned Howard to build one of the city's

Fig. 8.3: John Galen Howard's own house, 2421 Ridge Road, Berkeley (1903). The tiled roof and campanile-like tower were inspired by California's missions.

simplest wooden houses on an enormous plot of land with a magnificent view (now Greenwood Terrace). They admired Worcester's manner of living, and their Berkeley home emulated Worcester's Piedmont house, which Jack London referred to as *"the bungalow with a capital B."* [19] When Worcester died in 1913, the Gregorys bought his Russian Hill house, perhaps as an expression of their admiration.

The Gregory house (Figs. 8.6, 8.7) was low-lying and seemingly foundationless, its brown shingles blending with the trees as if it were a spontaneous creation rather than an architect-designed house. A long verandah and patio extended the living and dining areas out of doors.

Howard designed a second house for the Gregorys (Figs. 8.8–8.10), with the understanding that the Howards would live there. Woodbridge quotes Janette Howard Wallace's 1987 memoir describing the luscious view and rural landscape surrounding them:

> *Warren and Sadie Gregory owned a large property a mile or so north of the campus, at the place where Leroy Avenue, then a dirt lane, ended at Rose Street . . . so the Howards named it "Rose Leroy."*
>
> *To the north of Rose Street were rolling hills covered with grass and studded with oak trees . . . although the Ridge Road house had been much more spacious and suitable for a family of seven, Rose Leroy had a spectacular view of the bay and was on the edge of open fields. Just below the house was an uncovered reservoir that looked like a large blue lake. At night they slept on open decks and often heard the howls of coyotes in the sparsely developed hills.* [20]

Fig. 8.4

Fig. 8.4: Charles Aikin house, 2750 Buena Vista, Berkeley (1940), by Bernard Maybeck. The pecky cypress between the ceiling beams adds texture, light, and shadow; the cutout flat-board balusters on the mezzanine repeat those Maybeck had used on the balconies of the 1906 Hillside Club's principal hall. (Illustrated in Kenneth Cardwell, *Maybeck, Artisan, Architect, Artist,* 92.)

Fig. 8.5: Aikin house, view: this is the last of many two-story living rooms designed by Maybeck.

Fig. 8.5

Fig. 8.6

Fig. 8.6: Warren Gregory house, 1459 Greenwood Terrace, Berkeley, California (1903; expanded 1906–7), by John Galen Howard.

Fig. 8.7: Warren Gregory house. John Galen Howard kept the Arts & Crafts woodsy feeling of the original house when expanding the living room; view: fireplace end of the 1906–7 addition.

Fig. 8.7

Howard designed two wings, visually tied together by horizontal bands of untreated redwood shingles laid in regular smooth courses like a tightly stretched skin, which responded to the angle of the property lines and to the hillside.

The San Francisco Fire and Earthquake

Worcester and Howard remained friends throughout Worcester's life and when it came time to flee San Francisco in the aftermath of the 1906 fire and earthquake, it was Howard who rescued Worcester and housed him until it was safe to return to Russian Hill. From Howard's home Worcester wrote his cousin Daniel Burnham:

Fig. 8.8: Warren Gregory house, view: art glass windows in the living room extension ca. 1906.

May 3, 1906 Berkeley

Dear Dan,

That Wednesday morning all the clocks of the city stopped at 5:16. We realized that we had been visited by an earthquake more destructive than any within our memory, but we had little idea of what was to follow. I think most people understood that their chimneys were unsafe, but the crossing of the electric wires was less considered, yet there lay the danger, and as soon as the cloud of dust ran from the City—little columns of smoke were seen one, two, three—until they c'ld [sic] not be counted. Yet the thought of a general conflagration did not occur to us, so reliant were we upon our fire-service and so still the wind.

The fire ran North along the water-front as far as Broadway, and there was checked, but it went South and along Market Street unchecked, and Wednesday night from our Hill, the whole South side between the water-front and Valencia St. was an unbroken furnace of fire. Towards morning we realized that it had crossed Market and was creeping up to Union Square. All day Thursday its march upon us was steady, and about four o'clock it was a roaring line on the South stretching from the waterfront over the Hill and out as far as Franklin St. Then we realized that there was no safety for us; the valuables which had been brought to us were being removed to the Presidio and Fort Mason, and the soldiers were on the Hill.

Mr. Howard had been on the Hill some hours waiting for me, and leaving my house with some of the fugitives I took up my march to the Ferry which we reached passing over Telegraph Hill. Mr. and Mrs. Richardson had sent on some of their things to Fort Mason, and would not leave their house so long as their retreat was not cut-off. The fire turned at Franklin St. and came back, sweeping everything before it, around our Hill and Telegraph Hill again to the waterfront. Ten houses on our hill were spared, and they stand like an oasis in a desert. The desolation is so complete that I dread to have you see it. And I can form no idea of the practicalability [sic] of the City's rebuilding, that occupies Mr. Howard's mind without admitting a doubt.

The spiritual side is most present with me; the good in people was never before so apparent, the selfishness also, and the separation of the evil from the good in the individual

Fig. 8.9: "Rose LeRoy," 1401 Le Roy
Avenue, Berkeley, California (1912),
by John Galen Howard. The garden
elevation features round and rectangular projecting bays that Howard used
at Cloyne Court in 1904 (Fig. 8.2).

Fig. 8.10: "Rose LeRoy," view: street façade. Howard devised an ingenious solution to the problem of a corner lot on a rise. The open deck on which they slept also provided magnificent views of San Francisco and the bay.

and the community, which is the meaning of purification by fire makes one think that it is the world of spirit and not the world of earth.

Mr. Howard is a most outspoken upholder of your plans, but all the City seems to be ready for them and for you, even the Mayor, though jealousy of Phelan may work adversely.

Mr. Keith saved from his studio 27 of his last pictures and is hard at work in his home, confident of doing his best work. Your most generous contribution to our needs is a very great and opportune gift [Burnham had sent money]*, but I am awaiting the more desperate need to follow.*

With great love,
Jos Worcester[21]

Fig. 8.11: Howard house, 2421 Ridge Road (1903; destroyed by the 1923 Berkeley fire), view: looking toward undeveloped hills. *"Whole house was constructed without blue prints. My father would stop by every morning for a conference with the building contractor . . . . [when] photos were taken our family lived on the large porch (called the Lanai) under a vast green and white canvas awning, with all our furniture."*[22]

Fig. 8.12: Aikin house (1940), view: detail of Maybeck's signature "dragon" and flat-baluster balcony.

Fig. 8.13: John Galen Howard, portrait.

Fig. 8.11

Fig. 8.12

Fig. 8.13

The California Shingle Style   9

Shingle and Mission Modes Coexist

REFERRING TO THE SEARCH FOR STYLES IN THE 1880s, RICHARD GUY WILSON WROTE: *"Many Americans recognized that the contemporary English architectural rummaging could be easily paralleled in the United States by a study of American colonial architecture."* [1]

Just as A. J. Downing before them had viewed architectural styles as convenient names for various cottage types, Charles Keeler and the Hillside Club did not advocate a single style for the simple home but felt any "old" building type, by which they meant vernacular and preindustrial, could express the qualities they espoused. No land was too distant, no architecture too foreign to be of interest. Worcester's circle of architects, joined by Julia Morgan, John Hudson Thomas, Louis Christian Mullgardt, and many others, increasingly adapted old styles and invented new features for homes that were no longer so "simple" or rustic, due in part to the increasing population, its growing wealth, and more diverse tastes. The Mission and Mediterranean styles in particular saw an upsurge in popularity, especially after the 1906 San Francisco fire and again after the 1923 Berkeley fire. Yet the rustic shingled house continued to be in demand as it is to this day. Thus the first two decades of the twentieth century present us with two competing visions of what might be considered California's authentic Arts & Crafts architecture: the California Shingle and the Spanish-Mission-Mediterranean traditions and their derivatives.

Arts & Crafts Organizations Proliferate

In addition to the San Francisco Guild of Arts & Crafts founded in 1894 (see Chapter 4) and the numerous Southern California Arts & Crafts organizations already mentioned, northern California's Arts & Crafts activities persisted and California became well-known as a center of Arts & Crafts to Europeans and Americans alike. *House Beautiful* (February 1901) featured the Swedenborgian Church, the *Craftsman* (February 1903) praised California's houses of local wood such as one in Menlo Park, south of San Francisco, and Keeler sang the area's praises in the

Fig. 9.1

Fig. 9.2

Fig. 9.1: Wyntoon (1903), by Bernard Maybeck, whose furniture and lighting solutions are visible in the dining room. The fixture recalls similar English Arts & Crafts designs as well as the Swedenborgian Church chandelier.

Fig. 9.2: First Church of Christ, Scientist, Dwight Way and Bowditch Streets, Berkeley (1910), by Bernard Maybeck. His unusual light fixtures contribute to the magical effect found in the sanctuary. Large saucer chandeliers with trefoil cutouts emit a soft glow while bright light twinkles from the tiny cylindrical fixtures.

Craftsman (August 1905).[2] When British Arts & Crafts architect Charles R. Ashbee visited the Bay Area in 1909, he credited Californians with launching the vogue for Arts & Crafts in America: *"Curious it is that the best work in Arts and Crafts in America is already being produced on the Pacific Coast,"* and on another trip he wrote, *"California speaks. . . . Here things were really alive— and the Arts and crafts that all the others were screaming about are here actually being produced.*[3]

United Crafts and Arts of California (a name that recalled United Crafts founded in 1899 by Stickley) was incorporated in San Francisco in 1903, and in that same year Paul Elder & Co. established a bookshop and printing business that displayed Arts & Crafts objects in a shop designed by Maybeck (1908). Frederick H. Meyer joined Maybeck in making chairs, tables, and chandeliers for the refectory of Wyntoon between 1898 and 1902 (Fig. 9.1), inspired by English and European vernacular furniture, and in 1907 Meyer launched the California College of Arts & Crafts. Worcester's friend John Zeile supported the Furniture Shop (1906–20), established by two other Worcester acquaintances, Lucia and Arthur Mathews, after the 1906 fire wiped out their other shop.[4] The longest of these to survive, along with the California School of Arts & Crafts (which still exists as the California College of the Arts), was the Copper Shop that Dirk van Erp opened in San Francisco in 1910, which finally closed in 1977. In the 1920s Old Mission Koperkraft stamped Mission Dolores' façade on their products to identify them as Californian, suggesting that the Mission Style and its derivatives were still considered appropriate Arts & Crafts design.[5]

The Craftsman Promotes the Swiss Chalet

As noted, a popular offshoot of the Arts & Crafts simple home was patterned after the Swiss chalet. Although its forms did not suggest reaching toward heaven as did the Gothic style, they did conjure up tree-covered alpine slopes and a rugged lifestyle—appropriate for houses built with nature in mind. The Swiss chalet had been a favorite style for picturesque American houses since the mid-nineteenth century. Pattern book writer Henry William Cleaveland described one of his chalets in *Village and Farm Cottages,* the 1856 book he co-authored, published in New York and marketed *"to the small farmer and laboring man generally"*:

> *Its principal feature is the verandah or gallery covered by the projecting roof, and supported by the open framework. This is at once bold and simple, suggestive of summer enjoyment and of winter protection.*
>
> *In its main characteristics this house resembles the Swiss cottage. Circumstances similar to those which make this style proper on the Alpine slopes often exist among us, and it is for some such position that the design is intended. It would suit well the southern slope of some steep and rugged hill . . .* [6]

European architects derived inspiration from mountain houses and chalets found in Germany, Switzerland, Poland, Romania, and elsewhere; in his 1904 book, *The Simple Home,* Keeler acknowledged its successful adaptation in California, as had Gustav Stickley's *Craftsman* magazine in 1903:

> *Instead of hiding materials employed and the methods of their employment, every effort is made to show the joints and their fittings, the boards and timber, so that what is there by necessity becomes an object of decoration and harmony.* [7]

Maybeck's first house at 1300 Grove Street, Berkeley (1892–94), was said to be *"something like a Swiss chalet,"* and after his European trip Maybeck returned to this style. The house he designed for the George H. Boke family in 1901 at 23 Panoramic Way, Berkeley (Figs. 9.3–9.5) features crossed and exposed framing members, a low-pitched roof with eaves extending well beyond the walls, and balconies with slats carved in a Swiss-inspired apple pattern, later repeated at the Schneider house (Figs. 9.6, 9.7).

Despite advocating truth to materials, Maybeck delighted in visual tricks and obviously felt no shame that his *"expressed structure"* on the southwest corner of the Boke house is fake: heavy beam ends or logs were attached as if structural, although they were not.

Repeating the Hall house open plan (1896), but this time L-shaped, Maybeck merged the living room with the dining room (Fig. 9.4). Supporting posts, combed with a delicate network of straight lines, stand before the living room windows rather than being integrated into the wall structure, and continue into the dining room in a Japanesque manner. Redwood board and batten left in its natural state, neither waxed nor stained, makes up the

Fig. 9.3: George H. Boke house, 23 Panoramic, Berkeley (1901–2). One cannot help wondering whether Maybeck himself did the cutout decoration over the mantelpiece.

Fig. 9.4: Boke house, view: from the living room into the dining room.

Fig. 9.5: Boke house, designed by Maybeck in the Swiss Chalet style. At the far right he attached fake beam ends as if they were actual exposed structure. The owners have restored the original smaller windows and removed the modern bay windows seen in this photograph.

Fig. 9.4

Fig. 9.5

Fig. 9.6

Fig. 9.7

remaining interior finish. The built-in benches, dining room cabinets, and pierced work cut into the boards above the fireplace mantel (Fig. 9.3) exhibit the craftsman touch and make the house a *gesamtkunstwerk* (total work of art) such as Ruskin and Morris had advocated since the 1850s and were being built in Darmstadt, Germany, ca. 1901.[8]

These and other Swiss Chalet characteristics appear on the Isaac Flagg house (1900–1), the Albert Schneider house (1905–6), the William Rees house (ca. 1906), and the Atkinson house in Berkeley (1908) as well as on his J. H. Hopps house in Ross (1905), which features an asymmetrically placed fireplace and three-foot-long redwood shakes often seen on barns. Maybeck enlivens the Schneider façade with Japanesque double gables and irregular massing, varying the surface by reversing the boards' direction: those on the first story are laid horizontally, those above vertically. The window frame (Fig. 9.7) and the balcony's pierced screens express his love of hand-carved details.[9] In these chalet-style houses, the overhanging gable eaves are supported by brackets that visibly branch from the framing members below.

Fig. 9.6: Albert Schneider house, 1325 Arch Street, Berkeley (1906–7), by Bernard Maybeck, in the Swiss Chalet style.

Fig. 9.7: Schneider house, view: the scroll-carved window frame looks as if Maybeck, an advocate of handmade things, made it himself.

The Brown Shingle Arts & Crafts House Flourishes

Coxhead's brown shingle churches and houses, among the earliest in California as noted, relate to the Arts & Crafts aesthetic and the simple home; prime examples are the Charles Rieber house (Fig. 9.9) and Frederic C. Torrey house (#15 and #1 Canyon Road) (Figs. 9.10–9.13). Torrey was a member of the prestigious San Francisco decorating firm of Vickery, Atkins, and Torrey that Keeler praised for *"fitting up apartments in the arts and crafts spirit which is constantly*

Fig. 9.8

educating the taste of the mass of the people."[10] Worcester and Keith knew the shop (they sold Keith's paintings) and perhaps recommended Coxhead.

The 1904 Rieber house recalls houses by Shaw and English architects Ernest George and Harold Peto. Its height, strengthened by the chimney's vertical thrust, gabled dormers, and steep roof suggest Shaw's own house on Ellerdale Road, Hampstead, London, and resemble George and Peto's "Waterside Westgate-on-Sea," England (Fig. 9.8).[11] In a planning tour de force, Coxhead placed both house entrances at the rear off a courtyard, perhaps inspired by the courtyard entry at Edwin Lutyens' Munstead Wood (1896) built for Gertrude Jekyll, confirming our suspicion that "simple" homes were never so simple, certainly not in terms of their planning. At the Rieber house, Coxhead doubled the width of the dormer windows and extended leaded panes (a frank tribute to Arts & Crafts medievalism) over only one-third of the window area of the projecting bay to obtain the widest possible view and to flood with light what might otherwise have been a dark room; the floor, walls, and boxed beam ceiling are redwood.

Unlike the open plan of some contemporaneous Maybeck houses, where certain sections of one large living space are simply designated living and dining room areas (e.g., Boke house in Fig. 9.4), the Torreys' generously sized rooms can be made into separate spaces by closing the built-in pocket doors. Despite the elegant classical details such as the carved foliate capitals and library bookcase topped by a broken pediment, the Torreys walked up log steps until the elegant stairs designed by Henry Atkins were installed ca. 1909 (Fig. 9.10–9.13).[12]

Fred Dempster, an easterner, designed his own unpainted shingle house at 2204 Glen (1907) with a verandah sweeping around a prominent tower, recalling eastern Shingle Style houses. The

Fig. 9.8: "Waterside Westgate-on-Sea," England (pre-1892), by British firm Ernest George & Harold Peto Architects. This is one of many British houses with a triple-peaked roof that may have inspired Coxhead to use three dormers in a row.

Fig. 9.9: Charles Rieber house (1904) at left and Frederic C. Torrey house (1905–6) at far right, both by Coxhead & Coxhead; Hutchinson House (1908) in the middle, by Julia Morgan.

Fig. 9.9

Fig. 9.10

Fig. 9.10: Frederic C. Torrey house, 1 Canyon Road, Berkeley (1905–6), by Coxhead & Coxhead. Torrey, an art dealer, had purchased Duchamps' revolutionary painting *Nude Descending a Staircase* from the 1913 Armory Show, a copy of which remained when this photograph was taken ca. 1972.

Fig. 9.11: Torrey house, view: redwood paneled library with Renaissance-inspired details.

Fig. 9.12: Torrey house, view: the elegant Beaux-Arts staircase (date unknown, ca. 1909?) was designed by Henry Atkins, Torrey's partner in the San Francisco fine arts firm Vickery, Atkins, and Torrey. It replaced the original log steps by which the Torreys gained access to the house, visible in Fig. 9.9.

Fig. 9.13: Torrey house, view: detail of carved-wood porch capital. See also 12.1.

Fig. 9.13

Fig. 9.11

Fig. 9.12

Fig. 9.14: Fred Dempster
house, 2204 Glen Street,
Berkeley (1907). Dempster,
who was an active member
of the Hillside Club, said
he designed this house
for himself.

varnished and polished oak stair hall, with a mirror, benches, and built-in cabinets, opens narrowly to the small separate spaces of parlor and dining room. Despite these Victorian and eastern touches, Dempster adhered to many of the Hillside Club recommendations: he stepped the shingled elevation against the hill, and exposed the verandah's structural crossed timbers.[13]

Greene & Greene: "The Ultimate Bungalow"

Charles Sumner Greene (1868–1957) and Henry Mather Greene (1870–1954) lived and practiced primarily in Pasadena and Los Angeles; however, one or both brothers visited northern California and at some point became acquainted with Maybeck and friends with John Galen Howard and familiar with his work.[14]

In his excellent book *Greene & Greene,* historian Edward R. Bosley details their development. Beginning in March 1901 Charles and Alice Greene spent their honeymoon traveling in Europe. They traveled to Paris, where they may have met Julia Morgan, Maybeck's young protégé; visited London's South Kensington Museum, renamed the Victoria and Albert Museum in 1899; and may have seen English country houses by Voysey and Baillie Scott.

Equally as important, writes Bosley, on their way home the couple stopped in Buffalo, New York, to visit the Pan-American International Exposition (1901) where they very likely saw four rooms filled with Gustav Stickley's United Crafts furniture and possibly Joseph P. McHugh's "Mission" furniture, which derived from the chair made for the Swedenborgian Church (see Chapter 3).

Although the exact date is unknown when Charles Greene began to subscribe to the *Craftsman* and clip articles from it, by 1902 his work began to reflect America's growing fascination with the Arts & Crafts movement. Thus, writes Bosley, within the space of only a few months the Greenes progressed from designing competent though uninspired Colonial Revival houses to producing a regionally astute adaptation of English Arts & Crafts architecture.[15]

Whether the brothers saw northern California houses firsthand or not, their bungalows share characteristics with them as well as with Swiss chalets and Japanese architecture[16]: shingled exteriors and all wood interiors; boldly exposed roof rafters and structural beams; wide, overhanging eaves; sleeping porches connecting bedrooms with the outdoors; handcrafted ornaments, including light fixtures and hinges; trellises that connect to or stand adjacent to the house; and architect-designed wood furniture with its joinery emphasized rather than hidden. All these elements, many of which Maybeck used from 1892 on, appear in the Greenes' work.

There is another coincidence: In 1896 Maybeck referred to his first house for Emma Kellogg as "Californian." About eight years later, in 1904 or early 1905, according to Bosley, Henry Greene designed "The California House." Perhaps Henry Greene knew Maybeck's "Californian" designs?[17]

The Greenes' interest in Japan accelerated when in 1904, at the urging (some might say "unambiguous summoning") of their Long Beach client Adelaide Alexander Tichenor, Charles Greene decided he should visit the Louisiana Purchase International Exposition being held in St. Louis. Seeing the splendors of the Japanese buildings and gardens on display—the Imperial Japanese Garden and Main (Japanese) Pavilion—along with Mrs. Tichenor's enthusiasm for things Japanese, reinvigorated his youthful interests. Before seeing the Japanese buildings in St. Louis, the Greenes furnished the White Sisters' house (1903) with boxy Stickley-like pieces,[18] and Charles Greene took credit for the William Morris–inspired interior of the James A. Culbertson house (1902).[19] By 1908–9, these Japanese (and perhaps Chinese?) influences had been fully assimilated and had become even more refined.

The handcrafted details of the William R. Thorsen house at 2307 Piedmont Avenue, Berkeley (1908–10) (Figs. 9.15–9.19), were executed with as high a quality of exceptional craftsmanship as their lumber baron client could afford.[20] Timbers and columns were hand-shaped, their corners and edges softened and rounded (Fig. 9.16), and several exotic woods were used in the interior.[21]

The L-shaped plan (9,200 square feet) separated the three-story service wing with its distinct entrance and its own address on Bancroft Way from the Thorsen living and guest quarters facing Piedmont Avenue. Bosley continues:

> *In late 1909 when the framing and sheathing of the house were completed and the interior was ready to be finished, Mrs. J. W. Beswick-Purchas wrote this no-nonsense critique to William and Caroline Thorsen, her brother and sister-in-law:*
>
> "You will want to know what I think of this house [for Robert Blacker and his wife, Nellie Blacker, who was Mrs. Thorsen's sister]. . . . Well—I find the outside of the house and the grounds very pretty and attractive—but this architect has let his fancy run riot in wood! There is so much wood about the outside that when one finds oneself encased in wooden rooms, wooden wall, wood ceilings, wood floors, wood fixtures for light—well, one has a little bit the feeling of a spider scrambling from one cigar box to another.
>
> ". . . I hope you won't have quite so much wood or people may say: Lumberman! hm!

Fig. 9.15: William R. Thorsen house, 2307 Piedmont Avenue, Berkeley (1908–10) by Greene & Greene. Wood column detail with rounded edges and metal strapping. As Randell Makinson put it: *"They are functional, they are bold, and they are beautiful."*

Fig. 9.16: Thorsen house, view: the second-floor guest bedroom with its own balcony and magnificent view; it hovers over the projecting dining room just below. The Greenes designed this "ultimate bungalow" for lumberman William J. Thorsen and his wife, Caroline, who selected Greene and Greene because they were building a house in Pasadena for her sister Nellie Blacker.

Fig. 9.17: Thorsen house, view: fireplace detail. On the fascia just above the tiled fireplace surround and exotic wood mantel, Charles Greene designed a painted plum tree frieze that spreads from wooden brackets whose shape recalls oriental urns.

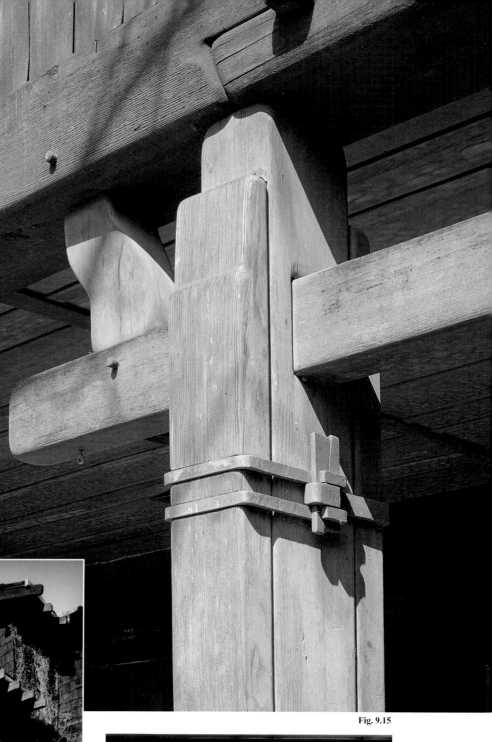

Fig. 9.15

Fig. 9.16

Fig. 9.17

*nothing like using up your own goods!
. . . All Mr. Green's [sic] woodwork is a
delight for the softness of its finish. It is
like fresh butter or paste squeezed out of
a tube—so soft are the surfaces and
the corners.*

Fig. 9.18

*"One more point. Don't let Green light
your rooms with lanterns of stained glass.
They are very artistic in shape and color-
ing perceived in the daylight but as points
of illumination they are rather negative
and one finds oneself in a 'dim religious
light' everywhere in the house.*

*"This is a damper to a natural buoyant
flow of spirits—a hindrance to work of any
sort, and very expensive—as one has to
turn on all the lights in a big room not to
feel that one is in moonlight. . . . I have
pointed out rather the faults* [in the Blacker
house] *which struck me unfavorably, that
you might get another point of view when*

Fig. 9.19

you are considering all these questions [for your own (Thorsen) house]."[22]

The Greenes considered their buildings collaborative efforts in the Arts & Crafts tradition.[23]
Charles Greene, who shared an interest in mysticism with Keeler, Maybeck, and Worcester,
believed all elements in their composition, from the garden gate to the smallest pegged joints,
were part of a higher unity, spiritual as well as physical.[24]

The Thorsen house is one of Greene & Greene's "ultimate bungalows," much more elegant
than Worcester's simple Piedmont bungalow (1876–78), which they may or may not have seen.
Nevertheless, the brick and shingle exterior recalls some of the more elegant examples of the rustic Arts & Crafts Shingle Style established in California by Worcester, Maybeck, Coxhead,
Schweinfurth, Howard, and perhaps by others yet to be identified twenty years before (from
1889), as well as Swiss Chalet and Japanese influences.

Fig. 9.18: Thorsen house,
view: the leaded-glass
recessed ceiling lights
probably resulted from the
Beswick-Purchas letter
warning the Thorsens that
single hanging leaded-glass
chandeliers do not produce
much more than moonlight.

Fig. 9.19: Thorsen house,
view: exterior of a California
"bungalow" with refined
Japanese touches and exqui-
site craftsmanship.

Rustic Barns Inspire Church and Home

Julia Morgan (1872–1957) was a petite woman with an iron will and an ability to manage multiple projects simultaneously. Born in California, she followed Maybeck's suggestion and obtained
a degree in engineering at Berkeley—the closest thing to an architectural degree available at the
time. She took "informal seminars" with Maybeck, helping him on his own house and the first
Lawson house (1895) (see Chapter 10). In 1896 she followed Maybeck's advice and became the
first woman to enter the architecture program at the École des Beaux-Arts (1896–1902). From her

Fig. 9.20: H. H. and Ellen Jenness house, 2706 Virginia Avenue, Berkeley (ca. 1908), attributed to Julia Morgan and Bernard Maybeck. The tree-shaped screen wall separating the entrance hall from the living room and fireplace inglenook recalls similar work by British Arts & Crafts architect Baillie Scott.

studies, travels, and work with Maybeck, she developed a personal interest in European medieval architecture and in the theories expressed by Viollet-le-Duc, Morris, and Ruskin.[25]

Although Morgan often designed Mediterranean-style mansions and is best known for the Hearst Castle at San Simeon, where she presided over what amounted to a guild of craftsmen, she found time for small Arts & Crafts homes. Morgan reportedly worked with Maybeck on the H. H. and Ellen Jenness house at 2706 Virginia Avenue, Berkeley (ca. 1908), in which posts separate the entrance hall from the living room and fireplace inglenook (Fig. 9.20). Perhaps the inspiration came from Baillie Scott, who had used tree-like posts as screen walls in 1898 for a large house at Lake Windemere.[26] Morgan also designed a striking shingle house (Fig. 9.21) for Joseph N. LeConte, son of renowned professor and geologist Joseph LeConte (1823–1901), who had been a close friend of Worcester's, and who had mapped much of Yosemite and the Sierra Nevada with John Muir.[27] According to Walter Steilberg, her structural engineer and friend:

> *Her criticisms were made in the form of quick but very definite sketches; to which she sometimes added this quotation from her friend and teacher Bernard Maybeck: "If you strike a difficulty, don't shy away from it; maybe it's an opportunity in disguise; and you can make a feature of it."*[28]

St. John's Presbyterian Church (1908–10) at 2640 College Avenue, Berkeley (Figs. 9.22–9.25), is arguably Morgan's most beloved rustic building.

As noted, the rural barn captured the imagination of Arts & Crafts architects from the turn of the nineteenth century. William Morris described an idealized house resembling a barn in his story "A Dream of John Ball" (1886, republished 1889), and in 1896 Morris invited Swedenborgian photographer F. H. Evans (1853–1943) to capture *"the quaint garrets among the timbers of the roof"* at

Fig. 9.21

Kelmscott manor, his sixteenth-century country retreat. Evans, like Worcester, associated all natural things with spiritual qualities and photographed the attic as carefully as if it were a church nave.[29]

At about the time the *Builder* published Morris' idealization of the barn, Howard published his artist's country house (see Chapter 8), including *"a studio facing out on a courtyard bordered by stables and stalls"*; in 1889 A. Page Brown published a design for stables at Seabright, New Jersey, not in an American magazine but in *British Architect;* and in 1895 Maybeck designed the Keeler living room open to the peak, leaving structural beams exposed *"as in a barn"* (Figs. 6.6, 9.26).[30]

When traveling in New England in 1883, William Keith wrote Worcester, praising old farm houses: *"The old rigid farm houses, grey & weather-stained are . . . affecting . . . in color they are so soft & harmonious in the landscape."*[31]

By the late 1880s many architects were sketching barns for their romantic and picturesque associations as well as for their connection with what they imagined to be the "simple life."

Apparently Morris and the *American Architect* agreed that barns, stables, and remote country places *"escaped the nineteenth-century orgy of styles"* most successfully.[32] St. John's followed the Bay Region tradition of domestically scaled, non-monumental churches inaugurated in San

Fig. 9.21: Joseph N. LeConte house, 19 Hillside Court, Berkeley (1908), by Julia Morgan.

Fig. 9.22: St. John's Presbyterian Church, 2640 College Avenue, Berkeley (1908–10), by Julia Morgan; view: facing the altar of the barn-like interior.

Fig. 9.23: St. John's Presbyterian Church, view: facing the doors to the sanctuary. Open timber structure and warm-colored wood walls contrast with brilliant light from the sanctuary doors and clerestory.

Fig. 9.22
Fig. 9.23

Fig. 9.24

Fig. 9.25

Fig. 9.26

Fig. 9.24: St. John's Presbyterian Church, view: chandelier inside the sanctuary reveals Julia Morgan's appreciation for the lowly lightbulb and straightforward construction.

Fig. 9.25: Ceiling of an eighteenth-century Japanese barn near Tokyo. Photo ca. 1971.

Fig. 9.26: Many Arts & Crafts architects delighted in the exposed structure found in barns, such as this eighteenth-century example at White Waltham outside London. This barn is now open to the public from June through September.

Francisco by Coxhead and Worcester. It appears modest from the outside, its mass low to the ground beneath wide spreading gables. Yet on the interior, the network of wood ceiling beams suggest an open-timbered barn.[33] As Berkeley expert Susan Cerny notes, the barn-like look may not have been all choice since their limited budget demanded creative thinking. Morgan left the studs, roof trusses, and other framing exposed to achieve a harmonious but inexpensive building.

John Hudson Thomas: A Master of Craftsman and Secessionist Styles

John Hudson Thomas (1878–1945) entered the University of California, Berkeley, Department of Architecture, in 1901, taking a three-year graduate course taught by Maybeck and Howard. In 1906 Thomas formed a partnership with George T. Plowman, and in 1910 established a long-lived independent practice. His English cottage houses include the half-timbered, shingled, and stuccoed H. L. Dungan house designed in 1911 (Figs. 9.27, 9.28), following Keeler's admonition to use wood in a manner befitting the material:

> . . . the man of average means must be content with wood. In this there is not hardship if the one essential rule be observed of using every material in the manner for which it is structurally best adapted. . . . the failure to observe this rule is the great sin in most of the domestic architecture of America. An arch of wood . . . has no structural value and is a mere imitation. . . . It is generally painted to imitate the effect of stone and thus sins even more seriously in becoming a sham. We feel that a woman with painted lips and cheeks is vulgar because she is shaming the beauty which only vigorous health can bestow; so also is woodwork vulgar when it is covered over to imitate the architectural form of stone . . . . [Such a house] is unworthy as the home of an honest man.[34]

As his son Mike Dungan related it, Maybeck was too busy to handle the job and told his friend Dungan *" . . . if you have doubts . . . build part of it and live in the unfinished house until the plan comes clearer."* [35]

The 1911 two-story redwood living room with its copper-hooded fireplace intentionally resembles the "gothic" living room–library Maybeck designed for Keeler, except this room arches gracefully over Harwood Creek—not exactly Falling Water but a dramatic use of the site. Dungan and Thomas certainly knew the earlier Moody house (Fig. 7.2), entered by crossing a bridge spanning a creek, as well as Maybeck's studio for Maurer (1907), which overlooks and almost sits on top of the same creek. Whether Muir's Yosemite cabin with the

Fig. 9.27

Fig. 9.27: H. L. Dungan house, 41 Oakvale, Berkeley (1911), by John Hudson Thomas, who used a combination of wood shingles and half-timbered walls to create an English cottage effect.

Fig. 9.28: Dungan house, view: Thomas designed the living room to form a bridge over Harwood Creek.

Fig. 9.28

brook running through it (see chapter 1) or other vernacular examples inspired these homes, only more detailed research might disclose.

Scholar Thomas Gordon Smith explains the 1912 James Hunt house (Fig. 9.29), also by John Hudson Thomas:

> *The surface above* [the lower half of the house] *is covered with horizontal tongue and groove redwood siding, superimposed with an external skeletal structure of redwood beams. A second story bay window nestled into the rhythm of the rafters is perched on a constructivist array of beams. Like Thomas' stucco buildings the actual construction of the Hunt house is invisible: the exhibition of structure is applied for decorative effect.*[36]

In contrast to these rustic Arts & Crafts houses, Thomas also designed in the Viennese Secessionist, Art Nouveau, Mission, Tudor, and other modes, as we will see in Chapter 10.

San Francisco Embraces the Arts & Crafts House

Despite the growing numbers of brown shingle houses in Berkeley, San Rafael, Belvedere, and San Anselmo, as well as the Coxhead houses on Pacific Avenue, most San Franciscans showed little interest in the unpainted wooden mode. Until 1904 when the Association for the Improvement and Adornment of San Francisco was formed, the city lacked a mobilized citizen group sensitive to the simple architecture of the Arts & Crafts movement that Berkeley had in the Hillside Club. Keeler (and perhaps Worcester?) did not sit passively by. In addition to *The Simple Home,* Keeler wrote promotional materials such as "San Francisco and Thereabout" (1902) and "As Others See Us" (1904) to encourage Californians to take an active interest in its architectural beauty and to advertise the state.[37] Keeler gave the association this advice:

> *What is needed is that persons having the authority of experience and taste would point out what to cultivate and what to avoid in home building. Ignorant contractors who style themselves architects are responsible for much of the mischief. . . . They should be bombarded with pamphlets giving pictures, plans, details and instructions for building picturesque homes. . . . In no way could so much good be quickly accomplished as in striking at the root of the evil and educating the designers of the architectural monstrosities that disfigure many of our streets. Now, when buildings are being erected, is the time to act. Let . . . public-spirited citizens start a campaign fund for the free distribution of literature upon the subject of making the mass of San Francisco homes more harmonious in form and color, more in keeping with the climate and life of the citizens and with more of sentiment and artistic motive in their conception.*[38]

Even before the fire and earthquake of 1906, which all but demolished San Francisco, Worcester and Polk were among those who had asked Daniel Burnham to develop plans for a grand urban design (see Chapters 1 and 3, and index). After the disaster, its citizens, seeking easily constructed and inexpensive housing, turned to the ideals of the simple home and often to the East Bay.

Several unpainted shingled houses survived the earthquake and fire. In addition to the Russian Hill enclave, Coxhead's houses still stand on Green Street and on the north side of the 3200 block of Pacific. Coxhead designed the house at 3234 Pacific for (and perhaps with) Bruce Porter, and also the one at 3232 Pacific (Fig. 9.30) for Porter's sister and her husband, Julian Waybur. Coxhead marked the Waybur entrance forcefully with a heavy rounded pediment framing a leaded-glass window above which a stepped balcony reflects and mimics the stairway inside. The resulting animated elegant façade differed radically from those he had designed for his earlier shingled homes.

Across from the Coxhead houses stand Maybeck's Samuel Goslinsky house (Fig. 9.31) at 3233 Pacific (1909) and Willis Polk's house for Bruce Porter at 3203 Pacific (1901). Both are brown shingled, but there the similarity ends. Polk ornamented his doorway from Georgian and

Fig. 9.31

Italian sources but did so in a dry and non-expressive manner, whereas Maybeck bowed to the simple and restrained only in the doorway pediment. He translated Gothic tracery into wood for one window; capped the plain windows with little eyebrow hoods, tilted and separated as if he were making a joke on the classical broken pediment; and crowned the peak of the lower roof with a dollhouse-like structure similar to one he used for the Keeler house fence and gate in 1895, and then repeated charmingly thereafter (e.g., at the Young and Chick houses). The result is a delightfully original, playful composition.

Maybeck's humorous architectural details may derive not only from his whimsical spirit but also from English sources. The playfulness in the Red House stairwell that Webb designed for Morris, with its castle-turreted newel posts, may have inspired Maybeck's delightful, sometimes childlike, architectural details. As Richard Guy Wilson expressed it: *"Red house was filled with sly jokes . . . that have been lost with time. . . . Canterbury Pilgrim's porch, murals of Morris and Jane dressed in medieval costume . . . the little stage up stairs and more."*[39]

Fig. 9.30 (facing): Julian Waybur house, 3232 Pacific Avenue, San Francisco (1902), by Coxhead & Coxhead, view: detail of the principal façade.

Fig. 9.31: Samuel Goslinsky house, 3233 Pacific Avenue, San Francisco (1909), by Bernard Maybeck, whose delightful sense of humor is reflected in this pastiche of a broken pediment along with a dollhouse roof topping the projection near the street.

British architects M. H. Baillie Scott and Edwin Lutyens also enjoyed playing the "game" of architecture.

These four houses still standing on the 3200 block of Pacific Avenue show how well the shingle mode worked for city townhouses as well as for suburban hilly towns.

Prominent English Architects Continue to Provide Inspiration

Maybeck continued to design with medieval European and English Arts & Crafts architecture in mind. As we have seen, he was acquainted with one of England's most famous vernacular revivalists, Richard Norman Shaw. Being fluent in German he may have possibly read Hermann Muthesius' groundbreaking volumes *Das Englische Haus* (published in 1904 after Maybeck's studies in Europe and after his trip to Europe for the University of California International Competition), which explained, detailed, and promoted English Arts & Crafts architecture to a German audience; e.g., superb Arts & Crafts examples can still be seen outside Berlin. Maybeck might even have met the author while they were both in London or perhaps during Maybeck's travels to his native Germany, although we have no proof to date and cannot say so with finality. Robert Craig, historian and Maybeck expert, points out that even if they did not meet, Maybeck and Muthesius shared parallel interests in rustic and primitive as opposed to artificially ornamental and urbane; and they shared interest in materials, in Nature, and in rustic building.[40]

Craig also tells us that Maybeck had possibly toured in the most picturesque of English districts, the Cotswolds, and if not he was certainly familiar with Cotswolds architecture from journals and books.[41] Some of the concepts of the Hillside Club may well have been derived from the observations of Maybeck and others about Shaw's work at Bedford Park (ca. 1875–81), which was referred to at the time as *"the source of the environment made art."*[42]

The Hillside Club library, which contained books illustrating club-sanctioned buildings, had at least one book of rural English architecture—W. D. Daire and E. S. Danker's *Old Cottages, Farm Houses and Other Stone Buildings in the Cotswolds District*—as well as copies of *International Studio*, a publication devoted to the English Arts & Crafts movement. Charles Keeler's personal library contained other books dealing with England and the Arts & Crafts movement, among them Aymer Vallance's study of *William Morris, His Art, His Writings and His Public Life* (1898); Malcolm Bell's *Sir Edward Burne-Jones, A Record and Review* (1910); and copies of the *Studio*, *House Beautiful*, and *Century Magazine*.[43]

The results of Maybeck's continued interest in England can be seen in his most famous house, the Leon Roos house at 3500 Jackson Street, San Francisco (1909). Guests approach the Roos house by a covered walk along the side of the house, lined with medieval-inspired leaded-glass windows that introduce light but shield one's view into the dining room on the other side. After passing through the low skylit entry, one's attention is drawn to the right where a sharply peaked living room soars upward, terminating not with a fireplace (although there is a magnificent baronial one along the side of the room) but with a rectangular bay that houses an enormous single-pane window, which seems to command us to approach and enjoy the captured view. To the left of the entry is the elegant, horizontally beamed dining room with a small fireplace enhancing that room's low-scaled intimacy. The dining room's leaded-glass bay projects toward Jackson Street,

providing perfect symmetry for the bay window at the other end of the vista in the living room. The hall connects both living and dining rooms. Thus all rooms are open to and visible from each other, a study in contrasts giving the clients the theatrical experience they sought.

As we see in the Roos presentation drawing (Fig. 9.32), flowers and other plants growing from built-in flower boxes were intended to add color and life to the exterior façades. At present, bright red geraniums complement the red edging of the freely interpreted "Gothic quatrefoils" inserted just under the eaves along the side elevation facing Locust Street. On the main façade under the broken pediment dormer facing Jackson Street, these quatrefoils flank a carved linenfold design, typically seen on late-medieval and Renaissance furniture and interiors, not on buildings, but Maybeck obviously delighted in quoting the linenfold on the building's exterior. The multiple dollhouse chimney tops add another playful touch, possibly springing from Maybeck's imagination or from examples still visible near Ravenna, Siena, Verona, and Vigevano, Italy (Fig. 10.2).

At the Roos house Maybeck did not leave the half-timbering rugged and irregular as he had seen it used in many German villages. Instead he placed the timbers in a regular vertical pattern, smoothed and darkened, setting them off against bare white walls. Maybeck could have seen this type of half-timbering in architectural magazines or while traveling in England, as it was typical of vernacular cottages from the fifteenth and sixteenth centuries in East Sussex, Surrey, and Kent. Or he could have seen Lutyens' surprising use of half-timbering on the gallery wall of the U-shaped court at Munstead Wood in Godalming, Surrey, just outside London. It was built for the famous landscape designer Gertrude Jekyll in 1895–96, the year before Maybeck arrived in Europe. In addition he could have known Baillie Scott's houses using vertical, smoothed, and

Fig. 9.32: Leon L. Roos house, 3500 Jackson Street, San Francisco (1909), by Bernard Maybeck. This presentation drawing shows the importance Maybeck gave to British Arts & Crafts architecture, and to plants and flowers and their softening and color effects. The vertical living room (right) placed under the high-peaked rear section terminates with a large window toward the spectacular view.

Fig. 9.33: J. B. Tufts house, 2733 Buena Vista, Berkeley (1931), by Bernard Maybeck, who designed the house with a dining area at one end of the living room, an enormous concrete fireplace, and half-timber interior walls for an English cottage effect.

darkened half-timbering set against white walls. Maybeck claimed to be satisfied with seeing unfinished irregular elements in the structure itself, but the client's budget often had a lot to do with the final design, as we see from the Roos house. Although his allegiance was to Pugin and his followers Ruskin and Morris, who equated morality and medieval architecture, Maybeck's open planning probably derives more from American domestic architectural developments than from English.[44]

In a manner distinctly different from the Roos house but nevertheless with English roots, Maybeck reinterpreted the Tudor cottage and used half-timbering for the J. B. Tufts houses (Fig. 9.33)—Tufts #1 at 14 Entrata Avenue, San Anselmo (1908); Tufts #2 at 245 Culloden Street, San Rafael (1908); Tufts #3 at 2733 Buena Vista Way, Berkeley (1931)—and the J. H. Senger house at Bay View Place, Berkeley (1907). At the Tufts house on Buena Vista in Berkeley, he used variegated colored shingles for the roof, and sloped it so far to the ground that the entrance is almost hidden from view (Fig. 7.19). Indeed, that wing of the house appears to be nothing but roof, recalling Coxhead's church in Monterey nicknamed "Saint Roofus" (Fig. 5.7). Although the half-timbering here is left rugged and unpainted, inspiration is still evident from Baillie Scott, who often bent his roofs almost to the ground to shelter the entrance.[45] In one of his delightful surprise moves, Maybeck also brought the half-timbering inside, using it for the dining room and living room walls as Baillie Scott had done at Blackwell.

Throughout Maybeck's long career he continued to cherish an interest in English architecture and the Arts & Crafts movement. It surfaced again in his last house, the Aikin house (1940), where his eye for a barn-like interior space merged with a taste for the baronial, resulting in a voluminous vertical space with a balcony—once again with flat boards cut into baluster shapes, recalling German *fachwerk* (half-timber) balusters—overlooking the living room.[46]

Arts & Crafts Expansion: Mission, Pueblo, and Mediterranean Styles 10

WHAT EASTERNERS FOUND IN OLD COLONIAL BUILDINGS, WESTERNERS FOUND IN THE architecture of Spanish California. As Charles Lummis wrote, *"Plymouth Rock was a state of mind. So were the California Missions."*[1]

Many architects saw inherent beauty in the nonmechanized construction and functionalism of the missions, their outlying buildings, and adobe dwellings, which represented a valid local past worth exploring, and which satisfied yearnings to find old roots in a new land. They also considered their rugged textures and unrefined atmosphere as perfectly suited to California's robust outdoor life as the rustic shingle style.[2] By 1903, *American Architect & Building News, The Craftsman, House Beautiful, House and Garden, Drake's Magazine, Out West, Scientific American, Building Edition*, and many more publications were featuring Mission and Mediterranean Style buildings.[3]

Interest in the Missions, 1883–1895

As noted, interest in the California missions was in the air by the time Helen Hunt Jackson's *Ramona* was first published in 1884. Several emerging leaders in the Bay Region showed early interest in missions. At Worcester's suggestion Keith had sketched the missions on his honeymoon trip in 1883, and in 1887 Polk had designed "An Imaginary Mission Church of the Southern California Type," which Longstreth suggests is *"the first known design to be directly fashioned after these buildings."*[4] John Galen Howard had sketched the missions in 1888 (see Chapter 8), and Bruce Porter drew several missions: *San Louis Aroyo; Narrow Passage in Santa Barbara Mission; Pala Mission, Calif.; Ramona's Marriage Place;* and *Ramona's Home.*[5]

Mission Revival scholar Karen Weitze points out that by 1889 Lummis had written "The Old Missions" for *Drake's Magazine* and had already attributed the vogue for missions to Helen Hunt Jackson's *Ramona: "... she has made all these crumbling piles dearer and more beautiful."* As early as 1895 Lummis noted that the missions were *"the best capital Southern California has."*[6]

As seen in Chapter 3, Stanford University (1887–91) was intended to be specifically mission-related; in 1887 Leland Stanford had already taken credit for proposing Olmsted adapt the *"adobe building of California"* with *"some higher form"* to create *"for the first time an architecture distinctively Californian in character,"* as noted in the *San Francisco Examiner,* April 28, 1887. This "higher style" ended up being Richardson Romanesque.[7]

When Stanford drove the "golden spike" into the last rail section at Promontory Point, Utah, in 1869, the event opened the first transcontinental railway. Central Pacific, Southern Pacific, and later the Santa Fe laid out towns and promoted land sales in California. The railroads became the biggest California boosters and promoted the missions and California's Hispanic past by constructing their stations in the Mission Revival style.[8]

Even though Polk's 1887 sketch of an imaginary Mission church had been published in *Architecture and Building* (April 12, 1890), he (and perhaps his friends) thought the general public and the commissioners (about to specify a style for the California State Building) remained uninformed. In 1890 Polk justified articles in *Architectural News* devoted to the missions because they were not familiar to most California residents: *"The story of the building of the missions is known to comparatively but few outside of the residents of the 'Golden State,' and in the same degree, perhaps, within its borders."*[9] In fact, *Architectural News* editors referred to their articles as *"both timely and useful"* in encouraging *"a semi-Spanish Renaissance in the architecture of California's buildings at the coming Columbian Exposition,"* to be held in Chicago in 1893, and argued for accurate restoration of the missions themselves rather than remodeling, but their author made no attempt to suggest the missions might serve as models for *domestic* architecture.[10]

In 1890 the San Francisco Sketch Club held a competition for the design of an adobe mission chapel, with the winning design to be published in *Architectural News.* As the basis for its competition, the club selected a

> *. . . revival of the feeling to be found in the sadly neglected mission buildings, which afford the only architectural type peculiar to the early history of California and which are in themselves a most interesting study aside from the fact that this State could not be more fitly represented in its buildings at the World's Fair.*[11]

Evidently their lobbying worked. Two competitions for the California State Building were held. When the first one (May–June 1891) did not produce a design acceptable to Daniel Burnham, the state committee in charge of California's exhibit indicated their partiality to the Mission Style.[12]

Six months later when the second competition guidelines were published in January 1892, they mandated a building in the "Mission-Moorish Style," and attracted thirty architects to compete further increasing interest in these historic mission buildings.[13]

Brown completed the winning design within a month. After its selection on February 11, 1892, numerous articles referred to the winning design as distinctly Californian and Mission in style. For example, an article in the *San Francisco Chronicle,* February 13, 1892, declared:

> *The State is to be congratulated; it will have a building that will be distinctive and purely Californian. . . . Although the proposal called for Mission-Moorish, Brown's plan is 99 and 100% Mission which is about right.*[14]

Brown staunchly advocated the Mission Style for California: *". . . no style has been offered since that brought by the Mission fathers which has given as universal satisfaction, and a revival of it may be looked for."* [15]

Who worked on the designs for the California State Building (Fig. 10.1) at the Chicago Fair is in dispute. As we have seen, Schweinfurth worked for Brown in 1893, and may have arrived in California in *late* 1892. But the drawings were made during January 1892 and the prize was awarded February 11, 1892. [16] There are no signs of Schweinfurth between 1891 and 1892: no signed projects or drawings; no contract notices; no competition entries or letters to the editor; no drawings out of Brown's firm that were signed or initialed by Schweinfurth. Nevertheless, he could have remained in Brown's New York office while Brown worked in California. My interest centers on Schweinfurth's whereabouts in 1891–92 and whether or not there was any connection between renewed interest in the Mission Style ca. 1890 and Schweinfurth. All available evidence suggests he had nothing to do with it. [17]

Fig. 10.1: California State Building, World's Columbian Exposition, Chicago (1892–93; demolished 1893). Originally published in *Shepp's World's Fair Photographed.*

Who in Brown's firm did work on the competition entry drawings for the California State Building? Polk is listed in the *San Francisco Directory* for 1891 and 1892 in partnership with Gamble, but he had worked for Brown and might have contributed ideas, if not drawings, to the design. Maybeck worked for Brown sporadically from 1891 to 1894–95, when he obtained his first clients, Charles Keeler and Andrew Lawson; and Maybeck did go to the Chicago Fair to work on the California Building even if he was not its supervisor of construction.[18]

Maybeck's personal interest in the Mission Style is demonstrated by his own submission to the competition. In January 1892, J. B. Mattheison and Maybeck submitted a competition entry for the California Building praised as even more purely Mission than Brown's, according to an unsigned article published in the widely read *American Architect and Building News* (March 1892).[19] This article attacked Brown's California Building as not pure Mission and commented: *"The Commission would have been wiser had they accepted the design of Messrs. Mattheison and Maybeck, which was unmistakably Californian. A combination of the two would have been best. The central feature was a low dome with four towers clustering around it. . . ."*[20] This description of Maybeck and Mattheison's submission sounds like a description of the building as built.

Cardwell suggests that although Maybeck submitted a separate design with Mattheison, he also worked on Brown's design, which seems likely: *"His contribution to Brown's design for the Columbian Exposition can be judged by the motif of the central dome which had as a prototype the one he or Hastings had designed for the Ponce de Leon Hotel* [in St. Augustine, Florida]*."*[21]

Ponce de Leon Hotel and the California State Building

Who actually designed the Ponce de Leon Hotel and the California Building (Fig. 10.1), which was inspired by the hotel's dome? Most of the February 1892 articles praising the building's winning design commented on the Mission Style and the exciting outline and form of the dome and surrounding roof garden. The *San Francisco Examiner* trumpeted: *"The crowning feature is the 'big dome and the roof garden.'"*[22]

If one compares the dome and roof garden of the Ponce de Leon Hotel by architects Carrère and Hastings, and the California State Building in Chicago, their resemblance is undeniably strong. This was Carrère and Hastings first commission. Perhaps Henry Flagler (the millionaire cofounder of Standard Oil with John D. Rockefeller) expected something exuberant; in any case, although they did not design anything quite like it after Maybeck left the firm in early 1889, when they designed the Ponce they were young architects with *"fertile imaginations,"* as we see in the hotel's towers and ornament.[23]

Hastings described the circumstances that led to their firm's being selected for the commission. Flagler had been a parishioner in Hastings' father's church and in 1885 asked Hastings for a "picture" of a hotel to be turned over to local builders,

> *. . . a mere sketch which I made of the plan and elevations while on our way to Saint Augustine in Mr. Flagler's private car in the early part of May 1885. After this we made more elaborate perspective drawings and studies and plans, but gradually transformed these drawings into more practical working drawings, finally figuring the plans.*[24]

It is very possible that Flagler, a very wealthy developer used to getting his own way, specified Spanish Renaissance style for the Alcazar and Ponce de Leon hotels.

Cardwell notes that in 1886, upon returning from five years in Paris at the École des Beaux-Arts, Maybeck joined Carrère and Hastings' firm in New York and began work on the Ponce, the very year in which they actually received Flagler's commission.[25] Maybeck's father traveled to Florida to oversee the installation of architectural carvings made by Pottier and Stymus *"while his son supervised the construction of the building."*[26] To suggest Maybeck made contributions to the hotel's design is not to suggest he actually designed the Ponce, just that he contributed to it, as with the Alcazar Hotel across the street.[27]

One can easily imagine either Maybeck or Schweinfurth proposing a similar dome to Brown for the California State Building in Chicago. However, Brown, a widely read and well-traveled architect (see Chapter 3 for the 1894 article he penned), may have admired the Ponce dome independently; he certainly would have seen drawings of it in various publications. On the other hand, it was Maybeck who brought firsthand experience with knowledge of its specifications and construction to Brown's firm.[28]

Mission Style: A Significant 1893 Choice

A much larger question is why the California World's Fair commission specified "Moorish-Mission Style" for the California State Building in the first place. Apparently *"Daniel Burnham . . . stipulated that the state buildings for the West and Southwest be mission in type."* Both Longstreth and Weitze state it was Burnham's decision. If it was Burnham's decision, it was not Schweinfurth's, and it was this decision that led to a major revival of the Mission Style.[29]

Is it possible that Worcester could have put the idea into his head? He was Burnham's cousin and close friend, expressed interest in documenting the missions as early as 1882, urged his friend Keith to spend his honeymoon painting them in 1883, and was a good friend of Charles Lummis and Willis Polk, both of whom were among the earliest promoters of the missions in 1889 and 1890. It is also worth remembering their frequent discussions of architectural matters as seen in letters cited throughout this book. Furthermore, Worcester's friend James Duval Phelan, mayor of San Francisco, was one of the competition judges. It would have been easy to whisper in his ear.[30]

Just as Schweinfurth or Maybeck could have suggested the Ponce as a model for the California State Building, Worcester too could have seen the Ponce drawings in the architectural press. *American Architect and Building News* featured the Ponce in 1888 with five full-page illustrations, including a double-page spread on the dome and roof garden about which the author crooned:

> *But there is another garden to see . . . a unique garden sixty feet above the court; between the two towers and looking down into the court on the one side, while it opens toward the interior of the dome on the other, It is a broad, paved terrace covered with an arbor of vines and plants. To this elevators ascend from the ground floor. This terrace is extended to the two sides of the building, forming thus a splendid promenade.*[31]

Furthermore, Worcester's correspondence with John Muir (see page 103 herein) shows that Worcester and Muir wanted a space at the Chicago Fair to feature California's native plants, one more reason for advocating a rooftop garden on the California State Building.[32]

However, the question remains: Whose hand, in addition to Brown's, may be detected in the project? Unfortunately, only Brown's name can be seen on the drawings or on the eight-foot-long watercolor Brown presented to the commission, nor can either Schweinfurth's or Maybeck's name or initials be found on any competition drawings or on any other drawings that came out of Brown's office; the Maybeck-Matheisen submission has disappeared; nonetheless, as mentioned, there are two independent accounts singing its praises.[33]

A large rendering of the California State Building drew accolades in many newspapers. For example, the *New York Times,* January 29, 1893, wrote: *"The huge watercolor of A. Page Brown's California building is on display in an exhibition of the Architectural League at the Fine Arts Building on West 57th Street."* Since the watercolors Schweinfurth submitted to the San Francisco AIA exhibition in early 1894 drew admiration (see Chapter 6), one might assume he was responsible for the large watercolor of the California State Building submitted by Brown's office; however, more than one person working for Brown (including Maybeck) was capable of creating high-quality watercolors and/or renderings. For example, a January 1895 article on the Ferry Building names the artist responsible for two enormous renderings: Charles Graham.[34]

Brown's Mission Style California Building drew so much acclaim that buildings designed in 1893 for San Francisco's 1894 Midwinter Exposition ended up being a polyglot collection of Mission and Mediterranean styles. Polk described them as *"East Indian, Egyptian, Moorish, Mission, Assyrian, and Conventional."*[35]

Mediterranean and Mission Influence on Domestic Architecture

In the early 1890s, if not before, architects also began to recognize the potential of early Spanish Mission architecture as a stylistic source for *domestic* building. Many architects incorporated Spanish as well as other Mediterranean themes into their non-shingled domestic buildings. They were attracted by hand-hewn beams, rough masonry textures, and heavy tiles, and by employing such features attempted to create another "authentic" California style. They used the same texts—Viollet-le-Duc, Ruskin, and Morris—to justify various Mediterranean styles as indigenous, vernacular, and suitably Arts & Crafts.

In 1893 Polk combined a Mediterranean-inspired exterior with an Arts & Crafts redwood interior for the Valentine Rey house in Belvedere (Fig. 10.3). Rey's devotion to settling in this new suburb and maintaining its rusticity may have been inspired by Polk or Worcester, both of whom he could have met on Russian Hill where he grew up, or through Keith, with whom his wife studied painting. In fact, Mrs. Rey's infatuation with sketching early California missions and adobes began just after Keith's did. Her interest may well have been encouraged by him and could explain why Polk synthesized Mission, Mediterranean, and Arts & Crafts characteristics in the Rey house. For the exterior walls Polk combined white plaster, numerous arches, and wood supports reminiscent of early Italian architecture (Fig. 10.2) while the inside is a study in contrasts. Writing in the *Wave* in 1897, Polk contended *"the missions ought not to be basely imitated"*; nevertheless, he

Fig. 10.2

happily interpreted Spanish California architecture and various Mediterranean styles if the client so requested. Frank McCullagh, a devotee of the missions, followed in Rey's footsteps. In 1901 he commissioned Polk to design a rambling Mission-Mediterranean-inspired house.[36]

Several Los Angeles architects built homes in the Mission Style. The W. S. Tevis house, "Los Portales," Bakersfield (1895), by Henry A. Schulze, was published in *California Architecture and Building News* in April 1895; the W. C. Stuart house, Pasadena (1895), by Frederick L. Roehrig, appeared in *House and Garden* in 1907; and the Harrison Gray Otis house (1898) (Fig. 10.4), by John Kremple, which displays a flamboyant touch, was published by the *Craftsman* in February 1904 (Otis was the editor of the *Los Angeles Times,* for whom Charles Lummis worked). The H. B. Sherman house, Pasadena (Fig. 10.5), by Blick and Moore, was published in the International Edition of *American Architect and Building News* on February 18, 1899; and W. H. Crocker hired A. Page Brown to create a series of five Mission Style houses in Santa Barbara (1894–98), which was published in the Imperial Edition of that same magazine on January 15, 1898.

Fig. 10.2: View of the *Effects of Good Government on the City Life* (1338–40), painted by Ambrogio Lorenzetti, Palazzo Publico, Siena. Italian Medieval architecture with arched openings and wood beams supporting a projecting upper story, balcony, or loggia may have provided inspiration to Arts & Crafts architects, especially those in the West.

Fig. 10.3: Valentine Rey house, 428 Golden Gate Avenue, Belvedere (1892–93), by Willis Polk. The combination of wood supports, tile roof, and arched openings recalls Italian architecture (Fig. 10.2), demonstrating the wide number of sources to which these architects turned.

Fig. 10.3

Early Mission-Influenced Buildings

Fig. 10.4

Fig. 10.5

Fig. 10.4: Harrison Gray Otis house (1898), by John Kremple. Mission advocate Charles Lummis worked for Otis, who was the publisher of the *Los Angeles Times.* In the February 1904 issue of the *Craftsman,* a much less expensive Mission Style house for the Consuelo family was published.

Fig. 10.5: The *Craftsman* featured Mission Style houses in many issues from February 1904. This expensive two-story Mission Style house reappeared in Gustav Stickley's *More Craftsman Homes: Floor Plans and Illustrations for 78 Mission Style Dwellings* (1912).

One of the first houses Maybeck designed was not shingled, as was the contemporaneous Keeler house, but rather what the *Oakland Enquirer* termed *"of Spanish style"*:

On Warring Street, near Dwight Way, Mr. J. H. Dingwell is constructing for Professor A. C. Lawson of the U.C. a two story house of ten rooms, under the plans of Instructor B. R. Maybeck of the U.C. This is one of the most unique houses now in course of construction. There will be no plaster in the interior which will be finished with redwood beams and heavy panels. The exterior, which is of Spanish style, will not be boarded, but plastered. As Professor Lawson says, "Mr. Maybeck has been turning things around in the architecture of Berkeley." Mr. Maybeck also drew the plans for Charles Keeler's new home on the Scenic tract north of the University grounds. It is one of the artistic additions of this growing district. [37]

Since the house was built in the flat part of Berkeley, Maybeck may not have felt the need to use unpainted shingles to make the house disappear into the hillside. Perhaps he wanted to attempt a domestic version of the Mission Style, or simply designed to suit his client. Looking at a photograph of the first Lawson house today (Fig. 10.6), it is hardly what we would term Mission or Spanish, although it does have a white "plaster" exterior, a vertical section perhaps inspired by Mission towers adds an asymmetrical note, and areas of wall divided by wood strips into panels, are vaguely reminiscent of English half-timbering. Two hipped roof wings enclose a court-like garden entrance (a circle drive on the right leads to it). Maybeck also used decks, pergolas, and a series of paired projecting beam ends, recalling Native American pueblos and early Mission buildings.

Other Mission Style buildings of the period are also in evidence. At the end of the century, Frank Miller hired Arthur B. Benton to transform his family's adobe boarding house into the well-known extravagant Mission Inn at Riverside. [38] William Curlett designed the Mission Style St. Mark's (Episcopal) Church in Berkeley in 1899 (dedicated 1902), and when he added to the church in 1904 and 1912, Polk retained Curlett's tall, squared bell towers, curved and squared gables, arched doorways and windows, and earth-toned walls, all taken directly from mission examples. [39]

In 1902 John Galen Howard designed his Ridge Road house (Fig. 8.3), with a Mission-referenced squared-off tower and arched openings; however, he finished the interior in the more rustic California style using natural redwood. The same year, Maybeck developed an innovative Mission Style exterior for the Faculty Club on the University's Berkeley campus (Fig. 10.7), but he kept the interior wood-beamed and medieval in feeling. In designing the Faculty Club,

Maybeck combined the two authentic California Arts & Crafts styles (as did Polk for the Rey house): Mission and rustic. Although the bare surfaces suggest Mission walls, Maybeck intended they be softened by foliage and by the weathered redwood trusswork outlining the gable. The arches and windows set in deep reveals, and the extension of the second story out over the first, cast shadows over the planar surface (Fig. 10.7). Unlike the ornamental orgy of the so-called Mission-inspired buildings at the California Midwinter Exposition, this severely plain exterior evokes the Spanish Franciscan friars' aesceticism in the historic California Mission prototypes.

The exterior of the Faculty Club does not reveal the surprisingly vertical great hall interior, which resembles the cathedral-ceiling living rooms of many Maybeck houses. Exposed rafters, windows on one side only, and a large fireplace recall the woodsy feeling of the Swedenborgian Church and the Keeler house. However, the hall is not as relentlessly rectilinear and devoid of other ornament as the Keeler house built seven years earlier. The large scale enabled some medieval grandeur: "gothic" trefoils open what could have been a dark area at the ceiling's peak, and paired beam ends carved as dragons mimic medieval gargoyles (Fig. 10.8).

Subsequently the Mission Revival underwent many more transformations. Maybeck's second house for Lawson (1907) (Figs. 10.9, 10.10) derives from Italian villas.[40] Lawson is said to have insisted the house be constructed of concrete, but Lawson's first house was not shingled either.

Despite concrete construction, the Lawson house exemplified the Hillside Club's aesthetic and had some handcrafted elements. Maybeck sited the house to capture the view and interact with

Fig. 10.6: A. C. Lawson house #1, 2461 Warring Street near Dwight, Berkeley (1895; demolished 1937), by Bernard Maybeck. The exterior was referred to at the time as in the *"Spanish style,"* but the interior was to be finished with *"redwood beams and heavy panels."*

the garden. Wood trellises are not an afterthought but an essential part of the plan as they were at Lawson's first house; they tie the house to its setting, modulate light on its surface, and link it to the garden in the "building with nature" manner. Maybeck decorated the arched openings at the back of the house with sgraffito such as he would have seen in many Italian and German towns; and in the mid-nineteenth century, shortly before his trip to London, sgraffito was used to decorate an entire façade (now hidden from public view) of the South Kensington Museum.[41]

The diamond pattern of incised lines and small colored tiles may have been inspired by J. E. A. de Baudot faience mosaic decorating the concrete structural members on Saint-Jean-de-Montmartre, begun while Maybeck was in Europe in 1897. His friend Otto Wagner in Vienna also used mosaic to decorate concrete. Closer to home, Frederick L. Roehrig, who had joined the San Francisco Sketch Club at the end of 1890, created a Pasadena house with diamond patterning on the walls and a fleur-de-lis in each diamond; the house was published in *American Architect and Building News* in 1898.[42]

The same year Maybeck built the second Lawson house, Irving Gill used concrete for the Homer Laughlin house in Los Angeles, and he and Frank Mead designed a concrete house for

Fig. 10.7: Faculty Club, University of California, Berkeley (1902; wings added 1903, 1904), by Bernard Maybeck. The original section of the club features arched openings, a tiled roof, stuccoed wall surfaces, and a tower, confirming Maybeck's statement that he took inspiration from the California missions.

Fig. 10.8: Faculty Club. Keeler referred to the main dining room, with its beamed cathedral ceiling and Maybeck's signature "dragons" (set atop wood posts that stand forward, distinctly separate from the walls behind them), as a "medieval hall."

Fig. 10.7

Fig. 10.8

Wheeler J. Bailey in La Jolla. Gill admired the missions as *"a most expressive medium of retaining tradition, history and romance, with their long, low lines, graceful arcades, tile roofs, bell towers, arched doorways, and walled gardens."*[43] Although he liked the modern structural possibilities of concrete, he shared with Arts & Crafts architects a desire to link his buildings to nature:

We should build our house simple, plain and substantial as a boulder, then leave the ornamentation of it to Nature, who will tone it with licens [lichen], chisel it with storms, make it gracious and friendly with vines and flower shadows as she does the stone in the meadow.[44]

The unornamented concrete exterior of the Bailey house (Figs. 10.18, 10.19) features arched openings on both levels, carved roof brackets, and a stepped roofline seen in mission architecture as well as on storefront façades in early California mining towns. In contrast, the wood posts of the Bailey house interior are so reminiscent of Maybeck's Boke house it is difficult to imagine Gill had not seen it.[45]

Fig. 10.9

Fig. 10.9: A. C. Lawson house #2, 1515 La Loma, Berkeley (1907–8), by Bernard Maybeck. As we see here on the south façade, Maybeck's skill extended beyond brown shingled homes to proficiency with Mediterranean styles.

Fig. 10.10: Lawson house #2, side view with sleeping porch.

Fig. 10.10

The Native American Pueblo Influence

Because of its handcrafted, carved-from-the-land quality, the southwestern Native American pueblo offered Arts & Crafts architects yet another inspiration for a suitably simple, contemporary architecture along with the Mission and Mediterranean styles. Lummis, who had contributed to the success of the Mission Revival by alerting westerners to the rich romance of their own past, also helped promote Native American culture. As noted, in 1889 Lummis had written "The Old Missions" for *Drake's Magazine*. In 1895 he became editor of *Land of Sunshine*, a magazine with 8,000 circulation, devoted to western history; the publication was re-titled *Out West* in 1902. [46]

Lummis published many articles about Native American traditions, architecture, and folklore, and articles devoted to the missions' founding, construction, and preservation. When a group of women urged action, he established a Landmarks Club (1895) to maintain and preserve historic California structures. In fact, Lummis so admired the Native Americans who built the missions that he imitated their methods in building his own home (Fig. 10.11), constructing his own furniture and utilizing hand-hewn rafters and adzed floor joints. [47]

As early as 1890 and perhaps before, Lummis became friendly with Worcester, Keith, Muir, and Keeler, eventually asking Keeler to write a feature article to be published in *Out West* about their mutual friend William Keith. [48]

When Keeler needed funds, Lummis helped him get a job writing the Santa Fe Railroad's tourist guidebook *Southern California*, illustrated with photographs and drawings by Keeler's wife, Louise. They were encouraged by Lummis to learn more about Native American culture.

> . . . *we were immensely interested in Aztecs, and Incas, in North American Indians and the Spanish California missions. . . . Lummis urged us to complete our education by going to live with the New Mexico Indians.*[49]

In fact they took Lummis' advice and traveled extensively, visiting old missions and Native Americans. Louise's numerous sketches and photographs document their travels. Keeler saw in Lummis' work an analogy between the American Arts & Crafts movement's attraction to Native American culture and the English Arts & Crafts fascination with European medieval culture: "[Lummis] *believed with all his heart in handmade things. He was a William Morris turned into a Mexican Indian.*"[50]

Schweinfurth, Hearst, and the "Pueblo Style"

As noted in Chapters 3 and 6, when William Randolph Hearst first hired Brown to remodel his Sausalito residence in 1894, he met Albert Schweinfurth; that same year they began discussing a much bigger project: the Hacienda del Pozo de Verona, an old-fashioned California hacienda (Figs. 1.1, 7.5, 7.6, 10.12, 10.13). [51]

The early 1894 date as the beginning of their collaboration is confirmed in two letters. The first mention of Schweinfurth occurs in an 1894 letter Hearst wrote his mother: "*Schweinfurth has completed all the drawings*" for the hacienda, "*I will forward copies in a few days,*" and the ground is being prepared for grass to replace weeds *"this Spring."*

Dear Mama,

Jack and I went to Sunol last Sunday. The men up there have ploughed over all those hills and done a lot of good work, so I imagine the ranch has been considerably improved and that grass will largely take the place of weeds this Spring. Schweinfurth has completed drawings for the house and I will forward them in a few days. I have had several talks with Edward. I think I shall bring him East with me when I come. What do you think?

The Call is still taking subscribers from us. . . . I am particularly annoyed at meeting this opposition just now as I hope soon to get my New York paper.[52]

Fig. 10.11: Charles F. Lummis' home, El Alisal ("The Place of the Sycamores"), 200 East Avenue 43, Los Angeles, California. Lummis built El Alisal with his own hands, beginning ca. 1896, filled it with Native American artifacts, and called it "El Museo." Lummis himself hewed some of the beams and chiseled much of the woodwork. El Alisal is open to the public.

Although Hearst wrote his mother quite often, he once offered this hilarious apology:

Dear Mama, 1894?
I am going to try to cultivate the habit of writing. It's more trouble for me to begin a letter than to start a newspaper.
Affectionately,
Will[53]

In a telegram from Hearst in San Francisco to his mother in Washington, D.C., dated February 4, 1895, he asks a question that reveals how deeply he was already into the hacienda: *"Whats money limit for country house. WRHearst"*[54]

In addition, two letters Schweinfurth wrote are published here for the first time.[55] They detail work that *had been done* and work *to be done* on the hacienda hereafter, and confirm that extensive planning for the hacienda, if not actual construction, started in 1894. Moreover, the letters shed light on Schweinfurth's disputed role at the Swedenborgian Church. As noted in Chapters 3 and 6, Hearst-related commissions made Schweinfurth's departure from Brown's firm possible in February 1894 and guaranteed him financial independence.

We can see from the first letter that much of the hacienda's basic construction seems to have been *completed* by November 25, 1895, when Schweinfurth updated Hearst, who by then was in

Fig. 10.12: Hacienda
del Pozo de Verona, Sunol,
California (1894–96), by
A. C. Schweinfurth.

Fig. 10.13: Hacienda
del Pozo de Verona,
east elevation.

Fig. 10.12

Fig. 10.13

New York City purchasing a newspaper. In the letter he asks Hearst for more detailed instructions on finishing the interiors.

While the November letter is fascinating, it is unclear whether Schweinfurth is advocating the "Spanish Renaissance" details he will copy directly from Spanish buildings, or whether he is satisfying his client's demands. At one point he argues for simplicity; later he states his preference for the even more elaborate *"Rococo,"* by which he probably meant Churrigueresque, a Spanish style with extremely rich ornamentation, developed in reaction to the more severe buildings of the Spanish Renaissance, such as L'Escorial.

November 25, 189? [probably 1895]
Mr. W.R. Hearst, #7 West 25th St., NY
My dear Sir,

To-day . . . I send working drawings and specifications for the decorations you wish for; also a fine book "Spanish Renaissance" the perusal of which I know will afford you much pleasure. There are in it some fine ceilings which are of course in much higher apartments but which could be made flatter and adapted to a lower room in case they strike your fancy. I did not use them [note the past tense] because I thought the sort of ceiling I did in the Library would be better adapted to the 'Painted Medallions' and leather treatment and would be more striking.

    The plans would take so long to trace . . . as I will have to draw out full size every scrap of carving . . . before it can be executed . . . and the work will take four months at least to execute. . . . As you definitely requested Spanish Renaissance for the Library I have kept straight to it and there is little . . . in the Library or Dining room which is not absolutely copied from renaissance work in Spain. . . . Had you not expressed a preference for this style I would perhaps have gone in a little more for the 'Rococo' . . . but I am satisfied that the style chosen is the more refined and will be less commonplace in general effect.

    You have enough plain leather for the Lobby and enough antique glass for the Hall windows [note that materials have already been purchased]. . . . To make the decorations perfectly satisfactory to you I would much like to have had at least as much instruction as you give your tailor when you order 'clothes' for I desire to make the things fit your ideas as much as any tailor ever did—but working as I did [note past tense] from the notes which Mr. Pancoast dictated to me . . . you must allow that I took chances of hitting what you were thinking of. . . . The andirons, beds, chairs and tables will be made . . . as soon as you decide if I have hit the character of the rooms as you wish them to be (I have them about half done at this writing).

    I should like to put leaded glass in all the principal downstairs rooms but . . . perhaps the plain long panes of clear glass are more to your taste.

    Also I wish to get your suggestions as to lighting. If you like the idea of floating tapers in oil I will make some sketches . . . or if you would accept candles (which I would prefer but if I remember correctly you are not greatly in favor of) I will make some designs for hanging lights and sconces. . . .[56]

The second Schweinfurth letter, December 20, 189?, probably dates from the end of 1895, judging from its contents. Mrs. Hearst had just taken, or was about to take, control of the hacienda, but when this letter was written they had not yet spoken. Schweinfurth explains to Edward H. Clark (whom he is asking to explain his position to Mrs. Hearst, having *"never talked"* with her) that certain things *"had already been built"* and completed; for example: *"the blue paint which has been applied to the doors and trim in Mrs. Hearst's room . . . was a suggestion of Mr. Hearst's. . . ."* Clearly, by the end of 1895, the time of this letter, the house is already built, some of the interiors painted, and Mrs. Hearst is about to take over the project.

In addition, in his December 1895 letter, Schweinfurth mentions that the building roofs had been completed and *"they are covered with . . . tin . . ."* He also indicates that Mr. Hearst opposed candles and *"at* [Mr. Hearst's] *request about a year ago* [in late 1894], *I got an estimate on an Electric light plant . . . to be placed in . . . the tank house which will have to be built eventually."*[57]

If Schweinfurth's November and December letters date from 1895, it is reasonable to conclude when he refers to "one year ago," he means work on the hacienda began in 1894 and continued into 1895.

Since numerous scholars writing after its construction, as well as those writing today, cite the Hacienda del Pozo de Verona's Pueblo style, we should note, as Calavan did,[58] that neither the tile roofs nor the columns (nor leaded-glass panes Schweinfurth preferred) would ever have been found on a pueblo.[59]

Pueblos, Modernism, and J. H. Thomas

Nevertheless, Schweinfurth's masterpiece with its romantic overtones conjuring up historic western culture—projecting gutter spouts, white walls, small windows, and low profile—deserves lasting acclaim. As a prototype for the Pueblo Revival, this important building is worthy of fur-

Fig. 10.14: Edwin R. Peters house, 18 Hillside Court, Berkeley (1914), by John Hudson Thomas. The "gothic" front door is flanked by Mackintosh-style windows, looking towards a mural of Indians on horseback.

Fig. 10.15: Peters house, view: front façade with cubistic/ Pueblo-style overhang protecting the "gothic" front door.

Fig. 10.14

Fig. 10.15

ther analysis. Although in California the Pueblo style never attracted the same following as did the Mission Style, Lummis and others writing even before him venerated the pueblos as the oldest and most original American architecture.[60]

Gustav Stickley used the *Craftsman* to link the pueblos, Indians, missions, and the Arts & Crafts movement for a nationwide audience. He presented pictures of Hopi Indians and published examples of traditional Native American arts, just as Lummis had in *Out West*. One *Craftsman* article had the amusing title "A California House Modeled on the Simple Lines of the Old Mission Dwelling; Hence Meeting All the Requirements of Climate and Environment."[61] In another article, a "mission bungalow" was described: *"The building is frankly modeled on the lines of the native Mexican and Spanish dwellings . . . and is clearly the outgrowth of the old Hopi Pueblo house. . . ."*[62]

In 1901, moreover, *House Beautiful*, an important promoter of the Arts & Crafts aesthetic, noted the mission-like characteristics of the Swedenborgian Church: *"In general lines the church follows the mission architecture of California."* Furthermore, the magazine criticized Californians for ignoring their architectural treasures *"fast melting into Mother Earth."*[63]

Although the Pueblo style never became as popular as the Mission Style, some architects, including the very talented John Hudson Thomas, designed several homes borrowing various elements from it. Indeed, Thomas' two houses for the Peters families (1914–15) synthesized the abstract forms of Native American Pueblos with the architect's interest in German Bauhaus architecture. In 1907, Picasso shocked the art world with his cubist painting *Les Demoiselles d'Avignon*. Le Corbusier and Gropius would soon design white-walled and flat-roofed houses totally devoid of ornament, and Frank Lloyd Wright and the German Jugendstil and Austrian Secessionists were adding banding and other simplified trim to their otherwise very spare block-like buildings. Thomas was not immune to these influences.[64]

At #14 and #18 Hillside Court, the George B. Peters and Edwin R. Peters houses (Figs. 10.14–10.17) of 1914–15 face each other across a courtyard, a pile of stacked cubes reminiscent of

Fig. 10.16: Peters house, view: living room fireplace. Thomas borrows from both Arts & Crafts copper hoods and Mackintosh's vertical linear decoration for the fireplace. Adding a humorous touch, each mantel-supporting caryatid reads an open book.

Fig. 10.17: Peters house, view: stairway with an Indian arrow motif brings the Native American motif inside.

Fig. 10.16

Fig. 10.17

the ascending blocks of pueblos. Decorative elements intermix Arts & Crafts and Austrian Secessionist influences with references to Native American culture. A living room mural shows Indians riding horseback on the plains, for example. Thomas's window frames, door moldings, and stair landing are decorated with arrows cut out of wood (Fig. 10.17). The incised designs on the fireplace hood (Fig. 10.14) echo Secessionist designs, and humorous caryatids (cross-legged men holding open books) call to mind Arts & Crafts tiles by Batchelder. Mixing styles still further, Thomas added squares, in relief, to punctuate and enliven the austere exterior in the Secessionist manner.

The Palace of Fine Arts and the Panama-Pacific Exposition

After the turn of the century, Joseph Worcester was by no means out of the picture. He continued to influence architects and artists as they all adapted to new trends. Maybeck in particular seems to have continued expressing sensitivities similar to Worcester's. In his 1915 feature essay on the Palace of Fine Arts for the 1915 Panama-Pacific Exposition in San Francisco, the design and color of which derive from the Mediterranean city of Rome, Maybeck stressed architecture's relationship to music, landscaping, and color. He also introduced a spiritual, mystical note of which Worcester, Keeler, Charles Greene, and other proponents of Arts & Crafts would have approved. The ideas they expressed were similar to those espoused by transcendentalists Ralph Waldo Emerson and Henry David Thoreau, and by Emanuel Swedenborg and Joseph Worcester. They all shared the belief that nature contains spiritual beauty and felt that the right kind of architecture, one which enhances and even brings nature into a building, could improve morality and mutual understanding.[65] Keeler expressed similar ideas:

> *The home must suggest the life it is to encompass. The mere architecture and furnishings of the house do not make the man any more than do his clothes, but they certainly have an effect in modifying him. . . .* [We are] *shaped and sized by the walls which we build about us.* [Furthermore,] *Emerson says that the ornament of a house is the friends who frequent it.*[66]

To Maybeck and Keeler, "gothic" architecture expressed aspiration and recalled the medieval period when, they imagined, people behaved morally. In addition they respected vernacular structures for their honest simplicity and were able to combine the two without a problem: Keeler described the cathedral ceiling of his home as *"pointing heavenward toward spiritual things unrealized"* and saw no contradiction in simultaneously connecting it to a barn (see Chapter 9).[67] Though Maybeck considered "gothic" an appropriate style for many houses, for others he was happy to revert to Spanish, Mission, or Mediterranean characteristics depending on the emotion he and the client wished to feel or convey. Thus Maybeck explained his retreat to classical Rome for the Palace of Fine Arts, stating that one must examine *"the historic form . . .* [to see] *whether the effect it produced on your mind matches the feeling you are trying to portray."*[68] Maybeck, like Worcester and Keeler, wanted the building to teach its lessons by conjuring up emotions and feelings indescribable in mere words. To make the Palace of Fine Arts' design and landscaping fit *"modified melancholy we must use forms in architecture and gardening that will effect the emotions. . . ."*[69]

Fig. 10.18   Fig. 10.19

The Arts & Crafts Influence on the
Panama-Pacific International Exposition of 1915

Both Maybeck and Worcester were concerned about the proper color for the Panama-Pacific Exposition buildings. Indeed Worcester worried so much that he lobbied to make sure Jules Guerin (1866–1946) took charge, as can be seen in the letter below to Burnham. Just as he took an interest in the California State Building at the 1893 Chicago Fair, the letter reveals Worcester's early involvement with those planning the 1915 Panama-Pacific Exposition for San Francisco. Perhaps he patterned himself on Burnham, whose *stupendous* accomplishments in Chicago he attributed to *". . . the inherent force of an idea when firmly grasped and held to."*[70]

In addition, Worcester regrets that Polk's early attempt to develop a Civic Center failed, but he (Worcester) resolved to make a difference at the exposition. In this case, as with Worcester's lobbying for John Galen Howard at the university, his determination helped obtain the desired result: Jules Guerin, the well-known muralist, was appointed director of color as Worcester had hoped. The letter to Burnham also suggests Worcester's likely involvement with the selection of architects to design the buildings for the exposition. His close friend Polk served as chairman of the Executive Council for Architecture for the exposition and, as such, he in turn appointed an Advisory Architectural Commission that included William Faville and Charles McKim, also friends of Worcester, as well as Louis Christian Mullgardt, whom Worcester undoubtedly knew through Mullgardt's work for Polk. The letter reminds us that Worcester may have been involved with San Francisco's Guild of Arts & Crafts through his friendship with Polk, Brown, and muralist Arthur Mathews:

January 16, 1912
1030 Vallejo, San Francisco
Dear Dan,
How deeply indebted you keep me! Yet I love to have it so. . . .
*   What you have been able to accomplish for Chicago seems stupendous, it shows the inherent force of an idea when firmly grasped and held to. . . .*

Fig. 10.18: Wheeler J. Bailey house, La Jolla, California (1907), by Irving Gill. The wood interior is very reminiscent of Maybeck's Boke house of 1902, and the living room balcony recalls balconies overlooking living rooms by Maybeck, Polk, and Howard.

Fig. 10.19: Bailey house, view: situated atop the La Jolla cliffs overlooking the ocean. This Mission-inspired house was built for a collector of American Indian art; its stepped gable recalls building façades seen in California mining towns.

Fig. 10.20 (facing): Alma
Kennedy studio, 1537
Euclid, Berkeley (built in
1914; demolished and
rebuilt in 1923 after the
Berkeley fire), by Bernard
Maybeck. The exterior
combines a "gothic"
window and balustrade
with a broken pediment
and Mediterranean-style
colored walls.

Now I am interested in holding our Exposition scheme to the simple but intelligent form and color which alone can distinguish it.

This afternoon I had a long talk with Faville; I went with the idea that he needed to be reinforced as to Guerrin [sic] as the only one who can be entrusted with the color. I was surprised to find him with Guerrin actually in his hand. He is much under the influence of Mathews who has done beautiful mural work here, but when I left him he was considering if Guerrin & Mathews could not work together.

Simplicity and breadth and [illegible word] *with the color refinement which Guerrin alone could give, would save the Exposition.*

When I think of the many things we could share with each other but for the physical distance. . . .

Yours,

Uncle Joseph [71]

Maybeck understood the importance of color at the Palace of Fine Arts and in what might seem a complete reversal from earlier Hillside Club recommendations to paint trim, if at all, with dark green or browns, he added touches of brilliant color to many of his Mediterranean-inspired houses, as evidenced at the Alma Kennedy studio in Berkeley (Fig. 10).

Maybeck asked one client if she would prefer *"a white house resembling a bird that has just dropped down on your hilltop, or an earth colored one that seems to rise out of it."* When she chose the latter, Maybeck invited her to participate in the process of spattering the walls with colored stucco; four pails of wet stucco were assembled, with different hues (pale chrome yellow, deep ocher, Venetian red, and gray) and each painter held a whisk broom with which to flick stucco onto walls. Maybeck directed the operation like a maestro: *"Red here. Ochre there. Now lighten with yellow. Now soften with gray."* When the job was finished, he announced approvingly that the walls vibrated. [72]

Mediterranean Styles Inspire Coxhead, Morgan, and Polk

The rustic shingle and Mission Styles continued simultaneously, as they do today. Coxhead too built several Mission-inspired houses. In 1906 he designed two houses for Mrs. Harriet Brakenridge, #6 and #10 Encina Place, Berkeley. For one of the houses, Coxhead used white stucco on the exterior and created a deep porch entered through arched openings; but he shingled number #6 from the start. He also designed a house for himself in the Mediterranean style at 76 Codornices Road (1925) as well as the Tyndall Bishop house, 1508 La Loma Street (1923–24). [73]

Some of Julia Morgan's most successful designs include versions of the Mediterranean mode. Her elaborate design for the Berkeley Women's City Club, 2315 Durant Street (1923), drew on Spanish Churrigueresque/Renaissance architecture. Her Seldon Williams house (Fig. 10.21), 2821 Claremont Boulevard, Berkeley (1926), had a sheltered interior courtyard with central fountain and a path-crossed garden. [74]

We can gather from Bruce Porter's letter to Willis Polk, written after Worcester's death, that Worcester would have loved a beautifully designed, well-landscaped Italian villa as much as he

Fig. 10.21: Seldon R.
Williams house, Berkeley
(1927–28), by Julia Morgan.
Hardly a "simple home," the
architect combines Mission
Style tile roofing with a
Gothic-inspired cloister, and
inserts a large tracery-filled
window to frame the view of
the client's lovely garden.

enjoyed the simpler Arts & Crafts homes that he had advocated earlier. Apparently Worcester adjusted to changing times as did his architect friends.

May 21, 1917

Dear Willis Polk,

Home from Blaney house, [Saratoga] . . . a straight "piece of enchantment." Exterior and interior are beautiful beyond any expectation of mine or theirs (or yours) and somehow as I walked around and through that house it seemed to me a fulfillment of all the things that Mr. Worcester used to find in your art, and I could hear his chuckle of pleasure in my ears, as I moved from one surprise to another.

It is not in any aspect, an imitation or affectation. You have merely picked up the spirit of the early spontaneous Italian work, and made it your own, you bring to it a sober roman- tic playfulness and poetry that is the very best of you. . . . The house might have been there forever, or it may after all be only a dream. It strikes me as the most enchanting structure I've ever seen and therefore may not be there when I go back. Yours always.

B.p. [Bruce Porter][75]

Although it may feel anachronistic from our point of view, late-nineteenth-century California architects treated the Mission Style as a variant Arts & Crafts building type—as valid as the California Shingle Style; thus, from as early as 1892 until well into the twentieth century, the mis- sions continued to influence the design of houses, churches, and public buildings.

Conclusion and Speculations: The Golden State Inspires America 11

FOR THE AMERICAN ARTS & CRAFTS MOVEMENT, CALIFORNIA TURNS OUT TO BE TRULY A "golden" state. It is always a bit risky to announce a "first," but the previous chapters have shown that: 1) the initial widespread development of "the humble cottage," advocated by John Ruskin and William Morris before 1850, was translated into "the simple home" in northern California beginning in 1876–78; it took flight from 1889 on, became popular in Pasadena and Los Angeles, and helped launch what became known as the Craftsman style across America[1]; 2) the first society for the Arts & Crafts in the United States was established in San Francisco in 1894 (the Guild of Arts and Crafts of San Francisco)[2]; and 3) the first Mission Style furniture was designed and made in San Francisco the same year.[3]

California deserves credit for helping to initiate influential and affordable interpretations of Arts & Crafts architecture in America, even if the suggestion may produce the kind of tirades that hounded Lewis Mumford,[4] who dared in his Skyline column (*New Yorker*, October 11, 1947) to praise *"that native and humane form of modernism which one might call the Bay Region style."* Two years later Mumford emphasized what he referred to as *"a serious omission in the existing histories of American architecture"* and acknowledged *". . . the existence of a vigorous tradition of modern building, which took root in California some half a century ago."*[5] Furthermore, he added, what Wendy Kaplan, Elizabeth Cumming, Karen Livingstone, and Linda Parry, among others, have recently demonstrated, and which this book confirms: *". . . this style was part of a worldwide movement in which no single country* [or state] *can claim preeminence . . . ."*[6] California helped lead Americans in the right direction[7]; however, exactly how the simple Arts & Crafts home spread across America merits more research.

Some scholars questioned the use in our 1974 book of the term "simple" to describe California architecture from this period. Therefore in this book I have tried to show that from the 1880s well into 1910, the term "simple" was used for its *positive* associations with anti-materialism and with the English Arts & Crafts "humble cottage" and its proponents Ruskin and Morris. "Simple" meant new, uncluttered, and without exuberant decoration so commonly seen at the time on so-called Victorian gingerbread, Aesthetic, Italianate, and Queen Anne homes. "Simple" houses were to be designed to satisfy the new, growing demand in Europe and America for middle-class affordable (i.e., simple) housing with an artistic, cottage, or bungalow feeling. As Morris put it: *"simplicity of life, even the barest, is not misery, but the very foundation of refinement."*[8]

In 1886 Bruce Price described the large Shingle Style cottages being built on the East Coast:

It is the fashion to call these country houses cottages but the cottage exists only in name.
The cliffs of Newport, the rocks of Mt. Desert . . . have cottages that would be mansions
in England, villas in Italy or Chateaux in France. The "cottage" is an amiable deception
. . . our countrymen . . . seek the beauties and comforts that wealth can furnish . . . .[9]

As we have seen, in 1890, about the time Stevens and Cobb published their 1889 book praising the small affordable house, Polk editorialized for simplicity, dignity and refinement, and he and Worcester built simple homes on Russian Hill. By 1891 Arts & Crafts shingle homes were being built in Berkeley and elsewhere in the Bay Area, and R. A. Briggs in England began promoting the bungalow-house as an inexpensive year-round Arts & Crafts house.[10] In 1899 the Vienna Museum of Art & Industry organized a competition called "For the Simple Household" to provide working and middle class families with well designed objects. In 1897, continuing the trend toward international exchanges, the Grand Duke of Hesse invited British artists C. R. Ashbee and M. H. Baillie Scott to Germany and two years later started an artists' colony in Darmstadt to improve German design and offer the average citizen well-built houses and a new quality of life; but the resulting houses, exhibited in May 1901, were branded luxurious and expensive by critics, who demanded the creation of simpler, affordable objects and houses.[11] At the time all this was happening, American versions of the Arts & Crafts simple home for the average middle-class family were being built in the United States.

After getting to know Maybeck around 1891, and working with him on his 1894–95 house, Keeler began promoting the simple home Arts & Crafts philosophy that his friends espoused. Those homes, said by Keeler to have been inspired by Worcester, and by the Swedenborgian Church (1892–95) he and his friends created, were by 1903 credited with influencing the Arts & Crafts movement: "*. . . the spirit of the church . . . which would have been a delight to William Morris . . . [was] so strongly rooted as to assume the aspect of a cult . . . .*"[12]

The *Craftsman* published not one but two articles on the church, increasing its status as an icon of the Arts & Crafts movement.[13]

As this book has shown, many of the group's ideas were codified in *Architectural News*, in Worcester's 1895 interview "A House that Teaches,"[14] and in Hillside Club pamphlets from 1898, and they were further detailed in Keeler's 1904 book, "*The Simple Home.*" In June 1904 Stickley, enamored of California and determined to build a cooperative community there, said: "*We shall live the simple life. Here in California you have ideal conditions . . . .*"[15] In 1905 Stickley added a subtitle to the *Craftsman*: "*an illustrated monthly magazine for the Simplification of Life.*" Clearly the move toward the "simple" and affordable middle-class house, a trend that accompanied the exodus from crowded cities, was international, and California played an important role in its American growth.

As we have seen, none of this might have happened without new clients flooding California's architects with work. Charles Lummis described them as "*progressive, adventurous, and dynamic simply by virtue of the fact that they had pulled up stakes back east or in the Old World and come to California.*" They were extraordinarily open to new ideas.[16]

Much work in this field remains to be done. Future research may well demonstrate that "simple Arts & Crafts homes" were built in California or elsewhere before Worcester's homes (1876 and 1888–90) became influential and the Arts & Crafts way of life blossomed. The ten-year period 1878 to 1888 merits more attention. Moreover, the numerous architects working before 1900, only touched on here, invite further study. In the San Francisco Bay Area, for example: Wright & Sanders, Clinton Day, Faville & Bliss, J. B. Mathisen (also spelled Matthisen, Matheisen), Walter Mathews, George Washington Pattiani, William Curlett, the Newsom Brothers, John White; and in the Los Angeles area: Frederick L. Roehrig, John Kremple, Myron Hunt, Elmer Grey, J. J. Blick, & Lester S. Moore, among others

Frederick Law Olmsted's impact on the early environmental movement and the development of California's architecture merits more attention; clearly, his influence permeated more than landscape design.[17]

I have devoted Chapter 10 to the Mission, Pueblo and Mediterranean versions of the early California Arts & Crafts tradition, but the full development of these modes and their relationship to the Arts and Crafts Movement warrant more research. Articles on the missions of the southwest appeared in Drakes Magazine in 1889[18] *Architecture and Building in 1890,*[19] *Land of Sunshine in 1896.*[20]

As early as 1903 the *Craftsman* tied the California Mission Style to the Arts & Crafts movement in America.[21] *International Studio* accepted the Missions' importance even earlier (February 1901), when it praised McHugh's Mission furniture, inspired by the Swedenborgian Church chair, as epitomizing an effort to capture the simplicity and harmony preached by William Morris and his followers.[22] As Richard Guy Wilson put it:

> *The term "Mission" came to mean more than just a furniture or building style; it became allied with home reform, based on the precept that a "missionary" intent should underlie both physical and spiritual life.*[23]

Gustav Stickley and the *Craftsman* have been studied extensively; but the major focus has been on Stickley's furniture, textiles, and metal work. I am suggesting, based on information below and that presented by others, that his *architectural* inspiration came largely from California, where architects before 1904 had created middle class homes by drawing inspiration from many sources, including Swiss chalets, Spanish missions, and Japanese architecture, as well as from European and American vernacular structures.

As Cathers, Stickley's biographer, points out: the first Craftsman House #1 published in January 1904 has *"low hipped roofs covered in unglazed red ceramic tiles, white roughcast exterior walls, and an arched entryway. These are components of mission architecture, although the article never alludes to that connection"*[24] (Fig. 10.5). In other words, Stickley promoted California's mission and shingle architecture for Craftsman homes without acknowledging the source, since there was no reason for him to do so.[25]

As noted, Swiss[26] and alpine prototypes, along with Japanese architecture[27] also inspired respect for wood, exposed structure, natural materials left in their natural state (e.g., trees with their bark on and knotted irregularities left visible). In October 1903, the *Craftsman,* published "The Use of Wood in Switzerland," and in November 1909 *House and Garden* published "A California Chalet."[28] In January 1912 the *Craftsman* published "Swiss Houses for People of Moderate Means;" and in May 1915 it published "The Swiss Chalet: Its Influence on American Architecture."

While visiting northern and southern California in 1904, Stickley had seen Swiss Chalet and Japanese architecture absorbed into Arts & Crafts houses for the average American family

Fig. 11.1 (facing): Louise and
Charles Keelers' bookplate,
hand-drawn by Louise Keeler.
See also Fig. 6.7.

especially in the work of Maybeck and Greene & Greene.[29] The range of interest in these matters was clearly ascendant during these years.

In 1912 the *Craftsman* acknowledged "California's Contribution to a National Architecture: Its Significance and Beauty as Shown in the Work of Greene & Greene Architects." The anonymous author of the article states:

> *The value of Western architecture, locally and to the nation at large, and its widening influence upon homebuilding all over the country, are facts not to be estimated lightly . . . . The East, on the whole, has still a good deal to learn—and perhaps even more to unlearn—before it can achieve much practical or artistic significance in the construction of its homes . . . .*[30]

This acknowledgment came the same year that Stickley published *More Craftsman Homes.*[31]

There may even be another first: Worcester's house 1876–78 may turn out to be the original American bungalow.[32] Anthony D. King associates the *Craftsman*, the bungalow and the Arts & Crafts movement: *"The Craftsman . . . was devoted to the development . . . of the three main principles of the Arts & Crafts philosophy—simplicity, harmony with nature, and the promotion of craftsmanship. The bungalow was to become the incarnation of all three."*[33]

As far as we know Worcester referred to his home as his "house" and used it year round until 1887 and frequently thereafter,[34] but by the time Jack London rented it in 1901–2, R. A. Briggs' book *Bungalows and Country Residences* would have had five editions, and his 1891 expression had become apt: *"a cottage is a little house in the country but a Bungalow is a little country house."*[35] In 1891 Briggs promoted the bungalow as suitable for suburban housing.[36] Therefore it is not surprising that, as noted in Chapter One, London referred to Worcester's house as the ultimate bungalow, *"a Bungalow with a capital B."*[37]

What we know of its plan corresponds in general with Anthony D. King's description of the Anglo-Indian bungalow as interpreted in California: the living room with a large fireplace flanked by cupboards and bookcases is entered directly from the verandah, supported on wood posts for a rustic effect; the open plan is very different from that seen on older houses; the Victorian hall and parlor have disappeared and the centrally placed living room takes on a new symbolic function. Whether a house or a bungalow, both the architecture and its owner were very influential.

As this book demonstrates ideas were received from the rest of the country and indeed the world, through individual travel and personal interaction; and via the architectural press. I have cited many instances whereby California's Arts & Crafts traditions were transmitted; but more research is needed to expand this aspect of the story.[38]

Charles R. Ashbee, the English Arts & Crafts architect and founder of the Handicraft Guild,[39] knew the American Arts & Crafts scene well, having traveled in the East and Midwest in 1896 and again in 1900–1. Ashbee visited both Northern and Southern California in early 1909 and wrote:

> *California speaks . . . Here things were really alive—and the Arts and crafts that all the others were screaming about are here actually being produced. Curious it is that the best work in Arts & Crafts in America is already being produced on the Pacific Coast.*

It is time for Americans to acknowledge what an Englishman recognized a century ago.

FROM · THE · LIBRARY
OF CHARLES · KEELER
AND LOUISE · KEELER

Abbreviations

A&B = Building (1882–1890);
Architecture & Building (1890–1936)

AABN = American Architect and Building News (1876–1909);
American Architect (1909–1936)

AB = Architect and Builder

AN = Architectural News

AR = Architectural Review: For the Artist and Craftsman
AR (Boston)
AR (London)

AT = Attic Trunk: A Publication of the Piedmont Historical
Society

AWMem = Alfred Worcester compilation: "Rev. Joseph Worcester:
A Memoir and Extracts from His Letters to His
Nephew, Alfred Worcester," in the Swedenborgian
Library and Archives, Pacific School of Religion,
Berkeley, California

BAHA = Berkeley Architectural Heritage Association

BL = The Bancroft Library, University of California,
Berkeley
BL: (Jean Murray) Bangs Papers
BL: (Ernest) Coxhead Papers & Architectural
Drawings
BL: (Sturla) Einarsson Papers
BL: (George and Phoebe Apperson) Hearst Papers
BL: (William Randolph) Hearst Papers
BL: (William Randolph) Hearst Papers
BL: (John Galen) Howard Papers
BL: (George H.) Howison Papers
BL: (Charles A.) Keeler Papers
BL: Keith-McHenry-Pond Family Papers
BL: (Bernard) Maybeck Family Papers
BL: (Julia) Morgan Papers & Architectural Drawings
BL: (Bruce) Porter Papers

BN = Building News

CABN = California Architect and Building News

CED = College of Environmental Design Library,
University of California, Berkeley
CED: (John Galen) Howard Papers
CED: Bernard Maybeck Collection

Chicago Fair = 1893 World's Columbian Exposition in Chicago

CHS = California Historical Society, San Francisco
CHS: (Emilie Price) Marshall Family Papers
CHS: (A. Page) Brown Scrapbooks #1 and #2

CMWFM = California's Monthly Worlds Fair Magazine (May
1891–June 1892); San Francisco: B. Fehnemann,
publisher; located in The Bancroft Library.

DHB = Daniel H. Burnham Collection, Ryerson & Burnham
Archives, The Art Institute of Chicago

EDA = Environmental Design Archive, College of
Environmental Design, University of California,
Berkeley
EDA: (Ernest) Coxhead Collection
EDA: (John Galen) Howard Collection
EDA: (Bernard) Maybeck Collection

EDA: (William) Merchant &
(William G.) Merchant Collection
EDA: (Julia) Morgan Collection
EDA: (Willis) Polk Collection
EDA: (Joseph) Worcester Collection

"FBT" = Keeler manuscript: "Friends Bearing Torches"
in BL: Keeler Papers

HB = House Beautiful

HCY = Hillside Club Yearbook

H&G = House and Garden

IS = International Studio

JVSA = Nineteenth Century, The Journal of the Victorian Society
in America

LC/MsDiv = Library of Congress/Manuscript Division,
Washington D.C.
LC/MsDiv: (John Muir) Collection
LC/MsDiv: (Frederick Law) Olmsted Papers
LC/MsDiv: (Charles Lummis) Collection

LHJ = Ladies Home Journal

NYSBA = New York Sketch Book of Architecture

OBA Directory = Husted's Oakland, Berkeley and
Alameda County Directory

RIBA = Royal Institute of British Architects

SABE = Scientific American Architects' and Builders' Edition
(1885–1895;)
Scientific American, Building Edition (1895–1905)

SAHJ = Society of Architectural Historians Journal

San Francisco Fair = California Midwinter International Exposition
held in 1894 (also known as the 1894 San Francisco
Midwinter Fair)

SCL = Swedenborgian Church Library, San Francisco

SF Call = San Francisco Call

SF Chronicle = San Francisco Chronicle

SF Directory = Langley's San Francisco Directory

SF Examiner = San Francisco Examiner

SHS = Swedenborgian House of Studies, Pacific School of
Religion, Berkeley, California

SLA = Swedenborgian Library and Archives, Pacific School of
Religion, Berkeley, California
SLA: (William) Keith Archives
SLA: (Othmar) Tobisch Archives
SLA: (Joseph) Worcester Archives

SM = Saint Mary's College of California, Moraga, California
SM: Brother (Fidelis) Cornelius (Braeg) Collection

TS = The Studio

UCB = University of California, Berkeley

UCSB = University of California, Santa Barbara

Endnotes

PREFACE
A Tribute and an Explanation

1. See bibliography for complete citations.
2. Keeler, "California in the World of Art,"
   BL: Keeler Papers, 7. He credits
   Worcester with having introduced
   the simple home to the San Francisco
   Bay Region.
3. Keeler, "FBT," BL: Keeler Papers, 36–37.
   He first expressed such sentiments
   much earlier: in *San Francisco and
   Thereabout,* repeats them in the
   Craftsman (August 1905): 592, and
   expresses them again in *Architect &
   Engineer* (1906): note 1.
4. Thompson, "Early Domestic
   Architecture," 18.
5. Bosley, "Schweinfurth," 13.
6. See notes 2 and 3 above.
7. Woodbridge, *Maybeck,* 24.
8. Woodbridge, *Howard & UC,* 46.

INTRODUCTION
Setting the Scene

1. Wilson, "Divine Excellence," 16–17.
2. Wilson, "Divine Excellence," 20.
3. On the architectural goals of the Arts &
   Crafts movement, see especially
   Kaplan, "Modern World," 10, and
   Cumming, "Sources and Early
   Ideals," 9–30.
4. See especially Kaplan, "America,"
   246–82.
5. Wilson, "Divine Excellence," 23. See
   also the *Craftsman* (February 1904),
   where George Wharton James praises
   the simplicity of the missions and
   comments that their color scheme
   harmonizes with foliage, making the
   buildings *"part of Nature"* itself.
6. On multiple architectural sources for the
   California Arts & Crafts home, see
   almost every chapter herein.
7. For example, *Architectural Record,* to
   which John Galen Howard subscribed,
   featured these articles between 1895
   and 1896: "Architecture in London,"
   "Japanese Architecture," "Architecture
   in Spain;" and "The Smaller Houses
   of the English Suburbs and Provinces.
   Part I, by Bannister Fletcher."
8. There were no plaster panels filled with
   sunflowers or other decorative
   designs, and they avoided towers,
   turrets or violently turned posts—
   to use Vincent Scully's phrase; and
   there were to be no decorated barge
   boards or Chippendale-style verandah
   railings. Unpainted shingles were to
   cover the entire exterior and wood
   trim was to be left unpainted or, if
   not, painted brown or green as was

also becoming more common in the
East. Also one might compare houses
illustrated in this book with those
illustrated in Scully, *Shingle Style.*
9. The house illustrated here (Fig. 0.3) is
   said to have been built by Bruce Price
   for J. V. Coleman in 1885. However,
   it is unclear whether Price built the
   original house or did extensive reno-
   vations for M. A. Hecht. Queen Anne
   plaster panels such as Price used in
   1879–80 at "The Craigs" on Mount
   Desert, Maine (Scully, *Shingle style,*
   fig. 40) are visible in San Francisco.
   Price's multiple designs for a client,
   presumably George Howard in San
   Mateo, seem never to have been built.
   See the many plans in Bruce Price,
   Country House.
10. *AABN,* no. 391 (June 23, 1883),
    illustration and text on 294.
11. Polk stressed *"simple homes"* in his
    magazine *AN* 1, no. 2 (December
    1890): 11, and Editorial in Contents
    on same page. Both quotes appear
    in Chapter 5.
12. Scully, *Shingle Style,* 155–56.
13. Thompson, "Domestic Architecture,"
    15ff.
14. Eisen, "Consistency," 53.
15. Oakey, *My Castle.*
16. Scully, *Shingle Style,* xxvii, xxxiii.
17. Morris, "Making the Best of It," 23, in
    Collected Works 22, cited by Wilson
    in "Divine Excellence," 17, 247n17.
18. Cathers, *Stickley,* 105. The architect for
    Craftsman House #1 was not identified.
19. Cited in Kaplan, "America," 248.
20. Cathers, "East Coast," 156: *"In May
    1903 The Craftsman published plans
    and perspective views of the first
    'Craftsman House.'"* The Craftsman
    House: Series of 1904, #1. The latter
    is illustrated and described as a
    Mission Style bungalow.

CHAPTER 1
Ruskin, Morris, and the
First California Arts & Crafts House

1. See bibliography and index herein.
2. Before becoming a very influential
   professor of art history at Harvard,
   Norton was coeditor of the *North
   American Review* from 1864 to 1868,
   and he helped found *The Nation* in
   1865. From 1874 to 1898 Norton lectured on the history of art at Harvard,
   where he was one of the most popular
   teachers of the day. In 1879 Norton
   established the Archaeological
   Institute of America. This was the first
   organization in the United States to
   promote archaeological research,

including investigating pueblos of the
Native Americans, which interested
Worcester also, and the study of
archaeology around the world.
Norton's friends embraced many literary men Worcester also admired,
including Ralph Waldo Emerson.
3. On Joseph Worcester's life, see
   Worcester, *Descendants,* 178. The
   best source for Worcester's life and
   letters can be found in AWMem.
4. Daniel H. Burnham to his wife,
   September 27, 1888, in DHB. See
   also Moore, *Burnham,* 1:14.
5. In AWMem, August 1, 1875, "William"
   is mentioned but no last name is
   given. For more on Worcester's friendship with William Keith and Willis
   Polk, see Cornelius, *Keith* 1, 343
   and index.
6. Cornelius, *Keith* I and II.
7. See unpublished correspondence
   between Keith and Worcester at SLA
   and SCL, Letter #8: November 1883;
   most of these letters were written
   while Keith was in Europe in 1883.
8. AWMem, June 11, 1871.
9. Cardwell, *Maybeck,* 17, 43.
10. For more on Howard's life and work,
    see Woodbridge, *Howard,* 11–52 and
    passim; see also Chapter 8 herein.
11. Longstreth, *Edge,* 299–300. For the
    relationship between Burnham,
    Polk, and Worcester, see ibid.,
    299–300, 392–93nn12–16, and
    letters quoted herein.
12. Keeler, "American Turner," 253–59. For
    Inness's work with Keith, see ibid.,
    257. For Ruskin's praise of Turner, see
    Hewison, "Ruskin, Turner, . . ."
13. *San Francisco Chronicle,* December 30,
    1894.
14. For those intervals when Worcester
    left the Swedenborgian Church, see
    AWMem, 5. For a letter suggesting
    Worcester had visited Bath and
    Yarmouth Port, see ibid., August 14,
    1872.
15. Ibid., August 1, 1875.
16. For the letter criticizing Florentine
    architecture, suggesting without
    definitely clarifying if Worcester had
    been in Florence or not, see DHB.
17. See Scully, *Shingle Style.* Worcester's
    architectural scrapbooks are in EDA:
    Worcester Collection.
18. AWMem, March 5, 1870.
19. Clipping from Viollet-le-Duc's
    Dictionnaire Raisonné inserted into
    one of Worcester's scrapbooks, EDA:
    Worcester Collection.
20. For Keeler's praise of Joseph Worcester,
    see Keeler, *Thereabout,* 41–42. For
    Worcester's influence on Polk and
    Coxhead, see Keeler, "Municipal Art,"

592. For more on Worcester, see Keeler, "FBT," 36–37. The Maybeck chapter can currently be found on the Internet at www.oregoncoast.net.

21. AWMem, 13.

22. Clipping with this advice inserted into one of Worcester's scrapbooks, EDA: Worcester Collection, n.d.

23. For Eastlake and Ruskin, see Scully, *Shingle Style,* 29n32.

24. AWMem, 8.

25. CHS: Brown Scrapbook #2.

26. DHB.

27. Ibid.

28. Mary Keith to Brother Cornelius, SM: Cornelius Collection, incoming "K."

29. AWMem, August 28, 1876.

30. Bosley, "Western North America," 192.

31. For Jack London's description of Worcester's Piedmont house, see Jack London to Cloudesley Johns, February 23, 1902, in Hendricks & Shepard, *London Letters,* 132–33. For the dates when the Londons rented Joseph Worcester's house and for more information on Worcester's cousins, Arthur Bowman and Henry Wright, and the cottage on their property, I am grateful to Gail Lombardi. See also Lombardi, "Oldest House," 1–7. See also Pattiani, *Piedmont,* for a general history of Piedmont with some errors.

32. See Scully, *Shingle Style,* xlii–xliii, for a discussion of how A. J. Downing, writing in 1850, *"attacks unnecessary ornament and advocates instead the planting of vines."* However, in his design for a "Small Bracketed Cottage" (ibid., fig. 6), Downing treats vines much as a carpenter would scroll ornament.

33. For the size of the house, see AWMem, Letters: February 23, 1879; see also London, *London Book,* 1:361.

34. Joan London's comments come from an unpublished statement given the authors by James E. Sisson in 1971.

35. For possible inspiration from Cape Cod houses, see Connally, "Cape Cod House."

36. For photographs of interiors of early Massachusetts homes, see French, *Colonial Interiors,* plate 106. The wood surrounding the fireplaces as well as the huge panels used for wainscoting were generally painted in eighteenth-century houses. The remaining wall area was horsehair plaster.

37. For the influence of the 1876 Centennial, see Scully, *Shingle Style,* 30.

38. For McKim's interest in vernacular architecture, the *NYSBA,* and the Bishop Berkeley house, see Wilson, "McKim," 248–49, who also notes that in the mid-1880s McKim and his colleague's interest in more formal Georgian styles supplanted their earlier interest in seventeenth-century American colonial and vernacular architecture. The Bishop Berkeley house is also discussed by Scully, *Shingle Style,* 26. Worcester pasted articles from the *NYSBA* in his scrapbook.

39. For the origins of the bungalow, the term *Anglo-Indian,* and its spread to the United States, see the classic work on the subject: Lancaster, American Bungalow (1995), and King, *Bungalow,* 144, especially the chapters on Britain and North America.

40. AWMem, October 21, 1876.

41. Ibid., January 8, 1878. I cannot help wondering: Did Worcester build the house himself? In AWMem, January 8, 1878, he apologized to Alfred about a letter dated October 21, 1877, that he forgot to mail. *"I was very soon began* [sic] *to build, and have been in a great tumult ever since."* What delayed its construction? What did he do in the interim?

42. Ibid., February 23, 1879.

43. On Swedenborgianism, see Silver, *Sketches,* 71ff. See also Wunsch, *Swedenborgian?* as well as Tobisch, *Christian, Why Swedenborgians,* and especially *Garden Church.* Swedenborg felt that natural objects hold specific spiritual significance and considered architecture a divine art: *". . . the art of architecture comes from heaven."* Rose, "Swedenborg on Architecture," cited by Bosley, "Schweinfurth," 20–21, 21n5.

44. I am grateful to Yosemite historian Linda Eade for pointing out the dates of Olmsted's Yosemite visits; see also Beveridge, *Papers of Olmsted 5.* Initial common goal derives from Olmsted, "Yosemite Valley." For other Olmsted citations, see Beveridge, "Olmsted's Theory," 32–37, on the Web site of the National Association of Olmsted Parks: www.olmsted.org.

45. AWMem, 3.

46. For Worcester's two trips to California, see AWMem, Introduction, 3. Although I checked passenger lists for boats arriving in San Francisco in 1864 and 1868, I was not able to find Worcester's name. The dates of christenings for Hutchings children might eventually help pinpoint Worcester's visits to Yosemite, although he could also have gone there at other times with his friend William Keith and/or with John Muir. Alice Burnham wrote to Brother Cornelius, *Keith* II, 102, a letter dated July 31, 1943, that she is "the grand niece" of Joseph Worcester and *"niece of Mr. D. H. Burnham, architect, of Chicago. . . . [and that] Mrs. Gertrude Hutchings Mills is one of my dearest friends. . . . The Hutchings children were the first white children born in the Yosemite and were christened by Uncle Joseph Worcester on one of his visits . . . ."* The Hutchings children were born as follows: Florence (August 1864), Gertrude (October 1867), William Mason (1869). See Sargent with Kaplan, "Yosemite Tomboy," 34.

47. See AWMem, March 5, 1869, where Worcester says he is happy to be back in California at a place he visited five years before, which would mean he was in California in 1864.

48. See AWMem., March 5, 1869, and AWMem, 3, for his work at Hutchings in Yosemite. Apparently the Hutchings were close friends of Daniel Burnham's family per letter from Alice E. Burnham to Brother Cornelius, *Keith* 2, 102; it is likely they were friends of Worcester's also as the Hutchings lived in Boston before moving to San Francisco before moving to Yosemite, schooled their children partly in San Francisco, and Worcester baptized their children, who were born in Yosemite.

49. Linda Eade informs me that he explored the high country with William Brewer and John C. Olmsted.

50. Frederick Law Olmsted to Mariana Griswold Van Rensselaer (draft, June 1893), LC/MsDiv: Olmsted Papers, cited in Beveridge, "Olmsted's Theory," note 1.

51. I am grateful to Charles E. Beveridge for pointing out the reference to Wilkinson in *Olmsted I,* 355, 357, and nn16–17.

52. Olmsted quote regarding *"style of the Beautiful"* is cited in Beveridge, "Olmsted's Theory."

53. Ibid.

54. Cheryl Robertson cites Ruskin in Trapp, *A&C California,* 95, taken from Sears, *Sacred Places,* 141.

55. For Olmsted citations, see Beveridge, "Olmsted's Theory," 32–37.

56. For the Muir letter, see Badè, *John Muir,* 1:207–8.

57. AWMem. March 5, 1869.

58. For descriptions and photographs of pre-1866 wooden buildings in Yosemite, see Russell, *100 Years,* 46–49, 95, 106. See also Royce, *Frontier Lady;* the description cited in Kirker, *Frontier;* and numerous photographs in BL. I am grateful to Yosemite historian Linda Eade for the information that Muir met Emerson in May 1871 in Yosemite and tried to convince Emerson to camp with him in the Mariposa Grove (not Wawona, as has been written). Could Worcester have been in Yosemite at that time? In his memoir, Alfred does not include any letters, if there were any, written between August 30, 1870 and June 11, 1871.

59. Badè, *John Muir,* 1:209.

60. AWMem, 3.

61. Uhte, *Pioneer Cabins.*

62. Kostura, *Russian Hill,* 51.

63. Worcester's interest in Ruskin has already been noted and will be mentioned several times again. For Ruskin's widespread influence, see Hitchcock, *19th and 20th Centuries,* 107n33, which provides evidence of the popularity of Ruskin's work in America from 1850 to 1900.

64. For an extensive discussion on the influence of the Arts & Crafts movement in America, see Kornwolf, *Scott,* still an excellent source, especially concerning architectural interchanges and cross-influences between England and the United States during the early Arts & Crafts period. Kornwolf is one of the few to point out how much the British Arts & Crafts architects took from the Americans and visa versa. See also Trapp, *A&C California.*

65. AWMem, January 17, 1873.

66. Keith painted Worcester's Piedmont house several times. One painting hangs in the Swedenborgian Church, 2107 Lyon Street, San Francisco. Another, illustrated in this book, is signed "William Keith," dated 1883, and belongs to Mr. and Mrs. Cameron Wolfe Jr. Another belongs to Sanford and Marilyn Goldeen. One version, from the collection of Richard Pettler, formerly belonged to Leonard G. Jordan, Worcester's classmate at the Swedenborgian seminary in Massachusetts in 1867. In 1877, Jordan came to San Francisco to replace Worcester, who had left the ministry to tutor. Other versions exist but I have not yet tracked their owners. One was sold in 1978 by Alfred Harrison, North Point Gallery, San Francisco, to Louis A. Capellino Antiques, Berkeley, who sold it to an owner who wishes to remain anonymous. Unfortunately, I have not found a single painting or sketch of Worcester's Russian Hill house by Keith, although he went there almost daily.

67. Keeler, "FBT," 226, and Chapter 3 herein.

68. Gail Lombardi researched the tax records and informed me that Worcester sold some of his 12.75 acres in 1904; in 1905 he sold his house and the remaining 8.5 acres to a Mr. Henshaw.

CHAPTER 2
Russian Hill:
An Early Arts & Crafts Neighborhood

1. AWMem, October 15, 1878.

2. Keith letters to Worcester, Letter #16: Munich, December 9, 1883, at SLA: Tobisch Archives.

3. Although Worcester moved to San Francisco, tax records prove that he kept his house in Piedmont. Worcester paid taxes on his Piedmont property; he complained to Alfred on January 24, 1887, that "an extraordinary tax bill for twice the value of my Piedmont property came." In *Edge,* 375n10, Longstreth convincingly demonstrates the completion dates of the Marshall houses as July 7, 1889, the date an application for water service was filed. Worcester's house on Russian Hill was finished a few months later in late 1889 or early 1890.

4. As this letter from Burnham demonstrates, Burnham considered Worcester almost "an architect." Worcester had sketched designs for his own house and the Marshall houses and sent them to Burnham by September 17, 1888. For the decision to build the Marshall houses with Worcester as architect, see CHS: Marshall Family Papers, as well as letters from Burnham to his wife, Margaret, about Joseph Worcester's architectural skill in DHB (1943.1, Box FF, Box 25, Folder 25.3). Sadly, the sketch of the Marshall houses mentioned in Burnham's letter was not filed with this letter, and no one at DHB seemed to know whether or not it might still exist.

5. For Alfred Worcester's comment on Joseph's Russian Hill house, see Alfred Worcester to Edmund Sears, July 8, 1930, SLA: Tobisch Archives. On page 110, Longstreth's apt characterization of rural inns as *"intentionally unassuming"* and his use of the term *"rustic city houses"* seems applicable to Worcester's own houses as well as to the Marshall houses he designed on Russian Hill, so I have used the term here. In Doughty, *New Church,* which is the Swedenborgian publication, SLA lists Worcester from February 1888 to January 1890 at 1407 Jones; for several months, from February 1890 through September 1890, no address is given in Doughty. (Did Worcester move into the Russian Hill house and then travel to Yosemite? Europe? Piedmont? Or was he working on the house?) In October 1890 he is listed at 1030 Vallejo.

6. The Worcester house has been demolished. William Kostura generously pointed out the photograph of the bay window end, *"large plate glass windows . . ."* of the living room, taken by Charles Lummis in 1898; the illustration (Fig. 2.4) corresponds with the description of Joseph Worcester's living room as described in Silver, *Sketches,* 120. The photograph of the fireplace in the living room (Fig. 2.3) was given to the authors of the 1974 edition *Building with Nature* by Eldridge T. Spencer, who lived in the Worcester house until 1969.

7. AWMem, 25. Worcester seems to have been invited out constantly; see Chapter 8 where Howard mentions his presence at every social occasion.

8. Keeler, "FBT," 16, in BL: Keeler Papers.

9. Edmund Sears Memoir, June 26, 1930, in SLA: Tobisch Archives.

10. For the Marshall house townscape, see Kostura, *Russian Hill,* 53, 56. William Kostura wrote, August 13, 2004, that *"all these Worcester houses were on one large lot"* and that *"he had located an abstract of a deed showing Marshall buying the lot in 1870. . . . It was a '. . . 50-vara lot,' or one-sixth of a square block. That's how the blocks were originally subdivided in the 1840s. In this case, it was the middle lot on the north side of Vallejo, between Taylor and Jones. Later, long after the four houses were built, it was split up. . . ."* This confirms that Worcester determined the dynamic placement of the houses in relationship to each other. Since he was not locked into small plots, Worcester was free to determine where the four houses should be built.

Kostura pointed out Bruce Price's San Francisco house (Fig 0.3). In addition to the houses and church, Worcester also designed "The Rock," a home for orphan boys (AWMem, 20). Per Kostura, he was assisted by Llewellyn B. Dutton, architect of record. Worcester undoubtedly knew Dutton through Burnham, as Dutton had worked for Burnham in Chicago.

11. Morphy, "Taylor Street," 61. For a more sober, and probably correct, analysis of how Willis Polk found this house, see Longstreth, *Edge,* 126, 134, 376n19.

12. See Kostura, *Russian Hill,* 64, for Willis Polk's renovation of the Livermore house and his role as spokesperson for Worcester. Kostura to the author, March 27, 2005: the house was added to and remodeled in the late 1880s; the redwood paneling was removed and then put back.

13. *AN* (December 1890): 11.

14. For the Goelet house, see Scully, *Shingle Style,* 138, 142, figs. 126–28; for the Newcomb house, Elberon, New Jersey, see 134–36 and fig. 121; and see throughout the book for multiple examples of eastern Shingle Style houses entirely different from Joseph Worcester's houses in Piedmont and on Russian Hill. In *Edge,* 114, Longstreth remarks on the earlier use of redwood in the East but without acknowledging that it was used for a completely different effect and purpose. The goal seems to have been elegance, and to that end the redwood was often elaborately turned, carved, and otherwise "improved."

15. Price, *Country House;* the preface, which was written by Bruce Price in New York, December 3, 1886, includes these statements. CED Library Microfilm: 17741.NA.reel 74:956

16. Scully, *Shingle Style,* 97.

17. Peixotto, "SF Architecture," 449–63; cited in Kostura, *Russian Hill,* 67.

18. Kostura, *Russian Hill,* 67.

19. For the Boericke commission and remodeling, see ibid. and Longstreth, *Edge,* 381n20, where he suggests Polk copied the half-timber façade from the "post-medieval" sixteenth-century Eastgate house illustration in ibid., 213, fig.170.

20. Longstreth coined this apt phrase, the rustic city house, in *Edge,* 107ff. For more-detailed excellent descriptions and photographs of the Polk-Williams duplex and the comparison with French medieval houses, a comparison first presented by Longstreth; see *Edge,* 117–19, and Kostura, *Russian Hill,* 67–70. Coxhead's design for All Saints Church (1888–89), Pasadena, presumably designed while Polk worked with Coxhead, features medieval-type half-timbering around its large Gothic window; it is illustrated in Longstreth, *Edge,* 49, fig. 28.

21. Kostura, *Russian Hill,* 70; for completion dates for the duplex, see ibid., 68. Note in the photo of Russian Hill, taken after the Marshall houses and Worcester's house were finished in 1889–90 (Fig. 2.5), that the duplex has not yet been built. The duplex is an unusual Polk house in that its exterior is extremely simple, having none of the historical trappings visible in his other designs, which can be seen in all three issues of *AN* and illustrated in Longstreth, *Edge.* The duplex structure is still numbered 1013–1015–1017–1019 Vallejo. See Mizner, *Many Mizners,* 75, for mention of architect Addison Mizner and other people living in various parts of the house. In 1892 Polk's father, Willis Webb, and brother, Daniel, lived at 1015 and 1017 Vallejo. See S. F. Voter Registration, October 17, 1892, in Kerrick, "Polk," 22. Beginning in late 1892, Willis Polk resided at 1015 Vallejo. See *OBA* and *SF Directories* as well as Kostura, *Russian Hill,* 67.

22. For Worcester's involvement with Russian Hill's development, see a copy of the letter Willis Polk wrote to Irving M. Scott in EDA: Polk Collection (1934–1, folder II.1, correspondence).

23. On Stevenson memorial, see *SF Examiner,* January 6, 1895, 7. I am very grateful to William Kostura, Anthony Bruce, and Daniella Thompson for helping me sort out the Stevenson connection with Worcester, Polk, Keeler, Russian Hill,

and Berkeley. John Muir may well have been part of this "Bohemian" group; his library contained books by Longfellow, Ruskin, Thoreau, and Stevenson, as well as two books on Swedenborgianism.

24. On Stevenson's shingling a Berkeley house, see Keeler, "FBT," 231: *"And finally, Mrs. Robert Louis Stevenson came and bought the old-fashioned house which stood just back of us on the canyon rim and made it over with a shingled exterior to conform to the group."* The property was located on the corner of Highland Place and Le Conte Avenue. The house belonged to Cora Tompkins in 1891 and to Samuel L. Osbourne in 1904; it was shingled, probably by Stevenson, in 1910. Samuel Lloyd Osbourne was Fanny Stevenson's son and Robert Louis Stevenson's stepson. It was for his amusement that Robert Louis Stevenson wrote *Treasure Island.* According to Daniella Thompson, Fanny never lived in this house; her home was in San Francisco. After 1900 she also lived off and on at her ranch, Vanumanutagi, in the Santa Cruz Mountains.

25. BL: Howison Papers. Stevenson's full name was Robert Louis Balfour Stevenson. Graham Balfour published *The Life of Robert Louis Stevenson* (New York: Scribners, 1901).

CHAPTER 3
The Swedenborgian Church and the First Mission Style Chair

1. Keeler, "San Francisco," 67, and similar sentiments in Keeler, *Thereabout,* 41–42. The Swedenborgian Church had become an Arts & Crafts icon by 1901 when Craft's "A Sermon in Church Building" was published in the widely read *HB* (February 1901). The feature story was eight pages long and included seven photographs, two of which were full page. The *Craftsman* published not one but two articles on it: Keeler, "Municipal Art," 592, and see also "Departure in Church Building, 330–34, with illustrations of both interior and exterior. Although the 1906 article is signed "By a Stranger," a letter to Mrs. Miller at 3369 Jackson Street, San Francisco, dated March 13, 1906, accepting *"your MS. about the charming little California Church"* remains in the SLA files and suggests that she authored it.

2. AWMem, March 1, 1892.

3. "A House that Teaches," *SF Examiner,* September 30, 1895; with multiple headlines: "A House that Teaches," "The Roof Supported by Madrone Trees just as they Left the Forest," "The Rev. Mr. Worcester's Church,"

and "Going to Service Through a Garden and Hearing a Sermon while Resting on Rush-Bottomed Chairs." The article is currently on the Internet at www.sfswedenborgian.org.

4. See Tuthill, *True and the Beautiful,* 72. Burnham also studied Ruskin; he wrote his mother December 1, 1867: *"I am studying John Ruskin's Stones of Venice evenings."* Letter in DBH. See also Hitchcock, *19th & 20th Centuries,* 107n33, provides evidence of the popularity of Ruskin's work in America from 1850 to 1900.

5. Keith to Worcester, May 18, 1884, in SLA.

6. Thomsen, *Its Lessons,* in SLA.

7. The difference between the Aesthetes and Ruskin and Morris is succinctly and clearly documented by curators of the Victoria and Albert Museum in its British Galleries.

8. AWMem, March 1, 1892.

9. Wood, "Muir Quotations"; Muir, *Yosemite,* 256; Wolfe, *Muir Journals,* 317.

10. McKail, "Morris," 39.

11. *SABE,* no. 2 (August 1899): 35; Craft, "A Sermon," *HB* 9, no. 3 (February 1901), 125–33.

12. For Richardson's visit to Morris, see Livingstone and Parry, *Arts & Crafts,* 25. Worcester's scrapbooks are in EDA.

13. DHB.

14. Ibid.

15. Ibid.

16. AWMem, March 1, 1892.

17. Letter to Warren (no first name given), in SLA: Worcester Archive, in a folder on Joseph Worcester and the Swedenborgian Church.

18. Copy of this survey remains in SCL.

19. Letter to Hinkley (no first name given) in SLA.

20. For convincing proof that Bernard Maybeck worked with Brown in 1893, see Cardwell, *Maybeck,* 30–32. Maybeck seems to have taken any job he could get as a newly married man needing work, so that between 1890 and 1892 he worked for Charles M. Plum furniture designer, Wright & Sanders architects, as well as for A. Page Brown, with Julius Kraaft and J. B. Mathiesen, and for himself. Woodbridge, *Maybeck,* 21: *"Maybeck seems to have been in several places at once during his first years in California, responding to the many opportunities that architecture on the western frontier offered."* Maybeck also planned to open a school of architecture, announced in the *Wave,* June 20, 1891.

21. Joseph Worcester to John Galen Howard (1900), in BL: Howard Papers. Worcester's letter and the following article present convincing evidence that Porter designed two windows. A paraphrase of the *Wave*

(August 4, 1897) follows: Bruce Porter is setting off for Southern France and Northern Italy. He brings all materials for his stained glass from New York; he has to reach across the whole continent for the colors. He will be gone 3 years. Earlier Bruce Porter *"designed the windows* [note the plural] *in the Swedenborgian church . . . ."*

22.Tobisch, "Garden Church," in SLA. Ruskin, *Seven Lamps,* 7, saw *"Venice and Verona, as representing the Italian Gothic colored by Byzantine elements."*

23. Worcester admits the church resembles one near Verona in "House that Teaches." In *Keith* 1, 366, Brother Cornelius repeats Miss Vesta Bradbury's story.

24. Porter to his brother, C. B. Porter, November 20, 1889, in BL: Porter Papers.

25. I am very grateful to Robert Judson Clark, who discovered this sketch by Trost, for first pointing it out and then for kindly letting us publish a photograph of it.

26. This bronze screen or grille is exhibited in the Art and Archaeology National Museum, Ravenna, Italy. Worcester and his friends could also have seen Blashfield, "Art of Ravenna," 37–57.

27. Dr. Richard C. Cabot to Mrs. Arthur Lyman, July 24, 1901, in SLA: Tobisch Archive.

28. Regarding Wright's Weed Vase, see Kaplan, "America," 265, plate 8.23. She writes that the Weed Vase was designed in 1893, made ca. 1898, and Wright used it in several of his houses.

29. *SABE* 28, no. 2 (August 1899): 35.

30. Craft, "A Sermon," 126, 131.

31. Neuhaus, *Keith,* 20–33, and Cornelius, *Keith* 1, 567.

32. William Keith to Judge Rearden, July 1, 1883, in BL: Keith-McHenry-Pond Family Papers.

33. *SF Call,* April 16, 1887, and *SF Examiner* April 28, 1887; cited in Turner, et al, *Stanford,* 70 and 80n8. Anthony Bruce and Lesley Emmington of BAHA pointed out that the chapel was not actually constructed until 1903 when Clinton Day carried out the Shepley, Rutan & Coolidge design, continuing the Richardson Romanesque style made famous by the firm's predecessor, Henry Hobson Richardson.

34. Turner, et al, *Stanford,* 26–27, and 66n52.

35. Jordan, *Days of a Man,* 1:212, 272, 372. Dr. James Lawrence of SHS believes Worcester knew Leland Stanford, one of the powerful San Francisco businessmen who contributed to Worcester's homes for ex-convicts and orphans. Lawrence suggested in a letter to the author on January 20, 2005, that *"the Stanfords were interested in Swedenborgianism. Stanford University was a memorial to their son, whose early death shook them to their core. The Stanfords developed a very deep interest in spiritualism and in information on life after death and contacts with the other world, and they established an endowment for a library to collect such literature at the campus; Worcester was also invited to be the annual Phi Beta Kappa speaker at Stanford in 1910; there is really no doubt that Worcester knew the Stanfords."*

36. Alice E. Burnham of Waltham, Massachusetts, to Brother Cornelius, July 31, 1943, in Cornelius, *Keith* 2, 103. For an image of Polk's Imaginary Mission Church, see Longstreth, *Edge,* 263, and fig. 204, or Weitze, *California Mission Revival.*

37. Brown, *SF Chronicle,* 1894. See also the Shipounoff introduction to Keeler, *The Simple Home* (1979), xxi; Shipounoff cites Keeler, who phrased his abhorrence a little differently from Brown: *"Keeler began to worry that others, less sensitive . . . to the landscape, would 'come and build stupid white-painted boxes all around' him."*

38. For A. Page Brown's complete article, see Brown, "Architecture in California,"16–17, although most of it is presented here and in Chapter 7.

39. "The Attractions of Blair Park," *Oakland Daily Evening Tribune,* June 20, 1891, 2/9.

40. For floor plans and elevations of a Japanese building, see *AB* 1, no. 2 (February 1894): 19.

41. CHS: Brown Scrapbook #2, December 1893, no. 11 in the scrapbook's table of contents lists "Japanese Life and Customs," Illus. by W. K. Burton, pages 449–55. The entire article is pasted into the scrapbook.

42. See Tobisch, *Garden Church.*

43. Dr. Richard C. Cabot to Mrs. Arthur Lyman, July 24, 1901, in SLA: Tobisch Archive.

44. Worcester's preference for asymmetry and his criticism of Brown's *"penchant for symmetry"* are expressed in his letter to Howison (1891), in BL: Howison Papers; see Chapter 5.

45. Letter entitled "Church of the Simple Life," given Reverend Tobisch in the 1940s by Alfred Worcester; it is not signed nor dated, but it is handwritten on the *back* of a sheet dated March 11, 1886. Since Alfred disposed of Joseph's effects, it is likely that he saved this letter from among Joseph Worcester's papers.

46. Craft, "A Sermon," *The House Beautiful,* 9, no. 3, 132. Worcester's version of how he obtained the Madrone trees appeared earlier in "A House that Teaches," *SF Examiner,* September 30, 1895. Worcester repeated the story to his nephew, Alfred, December 11, 1912, in SLA: Worcester Archive.

47. Worcester's diary remains in SCL. Brother Cornelius records the same story in *Keith* 2, 102. The roof was constructed by N. Clark & Sons, 17 & 19 Spear Street. The original bill is also in SCL.

48. Kostura, *Russian Hill,* 51.

49. Maybeck told Cardwell he worked with Wright & Sanders in 1890, and, indeed, he was sent by that firm to Salt Lake City before May 1890, the date when he patented a design for a fan there. See Cardwell, *Maybeck,* 27. More research on the San Francisco Theological Seminary and its Wright & Sanders houses and buildings in San Anselmo may well uncover information on the firm and Maybeck's possible contributions.

50. See "Maybeck: A Gothic Man in the Twentieth Century" in Keeler, "FBT," in BL: Keeler Papers. Maybeck would have met Worcester through Brown and Polk, whether they were neighbors or not; however, the fact that he rented a cottage, very possibly owned by Worcester's cousins, very near Worcester's, and that he was a young architect who admired Ruskin and Morris and worked for Worcester's friend Brown makes this story ring true.

51. Keeler, "FBT," 228–29.

52. Ibid.," 227.

53. *AR* (Boston) (1904); also cited in Cardwell, *Maybeck,* 53.

54. For Schweinfurth's comment on Maybeck, see Schweinfurth, *Wave,* November 28, 1896, letter to the editor, headlined "Communication," 3.

55. Cardwell, *Maybeck,* 18; for Maybeck's sentiment as an echo of Viollet-le-Duc's description of Art's capacity *"to strike deep-seated chords in the soul,"* see Craig, *Maybeck,* 33.

56. AWMem, June 11, 1871.

57. Schweinfurth to William R. Hearst, November 25, 189? (year unknown, probably 1895); see Chapters 7 and 10 for more on this letter. I am grateful to Richard Longstreth for sharing with me these two rare Schweinfurth letters, one to Hearst and one to Clark and will give BL copies.

58. Letter from Schweinfurth to Edward H. Clark in San Francisco regarding the Hacienda del Pozo de Verona, December 20, 189? (probably 1895).

59. For reasons why the hacienda may well have been started in 1894 and for reasons why this letter probably dates from 1895, see Chapter 10.

60. Calavan, "Schweinfurth," 7; see also Chapters 7 and 10 of this book. Since the publication of Richard Longstreth's *Edge* in 1978, many scholars have followed Longstreth's

lead and assumed that Schweinfurth designed the Swedenborgian Church. But whether the facts support this contention remains unclear. For those interested in Schweinfurth's role and for a different view from that presented here see Longstreth *Edge.*

61. Was Schweinfurth in San Francisco when the church was being planned, probably late 1892 as the completion of the round window suggests. In 1892 Brown may have sent Schweinfurth to Lima, Peru, to work on the Grand Market, an enormous project ($800,000–$1,000,000) whose drawings were published in August and November 1892, or Schweinfurth may have had another episode of depression (mentioned by Longstreth) or have been working for Brown in the New York office Brown maintained into 1892. Schweinfurth's obituary in *Inland Architect and News Record* 36, no. 4 (November 1900): 32, states that he married Miss Fanny Goodrich in 1888, so he could have been on a honeymoon; but he does not list a wife in the *SF Directory* until he is listed in the blue book in 1897–98. Without more evidence we only know that he arrived in time to be listed in the 1893 *SF Directory,* published in May of the year. On Schweinfurth, Brown, and the Grand Market for Lima, Peru, see Longstreth, *Edge,* 384n34; 388n24, and 438, which mentions the two articles on the market.

From the enormous size of the Lima project described in these two articles, it would seem possible that "an agent," possibly Schweinfurth, representing the architect A. Page Brown, might have been detailed to the San Francisco firm of Rix and Birrell, engineers. If so, that would explain why Schweinfurth does not appear in the *SF Directory* until 1893. However, in the end, despite the articles and drawings, the Grand Market appears not to have been built because there seems to be no subsequent articles on it, nor does it appear in any of the guidebooks I checked. There is a major market in Santiago, Chile, by Gustave Eiffel, the architect of the famous Eiffel Tower. Its size, prominence, and the fact that Chileans chose a French architect shows that this type of building would have been a major commission for Brown, and he may well have detailed Schweinfurth to deal with it.

62. Longstreth, *Edge,* 369n1.

63. Without sure proof that Schweinfurth designed the Lemon Curer Warehouse, we lack proof that Schweinfurth worked for brown in California or anywhere else in 1891. On Crocker & Co. Lemon Curer

Warehouse, see Longstreth, *Edge,* 88–89. In a reply to my e-mail query asking Longstreth if he had proof that Schweinfurth drew and or designed the Lemon Curer Warehouse, published as Brown's work in *A&B* (December 5, 1891), Longstreth replied on March 29, 2005: *"With no paper trail for these works, they are all attributions. My basis, as I recall, was that Schweinfurth did the rendering and that the quality of expression seemed to be his, irrespective of motifs. Moreover, Schweinfurth was Brown's chief designer at that time. I found a reference, which I cited in the book, that Brown delegated the designing to talented assistants."* (For a discussion of Schweinfurth's role in Brown's firm, see also Chapters 7 and 10 of this book.) However, Brown could well have designed the Lemon Curer Warehouse himself. It could even have been drawn by Willis Polk, who delineated for Brown the old People's Home, which has similar motifs. Compare Lemon Curer illustration in *Edge,* 89 fig. 46, with the Old People's Home herein, Fig. 5.2, 74. The facts remain to be uncovered.

64. I am basing this conclusion on detailed analyses of Schweinfurth's work and career by Longstreth, *Edge;* see also Calavan, "Schweinfurth," and on new information presented here and in Chapters 7 and 10. For the independent listing of his architectural firm by Schweinfurth in an office separate from Brown, see *SF Directories* for 1893, 1894, 1895–98. The *SF Chronicle,* February 26, 1894, 9/2, reports Schweinfurth's departure from Brown's firm.

65. For Maybeck's work with Brown in 1892, see Longstreth, *Edge,* 371n10. See also Cardwell, *Maybeck,* for biographical details and numerous references to Maybeck's work with Brown. In "California Exposition," 449–63, Phil Weaver describes the haste with which the buildings were being erected; clearly, they had been designed earlier in the year.

66. In *Edge,* 88–89, 371n10, Longstreth has Maybeck leaving Brown's firm to teach at the University of California, Berkeley, in 1894. But Maybeck is not listed in the *UC Annual Announcement of Courses of Instruction in the Colleges at Berkeley for the Academic Year 1894–95,* published in 1894. In conclusion, the evidence suggests that even if Maybeck did begin teaching at the university or taught informal seminars out of his home in 1894, he was doing it on a part-time basis, and even in 1895 he was only hired to teach part-time; thus, he did not have to leave Brown's

firm to take up his teaching, and so was available to work on the Swedenborgian Church.

67. Longstreth, *Edge,* 371n10.

68. Ibid., 273.

69. *SF Chronicle,* February 26, 1894, 9/2.

70. Longstreth, *Edge,* 279. Hearst asked Brown to renovate his Sausalito house before April 1894, because this information was discussed in "Town Talk," April 7, 1894, cited by ibid., 441. The microfilm editions of the William Randolph Hearst letters in BL now make it possible to date the Hacienda del Pozo de Verona's beginning to 1894. See Chapters 7 and 10.

71. Longstreth, *Edge,* 389n29.

72. Longstreth *Edge,* 85: "Schweinfurth held control for the next four years; once he departed in 1895 . . . ." One must ask which four years. Schweinfurth practiced in Denver in 1890 and there are no known Schweinfurth projects for Brown in 1891 or 1892 and he departed the firm February 1894, not 1895. For convincing proof that Bernard Maybeck worked with Brown in 1893, see Cardwell, *Maybeck,* 30–32.

73. Alfred Worcester's account of the building of the church, December 11, 1912, in SLA: Worcester Archive. Worcester must not have remembered precisely the fellow worker's name, as there is a question mark after the name "Richardson" in Alfred Worcester's transcription of his discussion with his uncle.

74. Historian Alan Thomsen reminded me of Ruskin's "The Poetry of Architecture."

75. *SF Examiner,* September 30, 1895

76. See Worcester's letter to George Howison denigrating Brown's *"penchant for symmetry"* in BL, cited in Chapter 5.

77. For illustration of E. C. Young, see Woodbridge, *Maybeck,* 148, plates 140 and 141.

78. Longstreth, *Edge,* 283.

79. For Mrs. John Baeck's letter to the editor, see *Berkeley Gazette,* November 5, 1964.

80. In August 2004 Dr. James F. Lawrence related via e-mail the stories of Brown's widow visiting the church and of his conversation with Mrs. Tobisch shortly before her death. Both confirm that Maybeck worked on the church. Neither woman mentions Schweinfurth. Cornelius, *Keith* 2, 101, also names Maybeck as the draftsman.

81. Thompson, "Domestic Architecture," 15–21.

82. Ibid., 18–21.

83. Thompson, "Early Domestic Architecture," 15ff. This article was published in 1951 when she was 40, appearing just three years after she had interviewed Porter.

Details of the Porter interviews as told to me by Richard Longstreth and Edward Bosley follow. Longstreth interviewed Thompson before the publication of *Edge* in 1983. Apparently Thompson told Longstreth during that interview that Porter had told her that Schweinfurth was the key figure (*Edge,* 389n28). Edward Bosley interviewed her again on March 15, 1995, when she was 84 years old, fifty-three years after her interview with Porter. (Thompson died March 27, 1998, at age 87. Her obituary states that she had a stroke in October, presumably in 1997, but no year is given.) During that interview, Bosley says Thompson told him that Porter had told her in 1948, that Schweinfurth had been "assigned" to design the Swedenborgian Church.

Neither Longstreth nor Bosley explain why Thompson did not credit Schweinfurth with the Swedenborgian Church in her 1951 article. In *Edge,* 88, Longstreth proposes that Schweinfurth served as Brown's principal designer, but as we have seen, there is no proof that Schweinfurth had been "assigned" to design the Swedenborgian Church.

Even if we accept the idea that Schweinfurth had been "assigned" by Brown to the Swedenborgian Church, Schweinfurth would have been working with or alongside Maybeck, whom everyone agrees was the draftsman. So the question really is: Considering how many details were determined by Worcester himself, what were Schweinfurth's and Maybeck's contributions to the design, if any?

84. Lawrence notes that Porter lived just two blocks from the Swedenborgian Church, and though Porter had ceased regular attendance at services by the time Tobisch assumed the pastorate in 1929, the two men nevertheless formed a warm friendship lasting more than two decades. Porter would certainly have told Tobisch that Schweinfurth designed the church if indeed he had. Information about Tobisch comes from James Lawrence, currently dean of SHS, who also knew his widow, Margit Tobisch, quite well and was her minister for eight years. He reports that Mrs. Tobisch was as devoted to the church as her husband, and was quite knowledgeable. Lawrence held two conversations with her, specifically on her belief about what was understood by the early principals as to the design of the church. She reported in 1992 that she had never heard the name of Schweinfurth.

85. A copy of the Maybeck drawing still hangs in SCL; the original was given to the San Francisco Museum of Modern Art and is catalogued as a Bernard Maybeck drawing.

86. Copies of Tobisch's 1945 Swedenborgian Church pamphlet are in SLA: Tobisch Archive.

87. SM: Cornelius Archive, August 15, 1939 (Folder T). The letter reveals that Tobisch was contacting persons intimately involved with the church as early as 1939.

88. For the date of the parsonage, see Bosley, "Schweinfurth," 11–22, especially page 15 where he states that *"the church and parsonage lots were purchased May 1, 1894, and construction contracts were signed for both buildings in August . . . ."* The first lot surveyed for the church, and then rejected, was at the corner of Taylor and Jackson, and was surveyed *"for Joseph Worcester by M. M. O'Shaunnessy; room 225 Crocker Building on March 13, 1893."* A copy of this survey is located in SCL. The lot on Lyon Street was surveyed August 28, 1894; a copy of this survey also remains in the Swedenborgian Church Library. For possible early dating of the design of the church to late 1892 or early 1893, see above discussion of Porter's window and fundraising in early 1893, page 38, letters to Warren and Hinkley.

89. On February 26, 1894, the *SF Chronicle* reported that Schweinfurth left Brown. Worcester documented the delivery of the trees in his diary, which remains in SCL. I am grateful to Edward Bosley and Alfred Einarsson for lending me the image of the church under construction. This photo was first published by Bosley as the frontispiece in "Schweinfurth," and was made from a glass negative in the Swedenborgian Church Library.

90. Regarding the photo of a man at construction site: William Gillitt, an architect, artist, and photographer, and an expert at three-dimensional overlays and Photoshop, was kind enough to overlay these portraits for me on January 9, 2005. His conclusions agree with another expert of Photoshop software, Maureen Taylor of Westwood, Massachusetts, who does historical photo analysis for a living. Both Gillitt and Taylor's results show that the man standing at the construction site is not Schweinfurth and is probably Brown. Taylor's results show that the man in the photograph at the work site during the building of Lyon Street church (late 1894), magnified 600 percent, when compared with a portrait photograph of Brown (1893) reveals six facial characteristics—ear, nose, brow, chin, side hairline, mustache—that are either wholly identical or so

close that no doubt can be entertained that they are the same person. If the ears are overlaid exactly, the man in the hat can be Brown but it is certainly not Schweinfurth. So for technical reasons as well as for the reasons given above, visible with the naked eye, Schweinfurth is not the man standing, wearing a hat, at the Swedenborgian Church construction site.

91. None of the architects or artists who were involved with Worcester or the Swedenborgian Church took credit for the design of the church, which is further confirmation that Worcester was probably the key designer working closely with his architect Brown, his draftsman Maybeck, and his many artist and architect friends.

92. For Schweinfurth's obituary, see *AABN* 70 (October 1900): 22, or the obituary in *Inland Architect and News Record* 36, no. 4 (November 1900): 32. For Brown's obituary, see *SF Examiner* (January 22, 1896).

Although the Swedenborgian Church had been praised in numerous articles in the San Francisco press, and had been featured in *Scientific American Building Edition* 28, no. 2 (August 1899): front page and 35–36; and in Craft, "A Sermon," 125–33, it was not attributed to Schweinfurth in *Architectural Review* 9 (March 1902; new series *AR* 4, no. 3, 76–81), published less than two years after his death and seven years after the church was finished. Swedenborg on architecture, cited in Bosley, "Schweinfurth."

93. Bosley, "Schweinfurth," 12. Several excellent scholars attribute the church's design to Schweinfurth, and it is possible that these same scholars may turn out to be right; only time and new evidence demonstrating that Schweinfurth was in San Francisco in 1892 and before March 1893 when the church was most likely being designed will finally tell.

94. Wilson "Divine Excellence," 28.

95. Craft, "A Sermon," 126–131. Craft notes on page 126 that *". . . the church follows the mission architecture of California with arches adapted from the Moorish . . . ."* Note that Craft links Mission and Moorish; see more on these linked styles in Chapter 10.

96. D'Ambrosio and Bowman, 11: *"McHugh was the self-proclaimed originator of "Mission" style furniture in America."* Ibid., 26nn32–47, cite numerous articles on McHugh's Mission Furniture including n36 a publication put out by McHugh himself: *"The 'Mission' Furniture of Joseph P. McHugh & Co: Its origins and Some Opinions by Decorative Authorities* (New York: Joseph P. McHugh & Co., 1901), Winterthur Library: Printed Book

and Periodical Collection. And see their n34, which states: *More than a Hundred Pen Sketches* [McHugh's catalog] *features eight pages of Mission designs.* The chair was first designed in late 1894, and Dudley, who drew up McHugh's version of the Swedenborgian Church chair, did not join McHugh until 1896. Evidence suggests McHugh first marketed the Mission pieces in 1898 in the catalogue mentioned above, *"More than . . . ."* See also Matlack Price, "Practicality, Imagination and the Designer: A Study of the Work of Walter J. H. Dudley," *Arts and Decoration* (July 1921): 166–68, Dudley's sketch for the *"first two pieces of Mission furniture."* I am not trying to suggest that McHugh's or Stickley's furniture was inspired only by the Swedenborgian Church chair; however, the church chair inspired McHugh to launch the first line of Mission furniture sometime between 1896 and 1898. I am very grateful to Arts & Crafts expert Harold Wright for several of the articles cited in this section.

97. For another point of view, see Cathers, "East Coast,"154–55, who discusses Stickley's desire to make "more meaningful work" but does not connect this desire with seeing McHugh's success. By September 1900, Stickley had hired LaMont Warner, a full-time designer. Warner had clipped English furniture designs published in International Studio, which he brought to the furniture he subsequently designed for Stickley. It would seem to me that Warner and Stickley were also aware of the competition's Mission line, as well as of British designs being published in International Studio. For a different point of view, see Cathers, *Stickley,* 36.

98. For *"no one would mistake it . . . ,"* see Cathers in "East Coast," 155. For Stickley steering clear of Mission, see Cathers, *Stickley,* 113. For *"over one hundred pages"* and Stickley's furniture as *"the structural style of cabinet making,"* see Cathers, "East Coast," 154–55. Although Stickley sometimes disparaged Mission furniture (Cathers, *Stickley,* 113) and emphasized his Craftsman label as distinct from the Mission Style, looking at his Arts & Crafts designs that began ca. 1900, the influence of his competitor's Mission line inspired by the Swedenborgian Church chair as well as recently published English furniture designs is evident. D'Ambrosio and Bowman, *McHugh,* 24, write: *"The similarity between McHugh's and Stickley's early designs is strong and implies some relationship, but the path of influence remains unclear.*

McHugh clearly viewed Stickley as one of his chief competitors and expended a great deal of energy in the effort to establish himself as the originator of the Mission style. . . . McHugh Mission was a trend setting product."

99. Cathers, *Stickley,* 124–25, notes that *"from 1904 onward Stickley turned increasingly to the more orthodox dictates of machines"* and cites Stickley, who wrote in his 1906 Craftsman catalog: *"To say in this day of well-nigh perfect machinery that anything that is good must be done entirely by hand is going rather far."* To achieve affordability and profitability, Stickley shifted toward *"plainness and standardization"* so that by 1904 he had turned to machine manufacture, as undoubtedly did McHugh and his other competitors, all of whom watched the bottom line.

100. Bowman in D'Ambrosio, *McHugh,* 24, states that half a dozen chairs were shipped from Martin Ingalsbe to McHugh *"in the spring of 1896 or possibly 1897,"* and that McHugh named it *"The Old Mission Chair of California."* For a slightly different view, see D'Ambrosio, *McHugh,* 18, where she credits Eudora Martin with sending McHugh *"a chair either from the Church of the New Jerusalem or one modeled on its chairs; McHugh sold it and a dozen or so more that Martin supplied."* For Candace Wheeler as *"the first professional woman interior designer,"* see Kaplan, "America," 252.

101. *SF Chronicle,* October 21, 1900, 30, tells the story of the Martin and Ingalsbe partnership, and mentions that Mary Ingalsbe worked for Mary Curtis (later Mary Curtis Richardson) and that Eudora Martin worked in the East for three years with Candace Wheeler, who handled draperies for "LaFarge and Tiffany."

The *SF Directory* listings for "Martin, Ingalsbe and Bruce Porter" appear in 1892, 1893, and 1894. But for 1886–1891 and 1895 the firm listed just Martin & Ingalsbe. Harold Wright kindly sent me this information. See also Kaplan, "America," 271. More research may uncover who actually sent the design or chair(s) to McHugh. For the description of Candace Wheeler and more on her work with Tiffany and Associated Artists, see Kaplan, ibid., 252; Kaplan also details the numerous "home industries" and "artistic craft" organizations that helped women from the 1870s on.

102. Despite the poor English in this contract, Forbes seems to have had an international clientele. In a letter to Worcester dated January 28 or 23,

1895, [writing unclear], written at 29 Glen Park Avenue, A. J. Forbes mentions making a cabinet for "Bismarck the chancellor" and a visit from the "archbishop of Paris" requesting a similar cabinet; however, Forbes writes that upon hearing that Forbes was not a Catholic, the arch-bishop withdrew the commission. Deanna Forbes, A. J. Forbes' great-granddaughter, sent me a copy of this letter, December 31, 2004. A copy was also given to SLA. Tim Hansen pointed out that the word "flag" in the contract refers to the rush from which the seats will be made.

103. Forbes' charming letter detailing his lack of religious feeling is cited in the *SF Examiner,* September 30, 1895. Forbes' original proposal is stored in SCL. See Cardwell, *Maybeck,* and elsewhere in this book for illustrations of the chairs being used in Bay Area houses.

104. Ann Baeck (granddaughter of Worcester's dear friend Judge Rearden), in a letter to the *Berkeley Gazette,* November 5, 1964, at SLA. One possible donor, Phoebe Apperson Hearst, was not only a friend of Worcester's but also Maybeck's and Schweinfurth's client. There are many letters from Worcester to Mrs. Hearst on micro-film at BL, but none found to date mention the chairs.

105. See note 100. I am grateful to Tim Hansen, who has extensively researched these chairs for the infor-mation that the McHugh chairs were scaled down. He also informed me that A. J. Forbes and Son is the firm's proper name.

106. *New-Church Pacific* 7, no. 7 (July 1894), at SLA.

107. Numerous mission sketches are found in BL: Keeler Papers and Porter Papers.

108. Howard's Mission sketching in 1887–88 is described at length by Woodbridge in *Howard,* 4–6. Keith's painting *San Juan Capistrano* was framed in the handicraft spirit by Lummis himself; see Moure, *Art in L.A.,* 25, fig. 10.

109. On Maybeck and Brown and the "Mission Style" California Building, see Cardwell, *Maybeck;* see also Chapter 10.

110. BL: Porter Papers. In July 1975 Willis Forbes told Longstreth that Forbes Manufacturing Company of San Francisco continued to make the chairs, but apparently Forbes did not tell Longstreth whether or not they were referred to as "Mission" or "Mission Style"; see Longstreth, *Edge,* 389n28.

111. *SF Examiner,* September 30, 1895, tells Forbes' story. For Forbes' reference to

cottage mats, see contract in text. Worcester may also have seen rush-bottomed chairs made by European designers (e.g., Voysey and Baillie Scott) or the Sussex chair made by Morris & Co. in the 1870s.

112. For Mackmurdo's ideals and travels with Ruskin, see Kaplan, "Simple Life." For an illustration of Mackmurdo's desk featuring the squashed foot, see Davey, *A&C Architecture,* 56.

113. For Mackmurdo and the spiritual see Kaplan, "Simple Life," as well as "America," 270–73. Kaplan referred to the foot as *"flared trumpet"* in the exhibition associated with her book.

Lethaby, too, like Worcester and Maybeck, emphasized the value of handwork, the craft of building, and the value of vernacular sources and local materials; he also believed there was mysticism connected with great architecture. R. Norman Shaw had admired Lethaby's writing about handicraft and brought him to his firm, where he remained for ten years (1879–89). Lethaby became friends with Ruskin and Morris, helped set up the Art Workers Guild and Arts & Crafts Exhibition Society, and published *Architecture, Mysticism and Myth* (1891) wherein he expected a future *"of nature and man, of order and beauty."* This information from Davey, *A&C Architecture,* 65–68, and Cumming and Kaplan, *A&C Movement,* 9, 39.

114. See Cardwell, *Maybeck,* 16–17, 22, for details of his work for Pottier and Stymus, pages 29–30 for Charles Plum, and for illustrations of many of Maybeck's furniture designs. For more on Maybeck's furniture, see figs. 3.16 and 3.25.

115. *SABE* (New York) 28, no. 2 (August 1899): 35.

116. Cardwell, *Maybeck,* 29, 30.

117. For example, Brown's December 1894 article, cited herein, indicates his familiarity with Vienna. Coxhead came from England; Maybeck studied at the École, Worcester clipped pictures of church chairs for his scrapbook, and all these architects followed architectural trends worldwide in the architectural press.

118. Keeler, "Mission Furniture." For A. Page Brown as designer of the chairs but indebted to Joseph Worcester, see *SABE* (New York) 28, no. 2 (August 1899): 35.

119. For Keeler's praise of Worcester, see Keeler, *Thereabout,* 41–42, and Chapter 3n1. For Worcester's influence on Polk and Coxhead, see Keeler, "Municipal Art," 592. See also Thompson, "Domestic Architecture," 15–21, for corroboration of Worcester's influence.

CHAPTER 4
The First American Arts & Crafts Society, San Francisco, 1894

1. For the "permanent" organization of the Guild of Arts and Crafts in San Francisco, see the *Wave* (September 22, 1894); for guild goals, see the *Wave* (October 27, 1894).

2. See Livingstone, "Origins and Development," 48. In 1883 five young assistants from R. Norman Shaw's office formed the St George's Art Society. The society discussed its worries about the growing practical and ideological separation of art and architecture, and the indifference to their ideas for reform in architecture shown by the official institutions such as the Royal Academy and the Royal Institute of British Architects. They soon realized that there was a need for a larger, broader society. In 1884 these same architects—Gerald Horsley (1862–1917), W. R. Lethaby, Mervyn Macartney (1853–1932), Ernest Newton and E. S. Prior—joined with another group, The Fifteen, led by Lewis F. Day (1845–1910) and Walter Crane (1845–1915), to form the Art Workers' Guild (1884). The guild actively promoted the theory of the interdependence of the arts, and its members were encouraged through lectures and discussion to understand each other's profession. Designers, artists, architects, and craftsmen were brought together as equals.

3. See these goals on stationery in EDA: Polk Collection (project 5 I: 4). The handwritten version, slightly different, as noted in the text also refers to the recent 1893 World's Columbian Exposition in Chicago.

4. The *Wave* (November 24, 1894): 7/1, and (October 27, 1894). Additional members were named by the *SF Chronicle,* November 23, 1894, 4/5: John Vance Cheney of the Public Free Library, J. O'H. Cosgrave, F. M. Gamble, C. O. Robinson, Horace G. Platt, Irving M. Scott, Charles F. Graham, M. W. Haskell, Professor Armes, Frank Burgess.

5. *SF Chronicle,* November 23, 1894.

6. The review of the San Francisco Guild of Arts and Crafts' exhibition by Austin Lewis appears in *Overland Monthly* (March 1896): 292–303. Its content shows how familiar architects and the press were with the Guild of Arts & Crafts in London's annual exhibitions and with *"the efforts of William Morris . . . and Walter Crane."*

7. "Second Exhibition of the Guild," *SF Examiner,* May 10, 1896, 12/3. See also reviews in *SF Chronicle,* May 9, 1896, n.p., and *The Wave,* May 23, 1896, 9/2.

8. For Keeler and the Ruskin Club, see biographical manuscript in BL: Keeler Papers (Keeler Scrapbook). See also Keeler, *Simple Home* (1979), Shipounoff introduction. Another Ruskin Club, which lasted eight years, was founded in Piedmont, November 1898, by A. A. Denison, Austin Lewis (who reviewed the San Francisco Guild of Arts & Crafts for the *Overland Monthly*), and Frederick Irons Bamford; Herman Sheffauer and George Sterling (poets) and Jacques Loeb (scientist). Jack London's first attendance was recorded January 6, 1900; information from Bamford, *Mystery of Jack London,* copy at Piedmont Historical Society. At the time, painter Xavier Martinez also formed part of Piedmont's bohemian crowd.

9. The *Wave* (April 24 1897): 3/3, described the petty rivalries in the Guild of Arts and Crafts; see also (May 23, 1896): 9/2, and (January 20, 1897): 7/3.

10. See Morris' frontispiece illustration in Winter, *Craftsman Style,* 18, or see Davey, *A&C Architecture,* 8.

11. Keeler, *Simple Home* (1979), xxxi–xxxii.

12. Kaplan, "America," 252.

CHAPTER 5
"A Cottage All of Our Own": Polk and Coxhead

1. Ruskin cited in Kornwolf, Scott, 14.

2. For Howison to Worcester and Howison to Pattiani Letters, see BL: Howison Papers (C-B 1037, incoming correspondence); BL: Worcester Letters (Box 6); BL: Pattiani Letters (Box 4). The first letter probably dates from early 1891. Paul T. Roberts, board president of the Victorian Preservation Center of Oakland, lectured on "Alfred Washington Pattiani: Victorian Designer-Builder" for BAHA, May 5, 2004, and kindly shared his knowledge of Pattiani and transitional shingle houses with the author. Roberts pointed out that contract details of construction progress and payment schedule were published in *CABN* 12, no. 6 (June 20, 1891): *"building, lot 36, Block E, George A. [sic] Howison. $4,763. A. W. Pattiani & Co. $1300, roof shingled & chimney built; $1,176 brown mortered & exterior primed; $1,100 completed; $1,187, 35 days."* The letters make it clear that Worcester also knew and respected architect Clinton Day (also a member of the San Francisco Arts & Crafts Guild and a friend of Worcester's), about whom more research needs to be done.

3. For Schweinfurth's arrival in San Francisco, the situation is not clear. Apparently something waylaid

Schweinfurth, as he did not appear in the *SF Directory* until 1893, and we know of no buildings or drawings done for Brown in 1891 or 1892. For more on Schweinfurth see especially Chapters 3, 7 and 10. The drawing of the old People's Home signed by Willis Polk (far left) is headlined (top left) A. Page Brown architect, New York and San Francisco. Did Schweinfurth remain in the New York office? Longstreth, *Edge,* 369n1, remarks that *"presentation drawings dated as late as 1892 refer to both offices . . . ."* Or did he have another breakdown? Anything is possible.

4. Paul Roberts located the Polk drawing in EDA: Polk Collection. See quote from Pattiani letter in BL: Howison Papers, as cited in note 2 above.

5. All correspondence mentioned is in BL; see note 2.

6. On Worcester's friendship with Polk, see Chapter 2 and Cornelius, *Keith* 1 and 2. See also Worcester to John Galen Howard, January 1, 1900, in BL: Howard Papers, and several other Worcester letters cited herein. As noted here, Polk published architecture from many places in *Architectural News,* 1890 and 1891.

7. See Polk's residence for H. R. Smith, Kansas City, Missouri, W. W. Polk and Sons, Architects, in *AABN* 23 (February 4, 1888): plate 632, signed "W. P., del. 1886, redrawn 1888." For the Presbyterian Church, see *AABN* 26 (August 24, 1889): plate 713. For the Lockwood house, see *AABN* 21 (March 12, 1887): 127.

8. See Longstreth, *Edge,* 364n20 and 262–63, who points out that Polk must have arrived in Los Angeles in late 1887 when he drew an imaginary mission church based on the "Southern California Type" and notes that Polk delineated for Coxhead the English Lutheran Church, Los Angeles (in *AABN* [May 19, 1888]), as well as two houses in Los Angeles and Santa Monica (in *AABN* [July 7, 1888]). Longstreth indicates that two designs, both labeled "Ernest Coxhead, architect, Willis Polk, del.," were published that year. See "House at Sta. Monica, Ca." in *AABN* 23 (July 7, 1888): plate 654, and "Lutheran Church, Los Angeles" in *AABN* 24 (May 19, 1888): plate 647. Longstreth also states that no two accounts of Polk's life agree.

9. *AABN* 26 (September 14, 1889): 716.

10. *AN* 1, no. 2 (December 1890): 11. Editors again cite Ruskin for support in *AN* 1, no. 3 (January 1891): 24.

11. For a review of John Calvin Stevens and Albert Winslow Cobb's book, see *AN* 1, no. 3 (January 1891): 33. Scully, *Shingle Style,* 114-19, also analyzes Stevens and Cobb's work

and cites their philosophy that *"was at the heart of the whole inventive American cottage development—in connection with a small house of their own."* Stevens and Cobb state: *"This simple cottage at Island Point, Vt., costs $2,300 complete. It exhibits the most primitive elements of architectural design. Such an authority as James Ferguson . . . might classify it as a specimen of 'mere building,' not architecture: but in our own terminology the word 'architecture' comprises in its meaning even so primitive a structure as this."* However, Scully acknowledges that most houses by either architect were neither small nor inexpensive.

12. *AN* 1, no. 2 (December 1890): 11; and on the same page under the heading "Contents: Editorial," there is more on the same theme.

13. Ibid.

14. See *AN* 1, no. 1 (November 1890) and all issues for images of buildings from all over the world showing that California architects were exceedingly well informed and up to date on architectural developments worldwide.

15. Longstreth, *Polk's Writings,* 15, with quotes from the *Wave* 1892–1899.

16. For the Avery house, see *AN* 1, no. 3 (January 1891): plates xvi, and 34. Longstreth, *Edge,* 428, cites "The Nook, Francis Avery House, 1890, by Polk and Gamble, 77 Buckley Drive, Sausalito. Demolished. Gates Extant."

17. For the Avery house, see *AN* 1, no. 3 (January 1891): plates xvi, and 34.

18. Photograph of Paget stair hall kept by Joseph Worcester was given to the author in the 1970s by Sturla Einarsson and will be donated to the BL in honor of Sturla Einarsson.

19. Information on the palatial Bourn house, 2550 Webster Street, San Francisco, is from Longstreth, *Edge,* 212–15, figs. 168 and 169, 430. For the Wheeler house, see Longstreth, *Edge,* 219, fig. 179. Longstreth also includes many other examples of Willis Polk's fashionable work and discusses and illustrates the McCullagh house in ibid., 290–91, figs. 228–29, 391n47.

20. The *Wave* (February 13, 1897): 3. I am grateful to Richard Longstreth for sharing this exchange with me. Ostensibly, Schweinfurth and Polk are criticizing the new planned post office but each also attacks the other with personal jibes.

21. For Coxhead's arrival in Los Angeles and for more biographical details, see Longstreth, *Edge,* 363n12 and index. Jeremy Kotas now holds the Coxhead papers, which formerly belonged to John Beach.

22. Letter from Worcester to Howard in BL: Howard Papers.

23. DHB.

24. Kornwolf, *Scott,* 13. Its interesting to consider how this principle and these ideas fit with Nikolaus Pevsner's famous statement from *European Architecture,* 19: "A bicycle shed is a building; Lincoln Cathedral is a piece of architecture."

25. Ibid., 14. For an excellent discussion of the roots of the Arts & Crafts movement, the development of the "artistic house," and the distinction between those for and against English socialism, see ibid., 11–15, and passim.

26. On English interest in the American Shingle Style as early as the 1880s, see ibid., 34–36; see also Longstreth, *Edge,* 48. For the international manifestation of Arts & Crafts in many countries, see Livingstone and Parry, *Arts & Crafts.* For more specifics on Voysey, see Gebhard, *Voysey,* 12–13; Kornwolf, *Scott,* 71–76; and Cumming, *Arts & Crafts,* 55–58.

27. On socialism in California after 1908 and its enormous popularity in Berkeley in the 1911 election, see Weitze, "Utopian Place Making"; Trapp, *A&C California,* 63; and Kornwolf, *Scott,* 13n9. Interestingly, in Boston there was a split between two Swedenborgians who were very active in the Boston Society of Arts & Crafts. Herbert Langford Warren was interested in the aesthetic aspect of the Arts & Crafts movement whereas Arthur Astor Carey was more interested in the laborer; see Meister, *A&C Boston,* 88.

28. For "The Poor Man's House of Today," see *AN* 1, no. 1 (November 1890): 1.

29. Kornwolf, *Scott,* 11–15. More research needs to be done on American influence on the Arts & Crafts movement.

30. Ibid. Kornwolf discusses Red House as *"the house as a vehicle for testing new, loftier objectives in architecture and design."* Excellent photographs and an informative discussion on Red House can also be seen in Davey, *A&C Architecture,* 39–45. See also Livingstone, "Origins and Development," especially plates 2.6 and 2.7, and Alan Powers, "Architecture and Gardens," 115. See Richardson's Trinity Church, a collaborative effort, discussed in Chapter 3, and Stevens and Cobb's interest in the small house discussed above in Chapter 5.

31. Kornwolf, *Scott,* 34–35nn67–76.

32. According to the late John Beach, the interior walls were covered with burlap and studded with brass tacks, clearly demonstrating Arts & Crafts influence. Interior walls are now painted white. The Church of the Holy Innocents was remodeled in 1913. For original drawing, see *AN* 1, no. I (November 1890); see also figs. 0.4 and 5.6 herein. Jeremy Kotas kindly

gave me permission to publish this beautiful watercolor of the church by Coxhead.

33. In *Edge,* 376n13, Longstreth mentions that Coxhead used redwood on two surviving churches from 1888 to 1889 but does not describe precisely how it was used—a critical point since Coxhead often outlined vaulting or domes with redwood molding. For painted clapboard churches, see Russian Orthodox Church, Menlo Park (1886), illustration in Olmsted, *Here Today,* 158; and Church of Nativity, Oak Grove, Atherton (1872), illustration in Gebhard, *Guide to San Francisco,* 145.

34. See Davies house in *AN* (January 1891): plate XIII. For Emerson's church, see Scully, *Shingle Style,* fig. 49. For shingled churches, see Sorell, "Silsbee," 5–16, and also Hasbrouck, "Wright," 5–16. It is also possible that contact with Worcester stimulated Coxhead's shingled church designs.

35. Coxhead was first listed at 2419 Green Street in *SF Directory 1894.* However, the house number is actually 2421.

36. *British Architect,* September 18, 1891, cited in Kornwolf, *Scott,* 73–78, fig. 45.

37. In June 1973 Richard Chafee located Coxhead's documents and identified the names of these visitors to the RIBA from 1876 through 1887. See Longstreth, *Edge,* 42–51, 362n7, for more on Coxhead. A brief summary follows: he worked for Frederic Chancellor restoring old churches, studied at the Royal Academy of Fine Arts, was elected an associate of the Royal Institute of British Architects in November 1886, won RIBA's silver medal; by January 1887 he had opened an office in Los Angeles with his older brother, Almeric, who served as business manager.

38. For Leyes Wood, Sussex (1868), see *BN* (March 31, 1871); republished in Scully, *Shingle Style,* fig. 6. Coxhead might have seen in British magazines such small, half timbered cottages as reinterpreted in the late nineteenth century; i.e., Ernest George's "House with Studio," Guildford, Surrey (ca. 1888), in the *Architect* (May 16, 1890), republished in Kornwolf, *Scott,* 25, fig. 8. Or he could have known Ernest George's work more directly from his time in England. See also Kornwolf, *Scott,* 74–78, figs. 47–48, for American Wilson Eyre as the first architect to be influenced by Voysey.

39. For Kornwolf on Coxhead, see ibid., 74–76, and floor plan & front façade of 2421 Green, 78, fig. 49. See the Kenley thatched cottage, signed "F. Merritt Del. 1891," in *AN* 1, no. 3 (January 1891): 25. For confirmation of the relationship between Coxhead's

houses and English work, see Longstreth, *Edge,* 374n4 and 377n21, where Longstreth writes that no record exists of architectural journals to which Ernest A. Coxhead subscribed except *AABN,* numerous illustrations from which survive in his papers; however, the multiple relationships between Coxhead's work and English work, then appearing in magazines such as *British Architect,* suggest he had access to such publications—and if he did not, his friends did.

40. For Polk's drawing after Ernest George, see *AN* 1, no. 1 (November 1890). For an excellent detail photo of the front steps that go under an arch cut through a wall at Coxhead's house on Green Street, see Longstreth, *Edge,* 130, fig. 76.

41. *AR* 5, no. 4 (April–June 1896): 321–46. For a building list and a brief biography of Ernest George, see Bloice, "Ernest George."

42. Longstreth, *Edge,* 129.

43. Such as Baillie Scott's proposed house, published in *BN* (December 4, 1891); see also his Red House, Isle of Man (1892–93), illustration in Kornwolf, *Scott,* fig. 53, p. 98. For Ivydene (1893–94), see ibid., 101–2, and 102, fig. 60.

44. W. E. Loy to "Dear Cousin Sue," March 29, 1893, Berkeley. A bill from Coxhead & Coxhead, architects, to W. E. Loy, July 7, 1893, indicates that discussion and planning of this house actually began January 1890.
    In an interview in the 1970s, Eleanor Chamberlain mentioned that she believed Joseph Worcester sent her grandfather William Loy to Coxhead.

45. For more on the Anna Head School, see Cerny, *Landmarks,* 189.

CHAPTER 6
Hillside Architecture:
Maybeck and Keeler

1. Keeler, "FBT," 223–24.

2. For the best, most recent explanation of André's and Viollet's influence on Maybeck, see Craig, *Maybeck,* 3, 27, 34, and passim. Maybeck knew Shaw well enough to stay at his home on Ellerdale Road in Hampstead (the northern part of London) and named him to the University of California, Berkeley design competition's jury (see Chapter 8); but he undoubtedly knew Shaw's work even earlier either via publications or by visiting London during vacations while a student at the École (1882–86). Shaw's work at Bedford Park was finished by the early 1880s.

3. See Craig, *Maybeck,* 45–49 and plates 1.19–1.21, for excellent illustrations of the Ponce de Leon Hotel; see also

Chapter 10 herein for discussion of the Ponce and its influence on the Mission Style via the California State Building for the 1893 Chicago Fair.

4. For Maybeck's positions in the San Francisco Bay Area from 1889 to 1895 (although no one has yet precisely defined the early chronology), see Cardwell's *Maybeck, which* seems the most accurate. Information from BAHA on Maybeck cottages near Grove and Berryman in addition to his own house. Lawson, Maybeck's second client, hired Maybeck the same year as Keeler did; see the first Lawson house, in the so-called Spanish style, discussed in Chapter 10.

5. Keeler, "FBT," 228–29.

6. For Ruskin Club and Handicraft Guild, see the Shipounoff introduction in Keeler, *Simple Home* (1979), xxxii, and biographical manuscript in Keeler's scrapbook, BL: Keeler Papers and chapter 4, note 8. For Keeler's drawing for beds made of wood with bowknot pegs, see BL: Keeler Papers.

7. In addition Maybeck had firsthand knowledge of Europe from his five years of study at the École des Beaux-Arts and his year organizing the university's international competition. Maybeck and Keeler undoubtedly had copies of the *Studio* and/or *International Studio* from 1897 as well as *Architectural Review: For the Artist and Craftsman* (from which Worcester clipped articles and to which Howard subscribed) in their own libraries in addition to having access to them in the Hillside Club library. These periodicals would have given them plenty of information and illustrations on the English Arts & Crafts movement from which to draw inspiration. For the importance of the *Studio* starting in 1893 as *"the principal showcase for British Arts & Crafts for about twenty years . . . widely read in Europe and the United States,"* and *Architectural Review, "edited from 1896 to 1900 by Henry Wilson, one of the most brilliant Arts & Crafts designers,"* see Crawford, "United Kingdom," 54.

8. McGrew house, contract notice, July 19, 1900, in Edwards Transcripts; information provided by BAHA. Paget was a professor of French, Spanish and Italian at UC Berkeley from 1887 to his death in 1903. According to Miss McGrew (interviewed in 1972), Keeler designed the house for her father while Maybeck was in Europe, and Keeler chose the roof, which looks like an English country inn.

9. Quote from 1908 unpublished manuscript "California in the World of Art," in BL: Keeler Papers.

10. Keeler to George Wilhelm, June 30, 1928, BL: Keeler Papers.

11. AWMem, May 20, 1871. Much later Worcester served on the Board of Managers of Arequipa (1911), which *"offered occupation to its patients in the form of a fully equipped pottery."* Information from Bosley, "Western North America," 193–93.

12. Keeler, "FBT," 225. Maybeck's house, though still standing on Grove near Berryman Street, Berkeley, has been altered considerably from its original appearance.

13. For the Wright and Sanders church with exposed structure, see fig. 3.17; it was originally published in *CABN* 88, no. 3 (March 1882): 38, 41, where it was described as *"recently built"* without specifying any date or location.

14. Longstreth, *Edge*, 323, fig. 248. John Arthur reminded me that the wood posts of the stave church very possibly had the bark left on them, and in any case were left very rugged. See *AN* 3 (January 1891): 23, which announced the forthcoming translation of Gottfried Semper's *Der Stil* (1860) by Bernard Maybeck.

15. Keeler, "FBT," 224.

16. Anthony Bruce to the author, October 2004.

17. Longstreth suggests that Maybeck's early drawing of the Keeler house strongly resembles Coxhead's Beta Theta Pi fraternity house built nearby just the year before; see Longstreth, *Edge*, 316, fig. 242. However, Maybeck could also have found inspiration for the Keeler house in late medieval townscapes he had seen firsthand while studying, reading, and traveling in Europe, 1882–86 and 1897–98.

18. BAHA provided the information on the Maher house (1890) and the Wilson-Arbogast house (1895).

19. BAHA files show the Murphy house contract notice in *CABN* (October 1891). Regarding the Sargeant house, it appears from the late Bill Sonin's unpublished notes at BAHA that John White, Maybeck's brother-in-law, arrived in 1893 and had a client, presumably Sargeant, in 1894 before Maybeck did. This is confirmed by the *Oakland Directory 1892–93,* which lists *"Bernard Maybeck, architect, res. Gilman nr. West, Berkeley"* and *"White, John draughtsman, res. Gilman near West, [Berkeley]."* BAHA supplied the Edwards contract notice, February 19, 1894, for Winthrop W. Sargeant house: Lot 2, Block 4, Daley's Scenic Park Tract; Architect: John White; $1,168.40 for a 1-1/2-story six-room dwelling.

20. The Wilson house, called Rosemond, was built at 2400 Ridge Road on the corner of Scenic Avenue. It was actually intended to be the barn and was going to serve as a temporary residence for the Wilson family while their mansion was being built. The family moved in on July 31, 1894, and remained there. The mansion was never constructed. The Wilson house was torn down in 1976 to make room for the Graduate Theological Union Library designed by Louis Kahn.

It is not known whether Frank Wilson knew Worcester or whether Worcester, Maybeck, or Keeler (or all three) encouraged Wilson to build in the rustic mode. However, it seems likely since Wilson sold Keeler his lot and sold John Galen Howard the Ridge Road parcel upon which Howard (also a close friend of Worcester; see Chapter 8) built his first Berkeley home. Furthermore, on April 28, 1899, Maybeck lectured on "Hillside Architecture" at the Wilson home, and at some point Wilson joined the Hillside Club. I am very grateful to Daniella Thompson for this information.

21. Keeler, "FBT, " 227. See Craig, Maybeck, for more on exposed structure, Viollet-le-Duc, and André's lectures at the École des Beaux-Arts.

22. Keeler, "FBT," 230. Note that the living room and library were one, in keeping with the Arts & Crafts ideal that books as well as one's architectural surroundings helped uplift the soul.

23. Ibid.

24. Ibid.

25. Baillie Scott quote from "The Decoration of the Suburban House," published in *The Studio* (April 1895): 15–16, and cited in Kornwolf, *Scott,* 124. Scott also wrote "An Ideal Suburban House" (January 1895): 127–32, and "On the Choice of Simple Furniture" (April 1897): 152–57, from the same publication. The *Studio* articles were extensively illustrated. See Kornwolf, *Scott,* 562ff, for a long list of Baillie Scott's publications. Just as Maybeck exposed wood structure, Scott exposed unplastered brickwork and/or stonework of his walls, insisted houses suit their landscape, and designed furniture that *"appears to grow out"* of the client's requirements and out of the architecture.

26. Note the Japanese lanterns hanging in the Keeler house living room–library in both the bookplate and the actual living room. The California Promotion Committee published *San Francisco and Thereabout,* thereby broadening interest in Japanese architecture to its readers in San Francisco and beyond.

27. For later Maybeck houses with exposed beams and decorative structure, see illustrations in Woodbridge, *Maybeck:* E. C Young house, San Francisco (1913), 148, fig. 140; and the S. H. Erlanger house, Forest Hills, near San Francisco (1916), 152, fig. 47.

28. "Early History of the Club," *SF Call,* Sunday Edition, 1898, reprinted in *Hillside Club Yearbook, 1911–12.*

29. Keeler, *Simple Home* (1979), Shipounoff introduction, xxi. BAHA reports that the white house to the left and above the Keeler house (seen in fig. 6.4) is the Wilson-Arbogast house (1895). The Arbogasts, the second owners, shingled the house in 1908.

30. The Davis contract notice appeared October 12, 1896, per BAHA. An illustration can be found in Longstreth, *Edge.* The dates and descriptions of Maybeck's earliest houses derive from Cardwell, *Maybeck,* 56–62, 240.

31. For Maybeck's early concern with open space planning in the Hall house, see Cardwell, *Maybeck,* 60–61. A summary from Cardwell follows: To enhance the splendid view of the San Francisco Bay, Maybeck moved the Hall house entrance from the front to the middle of the side of the house. From the entrance, one stepped into a long open space made up of the living room, dining room, and hall. Pocket doors allowed the rooms to be separated as needed. By banding the rooms with casement windows, Maybeck flooded them with light; by adding narrow balconies, he made the views even more accessible. As in Frank Lloyd Wright's Ward Willits house (1902), Maybeck plans with an openness that we see again in the Boke house (1902) and the Roos house (1909), among many others.

32. *Palo Alto Live Oak,* November 6, 1896, cited in Cardwell, *Maybeck,* 66.

33. Anthony Bruce at BAHA writes of the Keeler studio: *"We never had a confirmed date of construction; it seems to have been built in 1905, according to tax assessment records."*

34. Obviously the architecture chosen for Berkeley was not Shaw's brick or Burnham's classical white; both architects, along with Ruskin, Morris, and the British Arts & Crafts movement, advocated architecture appropriate for a particular region. For Keeler, Maybeck, and the Hillside Club, wood was the material best suited to simple homes. The City Beautiful movement was conceived as explicitly reform-minded; Daniel Burnham was a leading proponent of the movement. A reform *"of the landscape,"* he suggested, would *"complement the burgeoning reforms in other areas of society."* See Hines, "Imperial Mall," 95. See also Tinneswood, *A&C House,* 126–29, on Bedford Park and planned worker housing.

35. "Early History of the Club," *SF Call,* Sunday Edition, 1898, reprinted in *Hillside Club Yearbook, 1911–12.* Keeler managed to get several friends to buy lots near his house. I am grateful to Anthony Bruce and Jerry Sulliger at BAHA, who researched the information that follows. Most of the houses built near Highland Place and Ridge Road after the opening of Daley's Scenic Park were painted Victorians. For example, at the end of Hearst Avenue, the Charles S. Bonham house (1890) at 2727 Hearst was painted. Keeler could also see the house that Mrs. Stevenson bought (originally the Cora Tompkins house), 1730 Highland Place and Le Conte (1891), which was later shingled. In historic photographs, one can see two homes below the Stevenson house: the J. Fishelbrand house (1893) at 1725 La Loma Avenue, and the Ella Wilson house (1895), to the northeast on what would have been the end of Le Conte Avenue, at 1732 La Vereda. Photographs reveal that all of these were later shingled. Keeler is correct that Keith, who was Worcester's closest friend, did buy a lot on which he intended to build another house (he owned one at 2727 Atherton); it was at the northeast corner of La Loma and Ridge Road, next to the Davis house and behind Keeler's house. Keith purchased lots 1, 2, and the south 20 feet of Lot 3, block 23, of Daley's Scenic Park from Raymond V. Wilson on December 5, 1900. The deed is recorded at Alameda County, Deeds, Book 745, pages 217–19. However, no improvement was made on the lot until 1907–8, and the house seems not to have been built until after 1911. Keith, who died in 1911, arrived in California in 1859 and had been a friend of Muir's and Worcester's from 1872 if not before.

CHAPTER 7
Early Environmentalists, Yosemite, and a Garden Suburb

1. For Olmsted's early conservationist role and attitude toward saving Yosemite, see McLaughlin and Beveridge, *Olmsted,* 30–34, 52nn 134–51. For further information on Muir, Olmsted, and Yosemite, see Chapter 1.
2. Ibid. All was not lost; in 1916 Frederick Law Olmsted Jr. used these recommendations to help create the National Park Service.
3. See Muir, "Wild Wool."
4. Muir, "National Parks," 271–84, 282–83. See also Wood, "Muir Quotations." Willis Polk designed the logo for the Sierra Club.
5. For these three brief articles, see *CABN* 3 (1882): "Logging in California," 132;

"Uses of the Steel Square," 141; and "The Redwoods," 153.
6. For more on native flora, see Chapter 10.
7. Microform edition, *The John Muir Papers,* © 1984 Muir-Hanna Trust, University of the Pacific at Stockton, California. Copy at BL (Banc mss 86/212c; Film Reel 7, 1893). I wish to thank documentary filmmaker Paul Bockhorst for questioning whether these early practitioners were "environmentalist" or not, and for pointing out that they simultaneously venerated and exploited redwood.
8. Quote from Margaret Herrick's letter to Brother Cornelius in Cornelius, *Keith* 2,101–2. For Worcester as an intimate friend of the Herrick family and Margaret studying painting with Keith, see ibid., 57.
9. See "Architecture in California," *SF Chronicle,* December 30, 1894, 16–17. See also Chapter 3 herein.
10. Sutliffe, "Description of Berkeley." See also Bartlett, "Ideal Village," cited in Ferrier, *Berkeley,* where the Sutliffe pamphlet and the entire final quote regarding the success of this society are referred to along with other useful information.
11. Sutliffe, "Description of Berkeley."
12. Ibid. Among the twelve elegantly housed professors, Sutliffe named Professor George Goodall, John Le Conte, and George D. Dornin.
13. The entire text of Olmsted's report appears in Ranney, *Olmsted Papers* 5. This report was also published in brochure form, which probably increased its circulation and helped create widespread knowledge of the plan at the time; see Olmsted & Vaux, "Berkeley Neighborhood."
14. Sutliffe, "Description of Berkeley." Friends of Piedmont Way is raising funds to restore "overbowering trees" to the sides and median of Olmsted's dual carriage way.
15. See McGuire, "Olmsted in California," 52–73. However, Lesley Emmington points out that *"the information in Diana Kostial McGuire's thesis is not inclusive of the true events of 1865 as she was unaware of Olmsted's Map being adopted in 1865 that laid out Piedmont Way, Hillside, Prospect, Channing and Bancroft almost exactly as they are reflected today."*
16. See Emmington, "Berkeley Legacy."
17. For excellent photographs and insights into the architecture of the Ames Gate Lodge, see Floyd, *Richardson,* 176. I am grateful to architectural historian Kathleen James-Chakraborty for focusing my attention on the Ames Gate Lodge in particular as a source of inspiration.
18. See Whitaker, "Berkeley," 138–45. For more on Shaw's designs for Bedford Park, see Greeves, *Bedford Park.* See also Davey, *A&C Architecture,* 48–50,

and Tinneswood, *A&C House,* 126–29. Closer to home, Maybeck and Keeler certainly knew about developments in Belvedere, see Longstreth, *Edge,* 146, fig. 93, and 378n6–7. Since Keeler cites the architect Bruce Price in Hillside Club pamphlets, he and Maybeck were undoubtedly familiar with Price's architecture and the way it fit into Tuxedo Park, New York. See Pierre Lorillard House at Tuxedo Park in Scully, *Shingle Style,* 126–27, and figs. 106 and 107; see also his William Kent house, figs. 108 and 109.
19. Keeler, "FBT," 231. Examples of Victorian houses that upset Keeler and his friends were at the end of Hearst Avenue: the Charles S. Bonham house, 2727 Hearst (1890); Keeler could also see the house that Mrs. Stevenson bought and which Keeler says she later shingled—the Cora Tompkins house, 1730 Highland (1891)—and below that the J. Fishelbrand house, 1725 La Loma (1893), facing La Loma Avenue; and the Ella Wilson house, 1732 La Vereda (1895), to the northeast on what would have been the end of Le Conte Avenue. Photographs at BAHA show that all of these were later shingled.
20. For Schweinfurth's problems in Denver, see Longstreth, *Edge,* 59 60, and 365n33: *"Irritated by* [Schweinfurth's] *assault on the booster spirit, the magazine's editor carped that Schweinfurth was 'an extremist of the more virulent type.'"* After this nasty exchange in 1890, Schweinfurth may have returned to the New York branch of Brown's firm rather than traveling to San Francisco. In any case no documentation of his presence in San Francisco nor any documented work for Brown in 1891 and 1892 have been found, although it is clear from Worcester's letter to Howison that Brown expected Schweinfurth to be in San Francisco in 1891. In a letter from Schweinfurth to William R. Hearst, November 25, 1895, Schweinfurth makes it clear that he knew New York intimately and had been there so recently that he was sure a dealer still displayed the same tapestry in the same place: he tells Hearst to see a tapestry *"at Johnson & Faulkner's, on 18th Street, between Broadway and 4th Avenue (just back of Everett House.) If I remember correctly they had upon the wall a large . . . tapestry . . . around it a wide border . . . ."* Perhaps Schweinfurth returned to, or did not leave, New York as he had intended in late 1891 or early 1892. The *New York Tribune,* January 1, 1893, praised Brown's design for the California State Building and for the Grand Market, Lima, Peru, both of which were on display at the architectural league exhibition in New York City. Perhaps the fact that Brown's

drawings were on display in New York means that Schweinfurth remained in that city. The *Tribune* article and others are pasted in CHS: Brown Scrapbooks, I:113.

21. For the Moody connection, see Lummis to Phoebe Apperson Hearst, BL: Hearst Papers (MSS 72/204; William Randolph Hearst, 1864–1919; Subseries 2.1; Reel 26, Box 18, Folder 22: 1859–1928, frame 000148), in which Charles F. Lummis wrote Mrs. Hearst on September 15, 1905, that *"Moody gave me news of your return,"* indicating Moody and Hearst were friends. For Bradford, see BL: Hearst Papers (MSS 72/204; William Randolph Hearst, 1864–1919: Subseries 2.1; Reel 15, Box 12, Folder 18) with correspondence between Olney Bradford and William R. Hearst confirming their friendship and suggesting that Hearst probably recommended Schweinfurth to Bradford. For an illustration of the Bradford house, see ibid., 292–94, fig. 230. All these Hearst commissions, along with the others discussed in Chapter 10, explain why Schweinfurth succeeded independently from Brown beginning in February 1894 and why Schweinfurth did not try to take over Brown's firm at Brown's death.

22. See Chapter 10 for an in-depth discussion on the California State Building's design and sources.

23. Schweinfurth's displayed drawings were praised in *CABN* (April 15, 1894): 38–41.

24. Only the Montalvo project and not the Winter residence design was published in *CABN* (April 15, 1894); cited in Calavan, "Schweinfurth," 5 and 43 (plate 3), and in Longstreth, *Edge*, 276, fig. 216. For more on Schweinfurth's first California work see Calavan, "Schweinfurth," 7, 19–21, 64n21. Calavan suggests Schweinfurth's Montalvo project might be a California interpretation of a proposed hotel for Mesilla Park, New Mexico (architect, Seymour Davis), which Schweinfurth would surely have seen in *AABN* 35 (January 1892): plate 839.

25. See Calavan, "Schweinfurth," 5, and illustrations. For a different point of view and many illustrations, see Longstreth, *Edge*, index. See Chapters 3, 7, and 10 herein for additional information on Schweinfurth's career and work, his interest in the Mission Style, a proposed re-dating of the Pueblo-style hacienda to 1894 96, and the start of his successful independent career to 1894. Perhaps upon arriving in California, Schweinfurth read one of the most popular books on Native Americans, and perhaps that contributed to his switch to a style steeped in California native

tradition. Longstreth, *Edge, 277*, notes that Lummis' book *Land of Poco Tiempo* (1893) *"was one of the most influential books in popularizing Pueblo culture . . ."* It is a shame that Schweinfurth's library and personal effects, if they exist, are not available in a public collection. For example, Schweinfurth Memorial Art Center, Auburn, New York, has little or nothing on Albert Cicero Schweinfurth. Longstreth mentions in *Edge*, 401, that much of Schweinfurth's *"work for Brown is recorded in two scrapbooks of photographs and sketches assembled by Brown and owned by a descendant."* According to conversation with Richard Longstreth on June 29, 2005, thirty years ago Sheila Mack of Los Angeles held these scrapbooks; they were Brown's scrapbooks, not Schweinfurth's, and the drawings in them were mostly published.

26. For Schweinfurth's obituaries, see Anon., "Schweinfurth," 77, and *SF Call*, October 10, 1900, 12. No one seems to know precisely when Schweinfurth left for Europe in 1898; those working on the design of the First Unitarian Church may want to research this date in order to determine how far the design and construction had progressed prior to Schweinfurth's departure.

27. Keeler, "FBT," BL

28. Description of the Moody house is from the *Berkeley Daily Advocate,* November 1896.

29. Keeler, *Simple Home* (1979), Shipounoff introduction, xiii. Explanation for Weltevreden courtesy of Daniella Thompson.

30. Moody's friendship with Schweinfurth is documented in Anon., "Schweinfurth," 77: *"The house reflects the architect's personality. It was built for an intimate friend who was in sympathy with his views . . . ."*

31. Living room description from *Berkeley Daily Gazette,* November 1896. Dining room description from "The Later Work of AC Schweinfurth," *Architectural Review* 9 (1902). Sadly, none of the original color is visible without paint analysis and, in contrast to the Thorsen house, which is being well maintained, this house is not being cared for very well.

32. Edwin Long house was published in the *Architect* (March 7, 1890), or see Kornwolf, *Scott,* 75, fig. 46.

33. *Berkeley Daily Gazette,* November 6, 1896. See Moody living room with its horizontal beams in Longstreth, *Edge,* 294, fig. 232.

34. It is also possible that either Schweinfurth or Moody was familiar with the Dutch Colonies through the press or firsthand. South African Cape Dutch architecture may have

been published before the two articles I located, which date from 1900; for Part 1, see *AR* (London) 7 (January–June 1900): 3–8, 51–57; for Part 2, see *AR* (London) 8 (July–December 1900): 147–52, and illustration #8. John Galen Howard's bookplate is inside most volumes of *AR* at CED.

35. Anon., "Schweinfurth," *AR* 9 (1902): 77.

36. Names of church members from Cerny, *Landmarks,* 161–62, and Longstreth, *Edge,* 391n48. The following information comes from Longstreth, *Edge,* 391n48, and Betty Marvin, assistant to the church archivist: The First Unitarian Church purchased the land on Bancroft Way in 1893 from William Carey Jones and apparently engaged architect Joachim B. Mathisen to design a building in ca. 1894. The drawing (published in newspapers and in Jones, *History of UC*) shows a large Romanesque-style building with tall tower. Longstreth suggests the building was too expensive and Schweinfurth was hired. *"Plans* [for the First Unitarian Church] *completed in January* [1898], *dedication Nov. 20."*

It is interesting that Joachim B. Mathisen, the first architect hired, knew Maybeck well. He and Maybeck submitted a plan for the California State Building competition, January–February 1892. Also, Mathisen had completed at least one rustic shingle house according to BAHA: see the house incorrectly attributed to Coxhead in Keeler, *Simple Home,* 27.

37. The *Unitarian Universalist Church of Berkeley's Official History* states that *"*[Schweinfurth] *had been instructed to use only the best materials for each purpose. Bernard Maybeck, then a young member of the congregation . . . may have helped with the church's design. A member gave the redwood pillars that graced the two front entrances . . . ."* See the *Official History,* 10–13, at the church.

38. Longstreth, *Edge,* 391n48, uncovered the role of E. S. Gray. Those who are especially interested in the First Unitarian Church might wish to investigate possible input from Maybeck, Keeler, Polk, Coxhead, Worcester, and the Warren Gregorys. Many members were Worcester's friends, so if he had expressed interest, and it is difficult to imagine that he did not, Worcester would have known about every detail of its construction and possibly could have influenced its design.

39. Cerny, *Landmarks,* 162.

40. See Wilson, "Big Gable."

41. Calavan, "Schweinfurth," 37–38, mentions J. C. Stevens' work and McKim's William Low house, Bristol,

Rhode Island, as possible sources for the broad gable, and wonders if Coxhead's shingle churches could also have provided inspiration. Longstreth, *Edge,* 294, points out the possible derivation from the Low House. Wilson "Big Gable," 52–57, notes that the Low house commission entered the McKim office in late 1886 but was not published until much later. However, Schweinfurth may have seen the drawings for it while still working in New York in Brown's office from 1885 to 1888.

Architect J. C. Stevens' "House by the Sea" (Fig. 7.8) was published by *AABN* 18 (September 12, 1885): Pl. 38–39, and is cited by Scully, *Shingle Style,* fig. 91. For Frank Mead's "Nest," see *AABN* (February 27, 1886), cited by Kornwolf, *Scott,* 70, fig. 42. Scully, *Shingle Style,* 159, also points out that Frank Lloyd Wright used the big gable in his adaptation of Price's W. Chandler cottage at Tuxedo Park (1885–86) on his own home in Oak Park (1889).

42. Woodbridge, *Maybeck,* 69.
43. Keeler, "FBT," 225.
44. John Arthur pointed out the painted chamfering on the Senger house.
45. If Maybeck somehow missed the tree columns at the artists' studios while working on the Ponce de Leon and Alcazar Hotels, he could have seen palm columns on many old St. Augustine houses. It would be interesting to know if Maybeck helped design the artists' studios requested by Flagler.

Longstreth, *Edge,* 58–59, noted that the Ponce de Leon Hotel *"had even more influence on Schweinfurth. . . ."* This seems likely, given Schweinfurth's appreciation of Spanish Renaissance architecture (see Chapter 10); furthermore, Schweinfurth's comment that Maybeck has a "great regard for architecture as an art" (see page 52) suggests he knew Maybeck's work on the hotel.

46. The non-tapered column has multiple derivations, from rustic cabins to Italian pergolas, as Longstreth points out in *Edge,* 282, fig. 222. However Schweinfurth may well have found his source closer to home: the columns supporting the pergola of Polk's 1893 Valentine Rey house appear to have the same non-tapered outline. See illustration in Longstreth, *Edge,* 166 fig. 120. It is interesting that Stickley features such columns on numerous Craftsman homes; for one example among many, see Stickley, *More Craftsman Homes* (illustrations on pages 68 and 69) illustrates a house with stout columns supporting a "pergola porch," pub-

lished earlier in *The Craftsman* (August 1909).

47. From a newspaper article about the Unitarian Church, probably *Berkeley Gazette,* July 9, 1898, sent to the author by Anthony Bruce at BAHA.
48. For quote regarding "staining," see ibid. John Arthur reminded me that the Swedenborgian Church also has industrial sash windows. Note that Maybeck too used them in the Keeler house (1895 and 1907? renovation), Maurer studio (1907), and elsewhere.
49. In *Edge,* 285, and fig. 225, Longstreth used "pervasive horizontality" to describe Schweinfurth's work at the Hacienda del Pozo de Verona.
50. I am grateful to Richard Longstreth for sharing two Schweinfurth letters with me. There is only one two-story living room to be seen in Schweinfurth's work and that was added to the hacienda in a separate wing *after* Schweinfurth had finished the original villa. Longstreth comments in *Edge,* 286, that these *". . . interior changes represented a compromise of the original plan."*
51. An illustration of Asistencia de Pala's beamed ceiling after restoration by Lummis' Landmarks Club can be seen Moneta, *Lummis.*
52. Although the building is no longer used as a church, its beauty, especially on the exterior, is still visible. The big beamed ceilings, ships knees, and arched windows can still be seen inside.
53. *AN* 1, no. 3 (January 1891): 25. This suggests that Henry Merritt traveled and sketched in rural England, one more proof of the extensive international exchange of architects and ideas going on in the late nineteenth century.
54. Hillside Club, *Suggestions,* and Keeler, *Simple Home,* 18ff.
55. Though Coxhead's, Polk's, or Schweinfurth's names do not appear on the Club's membership rolls, Hillside Club members hired them.
56. Keeler, "FBT," 231. List of charter members (1902), sent by Fred H. Dempster, Berkeley. It was Mrs. Oscar Maurer's idea that a club should be formed to carry out their goals. See also Keeler, "Retrospection," 2, and "Early History," in BL: Keeler Papers.
57. The Landmarks Club was officially incorporated in 1895. For further information on Tessa Kelso and Charles Lummis, see Moneta, *Lummis,* 68. Weitze, *Mission Revival,* 141n23, states that Kelso established the Association for the Preservation of the Missions in 1888.
58. Of course Berkeley was not a totally planned "garden suburb," but the Hillside Club was influenced by the movement and adapted many of its

ideas. See Madge Robinson's article in *HB* 6, no. 1 (June 1899).

59. The architect of the Hillside School was Louis Stone; see Shipounoff introduction to Keeler, *Simple Home* (1979), opposite page xxix. Mention of a Hillside School inevitably calls to mind the much better known Hillside Home School (1887), an early Frank Lloyd Wright work, nominally a Silsbee commission, which was *"rather a provincial specimen of a Shingle-style house and was later demolished by Wright himself"*; see Hitchcock, *19th & 20th Centuries,* 270.
60. For corroboration that the Hillside School followed plans developed by the Hillside Club, see *Berkeley Gazette,* July 31, 1900, 6. Notes from conversation, n.d., with Mrs. Frank M. Todd in connection with a skit on the founding of the Hillside Club, were sent to the author by Fred H. Dempster, November 3, 1972.
61. Published as an interview with Charles Keeler while he was on a speaking tour in New Zealand during 1901, in Keeler's scrapbook in BL: Keeler Papers.
62. Undated newspaper clippings in Keeler's scrapbook (ca. 1899), BL: Keeler Papers. For illustration of Rieger house (demolished), see Longstreth, *Edge,* 332, and fig. 253 on 331.
63. *HCY, 1902.* Club members included Mrs. W. H. Marston, one of the founders of the local PTA; Mrs. C. Germain Potwin and Miss Annie Woodall, school principals; Mr. and Mrs. Warren Gregory, close friends of Howard and Worcester, and members of the Swedenborgian Church and the First Unitarian Church; Miss Elinor Carlisle; Mr. G. Bradley.
64. Hillside Club, "Advocates," 6–7, in BL: Dempster Papers or at BAHA.
65. *HCY, 1906–1907.* Berkeley Path Wanderers Association works toward the preservation of paths, connecting steps and walks. Piedmont also has many connecting steps and paths, and residents keep an eye on these cut-throughs; Gail Lombardi suggests they were probably established by the Key System to make it easier for customers to reach their streetcars (and later to reach busses).
66. Notes from conversation, n.d., with Mrs. Frank M. Todd in connection with a skit on the founding of the Hillside Club, were sent to the author by Fred H. Dempster, November 3, 1972.
67. Hillside Club, "Advocates," 6.
68. *HCY, 1907–1908.*
69. Morris, *Collected Works,* 22:72–73.
70. Original story from Fred H. Dempster to the author, November 3, 1972.
71. On Unwin and Parker, see Powers,

"Architecture and Gardens, 119–20, Plate 7.9; see also Creese, *Environment,* and Tinneswood, *Arts & Crafts House,* 129.

72. Hillside Club, "Advocates," 6; available at BL.

73. Hillside Club, *Suggestions.*

74. *HCY, 1906–1907;* available at BL.

75. Keeler and Maybeck undoubtedly knew and admired Price's work at Tuxedo Park, New York, from the mid-1880s. More research needs to be done on Price and his California work. The house Price designed or renovated at Octavia and Washington in San Francisco (Fig. 0.3) was a complex Queen Anne–Shingle Style, the opposite of what Keeler and his friends were advocating for "simple" and appropriate house design in California.

76. Hillside Club, "Advocates," 6; available at BL.

77. *HCY, 1906–1907.*

78. Hillside Club, "Advocates," 6–7; available at BL. See also Keeler, *Simple Home,* 17ff.

79. Craig, *Maybeck at Principia,* 36. Craig also convincingly points out (page 31) that *"Viollet's sensitivity to art, sculpture, music and poetry and their affect on the senses and the soul also appealed to Maybeck."* This theme of "architecture as expression" and the empathetic response of the observer to beauty is a major focus of *Maybeck at Principia.*

80. Keeler, *Simple Home,* 31–34, 43, 50, 54–55; see also Kornwolf, *Scott,* Chapters 2 and 3.

CHAPTER 8
John Galen Howard and "His Wizard" Continue the Two Arts & Crafts Traditions

1. For Worcester's influence on UCB architecture, see Cornelius, *Keith* 1, 101, 343, where Cornelius states that the architects planning the university buildings sought suggestions from Worcester. For a full discussion of Joseph Worcester as "wizard" and his connections mentioned here with Maybeck, Coxhead, Porter, and Howard about UCB, see Woodbridge, *Howard,* especially 46ff and 68ff.

2. Worcester to Howard, October 13, 1899; see BL: Howard Papers. Worcester's mention of Faville and Bliss and of Arthur Mathews indicates that Worcester's circle included more architects, artists, and friends than we have been able to discuss here.

3. Worcester to Howison, January 1, 1900, in BL: Howison Papers.

4. Woodbridge, *Howard,* 46. Weitze, *Mission Revival,* 26, notes that Howard came to San Francisco hoping to take charge of the Shepley,

Rutan and Coolidge (successor to Henry Hobson Richardson) branch office, which was handling Stanford University. When the position did not materialize, he moved to Los Angeles. It is quite likely that Worcester met Howard while he was in San Francisco, liked him, and decided to push for his appointment when Benard turned out to be a disappointment. As Woodbridge notes on page 38: *"Howard was not considered a foreigner. He had lived and worked in California, if not in the San Francisco Bay Area and was personally acquainted with local architects."*

5. Keeler, "FBT."

6. Ibid.

7. *The Wave,* January 29, 1898. For Worcester's influence, Howard's social schedule, and Polk's comments, see Woodbridge, *Howard,* especially 4–9, 36–38, 44–46. Worcester's scrapbooks include a complete prospectus and jury report of the "Programme for an International Competition for the Phoebe Apperson Hearst Architectural Plan for University of California, Berkeley, December 3, 1897."

8. Woodbridge, *Howard,* 46, and see 68: *"The Reverend Worcester continued to be a mainstay in Howard's life* [even after Howard had moved to Berkeley, as we shall see]."

9. Howard's letters regarding mission and adobe buildings, in ibid., 4–7.

10. Ibid., 6.

11. See illustration of Howard's "Artist's Country House" in Kornwolf, *Scott,* 63, fig. 33. The shingle roof unified the composition. Kornwolf, 62–63, sees no English precedent for this handling of the roof and suggests it came from *"American barns and stables, especially those with lean-to additions."* On McKim's interest in vernacular architecture, see Wilson, "Big Gable" and "McKim." On the international Arts & Crafts movement and its regional and nationalistic inspiration all over Europe from the late 1880s on, see Kaplan, *Arts & Crafts in Europe & America;* see also Livingstone and Parry, *Arts & Crafts.* Howard's original bookplate remains in many issues of *AR,* now in CED.

12. Kornwolf, *Scott,* 63. For Voysey's "Artist's house," see the *British Architect* (February 1, 1889); Howard's design appeared in the *American Architect* (May 5, 1888); for A. H. Mackmurdo's very different design for an "Artist's house" (1887), see *Hobby Horse* (1888) and the *British Architect* (January 4, 1889). All three are illustrated and described in Kornwolf, *Scott,* 60–66.

13. Worcester to John Galen Howard, January 8, 1902, in BL: Howard Papers.

14. For Cloyne Court as a project of the

University Land and Improvement Company, a development group, see Woodbridge, Howard, 73. For "the Ark" and the role of Howard and the university, see ibid., 93–95. *"Contract details on Cloyne Court supplied by BAHA: SE Corner Ridge Road & Le Roy Avenue; $4,340 for excavations and foundations for Cloyne Court, an apartment hotel; owner: University land Improvement Co.; architect: John Galen Howard; contractor: Oakland Paving Co.; completed: December 24, 1904; May 31, 1904; all work for Cloyne Court; cost $40,796; contractor: Kidder & McCullough."* For Senior Men's Hall by Howard, see ibid., 95.

15. Development group for Cloyne Court included Phoebe A. Hearst, Jane K. Sather, James K. Moffitt, and John Galen Howard. For more on Cloyne Court see Woodbridge, *Howard,* index.

16. Woodbridge, *Howard,* 69–73. This living room with balcony reflects Maybeck's influence; see illustration on page 72. Robert B. Howard to author, March 20, 1971: *"As I remember, the interior of 2421 Ridge Road was mostly natural redwood, not white except the bedrooms on second floor."*

17. Keeler, FBT.

18. For Mathews house built for "Borax" Smith in Oakland near East 28th Street (destroyed), Mathews' inspiration from Henry Hobson Richardson, and eastern Shingle Style architects, see Hildebrand, *Borax Pioneer.*

19. Jack London's statement was transmitted via Joan London, Jack's oldest daughter, to James Sisson and then to the author, March 21, 1973; Joan London wrote: *". . . the Bungalow, always capitalized thus when written, and pronounced by Mother and Daddy so that the large B was almost visible. . . . How well it began, the year and a half we were to live in the Bungalow . . . ."* BAHA supplied contract notice for the Gregory house on Greenwood Terrace: *Edwards Transcript of Records for Alameda County, April 17, 1903: "Lot south of Rose Street and east of Greenwood Terrace, Lot 6, La Loma Tract, $2475 for a 2-1/2-story frame building; owner: Warren Gregory; architect: John Galen Howard; contractor: Nelson & Bigelow."* The Gregorys added to the house in 1906–7: *"February 12, 1906, Lot 7, La Loma Park all work for alterations & additions to house, $4,660; owner: Warren Gregory, Esq.; architect: John Galen Howard; contractor: Nelson & Boldt."*

20. Woodbridge, *Howard,* 129. Howard to author, March 20, 1971: *"Interior of Rose LeRoy dining room had burlap*

on walls and redwood trim, stained pale grey, both new ideas."

21. For Worcester's letter describing the 1906 earthquake and fire, see DHB. In 1905 Worcester sold his house and 8.5 of the original 12+ acres he still owned to a Mr. Henshaw. I am grateful to Gail Lombardi for checking tax records for me.

22. Robert B. Howard to author, March 20, 1971. Photo dated 1903.

CHAPTER 9
The California Shingle Style

1. Wilson, "McKim," 235–67. On Downing's many cottage styles, see Scully, *Shingle Style*, xl/n49.

2. The *Craftsman* published and Stickley republished many California houses in his books *Craftsman Homes* (1909) and *More Craftsman Homes* (1912). These are most easily accessible in the book *Craftsman Bungalows: "This is a new selection of 36 articles from . . . The Craftsman, . . . originally published monthly from 1901 through 1916."* In *Craftsman Bungalows,* see "The California Bungalow: A Style of Architecture Which Expresses the Individuality and Freedom Characteristic of our Western Coast (October 1907) 12–25; and on page 17*: "Messrs. Myron Hunt and Elmer Grey, the architects who designed the houses shown here, are pioneers in the development of the new American architecture."* For more on Craftsman housing's inspiration coming from California, see Chapter 11 herein.

3. Cited in Wilson, "Divine Excellence," 13.

4. Mathews was also a director of the Guild of Arts & Crafts of San Francisco; see Chapter 4. On Paul Elder's bookstores, see Cardwell, *Maybeck,* 94–95, 241–42.

5. Trapp, "A&C Movement," 129–61. Wyntoon is generally dated 1902–3, but if Trapp is correct, its planning probably began earlier along with its furniture manufacture.

6. Scully, *Shingle Style*, xl–xlvi, liii.

7. See Cothrell, "Use of Wood in Switzerland," 31–41, well illustrated with chalets. Cothrell's ideas resemble Keeler's in Hillside Club pamphlets. For additional praise of chalets, see Anonymous, "Wood in Switzerland," 37.

8. For more information on Darmstadt and the artists colony established there, see Ulmer, "Germany," 204–17.

9. Some of Maybeck's fascination with Swiss chalets probably derived from the fact that his mother was Swiss. His family came from Westphalia and he traveled extensively in Europe, where he would undoubtedly have seen all wood mountain houses or chalets with overhanging eaves, balconies, wood structure, and exposed wood inside. Scully, *Shingle Style,* xxxv and ff, points out that the Swiss chalet conveniently answered the mid-nineteenth-century need for structural expression as well as for a bit of romance.

For an enlightening discussion of "romantic rationalism," and for Viollet le Duc and Ruskin as "the best known protagonists of that point of view," see Scully, ibid., 36. See also Robert Craig, Maybeck at Principia, index, for Viollet's influence. BAHA dates the Schneider house (1905–6); the contract notice appeared December 12, 1905.

10. Keeler, "World of Art," 29, in BL: Keeler Papers.

11. Fletcher, "Smaller Houses," 321–46. Coxhead may have worked in George and Peto's firm as did Lutyens and many other Arts & Crafts architects, before moving to America. Lethaby tucked his entrance into a courtyard at the angle of the building in his Mesletter house, Orkney (1898), "as Webb had at the Red House." See plan of Mesletter and this statement in Cumming, "Architecture in Britain" and in Cumming and Kaplan, *A&C Movement,* 38. Entrance at Munstead Wood by Lutyens is also tucked into the courtyard (1896). See Munstead Wood Plan in Davey, *A&C Architecture,* 171.

12. Janice Thomas from BAHA supplied this fascinating tidbit: "Early pictures show that originally the Torreys walked up log steps, rather than up the elegant Beaux-Arts staircase we see today. The stairs have a nice landing, at which point they go off in two directions; that is, toward the Torrey House at 1 Canyon to the right and toward the Hutchinson house (1908) at 9 Canyon, designed by Julia Morgan, to the left. The stairs were designed by Henry Atkins, as were the Orchard Lane steps; Warren Cheney, who developed Panoramic Hill and served as the former editor of a literary magazine titled *The Californian,* commissioned Henry Atkins to build Orchard Lane stairs in 1909. Either Cheney or Torrey could have commissioned Atkins to build the matching stairs to the Torrey, Rieber, and Hutchinson houses. Atkins and Torrey were partners in their fine arts firm (Vickery, Atkins, and Torrey) in San Francisco, which launched the careers of such notable artists as Imogen Cunningham and Maynard Dixon. Orchard Lane, a public pedestrian corridor that winds up the hill, was also designed by Henry Atkins. The Atkins stairs presumably date from after construction of the 1908 Julia Morgan house.

13. Fred H. Dempster to the author November 3, 1972, describing his family's library of Hillside Club literature and how the Dempster house was designed.

14. Bosley to author, June 19, 2005: *"I don't know if Maybeck and Greene were friends, but they certainly knew each other. (There is a telegram from Maybeck to the California AIA saying nice things about the Greenes.) Greene and John Galen Howard, on the other hand, were definitely friends."* I am grateful to Robert Judson Clark, who is preparing a book on the Thorsen house, and to Edward R. Bosley for helping me pin down details cited in this section.

15. Bosley, *Greene & Greene,* 50. Information on Greene & Greene in this section comes primarily from Bosley's superb book. For the honeymoon in Europe and its influence, see 47–50.

16. Ibid., 51. Bosley notes that at some point, Charles began to clip articles from the Craftsman, which featured articles on both Swiss chalets and Japanese architecture: "Some Phases of Japanese Art" (February 1903), "Japanese Gardens" (March 1903), "The Use of Wood in Switzerland" (September 1903), "The Evolution of the Japanese Carpenter" (October 1905), and "Japanese Architecture and its Relation to the Coming American Style" (May 1906). It's unclear whether the Greenes had seen, firsthand or in the architectural press, houses by Arts & Crafts architects working in the Bay Area and whether these houses provided inspiration in addition to what they gleaned from Japanese and Swiss examples. Dates for the Thorsen house were supplied by Bosley: by November 1908 preliminary sketches had been prepared, working drawings date from March 1909, and the house was completed in 1910. Compare the Arturo Bandini house by the Greenes (1903, demolished), illustrated and described in Bosley, *Greene & Greene,* 60, fig. 44, 59–60, with Bay Area "simple homes" that had been built in the San Francisco area from 1890.

17. On Maybeck's "Californian" Emma Kellogg house, see Cardwell, *Maybeck,* 66, where he cites an article quoting Maybeck from *Palo Alto Live Oak,* November 6, 1896. See Bosley, *Greene & Greene,* 69–70, on Henry Greene's "The California House," intended to *"satisfy the basic needs of upper middle-class homebuilding."*

18. Bosley to author, February 3, 2005. For more on the furniture for the White sisters and for Stickley's influence on

its design, see Bosley, *Greene & Greene*, 53–54.

19. Bosley to the author, February 3, 2005. For more on Culbertson house, see ibid., 48–53. On the change in furniture design and on Charles Greene's interest in things Japanese, see ibid., 16, 67–68, where he clarifies the change in the Greene's furniture from being Stickley-like to their own more elegant, oriental-influenced style. See also Bosley's "The Beauty of Life" in Waggoner, *Morris.*

20. Bosley, *Greene & Greene*, 132–36, 222n47, *"Since 1943, the Thorsen house has been home to the Alpha of California chapter of the Sigma Phi Society, a college fraternity. Through their efforts the house has been maintained well in its near-original state. The furniture, however, was removed at the time of sale, and is now in the collection of The Gamble House, USC, and is on exhibit at the Huntington Library's Virginia Steele Scott Gallery, San Marino, California."* It's a shame that the students living in Howard's Cloyne Court and Schweinfurth's Moody House do not maintain their historic houses as the Alpha of California chapter of the Sigma Phi Society maintains the Thorsen house.

21. For much more on the Greenes and the Thorsen house, see Bosley, *Greene & Greene*, 132–36 and index. See also Makinson, "Greene and Greene," 103–48; and Gebhard, *Architecture in California*, 13–15. For the Greenes, Tichenor, and Japanese architecture, see Bosley, *Greene & Greene*, 67–69, as well as Makinson's "Charles and Henry Greene," 123–35, and *Greene & Greene: Fine Art*, 94–96.

22. Bosley, Greene & Greene, 134–35, 222n44: Mrs. J. W. Beswick-Purchas to Mr. and Mrs. William R. Thorsen, December 17, 1909, unpublished typescript courtesy of Robert Judson Clark, originally from the collection of Mr. and Mrs. Eric Thorsen.

23. See Bosley, *Greene & Greene*, 136; it was a collaborative effort. On the craftsmanship, see also Makinson, *Greene & Greene: Fine Art*, 175–78.

24. For more on mysticism and the Arts & Crafts Movement, see Wilson, "Divine Excellence," 33. Bosley to the author, February 3, 2005, suggests that probably only Charles Greene shared this interest.

25. All biographical information and much more on Morgan can be found in Boutelle, *Morgan*, 7ff.

26. For later English interiors with tree-like posts as screen walls, see Kornwolf, *Scott*, especially 187, fig. 98, and 218, fig. 114. Information that Morgan and Maybeck collaborated on the Jenness house is derived from later owners Dorothea Lange and family. They were told *"that Maybeck had suggested a floorplan by making a rough sketch on a paper bag when the Jenness's had decided to build."* The Jenness family bought the lot in January 1906. It originally fronted on LeConte, so the brick path leading to Virginia may not be original. Anthony Bruce, executive director of BAHA, kindly supplied this information.

27. See Armes, *Joseph Le Conte.*

28. See the unpublished biography of Julia Morgan by her structural engineer, Walter Steilberg, on deposit in the AIA Archives, Washington, D.C.

29. Kornwolf, *Scott*, 37, reprints Morris' poem, published originally in the *Commonweal,* a socialist journal, in 1886, and republished in *the Builder* (September 7, 1889). For Morris hiring the photographer Evans, see Livingstone and Parry, *Arts & Crafts,* 135–37.

30. For Seabright stables, see Kornwolf, *Scott*, 37. The A. Page Brown stable design appeared in the *British Architect* (December 6, 1889), reprinted in Kornwolf, *Scott,* 64, fig. 34, but incorrectly assigned to Great Barrington, Massachusetts. Howard's design appeared in *AABN* (May 8, 1888), and seems to have been the first "Artist's Country House" published, per Kornwolf, *Scott,* 42. See also Scully, *Shingle Style*, 105. For the Keeler comment on his house as a barn, see Keeler, *Simple Home,* 30. In 1894 Fred Esty decided to make his home a structure originally designed as a barn; see Chapter 5.

31. Letter #1, September 23, 1883, Great Barrington, Massachusetts. Copies of the extensive exchange of letters between Keith and Worcester can be found in SCL and SLA.

32. For a description of several attitudes toward the barn, see Kornwolf, *Scott,* 37–39.

33. Cerny, *Landmarks,* 220–21.

34. Keeler, *Simple Home,* 17–20. For details of Thomas' life, see Smith, "Thomas," 24.

35. Told to the author by Mike Dungan in June 2004.

36. See Smith, "Thomas," 45.

37. See Keeler, *Thereabout;* for "As Others See Us," see *SF Chronicle,* October 9, 1904. Keeler's writing was often paid for by promotional groups, and is very upbeat and positive about the glories of California.

38. Keeler, "San Francisco, California" (1904), in BL: Keeler Papers.

39. On the Red House and its popularity, see Cumming, "Architecture in Britain," 31–66. Wilson to the author, September 5, 2004. As of 2004 Red House is open to the public by reservation. See Craig, *Maybeck,* 491–92n19, on Lutyens playfulness.

40. Robert Craig to the author, February 7, 2005, noted that Maybeck and Muthesius might have been kindred spirits. But we do not know if Maybeck actually read Muthesius, as his library was destroyed in the 1923 fire. Said Craig, *"It is a case of an affinity, perhaps an inspiration."*

41. For Maybeck's possible Cotswolds inspiration, see Craig, *Maybeck,* 37–38, 104–6, where Craig notes that Maybeck's interest in the vernacular and picturesque led him to use illustrated books and journals for source material, combined with extended travels, the details of which are not recorded. Oxford is the only specific place Craig knows that Maybeck actually "saw" because he references it in a letter. Craig presents other towns and villages in his book as places in the Cotswolds that Maybeck would have (or could have) seen in books.

42. Kornwolf, *Scott,* 12, 12n3, cites "The Ballad of Bedford Park" (1881). It is also possible that Maybeck learned something about town planning from Viennese architect Otto Wagner. Maybeck visited Wagner on his 1897–98 trip to the capitals of Europe and may have been influenced by him, just as Wagner learned from Maybeck. For example, Wagner's Interimskirche is a structural reiteration of Maybeck's Hearst Hall. On Maybeck and Wagner, see Geretsegger & Peinter, *Wagner,* 14.

43. Taken from a list entitled "Some of the Books included in the Hillside Club Library," *HCY, 1912–13,* 17. Books in Keeler's personal library compiled by Keeler's daughter, in BL: Keeler Papers.

44. For the statement equating morality and medieval architecture, see Kornwolf, *Scott,* 90, who attributed this belief to Baillie Scott; however, it applies equally to Maybeck.

45. Compare Maybeck's Roos house with Baillie Scott's Red House, Douglas, Isle of Man (1892–93), published in the *Building News,* April 21, 1893; illustrated in Kornwolf, *Scott,* figs. 58 and 59. For Scott's half-timber technique and roofs, see ibid., figs. 61, 63, and 64. Excellent photograph of the linenfold design can be seen in Woodbridge, 128, fig. 112, and 130, fig. 114.

46. Maybeck used the two-story living room with balcony many times. Howard used a mezzanine balcony in the living room of his Ridge Road house. Polk's Russian Hill duplex employed a tight two-story living room with balcony. However, to my knowledge, only Maybeck's balusters are cutout boards. Half-timber balus-

ters and imaginative Arts & Crafts stuccowork can be seen in German half-timbering, or *fachwerk*. An easily accessible example is Berlin's Bieberbau restaurant, completed in 1894.

CHAPTER 10
Arts & Crafts Expansion: Mission, Pueblo, and Mediterranean Styles

1. Lummis, *Spanish Pioneers;* cited by Weitze, *Mission Revival.*
2. Moreover, after the 1906 San Francisco earthquake and fire and the 1923 Berkeley fire, there were practical considerations: stucco houses, especially those with tile roofs, seemed less susceptible to fire (even if they probably weren't).
3. The *Craftsman* magazine ran articles on the Mission Style in 1902, 1903, and 1904. For example, see these Craftsman articles: "Traces of the Franciscans in California," vol. 1 (February 1902): 29–30; "Sermons in Sun Dried Bricks from Old Spanish Missions," vol. 5 (December 1903): 212–16; George Wharton James articles on the missions and Indians in *Craftsman* 4–6 (1904–5). For more articles, see Conclusion, n21, herein.
4. Longstreth, *Edge,* 262–63, and 263, fig. 204. It was originally published in *A&B* (April 12, 1890).
5. BL: Porter Collection (Box 1978.100 ax; Folder 1978.125 1–25 AX); none of the drawings are dated. I am grateful to Robert Craig for helping me with this section.
6. For much more on the Mission Revival, see Weitze, *Mission Revival,* 15, and index. For Lummis on Pueblo style, see Calavan, "Schweinfurth," 5n4, who cites an article on the Pueblo style by Lummis in "City of the Sky," 32.
7. Jordan, *Days of a Man,* 1:3 and 1:212, 272, 372, states that, architecturally, Stanford's buildings derive from California's Franciscan missions, San Juan Capistrano having *"doubtless furnished the acceptable motive. . . ."* However it is also true that H. H. Richardson's Richardson Romanesque style affected the Stanford design, carried out after his death by his successor firm Shepley, Rutan, and Coolidge. Leland Stanford apparently saw an affinity between Mission and Romanesque and felt the two styles could be meshed.
8. Winter, in Gebhard, *Newsom.*
9. *AN* 1, no. 1 (November 1890): 8.
10. Ibid., prospectus page; and ibid., no. 2 (December 1890): 14.
11. Ibid., no. 3 (January 1891): 24; first-place sketch for adobe mission chapel, won by R. M. Turner.

12. Weitze, "Origins and Early Development," ix. See also Longstreth, *Edge,* 263: *"Daniel Burnham . . . stipulated that the state buildings for the West and Southwest be mission in type."*
13. It is not clear what the committee setting the guidelines meant by Moorish. Perhaps they considered Spanish California missions to have Moorish roots as did some Spanish architecture. Even into 1901 Mission and Moorish were associated. See Craft, "A Sermon," 126: "In general lines the [Swedenborgian] church follows the mission architecture of California, with arches adapted from the Moorish and a tower that gives dignity . . . ." Perhaps the guideline committee considered Spanish California missions to have Moorish roots as did some Spanish architecture? Or perhaps "things Moorish" were in vogue as Weitze notes in *Mission Revival,* 140n13: Washington Irving's The Alhambra introduced the term "Moorish." Weitze also cites Berstein, "Islamic Form," 33–42, 44, and remarks that mid-nineteenth-century painters (1830s–1860s), such as Delacroix, Gerome, Courbet, and Manet, borrowed and popularized Islamic and Spanish themes. Subsequently, Moorish lost out to Mission with one exception: Temple Emanu-El in San Francisco (1926). In Maybeck's autobiographical notes, EDA: Maybeck Collection, cited by Woodbridge, *Maybeck,* 214, he lists himself as advisory architect to Arthur Brown Jr., architect of Emanu-El.
14. Copy in CHS: Brown Scrapbooks.
15. See entire Brown article, December 30, 1894, cited in Chapters 3 and 6 herein.
16. See Weitze, "Origins of Mission Revival."
17. In 1890 when Polk was urging the Mission Style on readers of *AN,* Schweinfurth practiced independently in Denver. For a different point of view on Schweinfurth and Mission Revival, see Longstreth, Edge, 263–64. The one known photo of Schweinfurth working dates to 1893 (see ibid., 5, fig. 4) one year after the California State Building had been designed. There is as yet no proof that he worked on the California State Building winning design in February 1892.
18. Cardwell, *Maybeck,* 31 writes that Maybeck was sent to the fair by Brown. Longstreth, *Edge,* 371n10, writes that Peter B. Wight was the building's supervising architect. For more on Polk & Gamble, see ibid., 372n12.
19. *AABN* (March 19, 1892): 187. Brown cut out the article and pasted it in his scrapbook, CHS: Brown Scrapbook 1;

#47. Unfortunately, the original design seems to be lost.
20. Ibid. Another article in Brown's scrapbook also praises Maybeck's submission. Thus we have two independent comments documenting the existence of a Maybeck submission. Oddly, Maybeck is not listed as one of the architects who submitted plans to the competition in *CMWFM.* In BL (F850 C247; v. 1: 1–8.) In vol. 1, no. 4, (1892): 60, there is a list of all thirty architects who submitted competition drawings, including two plans by *"J. B. Mathisen, Plan no. 1, San Francisco"* and *"J. B. Mathisen, Plan no. 2, San Francisco."* Perhaps Maybeck was working for Brown and did not want his name on the Mathisen plans. Or perhaps this magazine made an error. (Note that the spelling of Mattheison changes often; he is also referred to as Matthisen, Mathisen, and Matheison.) Mattheison and Maybeck are each listed as architects at 23 Post Street in the *San Francisco Directory* for the year commencing May 1, 1892, but they do not list themselves in partnership. Neither the California State Library nor the California State Archives in Sacramento could locate any drawings by Maybeck and/or Mattheison, nor any signatures other than A. P. Brown's on his submissions. In an e-mail to the author, June 2005, Robert Craig pointed out that when Mark White assembled the firm's 1947 list of works, he wrote: *"Mr. Maybeck made some drawings for restoration of some of the missions, but* [I] *can't give you dope on these, although I worked with him on the Carmel mission."*
21. Cardwell, *Maybeck,* 30
22. *SF Examiner,* February 12, 1892, pasted in Brown Scrapbook #1, at CHS. Nationally known critic Montgomery Schuyler characterized the California Building's dome *"as a quite original feature."* Cardwell also notes the *"ornamental capitals of the piers & coved eaves* [of the California State Building's Roof Garden restaurant] *repeat a decorative scheme used in the Ponce de Leon hotel."* Maybeck went to Chicago, and Cardwell tells us "[Maybeck's] *reports of the Exposition were laudatory; he liked the scale and vigor of its buildings. . . ."* Maybeck told Cardwell he assisted at the 1893 Chicago Exposition, and since several details of the California Building reflect Maybeck's exuberance, it is likely he was sent there to help with its construction, even if he did not hold the title "site supervisor." For Schuyler quote and information in this note, see Cardwell, *Maybeck,* 30–32.
23. Cardwell, *Maybeck,* 22; Carrère &

Hastings did design an exuberantly decorated hotel in a comparable Mediterranean style—the Jefferson Hotel in Richmond, Virginia, in 1895—patterned after the Villa Medici. I am indebted to Richard Guy Wilson for noting this related commission.

24. "A letter from Thomas Hastings, FAIA, Reminiscent of the Early Works of Messers Carrère and Hastings, Archts," in *AA* (July 7, 1909): 3–4. Cited in Blake, "Carrère & Hastings," 102). McCoy, *Five California Architects*, 5, published just three years after Maybeck's death, had information from from William Gray Purcell, who had interviewed Maybeck. She writes: *"Hastings, with Maybeck at his elbow (1886) did most of the preliminary planning of the enormous Spanish Renaissance hotel."*

25. Cardwell noted in Maybeck, 23, 23n3, that when the drawings were published, sketches signed by both Maybeck and Hastings were used as illustrations. See "Plans of the Hotel Ponce de Leon, the Alcazar and the Methodist Episcopalian Church, St. Augustine, Fla.," in *AABN* 24 (August 25, 1888): 87–88. The drawings in this article are all signed "Carrere & Hastings" or "Thomas Hastings del." See also *AABN:* (June 13, 1896), (June 20, 1896), and (July 18, 1896). However, Longstreth, *Edge*, 366nn39–40, refers to Frederick Nichols, "A Visit with Bernard Maybeck" 31, which confirms what Maybeck told Cardwell.

26. Cardwell, *Maybeck*, 22; Cardwell knew Maybeck for many years. He interviewed him often for his research, and Maybeck told Cardwell of his work on the Ponce. For excellent photos and discussion on the Ponce de Leon Hotel, see Craig, *Maybeck at Principia*, Plates 1.19–1.21. On page 47, Craig seconds Cardwell's viewpoint and demonstrates the extent of Carrere & Hastings' faith in Maybeck: *"Architectural ornament for the hotel was provided by Pottier and Stymus, the Paris and NY firm . . . for which Maybeck's father . . . was foreman of carving. The elder Maybeck supervised the installation of the Ponce . . . ornamental carvings while his son supervised the building's construction."* Furthermore, Maybeck lists Carrère & Hastings as one of the firms that knew him and his work sufficiently to provide a good reference. EDA: Maybeck Collection.

27. Longstreth, *Edge*, 62–63, 366nn39–42. Longstreth agrees with Cardwell that Maybeck returned to New York, joined the firm, and worked closely with Hastings, but he does not credit

Maybeck with any of the Ponce design. He does, however, compare the Alcazar decorative details with the Palace of Fine Arts, San Francisco. There is no reason to doubt Hastings, who states that Henry Flagler intended to build the Ponce de Leon Hotel in 1885 with local contractors, and that he and Carrère did not get a contract until 1886, by which time Maybeck was on board.

28. See notes 25 and 26 above for Maybeck's experience at the Ponce.

29. Weitze, "Origins of Mission Revival," ix. See also Longstreth, *Edge*, 263.

30. We have seen how influential Worcester was. It is worth remembering that Worcester influenced the selection of John Galen Howard as university architect (Chapter 8 herein), and he influenced the 1915 Panama Pacific Exposition in San Francisco, as we will see.

31. See *AABN* (August 25, 1888): 88. Unsigned article. Many praised the dome and roof garden design of the California State Building for the 1893 Chicago Exposition. See, for example, *SF Examiner*, February 12, 1892, and CHS: Brown Scrapbooks.

32. See Worcester correspondence with Muir in Chapter 7 herein.

33. See note 20.

34. *SF Examiner*, January 11, 1895, mentions that *"in January 1893 the* Examiner *published a drawing of the Ferry Building from the Market Street side. . . . The original colored drawing is the work of Charles Graham, whose reputation was made in the colored panoramic view of the World's Fair, copies of which in colored lithographic form were so widely distributed. He has spent weeks in the preparation of the drawing making sketches of the wharves, . . . the vessels and the city which stands behind the site on which the building is to stand. The building itself was . . . reproduced from the plans made by the architect, A. Page Brown. . . . The watercolor drawing has been made for the Harbor Commission* [on which Brown sat]." It is also worth noting that the *New York Times* covered California's design, bringing it to the attention of many readers.

35. "An Architectural Controversy," *The Wave* (February 13, 1897): 3; cited by Longstreth in *Edge*, 289–91, 390–91nn43–46.

36. Frank McCullagh house, Los Gatos (1901), Longstreth, *Edge*, 290–91nn45–47, illustrated on pages 228–29. For Polk's opposition to *"basely imitating"* missions, see ibid., 289–91, 391n45. For the Rey house, see ibid., 163 and 379nn16–17.
   Karen Weitze, *Mission Revival*, 45, points out that an even earlier partially Mission Style house was designed by

the San Francisco firm of Percy and Hamilton. In *CABN* (September 1892), they published the "Residence of S. Taylor" with an enclosed patio, a fountain, and palms; and they used concrete and stucco, making them among the first to adapt Spanish Mission architecture for residential use. Note that a one-story inexpensive "simple cottage" version of the house illustrated here (Fig. 10.5) appeared in the *Craftsman (*February 1904) along with the Otis house.
   Mission Style was justified for the same reasons as the Shingle Style. George Wharton James wrote about the one-story Mission Style house in the *Craftsman* (February 1904): 467: The Consuelo residence is a *"simple cottage. . . . While fanciful and florid architecture may captivate for the moment . . . it soon produces . . . a longing for the simple."* He goes on to praise the Mission Style houses for their *"broadly reaching or widely projecting eaves"* and *". . . a color scheme which harmonizes with foliage and makes the missions 'part of Nature herself.'"*

37. *Oakland Enquirer*, September 28, 1895. Anthony Bruce at BAHA uncovered this article. Apparently Morgan worked on the first Lawson house with Maybeck. Lilian Forney McMurray, who was Julia Morgan's private secretary for thirty years, owns a photo of the first Lawson house, labeled "Lawson House" in Julia Morgan's handwriting on the back.

38. For more on the Mission Inn, see Weitze, "Utopian Place Making," 81.

39. Information on St. Mark's Church was compiled from church minutes and archives. However, records were unclear as to what these additions were. The booklet titled *St. Mark's*, 19, states that in 1911 the Parish House was *"designed by Willis Polk in harmony with the architecture of the church. . . ."* The chantry was added that same year, but the architect's name is not mentioned.

40. On Maybeck's use of color and for his inspiration from Italian villas and Pompeii, see Cardwell, *Maybeck*, 88, 98–99; Woodbridge, *Maybeck*, 118–25; and Craig, *Maybeck at Principia*, 25–26. Craig's index on page 503 lists no fewer than thirty-five references to color in his discussion of Maybeck.

41. Sgraffito work at the South Kensington Museum (now the Victoria and Albert Museum) is visible if one passes under the building, just beyond the side entrance, through an arched opening. After passing a guard station, one enters a courtyard with the sgraffito work. Sgraffito can also be seen in Maybeck's set design for Ernest Flagg's play *Circe,* illustrated

in Wilson, "Divine Excellence," 22, plate 9. On the lack of tile roof for Lawson, see Woodbridge. *Maybeck,* 121. However, judging from the flat-roofed "classical" temples in the *Circe* set design, Maybeck might have liked the almost flat roof look. There were two contrasting hillside aesthetics. The wood and shingles house derives from California vernacular and other sources previously discussed; the other is the Mediterranean and Mission aesthetic, where softly colored stucco and concrete buildings may "feel" right but do not disappear in the land-scape. Maybeck recognized the two choices when he asked Mrs. Joralemon what kind of house she would prefer: *". . . a white house resembling a bird that has just dropped down on your hilltop, or an earth colored one that seems to rise out of it."*

42. *AABN* (February 18, 1898). Sir Nikolaus Pevsner pointed out the relationship to Roehrig's design when Elisabeth Sussman and I gave him a tour of Berkeley's architecture in the early 1970s. Roehrig's member-ship in the San Francisco Sketch Club is mentioned in *AN* 1, no. 2 (December 1890): 21. On the possibility that Maybeck found inspiration for the Lawson house diamond patterning in Gottfried Semper, see Craig, *Maybeck at Principia,* 466n71.

43. McCoy, *Five Architects,* 61ff.

44. *The Craftsman* (May 1916), cited in McCoy, *Five Architects,* 61.

45. For an illustration on the Bailey house interior and exterior, see Figs. 10.18, 10.19 herein.

46. Circulation number (large for that day) derives from a letter written by Charles F. Lummis to John Muir, June 14, 1895; in LC/MsDiv: John Muir Finding Aid, 123 (microfilm 1 A/08/04924).

47. "FBT," 231ff. See also Moneta and Butz, "Lummis in California Life," 49–60. For letters from Lummis to Muir and Keeler discussing articles they might write for Lummis, see LC/MsDiv: Lummis and Muir Collections (microfilm).

48. Keeler, "The American Turner," 253–59. For further proof of their friendship with Lummis, see Mary Keith to Brother Cornelius, July 3, 1930, in SM: Cornelius Collection (Box 302, Folder 1929–30): *". . . Chas. Lummis, Charles Keeler, Charles Warren Stoddard & so on were habitués of* [Keith's] *studio. . . ."*

49. Keeler, "FBT," 210–12. The Keeler guidebook was published in Los Angeles by Passenger Department, Santa Fe Route, 1898. Exchange of letters about the guidebook can be found in LC/MsDiv: Lummis Collection. According to the Lummis

diary at the Braun Research Library and Lummis Archive Southwest Museum in Los Angeles, Lummis was in San Francisco from March 14 through May 27, 1898.

50. Keeler, "FBT," 220. Sketches by Louise Keeler are in BL.

51. Longstreth, *Edge,* 279.

52. This letter confirms that Schweinfurth completed all the drawings in 1894. William Randolph Hearst to his mother Phoebe Apperson Hearst, in BL: Hearst Papers (MSS 72/204; William Randolph Hearst, 1864–1919: Subseries 2.1; Reel 6, Box 7, Folders 1–4). Although 1894 is penciled on the letter by someone, the date is con-firmed by the fact that it is written on *SF Examiner* stationery, and Hearst mentions in the letter that he has not yet purchased the *New York Journal,* which he did in 1895. The 1894 date is also confirmed by a November 8, 1894, telegram to Mrs. Hearst, 1400 New Hampshire Avenue NW, Washington, D.C.: *"Can't come East yet. . . . WRHearst."* I have not been able to locate the Schweinfurth drawings Hearst mentions as being forwarded to his mother in this letter. Perhaps they remained in Washington where she was at the time.

53. Ibid.

54. Ibid. I have not been able to locate the reply from Mrs. Hearst stipulating the *"money limit."* It does not seem to be in BL or in the Hearst Papers on microfilm.

55. I am grateful to Richard Longstreth for sharing these two Schweinfurth letters with me.

56. Longstreth dates both November and December letters to 1895. As noted in Chapter 3, the November letter continues by decrying architectural "soaring," and Schweinfurth mentions the (Children's) hospital as finished. This hospital seems to have been the first commission from Hearst (1894, per Longstreth, *Edge,* 279) and it was probably this large job that caused Schweinfurth to leave Brown, as reported in February 1894. Schweinfurth mentions that the hospital is finished: *". . . photo-graphs* [of the hospital] *are to be sent to you in a day or two,"* and states that *"the hospital people are pleased . . . ."* We can conclude that by the end of 1895 the hospital was finished and design and construction on the hacienda was also quite advanced.

57. The December 20, 189?, letter to Mr. Edward H. Clark's office, Room 33, Mills Building, San Francisco. In the letter Schweinfurth is replying to notes transmitted to him *"yesterday afternoon"* on behalf of Mrs. Hearst. Schweinfurth asks Clark to convey his thoughts to Mrs. Hearst. Longstreth, *Edge,* 442, notes that Mrs. Hearst

made *"additions and minor alterations in 1896."*

58. Calavan, "Schweinfurth," 10.

59. Ibid., 20. One should also note that pueblos like those that inspired Schweinfurth were to be found in the Southwest, not in California, such as the one Longstreth illustrates in Taos, New Mexico, in *Edge,* 278, fig. 217; but the entire western heritage was considered exciting, romantic, and of interest to Californians. And Indians did live in California; in fact, Indians lived in Sunol.

60. For quotes praising the pueblos in the 1880s and for more on pueblos and the architecture of the Hearst hacienda, see ibid., 277–88, and notes.

61. *The Craftsman* 11 (November 1906): 208–21. The full color cover of the *Craftsman* (January 1904) features a single-story Mission Style house. An article on "A Craftsman House," page 399, features a two-story Mission Style house *"with a roof Ruskin might describe as neither 'scowling' or 'frowning' . . . and an exterior which employs . . . constructive features as the only means of decoration."* On the interiors, 400–1: *"Dining room and living room walls are of lacquered chestnut and the ceilings are beamed."* However, on page 403, for *"the deco-rative scheme . . . the walls will be covered with moss green canvas . . . reaching to a frieze of fabric . . . ."* The interior furniture, curtains, etc., are described in detail to increase sales of Stickley designs. Indian rugs and patterned fabrics are specified.

62. *The Craftsman* 11 (November 1906): 208–21.

63. Craft, "A Sermon," 127.

64. Warren Perry interview with the architect's son, John Wickson Thomas, ca. 1973.

65. On spirituality and mysticism in Arts & Crafts, see Wilson, "Divine Excellence," 26–32.

66. Keeler, *Simple Home,* 3. As noted in Chapter 1, Emerson's love of nature led him to meet Muir in Yosemite in May 1871. On Maybeck's view of architecture as an embodiment of the spirit of the client and its expressive power to influence the character of the client, see Craig, *Maybeck at Principia,* especially Chapter 1.

67. Ibid., 25.

68. Woodbridge *Maybeck,* 105, cites an unpublished version of Maybeck's comments on the Palace of Fine Arts. Maybeck expresses similar thoughts in his published essay, "The Palace of Fine Arts and Lagoon/Panama Pacific International Exposition," published in 1915 by Paul Elder & Co.; republished by the Maybeck Foundation in *A Vision for the Ages,* 14–20.

69. Maybeck, *Palace,* 14–20.

70. DHB: Worcester to Burnham, January 16, 1912.
71. Details on the architectural council and commission from Woodbridge. In an e-mail to the author, June 23, 2005, Robert Craig pointed out that the very first world's fair had a color scheme in Owen Jones's color plan for the Crystal Palace (painting of iron interior).
72. For Maybeck on color at the Palace, see Maybeck, *Palace,* 14–20. And on color for a client, Dorothy Rieber Joralemon, see Woodbridge, *Maybeck,* 10, 219n1, where she cites Mrs. Joralemon's journals.
73. . Details on Brakenridge houses courtesy of Anthony Bruce at BAHA; see also BAHA's booklet entitled *Claremont.*
74. Morgan's Seldon Williams house uses Venetian gothic tracery similar to that seen in Polk and Polk's 1893 house for John Kilgarif, illustration in Longstreth, *Edge,* 162n114.
75. Letter about Blaney house (1917), written by Porter from 3234 Pacific Avenue, in EDA: Polk Collection.

CHAPTER 11
Conclusion and Speculations:
The Golden State Inspires America

1. *HB* 6, no. 1 (June 1899), a national magazine, published Madge Robinson's article, featuring California houses of native materials designed to fit into and enhance the landscape; it was entitled "Hillside Architecture." See also Cathers, *Stickley,* 108–9: *"Stickley published numerous articles on the American West as his interest and plans to visit California grew;"* and Cathers remarks on *"two wonderfully lush and evocative California essays"*: "The Colorado Desert and California" (June 1903) and "Nature and Art in California" (July 1903).
2. See Chapter 4.
3. D'Ambrosio and Bowman (*McHugh,* 25) write: *"The [Mission Style] furniture McHugh produced [1898 and thereafter, inspired by the Swedenborgian Church chair] was a catalyst in disseminating the American Arts & Crafts style. . . . McHugh made the Arts & Crafts style affordable to the middle class and, in so doing, helped bring about the broad acceptance of the movement."* Although Stickley denied influence from mission furniture, the table he published in the *Craftsman* (February 1902): 5, as "Simple Furniture by the United Crafts" appears to be a direct quote from the table seen in photographs of Wyntoon's refectory, created by Maybeck and Meyer from 1901 and possibly before because, according to Cardwell, *Maybeck,* 53, much "medieval furniture" from Hearst Hall (1899) was moved to Wyntoon. See Wyntoon table illustrated here (Fig. 9.1).

4. For the tirade against Mumford, see Weingarten, *Bay Area Style,* 7–9. His lively text describes the attack on Mumford at the symposium on "Modern Architecture," 18–19.
5. See Mumford, "Introduction."
6. See Livingstone, Parry, Cumming, and Kaplan in bibliography.
7. See all notes in this section.
8. Morris, "Birmingham Art Students," 30.
9. For Price's statements, see "Preface."
10. Briggs' Preface to *Bungalows and Country Residences* advocated the same thing on a much more modest level; both cited in King, *Bungalow,* 105.
11. Renate Ulmer, "Germany," 214.
12. Keeler, *Thereabout,* 41–42. The same thought was repeated in *The Craftsman* 6, no. 1 (August 1906), 67.
13. Keeler, "Municipal Art," 592; see also *The Craftsman* (June 1906). "A Departure in Church Building," 330–34, with illustrations of both interior and exterior.
14. *SF Examiner,* September 30, 1895: currently on the Internet at www.sfswedenborgian.org
15. Cathers, *Stickley,* 113, quotes from an interview with Stickley regarding his trip to California published in *Furniture World.*
16. Mark Thompson, *American Character,* 85. These quotes are extrapolated by Thompson from many of Lummis' articles published 1886–87 in the *Los Angeles Times.*
17. See especially discussion of his contributions to Stanford and suggestions regarding Berkeley's architecture.
18. Weitze, *Mission Revival,* mentions an article by Lummis for Drakes' Magazine in 1889. The eclectic "Spanish Renaissance" architecture of Carrère and Hastings' Alcazar Hotel was featured in *AABN* (August 1888). Many architects and readers saw relationships between the California Spanish Missions and the Ponce de Leon and Alcazar Hotel designs. See Chapter 10 for more on this connection.
19. Willis Polk's Imaginary Church of the Mission Type appeared in *A&B* (April 19, 1890), spreading interest in the mission type outside California.
20. Mission Style house, "La Mita," by Mausard-Collier for John W. Mitchell, Cahuenga, California (1896), was published in *Land of Sunshine* (May 1896), cited by Weitze, *Mission Revival,* 60, fig. 67.
21. Cathers, *Stickley,* 110, notes about Harvey Ellis' essay on "Missions of the Southwest," *The Craftsman* (December 1903). "[Ellis] *called them proper models for modern domestic architecture* [in America]." and notes that *"other Craftsman architects would later design houses guided by this insight."* And as noted, the *Craftsman* (February 1904) published a Mission Style house along with a mansion for Harrison Gray Otis. Montgomery Schuyler, "Round about Los Angeles," *AR* (December 1908), praised the missions *"quietness and moderation . . . for direct imitation,"* and "A Craftsman House" in the mission style was published

in G. Stickley, *Craftsman Homes* (1909), both cited in Weitze, *California Missions,* 112. And Kaplan, "Regionalism in America," 107, writes: ". . . *every area of the country had Mission-style bungalows."*
22. "American Studio Talk," cited by Catherine Zusy in Kaplan, *A&C Movement in America, 1875–1920,* 185n5, entry 71.
23. Wilson, *"Divine Excellence,"* 16
24. Cathers, *Stickley,* 105.
25. However, in 1909, Stickley illustrated what appears to be a composite version of Maybeck's Flagg and Schneider chalets, with some of Greene and Greene, and a Maybeck-type pergola, and he acknowledges *"its design is primarily that of a California house."* The house was published in the *Craftsman* (January 1909). See illustration in Stickley, *Craftsman Homes: Architecture and Furnishings,* 42–44.
26. Cited in Robertson, "Resort to Rustic," 103. The article featured "Felsengarten," Ojai, California, by Myron Hunt and Elmer Grey, built three years before the article appeared in 1906.
27. Clay Lancaster, *Japanese Influence,* especially 111, 113, 122, 124–25, 130.
28. Robertson "Resort to Rustic," 103, also cites Stellmann, "Swiss Chalet Type," 290. Ibid., 102–3, lists reasons why the alpine house appealed to Californians and to the Arts & Crafts movement.
29. For Stickley's seven-week transcontinental trip to the West Coast beginning March 1904, which included San Francisco, the East Bay, Los Angeles, and Pasadena, see Cathers, *Stickley,* 108, 114–17. Cathers points out that Stickley's interest in California and the West preceded the trip and that *"In the months leading up to this trip, Stickley's magazine had been paying an increasing amount of attention to the American West."* Furthermore, in ibid., 117, Stickley furnished the California Building at the 1904 Louisiana Purchase Exposition in St. Louis, and *"California continued to be important to Stickley, with his Craftsman furniture in daily use in the mission-style California building."*
30. *The Craftsman* (August 1912), 532.
31. The subtitle of the publication was even more California inspired: *Floor Plans and Illustrations for 78 Mission style Dwellings.* The book includes many Mission Style houses as well as wood bungalows and most combine various styles and materials into all sorts of middle class house types.
32. Robert Winter, *American Bungalow Style,* writes: *"The first American house actually called a bungalow was designed in 1879 by William Gibbons Preston. Contrary to the usual definition, it was a two-story house built at Monument Beach on Cape Cod, Massachusetts. It was probably called a bungalow because it resembled resort architecture."* And he continues, *"The first California house dubbed a bungalow was designed by the San Francisco architect A. Page Brown for*

J. D. Grant in the early 1890s. A true bungalow, this one-and-a-half story residence was set on a high foundation and located on a hillside. It was a strange blend of Bengalese, Queen Anne and Swiss chalet architecture." However, the Worcester house preceded the Grant house by twelve years. The Grant house may have been designed by Maybeck; it closely resembles the "The Swiss Chalet Motif" illustrated in "Hillside Architecture" published in 1898 by Margaret Robinson, a member of the Hillside Club established by Maybeck and Keeler; this article is currently at www.berkeleyheritage.com.

33. King, *The Bungalow,* 95, caption for Fig. 3.1.

34. After his move to San Francisco in 1887 Worcester returned to the Piedmont house as often as his duties at the Swedenborgian Church were minimal compared to those of today's ministers. Except for Sunday services and raising money quietly to build a little church, he was basically free and spent much of his time with the region's architects, as we have seen. In 1902 Worcester still owned and paid taxes on 8.50 acres. He once owned 12.75 acres. I am grateful to Gail Lombardi for tracking down this information.

35. King, *The Bungalow,* 95, caption for Fig. 3.1.

36. For Briggs' statement on the suburbs, see King, *The Bungalow,* 105, 134–35.

37. Jack London's statement was transmitted via Joan London, Jack's oldest daughter, to James Sisson and then to the author March 21, 1973: *". . . the Bungalow, always capitalized thus when written, and pronounced by Mother and Daddy so that the large B was almost visible."* For more of London's description of Worcester's Piedmont house, see Chapter 1. On R. A. Briggs, see King, *The Bungalow,* 95, where he writes that the five editions of Briggs book published between 1891–1901 *"had considerable influence in spreading the bungalow ideology on both sides of the Atlantic."* For a description of a typical bungalow see ibid., 146, where he notes that the bungalow's popularity developed simultaneously with the Arts & Crafts movement.

38. David Cathers, *Stickley,* 51, refers to the *Craftsman* as *"by far the most important periodical to come out of the American Arts & Crafts movement."* Cathers, ibid., entitles an entire chapter, "The Pivotal Year, 1904," 104–23. That year Stickley traveled to Palm Springs,

Mission Inn in Riverside, Los Angeles, Pasadena, Santa Barbara, and photographed Mission San Miguel, visited San Francisco and the East Bay, and then went back to Southern California before heading home. However, even before the actual trip, the *Craftsman* saw that other magazines were promoting California and the West and jumped on that bandwagon. The San Francisco Swedenborgian Church was featured in major magazines; e.g. Craft, "A Sermon," 125–33, and *SABE,* no. 2 (August 1899): front page, 35–36. Articles on California's architecture and lifestyle, along with features on Swiss chalets, English and other Arts & Crafts developments, and Craftsman houses influenced by these styles helped expand the growth of the Craftsman movement in the United States; see bibliography. More articles on the missions and their interest to those designing Craftsman houses are cited in Chapter 10 herein. See note 1 for some of the articles the *Craftsman* published on California.

39. Ashbee quotes from Charles Robert Ashbee Journals (January 1909), King's College Library, Cambridge, were published by Wilson in "Divine Excellence," 13. See also Crawford, *C. R. Ashbee,* 151–53.

Fig. 12.1   **Fig. 12.2**

Fig. 12.1: Wintermute house, 227 Tunnel Road, Berkeley (1913), by John Hudson Thomas. Living room detail of Arts & Crafts wood carving.

Fig. 12.2: Wintermute house, view: the conservatory shows Secessionist Style detailing that Thomas used in combination with Arts & Crafts style.

Bibliography

A

Anonymous. "A Departure in Church Building—The Second New Jerusalem Church in California: By a Stranger," *The Craftsman* (June 1906).

———."A House that Teaches; The Roof Supported by Madrone Trees, Just as they Left the Forest; The Rev. Mr. Worcester's Church; Going to a Service through a Garden and Hearing a Sermon While Resting on Rush Bottomed Chairs." *San Francisco Examiner,* September 30, 1895.

———. "The Later Work of A. C. Schweinfurth," *Architectural Review* 9, no. 3 (March 1902): 76–79; new series: vol. 4: 3.

———. "Logging in California," *California Architect and Building News* 3 (1882).

———. "The Redwoods," *California Architect and Building News* 3 (1882).

———. "Uses of the Steel Square," *California Architect and Building News* 3 (1882).

———. "Wood in Switzerland," *The Craftsman* 5 (1903).

Anscombe, Isabelle, and Charlotte Gere. *Arts & Crafts in Britain and America.* London: Academy Editions, 1978.

———. "The Attractions of Blair Park," *Oakland Daily Evening Tribune,* June 20, 1891, 2/9.

Armes, William Dallam, ed. and comp. *Autobiography of Joseph Le Conte,* New York: Appleton & Co., 1903.

Ashbee, C. R. Journals, January 1909, King's College Library, Cambridge; in Wilson, "Divine Excellence: The Arts and Crafts Life in California," in Trapp, *The Arts and Crafts Life in California* (1993).

B

Badè, William Frederick. *The Life and Letters of John Muir.* Boston: Houghton Mifflin, 1924.

Bamford, Georgia Loring, *The Mystery of Jack London: Some of His Friends, Also a Few Letters; A Reminiscence.* Oakland, California: Piedmont Press, 1931.

Barrett, Benjamin Fiske, ed. *The Swedenborgian, Devoted to the Advocacy of Spiritual Christianity, and Religious Liberty.* Monthly, 4 vols. New York: American New Church Association, January 1858–1860.

Bartlett, William C. "The Ideal Village," *San Francisco Bulletin,* March 19, 1880.

Berstein, G. S. "In Pursuit of the Exotic: Islamic Form in Nineteenth Century American Architecture." Dissertation, University of Pennsylvania, 1968.

Beveridge, Charles E. "Frederick Law Olmsted's Theory on Landscape Design." Reprinted from the *Twenty-fifth Anniversary Issue of Nineteenth Century,* the *Journal of the Victorian Society in America* 20, no. 2 (Fall 2000): 32–37. Also located on the Web site of the National Association for Olmsted Parks: www.olmsted.org.

Beveridge, Charles E. *The Papers of Frederick Law Olmsted, Vol. 5: The California Frontier, 1863–1865.* Ed. by Victoria Post Ranney (1990). Baltimore: Johns Hopkins University Press, 1977– .

Blake, Curtis Channing. "The Architecture of Carrère and Hastings." PhD dissertation, Columbia University, 1976.

Blashfield, E. H., and E. W. Blashfield. "The Art of Ravenna," *Scribner's* Magazine 12, Issue 1 (July 1892): 37–57; published by Charles Scribner's Sons.

Bloice, Brian. "E. G., Gentleman Architect: A Profile of Sir Ernest George, R. A. 1839–1922," *Insights.* Vauxhall Society Newsletter. London: Southwark & Lambeth Archaeological Society (August 1984): 4 pp.

Bonnett, Wayne. *Victorian Classics of San Francisco.* With an introduction by Alex Brammer. Sausalito, California: Windgate Press, 1987.

Bosley, Edward R. "A. C. Schweinfurth," in Winter, *Toward a Simpler Way of Life* (1997).

———. *Greene & Greene.* London: Phaidon, 2000.

———. "Western North America: Nature's Spirit" in Livingstone and Parry. *International Arts & Crafts* (2005).

———, Robert Judson Clark, and Randell L. Makinson, eds. *Last of the Ultimate Bungalows: The William R. Thorsen House of Greene and Greene.* Pasadena California: The Gamble House, privately published 1996.

Boutelle, Sara Holmes. *Julia Morgan, Architect.* With photographs by Richard Barnes. New York: Abbeville Press, 1995; © 1988 Cross River Press, Ltd.

Briggs, Robert Alexander. *Bungalows and Country Residences.* London: B. T. Batsford, 1891.

Brooks, H. Allen. *The Prairie School: Frank Lloyd Wright and His Midwest Contemporaries.* Toronto and Buffalo: University of Toronto Press, 1972.

Brown, A. Page. "Architecture in California," *San Francisco Chronicle,* December 30, 1894.

C

Calavan, Carol Louise. "A. C. Schweinfurth in California, 1893–1898." MA dissertation, University of California, Santa Barbara, 1972.

Camp, Charles L., Collection of Stereographs, ca. 1867–95, Boston Public Library. Photographer: Carleton Watkins or J. J. Reilly. Photographer's # 413. Publ.: Yosemite Valley, California. Photographer's series: Photographic Views of American Scenery: 16340.

Cardwell, Kenneth. *Maybeck, Artisan, Architect, Artist.* Salt Lake City: Peregrine Smith, 1977.

Cathers, David. *Gustav Stickley.* London: Phaidon, 2003.

———. "The East Coast: 'Enterprise upon a Higher Plane,' " in Livingstone and Parry, *International Arts & Crafts* (2005).

Cerny, Susan Dinkelspiel. *Berkeley Landmarks: An Illustrated Guide to Berkeley, California's Architectural Heritage.* Revised edition. Berkeley: Berkeley Architectural Heritage Association, 2001.

Claremont and the Uplands: Gateway to a Private Residence Park at Berkeley. Pamphlet issued by Berkeley Architectural Heritage Association, 1998.

Clark, Robert Judson. "Louis Christian Mullgardt," in Winter, *Toward a Simpler Way of Life* (1997).

———. *Louis Christian Mullgardt 1866–1942.* University of California, Santa Barbara: The Art Galleries, 1966.

———. "Louis Christian Mullgardt and the Court of Ages," *The Journal of the Society of Architectural Historians* (December 1962).

———, ed. *The Arts and Crafts Movement in America, 1876–1916.* Princeton, New Jersey: Princeton University Press, 1972.

Cleaveland, Henry W., William Backus, and Samuel D. Backus. *Village and Farm Cottages: The Requirements of American Village Homes Considered and Suggested, with Designs for Such Houses of Moderate Cost,* 8 vols. New York: D. Appleton, 1856.

Connally, Ernest Allen. "The Cape Cod House: An Introductory Study," *Society of American Historians Journal* 19, no. 2 (May 1960).

Cornelius, Brother. *Keith: Old Master of California, Vol. 2: A Supplement.* Fresno, California: St. Mary's College, 1957.

Corthell, Wendell G. "The Use of Wood in Switzerland," *The Craftsman* 5, no. 1 (September 1903).

Covell, Alwyn T. "The Real Place of Mission Furniture," *Good Furniture* 4 (March 1915).

Craig, Robert M. *Bernard Maybeck at Principia College: The Art and Craft of Building.* Salt Lake City: Gibbs Smith, Publisher, 2004.

Craft, Mabel Clare. "A Sermon in Church Building," *House Beautiful* 9, no. 3 (February 1901).

Crawford, Alan. *C. R. Ashbee: Architect, Designer and Romantic Socialist.* New Haven, Yale University Press, 1985.

Crawford, Alan. "United Kingdom: Origins and First Flowering," in Kaplan, *The Arts & Crafts Movement in Europe & America* (2004).

Creese, Walter C. *The Search for an Environment.* New Haven: Yale University Press, 1966.

Cumming, Elizabeth. "Architecture in Britain," in Cumming and Kaplan, *The Arts and Crafts Movement* (2002).

———. "Sources and Early Ideals," in Cumming and Kaplan, *The Arts and Crafts Movement* (2002).

———, and Wendy Kaplan. *The Arts & Crafts Movement.* London: Thames & Hudson, 1991, 2002.

D

D'Ambrosio, Anna Tobin. *The Distinction of Being Different: Joseph P. McHugh and the American Arts & Crafts Movement.* Essay and exhibition, with essays by Anna Tobin D'Ambrosio and Leslie Greene Bowman, at the Munson-Williams-Proctor Institute, October 2, 1993–January 30, 1994.

Davey, Peter. *Arts and Crafts Architecture.* Hong Kong: Phaidon Press Ltd, 1995.

Doughty, J., ed. *New Church Pacific.* Monthly, 8 vols. San Francisco: Swedenborg Library and Tract Society, 1888–February 1894; San Francisco: Pacific Coast New-Church Association, March 1894–December 1895.

Downing, Annette, and Vincent Scully. *The Architectural Heritage of Newport, Rhode Island.* Cambridge: Harvard University Press, 1952.

Drexler, Arthur, ed. *The Architecture of the Ecole des Beaux-Arts.* With essays by Richard Chafee, Neil Levine, and David Van Zanten. New York: Museum of Modern Art, 1977.

E

Eastlake, Charles Locke. *Hints on House-hold Taste: The Classic Handbook of Victorian Interior Decoration.* Originally published in London, England, 1868; reprint of 4th edn. (1878); New York: Dover Publications, 1969.

Eisen, Theodore A. "The Consistency of San Francisco Architecture," *California Architect and Building News* 3, no. 4 (April 1882).

Emanuel, Frank L (author and illustrator). "British and Dutch Architecture in South Africa. Part 1: Capetown and Kimberly," *Architectural Review* (London) 7 (January–June 1900): 3–8.

———. "British and Dutch Architecture in South Africa. Part 2: Johannesburg, Durban, East London, Port Elizabeth," *Architectural Review* (London) 7 (January–June 1900) 51–57.

Emmington, Lesley. "Introduction," *Frederick Law Olmsted's Berkeley Legacy, Piedmont Way and the Berkeley Property Tract.* Berkeley, California: Berkeley Architectural Heritage Association (BAHA), 1995.

F

Ferrier, William Warren. *Berkeley, California: The Story of the Evolution of a Hamlet into a City of Culture and Commerce.* Berkeley: Ferrier, 1933.

Fletcher, Bannister. "The Smaller Houses of the English Suburbs and Provinces, Part I," *Architectural Review* 5, no. 4 (April–June 1896).

Floyd, Margaret Henderson. *Henry Hobson Richardson: a Genius for Architecture.* New York City: Monacelli Press, 1997.

French, Leigh, Jr. *Colonial Interiors: The Colonial and Federal Periods.* New York: Bonanza Books, 1923.

Freudenheim, Leslie. *Building with Nature: Inspiration for the Arts & Crafts Home.* Salt Lake City: Gibbs Smith, Publisher, 2005.

———, and Elisabeth S. Sussman. *Building with Nature: Roots of the San Francisco Bay Region Tradition.* Salt Lake City: Peregrine Smith, Inc., 1974.

G

Gebhard, David. *Architecture in California, 1868–1968: An Exhibition.* Held April 16–May 12, 1968, at the Art Gallery, University of California, Santa Barbara, to celebrate the centennial of the University of California. Santa Barbara: Standard Printing, 1968.

———. *Samuel Newsom and J. Cather Newsom: Victorian Architectural Imagery in California 1878–1908.* Exhibition and catalog for the University of California, Santa Barbara, Art Museum, April 4–May 6, 1979; The Oakland Museum, May 22–August 12, 1979.

———, Robert Winter, and Eric Sandweiss. *The Guide to Architecture in San Francisco and Northern California.* Santa Barbara: Peregrine Smith, 1973; 2d ed., 1976; 3rd ed., Salt Lake City: Peregrine Smith, 1985.

———. *Charles F. A. Voysey, Architect: An Exhibition Organized by David Gebhard for The Art Galleries, University of California, Santa Barbara.* Santa Barbara: The Regents, University of California, 1970.

Geretsegger, H., and Max Peinter. *Otto Wagner 1841–1918.* New York: Praeger, 1970.

Greeves, T. Affleck. *Bedford Park: The First Garden Suburb.* United Kingdom: Anne Bingley, 1975; reprinted by the Bedford Park Society, London, 1999.

H

Hasbrouck, W. R. "The Earliest Work of Frank Lloyd Wright," *The Prairie School Review* 7, no. 4 (4th quarter, 1970).

Hendricks, King, and Irving Shepard, eds. *Letters from Jack London.* New York: Odyssey Press, 1965.

Hewison, Robert. *Ruskin, Turner and the Pre-Raphaelites* (catalog:Tate Britain Exhibition, March 9–May 29, 2000).

Hildebrand, George Herbert. *Borax Pioneer, Francis Marion Smith.* San Diego: Howell-North Books, 1982.

Hillside Club. "What the Club Advocates." From a booklet issued by Advisory Board of the Club, 1898; reprinted in *Hillside Club Yearbook, 1911–1912,* 6–7; located in The Bancroft Library.

Hillside Club Suggestions for Berkeley Homes. Issued by the Hillside Club, 1901; The Bancroft Library: Keeler Papers.

Hines, Thomas S. "The Imperial Mall: The City Beautiful Movement and the Washington Plan of 1901–02," in *The Mall in Washington, 1791–1991.* Washington: National Gallery of Art, 1991.

Hitchcock, Henry-Russell. *Architecture: Nineteenth and Twentieth Centuries.* Baltimore: Penguin Books, 1958, 1963.

———. *The Architecture of Henry Hobson Richardson and His Times.* Cambridge: MIT Press, 1966.

———. *Rhode Island Architecture.* Providence: Rhode Island Museum Press, 1939.

I

Irving, Washington. *The Alhambra:A Series of Tales and Sketches of the Moors and Spaniards,* vols. 1 & 2. Philadelphia: Carey & Lea, 1832.

J

Johnston, Hank. *The Yosemite Grant, 1864–1906: A Pictorial History.* Yosemite Association, November 1995.

Jones, William Carey. *The Illustrated History of the University of California.* Berkeley: Student's Cooperative Society; San Francisco: Frank H. Dukesmith, 1895.

Joralemon, Dorothy Rieber. "Memories of Bernard Maybeck, 1923: From the Journal of Dorothy Rieber Joralemon," 1977. Cited by Woodbridge in *Bernard Maybeck: Visionary Architect* (1992).

Jordan, David Starr. *Days of a Man,* 2 vols. Yonkers on Hudson, New York: World Book Company, 1922.

Jpooien, Ròdigger. "Germany: a New Culture of Things," in Kaplan, *The Arts & Crafts Movement in Europe & America* (2004).

K

Kaplan, Wendy, ed. *"The Art That Is Life": The Arts & Crafts Movement in America, 1875–1920.* Boston: Little, Brown and Company and the Museum of Fine Arts, Boston, 1998.

———. *The Arts & Crafts Movement in Europe & America: Design for the Modern World.* With contributions by Alan Crawford, Rudiger Jpooien, Juliet Kinchin, Amy F. Ogata, Elisabet Stavenow-Hidemark, and Christian Witt-Dorring. Los Angeles: Los Angeles County Museum of Art, 2004; New York: Thames & Hudson, Inc., 2004.

Kaplan, Wendy, ed. "Design for the Modern World," in Kaplan, *The Arts & Crafts Movement in Europe & America* (2004).

———. "America: The Quest for Democratic Design," in Kaplan, *The Arts & Crafts Movement in Europe & America* (2004).

———. "Regionalism in America," in Cumming and Kaplan, *The Arts and Crafts Movement* (2002).

———. "The Simple Life: The Arts and Crafts Movement in Great Britain," *Antiques Magazine* (October 1999).

Keeler, Charles "The American Turner: William Keith and his Work," *The Land of Sunshine* 8, no. 6 (May 1898).

———. "As Others See Us" (1904), in BL: Keeler Papers.

———. "California in the World of Art." Unpublished manuscript, ca. 1908.

———. "Early History of the Club," *Hillside Club Yearbook, 1911–12.*The Bancroft Library: Keeler Papers.

———. "Friends Bearing Torches." Unpublished manuscript, n.d. The Bancroft Library: Keeler Collection.

———. "Municipal Art in American Cities: San Francisco," *The Craftsman* (August 1905).

———. "A Retrospection," *Hillside Club Yearbook, 1907–8.* The Bancroft Library: Keeler Collection.

———. "San Francisco, the Home of Mission Type of Furniture," *Architect and Engineer* 6, no. 1 (August 1906).

———. *San Francisco and Thereabout,* 2nd edn. San Francisco: California Promotion Committee, 1902.

———. *The Simple Home.* San Francisco: Paul Elder and Co., 1904. Reprinted with an introduction by Dimitri Shipounoff, Salt Lake City: Peregrine Smith, 1979.

Kerrick, Jane Berry Kerrick. "Willis Jefferson Polk, San Francisco Architect." Master's thesis, Mills College, 1965.

King, Anthony D. *The Bungalow: The Production of a Global Culture.* New York & Oxford: Oxford University Press, 1995.

Kirker, Harold. *California's Architectural Frontier: Style and Tradition in the Nineteenth Century.* San Marino, California: Henry E. Huntington Library and Art Gallery, 1960; reprinted with new material, Salt Lake City: Peregrine Smith, Inc., 1973.

Kirkham, Pat, ed. *Women Designers in the USA, 1900–2000.* New Haven, Connecticut: Yale University Press, 2002.

Kornwolf, James O. *M. H. Baillie Scott and the Arts and Crafts Movement.* Baltimore & London: The Johns Hopkins Press, 1972.

Kostura, William. *Russian Hill: The Summit, 1853–1906, Vol. I: A Neighborhood History.* San Francisco: Aerie Publications, 1997.

L

Lancaster, Clay. *The American Bungalow, 1880–1930.* New York: Abbeville Press, 1985; Dover Publications, 1995.

Lancaster, Clay. *The Japanese Influence in America.* New York: Walton H. Rawls, 1963.

Livingstone, Karen, and Linda Parry, co-eds. *International Arts & Crafts.* London: Victoria & Albert Museum, 2005.

Livingstone, Karen. "Origins and Development," in Livingstone and Parry, *International Arts & Crafts* (2005).

Lombardi, Gail. "The Oldest House in Piedmont," *The Attic Trunk* 5, no. 2 (Fall 2001). Edited by Stafford Buckley; Piedmont, California: Piedmont Historical Society.

London, Charmian. *The Book of Jack London.* New York: The Century Co., 1921.

Longstreth, Richard. *On the Edge of the World: Four Architects in San Francisco at the Turn of the Century.* Los Angeles, London: University of California Press, Berkeley, 1998.

———, ed. *A Matter of Taste: Willis Polk's Writings in* The Wave. San Francisco: Book Club of California, 1979; copy in Environmental Design Archive, College of Environmental Design, University of California, Berkeley.

Lummis, Charles. "The City of the Sky—Acoma," *California Illustrated Magazine* 1, no. 2 (February 1891).

———. "The Old Missions," *Drake's Magazine* 7 (March 1889): 191; cited by Weitze in *California Architecture and Architects 3: California's Mission Revival* (1984).

———. "The Right Hand of the Continent," *Land of Sunshine* 17, no. 2 (August 1902).

———. *The Spanish Pioneers and the California Missions.* Chicago: A. C. McClurg & Co., 1914; Glorieta, New Mexico: Rio Grande Press, 1963.

M

Makinson, Randell L. "Charles and Henry Greene," in *Toward a Simpler Way of Life.* Edited by Robert Winter. Berkeley: University of California Press, 1997.

———. "Greene and Greene," in McCoy, *Five California Architects* (1960).

———. *Greene & Greene: Architecture as a Fine Art.* Salt Lake City: Peregrine Smith, Inc. [Gibbs Smith, Publisher], 1977.

———, and Thomas A. Heinz. *Greene & Greene: Creating a Style.* Gibbs Smith, Publisher, 2004.

Maybeck, Bernard R. *Palace of Fine Arts and Lagoon/Panama Pacific International Exposition, 1915.* San Francisco: Paul Elder and Company, 1915. Republished in *A Vision for the Ages: Essays on the Life and Architecture of Bernard Maybeck, Reflections by Bernard Maybeck on his First Church of Christ, Scientist, Berkeley, and his Palace of Fine Arts.* Special Premiere Edition, Scholar's Insert of the Newsletter of the Maybeck Foundation, Berkeley, California, 1998.

Maybeck, Jacomena. *Maybeck: The Family View.* Berkeley, California: Berkeley Architectural Heritage Association (BAHA), 1991.

McCoy, Esther. *Five California Architects.* New York: Reinhold Publishing Corp., 1960.

McGuire, Diana Kostial. "Frederick Law Olmsted in California: An Analysis of his Contributions to Landscape Architecture." Master's thesis, University of California, Berkeley, 1956.

McKail, J. D. "The Life of William Morris," reviewed by "E. R." in *Architectural Review* (London) 8 (July–December 1900).

McLaughlin, Charles Capen, ed., and Charles E. Beveridge, assoc. ed. *The Papers of Frederick Law Olmsted. Vol. 1: The Formative Years, 1840–1852.* Edited by the Olmsted Papers Project (1977). Baltimore: Johns Hopkins University Press, 1977– .

Meister, Maureen. *Architecture and the Arts and Crafts Movement in Boston: Harvard's H. Langford Warren.* Hanover, New Hampshire: University Press of New England, 2003.

Mizner, Addison. *The Many Mizners.* New York: Sears Publishing Co., 1932.

Moneta, Daniela P., ed. *Chas. F. Lummis: The Centennial Exhibition.* Los Angeles: Southwest Museum, 1985.

———, and Patricia A. Butz. "Lummis in California Life," in Moneta, *Chas. F. Lummis: The Centennial Exhibition* (1985).

Moore, Charles. *Daniel H. Burnham: Architect Planner of Cities,* 2 vols. Boston: Houghton Mifflin Co., 1921.

Morphy, Edward A. "San Francisco's Thoroughfares: Taylor Street," *San Francisco Chronicle,* August 11, 1918.

Morris, May, ed., with introductions by his daughter. *The Collected Works of William Morris.* London: Longmans Green and Company, 1868, 1910–1915.

Morris, William. "Address to Birmingham Art Students" (1894), in Morris, *The Collected Works of William Morris* (1868, 1910–1915).

Morse, Edward S. *Japanese Homes and Their Surroundings.* Boston: Ticknor and Company, 1886.

Moure, Nancy. *Loners, Mavericks and Dreamers: Art in Los Angeles Before 1910.* Laguna, California: Laguna Art Museum Catalog, 1993.

Muir, John. "The National Parks and Forest Reservations," *Sierra Club Bulletin* 1, no.7 (January 1896).

———. "Wild Wool," in *Steep Trails: California - Utah - Nevada - Washington - Oregon - The Grand Canyon.* Edited by William Frederick Badè. Boston and New York: Houghton Mifflin Company, 1918. "Wild Wool" originally appeared in *Overland Monthly* (1875).

———. *The Yosemite.* New York: The Century Co., 1912.

Mullgardt, Louis Christian. *The Architecture and Landscape Gardening of the Exposition.* San Francisco: Paul Elder & Co., 1915.

Mumford, Lewis. *Roots of Contemporary American Architecture.* New York: Reinhold, 1952.

———, as quoted in "What Is Happening to Modern Architecture? A Symposium at the Museum of Modern Art," *New York Museum of Modern Art Bulletin* 15, no. 1 (Spring 1948): 1–21.

———. "Introduction," *Domestic Architecture of the Bay Region.* Exhibit for the San Francisco Museum of Art, 1949.

N

Neuhaus, Eugen. *William Keith.* Berkeley: University of California Press, 1938.

Newcomb, Rexford. *Spanish Colonial Architecture in the United States.* New York: JJ Augustin, 1937.

Nichols, Frederick. "A Visit with Bernard Maybeck," *Society of Architectural Historians Journal* (October 1952).

O

Ogata, Amy F. "Belgium and France: Arts, Crafts and Decorative Arts," in Kaplan, *The Arts & Crafts Movement in Europe & America* (2004).

O'Gorman, James F. *Living Architecture: A Biography of Henry Hobson Richardson.* New York: Simon and Schuster, 1997.

Oakey, Alexander F. *My House Is My Castle.* San Francisco: The Pacific States Savings and Loan Building Co., 1891.

Ochsner, Jeffrey Karl. *H. H. Richardson, Complete Architectural Works.* Cambridge and London: The MIT Press, 1982.

Olmsted, Frederick Law, and Olmsted, Vaux & Co. "Study for Laying Out the Berkeley Neighborhood Including the Grounds of the College of California," *Report upon a Projected Improvement of the Estate of the College of California, at Berkeley, Near Oakland.* New York: Wm. C. Bryant & Company, Summer 1866. Republished, San Francisco: Towne and Bacon, Fall 1866.

Olmsted, Frederick Law, Sr., with an introductory note by Laura Wood Roper. "The Yosemite Valley and the Mariposa Big Trees," *Landscape Architecture* 43, no. 1 (October 1952).

Olmsted, Roger, and T. H. Watkins, *Here Today: San Francisco's Architectural Heritage.* San Francisco: Chronicle Books, 1968.

P

Pattiani, Evelyn Craig. *Queen of the Hills: The Story of Piedmont, A California City.* Oakland: Yosemite-DiMaggio, 1982 edition; originally published by The Academy Library Guild, 1954; originally published in 1943.

Pevsner, Nikolaus. *An Outline of European Architecture.* Baltimore: Penguin, 1957.

Piexotto, Ernest. "Architecture in San Francisco," *Overland Monthly* (May 1893).

Powers, Alan. "Architecture and Gardens," in Livingstone and Parry, *International Arts & Crafts* (2005).

Price, Bruce. *A Large Country House: Modern Architecture* 1. New York, 1886.

Price, Matlack. "Practicality, Imagination and the Designer: A Study of the Work of Walter J. H. Dudley," *Arts and Decoration* (July 1921): 166–68.

Purcell, William Gray. "Bernard Maybeck, Poet of Building." Typescript of Purcell's interview with Maybeck, written down in 1949 for Mrs. Harwell Harris (Jean Murray Bangs); The Bancroft Library: Jean Murray Bangs Papers; Environmental Design Archives: Maybeck Papers. Also cited in Woodbridge, *Bernard Maybeck* (1992).

R

Ranney, Victoria Post, ed. *The Papers of Frederick Law Olmsted, Vol. V: The California Frontier, 1863–1865.* Baltimore: The Johns Hopkins University Press, 1990.

Reid, Arthur H. "Architecture of the Past in South Africa. Part 1: Capetown," *Architectural Review* (London) 8 (July–December 1900): 147–52; plate 8.

———. "British and Dutch Architecture in South Africa. Part 2: Johannesburg, Durban, East London, Port Elizabeth," *Architectural Review* (London) 7 (January–June 1900): 51–57.

Roberts, Paul T. "Alfred Washington Pattiani: Victorian Designer-Builder." Lecture for the Berkeley Architectural Heritage Association, Berkeley, California, May 5, 2004.

Robertson, Cheryl. "The Resort to the Rustic," in Trapp, *The Arts and Crafts Life in California* (1993).

Rose, Donald L. "Swedenborg on Architecture," *Chrysalis: Journal of the Swedenborg Foundation* 2 (Summer 1987).

Royce, Sarah. *A Frontier Lady.* New Haven: Yale University Press, 1933.

Runte, Alfred. *Yosemite: The Embattled Wilderness.* Lincoln: University of Nebraska Press, 1990.

Ruskin, John. *The Seven Lamps of Architecture.* Boston: Dana Estes and Company, n.d. Originally published in London, 1849; reprinted, New York: Noonday Press, 1961.

———. "The Poetry of Architecture." A series of articles in the *Architectural Magazine* (1837). Reprinted in *Works of Ruskin.* New York: John Wiley, 1885.

Russell, Carl Parcher. *One Hundred Years in Yosemite: The Story of a Great Park and Its Friends.* London: Oxford University Press, 1931.

Rybczynski, Witold. *A Clearing in the Distance: Frederick Law Olmsted and America in the 19th Century.* New York: Touchstone, 1999.

S

Sargent, Shirley, with Ray Kaplan. "Yosemite Tomboy," *Yosemite, Saga of the Century.* Oakhurst, California: Sierra Star Press, 1964.

Schuyler, Montgomery. "Round about Los Angeles," *Architectural Record* (December 1908).

Schweinfurth, A. C. "Communication," *The Wave,* November 28, 1896.

Scully, Vincent J., Jr., *The Shingle Style and The Stick Style: Architectural Theory and Design from Richardson to the Origins of Wright.* Revised edition. New Haven and London: Yale University Press, 1971.

Sears, John F. *Sacred Places: American Tourist Attractions in the Nineteenth Century.* New York: Oxford University Press, 1989.

Seventy-five Years of St. Mark's. Berkeley: St. Mark's Episcopal Church, 1952.

Silver, Ednah C. *Sketches of the New Church in America.* Boston: New Church Union, 1920.

Smith, Thomas Gordon. "John Hudson Thomas: and the Progressive Spirit in Architecture, 1910–1920." Master's thesis, University of California, Berkeley, 1970.

Sorell, Susan K.. "Silsbee: The Evolution of a Personal Architectural Style," *The Prairie School Review* 7, no. 4 (4th Qtr., 1970).

Stellmann, Louis J. "The Swiss Chalet Type for America," *House and Garden* 20 (November 1911).

Stevens, John Calvin, and Albert Winslow Cobb. "Review: *Examples of American Domestic Architecture,*" *Architectural News* 1, no. 3 (January 1891).

Stickley, Gustav. *Craftsman Bungalows, 59 Homes from "The Craftsman."* Edited by Gustav Stickley. New York: Dover Publications, 1988.

———. *Craftsman Homes 1848–1952.* New York: The Craftsman Publishing Company, 1909.

———. *Craftsman Homes: Architecture and Furnishings of the American Arts & Crafts Movement.* New York: Dover Reprint, 1995.

———. *Craftsman Homes: Mission Style Homes and Furnishings of the American Arts & Crafts Movement.* Original 1909 edition reprinted, New York: Gramercy Books, 2005.

———. *More Craftsman Homes.* New York: The Craftsman Publishing 1912; republished with 1905 and 1909 editions in one volume, New York: Dover Publications, 1982.

Sutliffe, Albert, comp. *A Description of the Town of Berkeley with a History of the University of California, Berkeley. Presenting the Natural and Acquired Advantages of a most attractive Place of Residence* (1881). The Bancroft Library: California Pamphlets microfilm (Film 858, C21 x, V. 6, 31ff).

T

Thompson, Elisabeth Kendall. "The Early Domestic Architecture of the San Francisco Bay Region," *Society of*

Moraga, helped find important letters in their mammoth Brother Cornelius archives. Mary K. Woolever, art and architecture archivist at the Daniel H. Burnham Collection, Ryerson & Burnham Archives, The Art Institute of Chicago, kindly supplied information both before and after my trip to Chicago, which saved hours of work. Thanks to persistent sleuthing by Kim Walters and Manola Madrid at the Lummis Archive in Los Angeles—encouraged by Marva R. Felchlin, director of the Autry Library Institute for the Study of the American West, Autry National Center, and also by Duane King, director of the Southwest Museum—who located Lummis' photographs of San Francisco and Worcester's San Francisco house. Betty Webster uncovered the original photographs of the First Unitarian Church in their archive, now in Kensington. Janene E. Ford, department coordinator, Holt-Atherton Special Collections, University of the Pacific Library, located Swedenborgian publications in John Muir's library.

Susan Snyder, head of Public Services, as well as Jessica Lemieux and the entire staff at the various desks in the Bancroft Library provided excellent assistance for months on end; Jack von Euw assisted with pictorial research; and David Kessler and David Farrell took the time to answer long distance requests to clear up details of Maybeck's hiring. In general the Bancroft Library staff could not have been more helpful. The librarians and rare book specialists at the College of Environmental Design Library, University of California, Berkeley, generously extended the time available for perusing rare books and periodicals. Joe Evans answered my research requests at the California Historical Society, as did dedicated staff at the California State Archives and Susan Goldstein in the History Room of the San Francisco Public Library. Those manning the Library of Congress' electronic reference desks were amazingly efficient and helpful.

I am very grateful to the many scholars who generously shared their expertise. Richard Longstreth, author of what is still the most important book on late nineteenth-century architecture in the San Francisco area, *On the Edge of the World: Four Architects in San Francisco at the Turn of the Century,* has been incredibly helpful. He located documents from his own files and very generously lent the publisher numerous photographs that appear in the book, as well as answering my many questions and sharing Schweinfurth's letters to Hearst with me. Edward R. Bosley, director of the Gamble House in Pasadena, kindly lent photographs of the Swedenborgian Church and also helped me improve the section examining Schweinfurth's role at the church as well as the paragraphs on Greene & Greene's Thorsen house. Kenneth Cardwell, whose book *Bernard Maybeck: Artisan, Architect, Artist* captures Maybeck's spirit and best clarifies his early career, lent photographs and kindly answered my questions. I received valuable assistance from many other scholars in this field: John Arthur, Robert Judson Clark, Robert M. Craig, Randell L. Makinson, Richard Guy Wilson, and Robert Winter. Thanks to Kathleen James-Chakraborty in the Architecture Department at University of California, Berkeley, I had access to Carol Louise Calavan's thesis on Schweinfurth, usually available only to staff on interlibrary loan. Kathleen also helped me recognize the influence Henry Hobson Richardson's Trinity Church, Ames Gate Lodge, and his shingle houses had on California

architects. William Kostura, the reigning expert on Russian Hill, pointed out the Bruce Price shingled house and checked the chapter on Russian Hill for accuracy; he also led me to the Lummis photograph of the bay-window end of the living room in Worcester's Russian Hill house, which has, as far as I know, not been published since Lummis published it in 1902. Susan Cerny took the time to show me some of Berkeley's treasures that her own book has helped preserve. Linda Eade, Yosemite historian, supplied many facts on Frederick Law Olmsted, John Muir, and James Lamon's Yosemite cabin, and helped me sort out the names of the photographers who might have worked with Worcester in Yosemite.

British scholars are cited in the notes and bibliography. At the 2005 Victoria and Albert Museum Conference on the Arts & Crafts, I met Alan Crawford, an expert on C. R. Ashbee, who kindly answered my questions regarding Ashbee's American trips; Alan Powers helped place the San Francisco Guild of Arts & Crafts in its proper English "guild" context. Brian Bloice shared his knowledge of English architects Ernest George and Harold Peto. David Cathers helped me put Gustav Stickley in context. Many other scholars made significant contributions through their excellent books and articles cited in the bibliography and notes.

Darrin Alfred at the San Francisco Museum of Modern Art allowed me ample time to closely examine the original Bernard Maybeck drawing of the Swedenborgian Church, now in their collection. Jeremy Kotas let me peruse the original Ernest Coxhead sketches and negatives he inherited from John Beach, which, I hope, will soon be given to EDA. Kent Mitchell and Robin Lakoff shared their Maybeck houses with me, and Kent supplied a photo of the strap hinges on his Keeler house door. The Wolfe family let me examine and reproduce their William Keith painting of Joseph Worcester's Piedmont cottage, and Sanford Goldeen and Richard Pettler let me examine their Keith paintings. Alfred Harrison at the North Point Gallery kindly duplicated many articles from the 1880s and 1890s that helped document the relationship between William Keith, Joseph Worcester, and John Muir, and Alfred helped me track down some of the other Keith paintings of Worcester's cottage. Nancy Boas helped me locate Alfred Einarsson. Mrs. Sturla Einarsson helped with the 1974 edition of *Building with Nature,* and in her honor I am donating Worcester-related materials to the Bancroft Library.

Frank Greene supplied excellent photographs of the S-curved Swedenborgian Church bench and strap-hinged door. Roselyn C. Swig, Steven L. Swig, and Al Schreck helped me obtain permission to publish a photograph of Maybeck furniture housed in a lodge in the redwoods. Nicky Oppenheimer took the wonderful picture of the barn at Waltham Place in Berkshire, England. Carlotta Montebello generously helped secure the photo of the Siena mural and the permission to publish it.

Finally, I want to thank my son Adam and his wife, Victoria, their children Susannah and Max; my son Sascha and his wife, Nina; and my 92-year-old mom, Elinor Mandelson, all of whom put up with multiple visits dedicated to research as well as to them.

So many people helped improve this book that if I have forgotten to acknowledge someone, I ask forgiveness.

Photo Credits

American Architect and Building News
Fig. 3.1 (November 17, 1894)

American Home and Gardens
Fig. 9.1 (February 1906)

Arts and Decoration
Fig. 3.24 (July 21)

Autry National Center, Los Angeles: Southwest Museum of the American Indian, Museum of the American West, Institute for the Study of the American West
Figs. 1.3 (#P32445A), 2.4 (#N922), 2.5 (#P14227), 7.14 Lummis Archive (Neg. 22,203), 10.11 (#P35555)

The Bancroft Library, University of California, Berkeley
Figs. 0.1 (Call # Pf F869 0237 R4), 0.3 (Call # 1905.02960: 20-PIC), 1.8 (#1905.16340-STER), 1.10 (#1905.16340-STER), 3.15 (#1978.059, Ser.7:2-PIC), 5.1 (#17037), 6.8 (#1959.078: 1-AX), 7.1 (#1905.17141), 7.2 (#1981.56.25), 7.6 (#1905. 11714-PIC), 9.2 (#1978.059 Ser. 1:150-PIC), 10.13 (#1905. 17710-PIC)

Berkeley Architectural Heritage Association (BAHA)
Figs. Frontispiece, 1.9, 6.1, 6.2, 7.18, 10.6

Blackwell, Ben
Fig. 3.19

Bosley, Edward
Figs. 3.4, 3.12, 3.20

California Architect
Fig. 10.3 (April 1894, 98)

California Historical Society
Figs. 3.21 (#FN-25365), 7.5 (#FN-19980)

Cardwell, Kenneth
Figs. 1.12, 3.25

Clark, Robert Judson
Fig. 3.7

Comune di Siena
Fig. 10.2

Dudley, W. J. H., original sketches by
Fig. 3.24

Einarsson, Mrs. Sturla
Figs. 0.2, 1.2, 1.5, 1.7 5.3 (to be given to The Bancroft Library on behalf of Mr. and Mrs. Sturla Einarsson); 2.3

Environmental Design Archives, University of California, Berkeley
Figs. 3.13, 3.18, 5.7, 8.1, 9.32

Environmental Design Library, University of California, Berkeley
Figs. 2.8, 6.4, 6.6 (#Neg. 194; per Richard Longstreth's instructions); 3.1, 3.17, 5.8, 5.10, 7.3, 7.4, 7.8, 9.8,

Freudenheim, Leslie
Figs. 0.4, 9.25

Greene, Frank
Figs. 3.16, 6.5a

Hiken, Ambur
© Leslie Freudenheim and Elisabeth Sussman
Figs. 2.1a, 2.1b, 3.2, 3.3, 3.8, 3.14, 4.1, 5.4, 5.5, 6.3, 6.8–6.13, 7.10, 7.15–17.17, 7.19–7.23, 8.4–8.10, 8.12, 9.3–9.7, 9.10–9.21, 9.23, 9.24, 9.33, 10.7–10.10 10.14–10.17, 10.20, 10.21, 12.1

Historical Works
Figs. 10.4, 10.5

Howard, Robert
Figs. 8.3, 8.11, 8.13

Kostura, William
Figs. 2.6. 2.9

Kotas, Jeremy, from the John Beach Collection:
Fig. 5.6

Livermore, George
Fig. 2.6, 2.9

Longstreth, Richard:
Figs. 1.4, 2.3, 2.7, 2.8, 2.10, 3.6, 5.2, 5.9, 5.11, 5.12, 5.14, 6.4, 6.6, 7.7, 9.1, 9.9, 10.1, 10.3, 10.13

Maybeck, Jacomena, *Maybeck: The Family View* (fig. 3)
Fig. 1.11

Morley Baer Photography Trust
© 2004. All production rights reserved:
Figs. 9.22, 9.27–9.31

Mitchell, Kent
Fig. 6.5b

Oakland Daily Evening Tribune
Fig. 3.11 (June 20, 1891; microfiche)

Oakland Museum of California
Fig. 5.13 (Neg. #75 334.942)

Oppenheimer, Nicky
Fig. 9.26

Piedmont Historical Society
Fig. 1.6, 1.6 (detail)

Saint Mary's College of California, Moraga, California: Brother Cornelius Collection
Fig. 2.2

San Diego Historical Society
Fig. 10.18, 10.19

San Francisco Examiner
Fig. 3.5 (September 1895)

San Francisco Museum of Modern Art
Fig. 3.19

San Francisco Newsletter & California Advertiser
Fig. 3.10 (December 24, 1887)

Stanford University Library
Fig. 3.10

Studio Lensini:
Fig. 10.2

Sue Tallon Photography
Figs. 1.6, 1.6 (detail)

Swedenborgian Church
Figs. 3.4, 3.12, 3.20, 3.23

Thompson, Daniella
Fig. 8.2

Unknown
Figs. 1.1, 3.9, 6.14, 10.12

Warshaw Collection of Business Americana-Furniture, Archives Center, National Museum of American History, Behring Center, Smithsonian Institution
Fig. 3.22

Unitarian Universalist Church of Berkeley Archives
Figs. 7.11–7.13

Wolfe Jr., Mr. and Mrs. Cameron, from the collection of,
Figs. 1.6, 1.6 (detail)

Index